きみにしか聞こえない

CALLING YOU

都筑せつり SETSURI TSUZUKI

原作／乙一 OTSUICHI

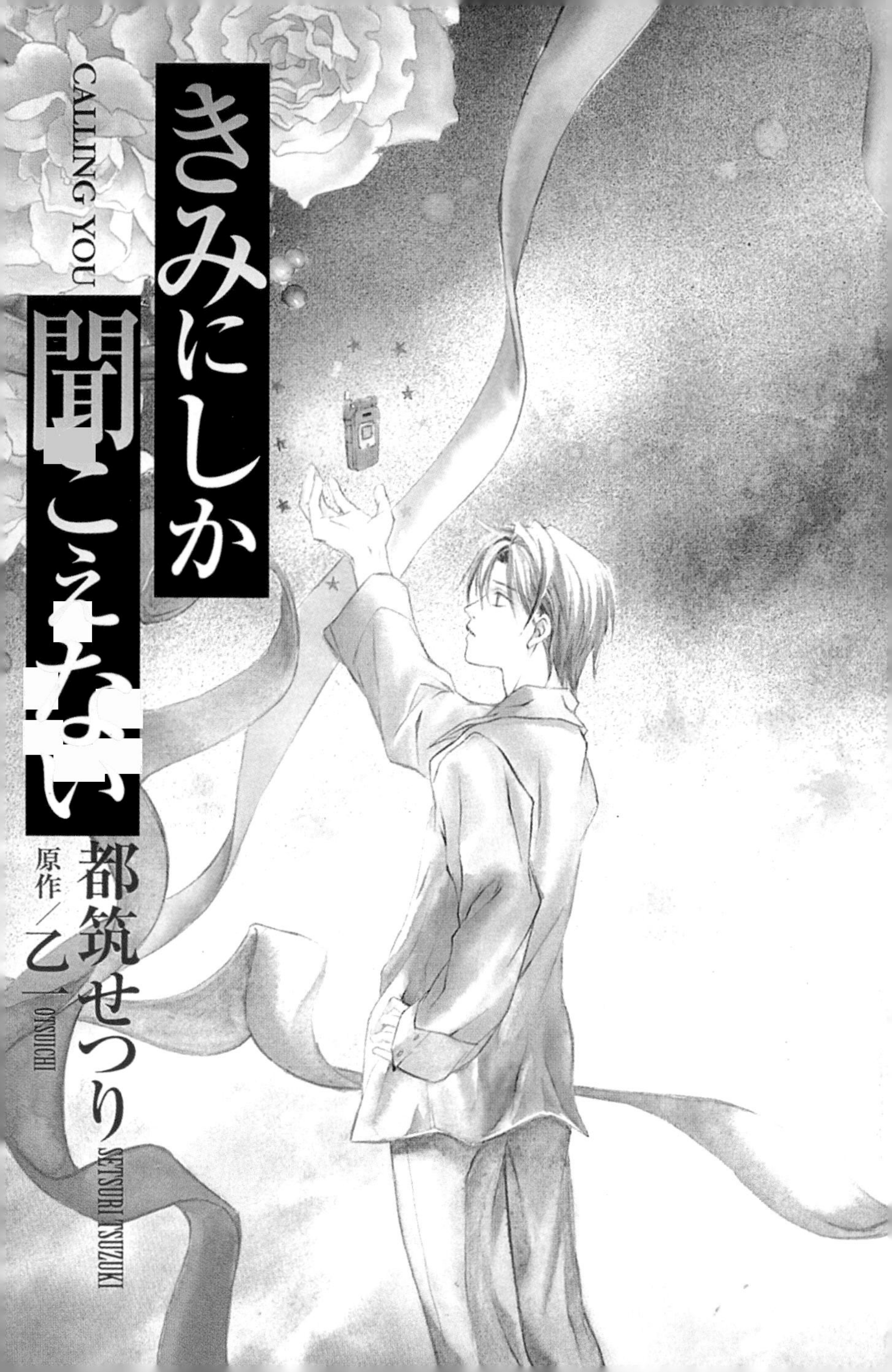

contents

KIZ / KIDS : Japanese Character reads 'kizu,' meaning wound or injury —it's a play on words.

Calling You™

Kimi ni shika Kikoenai

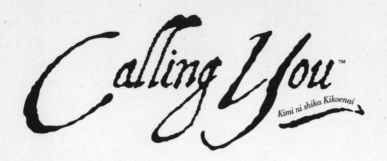

By Setsuri Tsuzuki
Original Story by Otsuichi

TOKYOPOP®

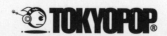

HAMBURG // LONDON // LOS ANGELES // TOKYO

Calling you Vol 1
Created by Setsuri Tsuzuki and Otsuichi

Translation - Yuko Fukami
English Adaptation - Carol Fox
Copy Editor - Stephanie Duchin
Retouch and Lettering - Kimie Kim
Cover Design - James Lee

Editor - Luis Reyes
Digital Imaging Manager - Chris Buford
Pre-Production Supervisor - Erika Terriquez
Art Director - Anne Marie Horne
Production Manager - Elisabeth Brizzi
Managing Editor - Vy Nguyen
VP of Production - Ron Klamert
Editor-In-Chief - Rob Tokar
Publisher - Mike Kiley
President and C.O.O. - John Parker
C.E.O. and Chief Creative Officer - Stuart Levy

A 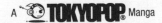 Manga

TOKYOPOP and 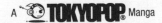 are trademarks or registered trademarks of TOKYOPOP Inc.

TOKYOPOP Inc.
5900 Wilshire Blvd. Suite 2000
Los Angeles, CA 90036

E-mail: info@TOKYOPOP.com
Come visit us online at www.TOKYOPOP.com

KIMINISHIKA KIKOENAI CALLING YOU
© Setsuri Tsuzuki 2003 © OTSUICHI 2003
First published in Japan in 2003 by KADOKAWA SHOTEN
PUBLISHING CO., LTD., Tokyo. English translation rights
arranged with KADOKAWA SHOTEN PUBLISHING CO., LTD.,
Tokyo through TUTTLE-MORI AGENCY, INC., Tokyo.

All rights reserved. No portion of this book may be
reproduced or transmitted in any form or by any means
without written permission from the copyright holders.
This manga is a work of fiction. Any resemblance to
actual events or locales or persons, living or dead, is
entirely coincidental.

English text copyright © 2007 TOKYOPOP Inc.

ISBN: 978-1-59816-931-7
First TOKYOPOP printing: January 2007
10 9 8 7 6 5 4 3 2 1
Printed in the USA

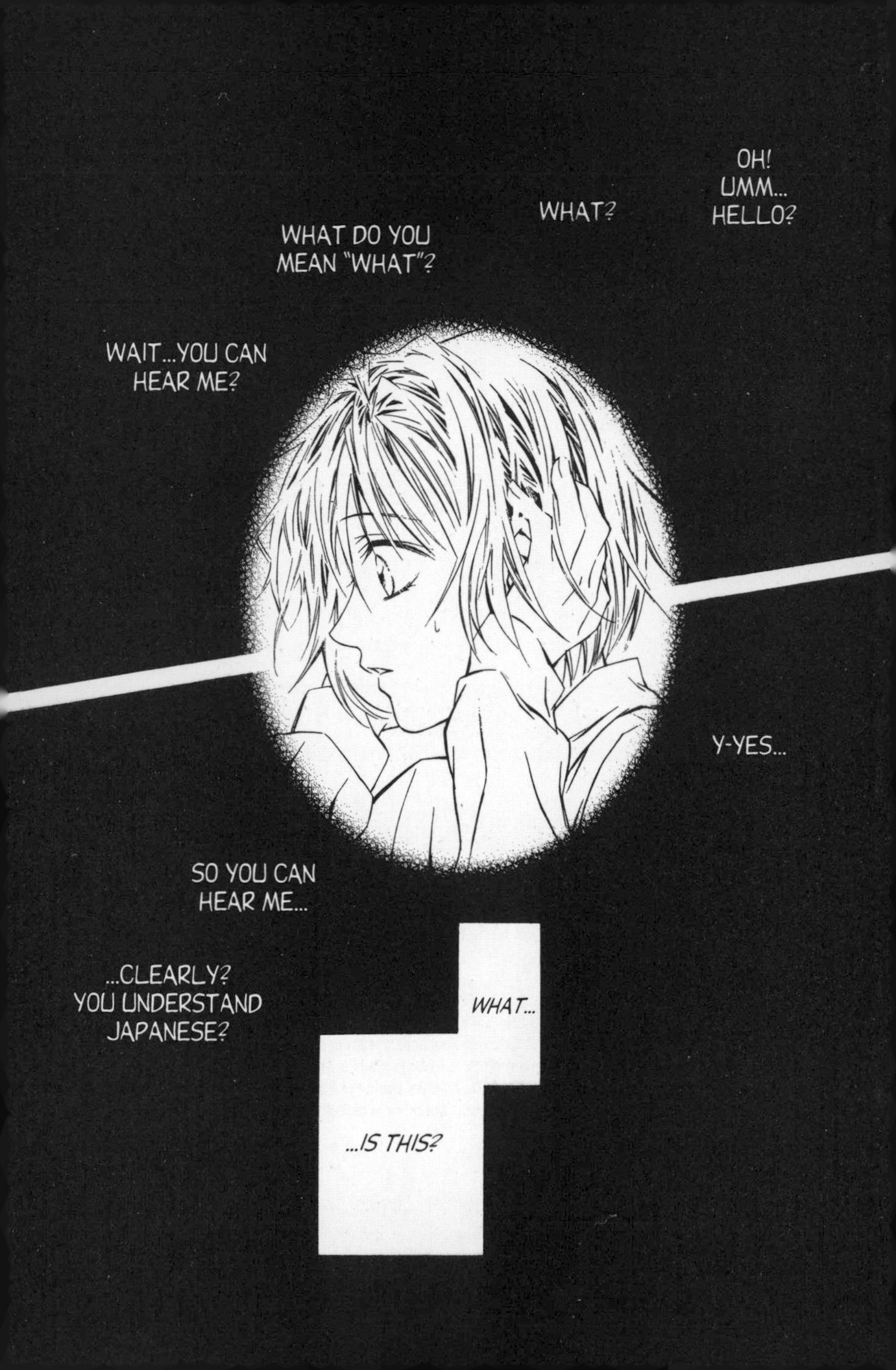
OH! UMM... HELLO?
WHAT?
WHAT DO YOU MEAN "WHAT"?
WAIT...YOU CAN HEAR ME?
Y-YES...
SO YOU CAN HEAR ME...
...CLEARLY? YOU UNDERSTAND JAPANESE?
WHAT...
...IS THIS?

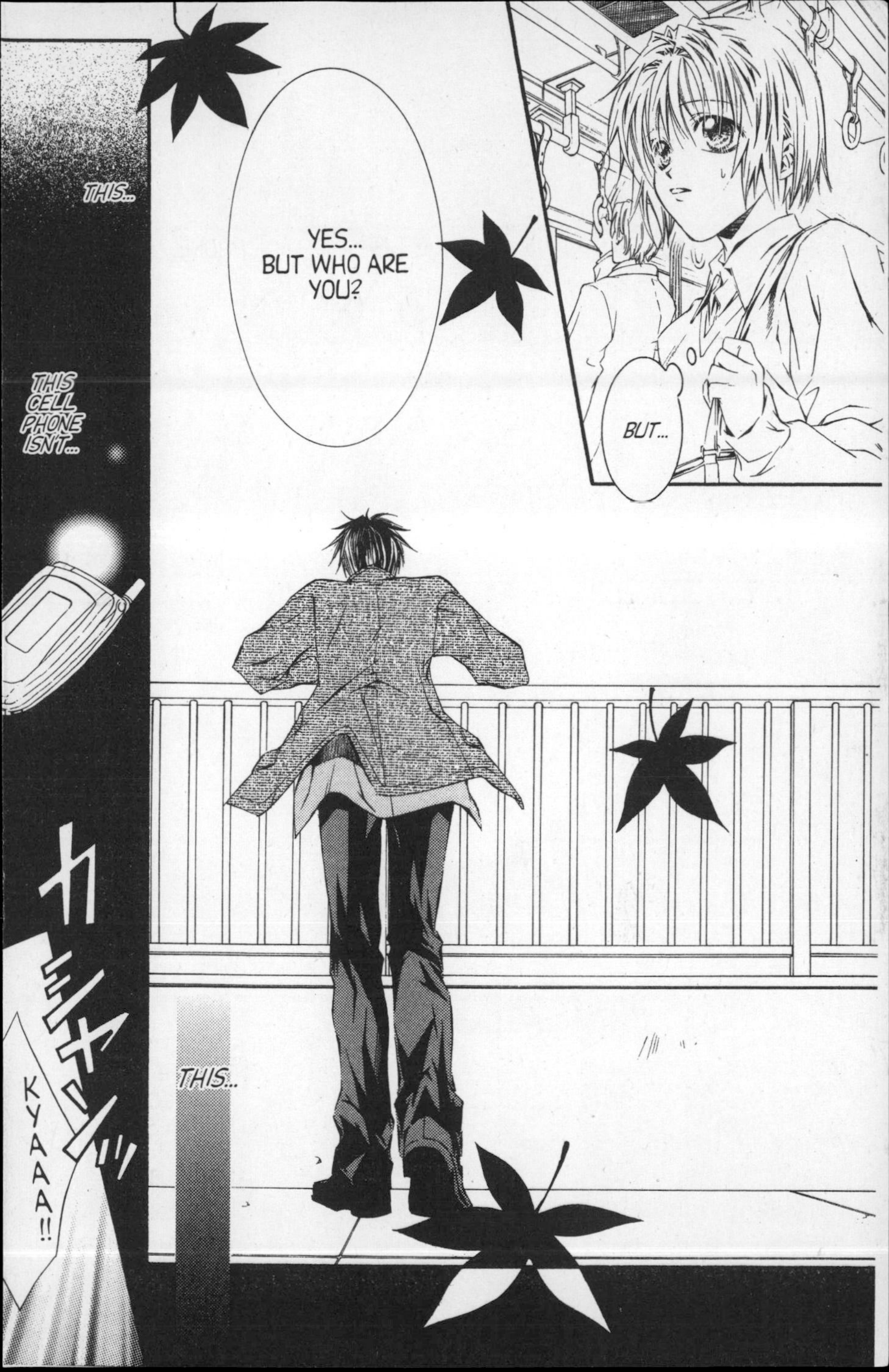
BUT...
YES... BUT WHO ARE YOU?
THIS...
THIS...
THIS CELL PHONE ISN'T...
KYAAA!!

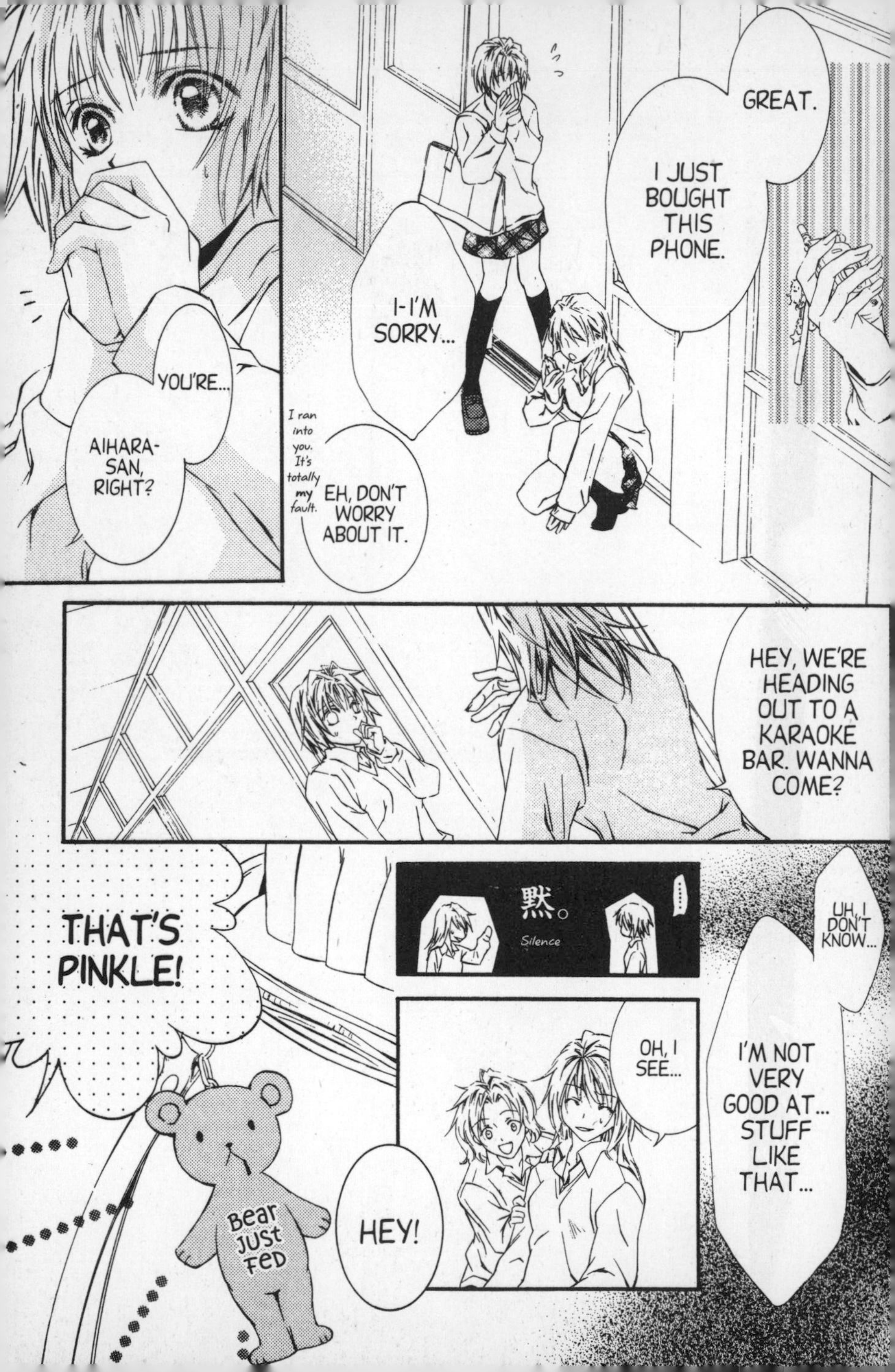
GREAT.
I JUST BOUGHT THIS PHONE.
I-I'M SORRY...
I ran into you. It's totally my fault.
EH, DON'T WORRY ABOUT IT.
YOU'RE...
AIHARA-SAN, RIGHT?
HEY, WE'RE HEADING OUT TO A KARAOKE BAR. WANNA COME?
UH, I DON'T KNOW...
I'M NOT VERY GOOD AT... STUFF LIKE THAT...
......
黙。
Silence
OH, I SEE...
HEY!
THAT'S PINKLE!
Bear JUST FED

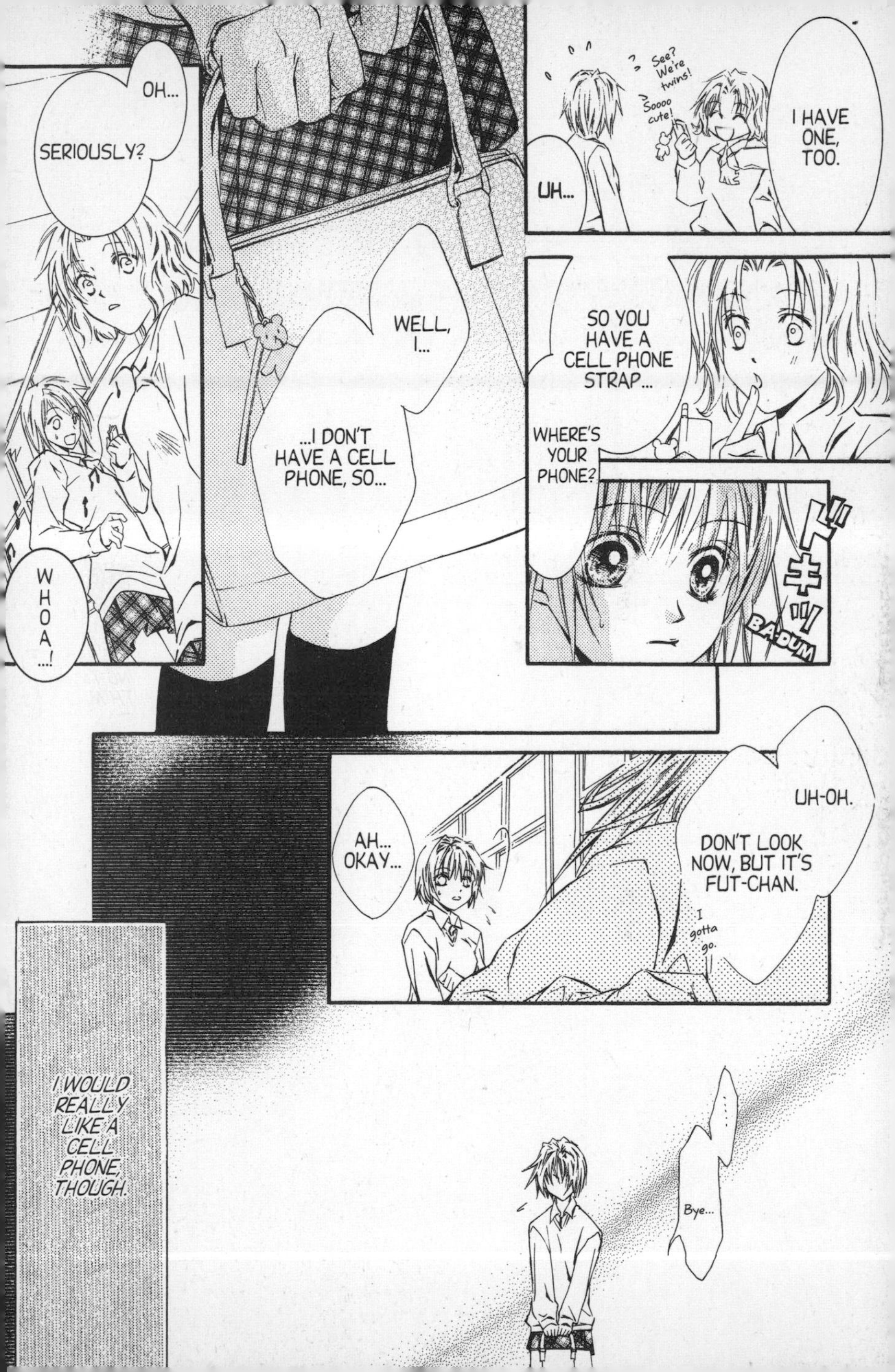
I HAVE ONE, TOO.
See? We're twins!
Soooo cute!
UH...
SO YOU HAVE A CELL PHONE STRAP...
WHERE'S YOUR PHONE?
ドキッ
BA-DUM
WELL, I...
...I DON'T HAVE A CELL PHONE, SO...
OH...
SERIOUSLY?
WHOA...!
UH-OH.
DON'T LOOK NOW, BUT IT'S FUT-CHAN.
I gotta go.
AH... OKAY...
...
Bye...
I WOULD REALLY LIKE A CELL PHONE, THOUGH.

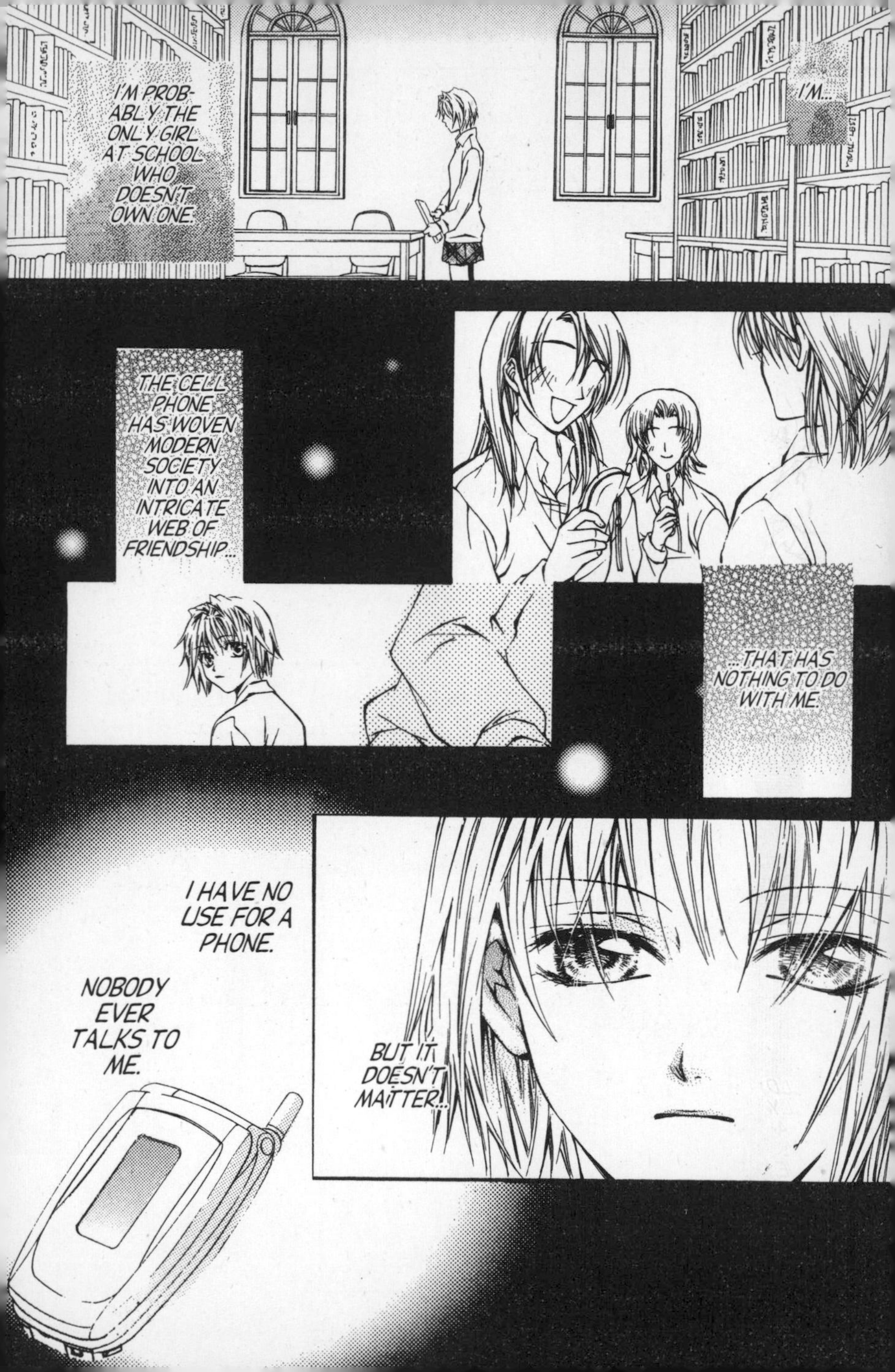
I'M...
I'M PROBABLY THE ONLY GIRL AT SCHOOL WHO DOESN'T OWN ONE.
THE CELL PHONE HAS WOVEN MODERN SOCIETY INTO AN INTRICATE WEB OF FRIENDSHIP...
...THAT HAS NOTHING TO DO WITH ME.
I HAVE NO USE FOR A PHONE.
NOBODY EVER TALKS TO ME.
BUT IT DOESN'T MATTER...

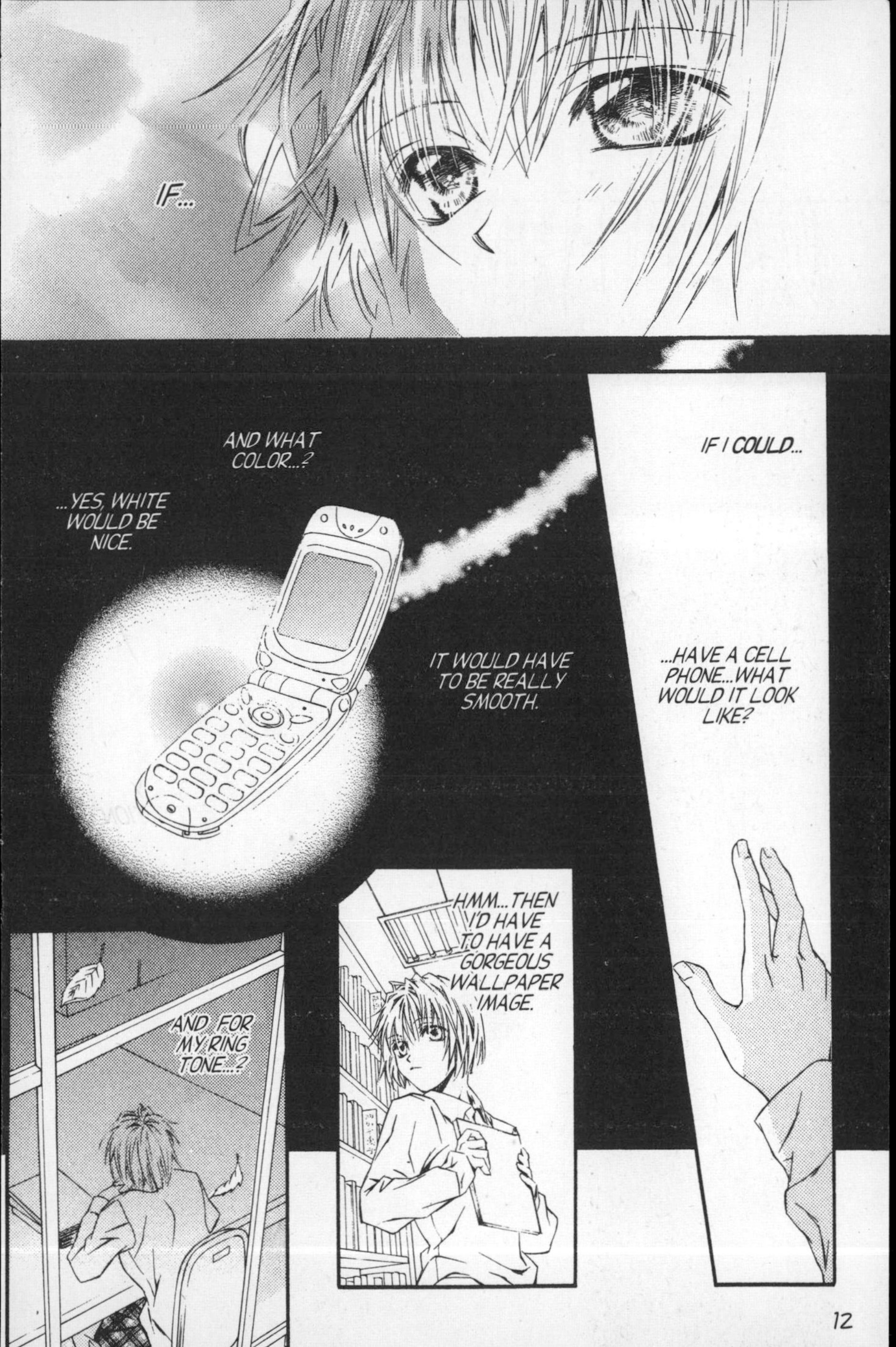
IF...
IF I COULD...
...HAVE A CELL PHONE...WHAT WOULD IT LOOK LIKE?
IT WOULD HAVE TO BE REALLY SMOOTH.
AND WHAT COLOR...?
...YES, WHITE WOULD BE NICE.
HMM...THEN I'D HAVE TO HAVE A GORGEOUS WALLPAPER IMAGE.
AND FOR MY RING TONE...?

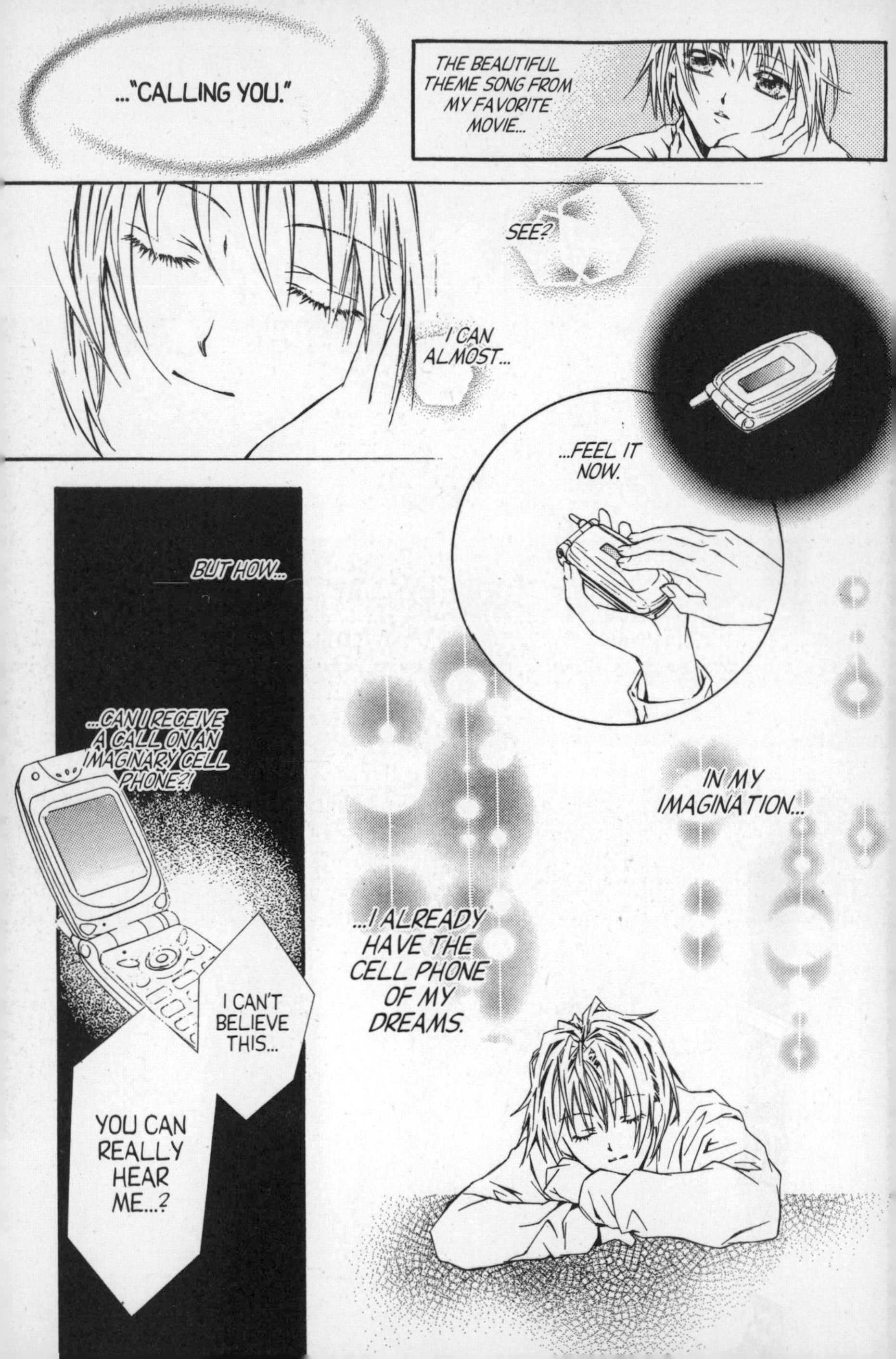
THE BEAUTIFUL THEME SONG FROM MY FAVORITE MOVIE...
..."CALLING YOU."
SEE?
I CAN ALMOST...
...FEEL IT NOW.
IN MY IMAGINATION...
...I ALREADY HAVE THE CELL PHONE OF MY DREAMS.
BUT HOW...
...CAN I RECEIVE A CALL ON AN IMAGINARY CELL PHONE?!
I CAN'T BELIEVE THIS...
YOU CAN REALLY HEAR ME...?

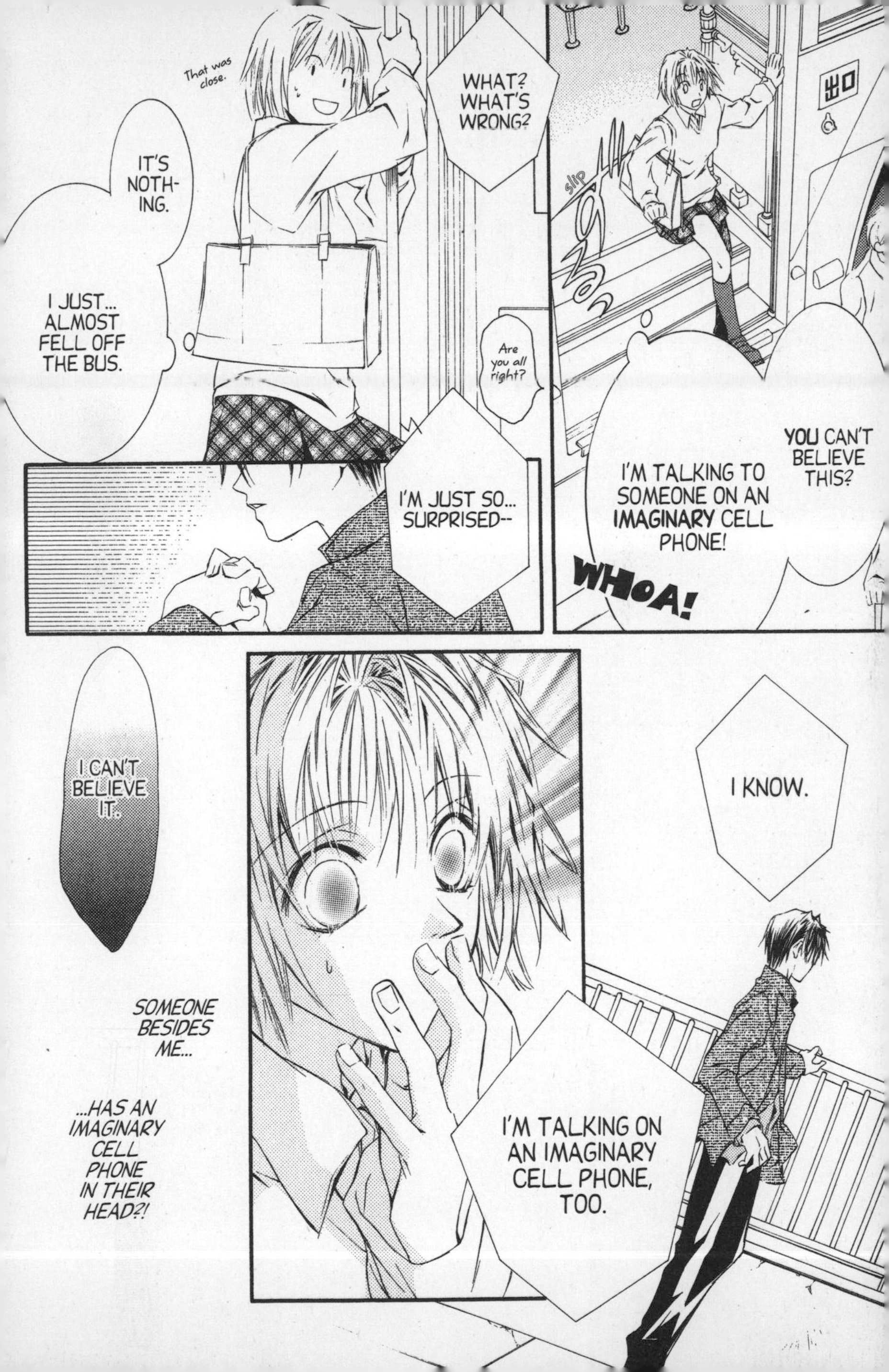

slip
YOU CAN'T BELIEVE THIS?
I'M TALKING TO SOMEONE ON AN IMAGINARY CELL PHONE!
WHOA!
WHAT? WHAT'S WRONG?
That was close.
IT'S NOTH-ING.
I JUST... ALMOST FELL OFF THE BUS.
Are you all right?
I'M JUST SO... SURPRISED--
I KNOW.
I'M TALKING ON AN IMAGINARY CELL PHONE, TOO.
I CAN'T BELIEVE IT.
SOMEONE BESIDES ME...
...HAS AN IMAGINARY CELL PHONE IN THEIR HEAD?!

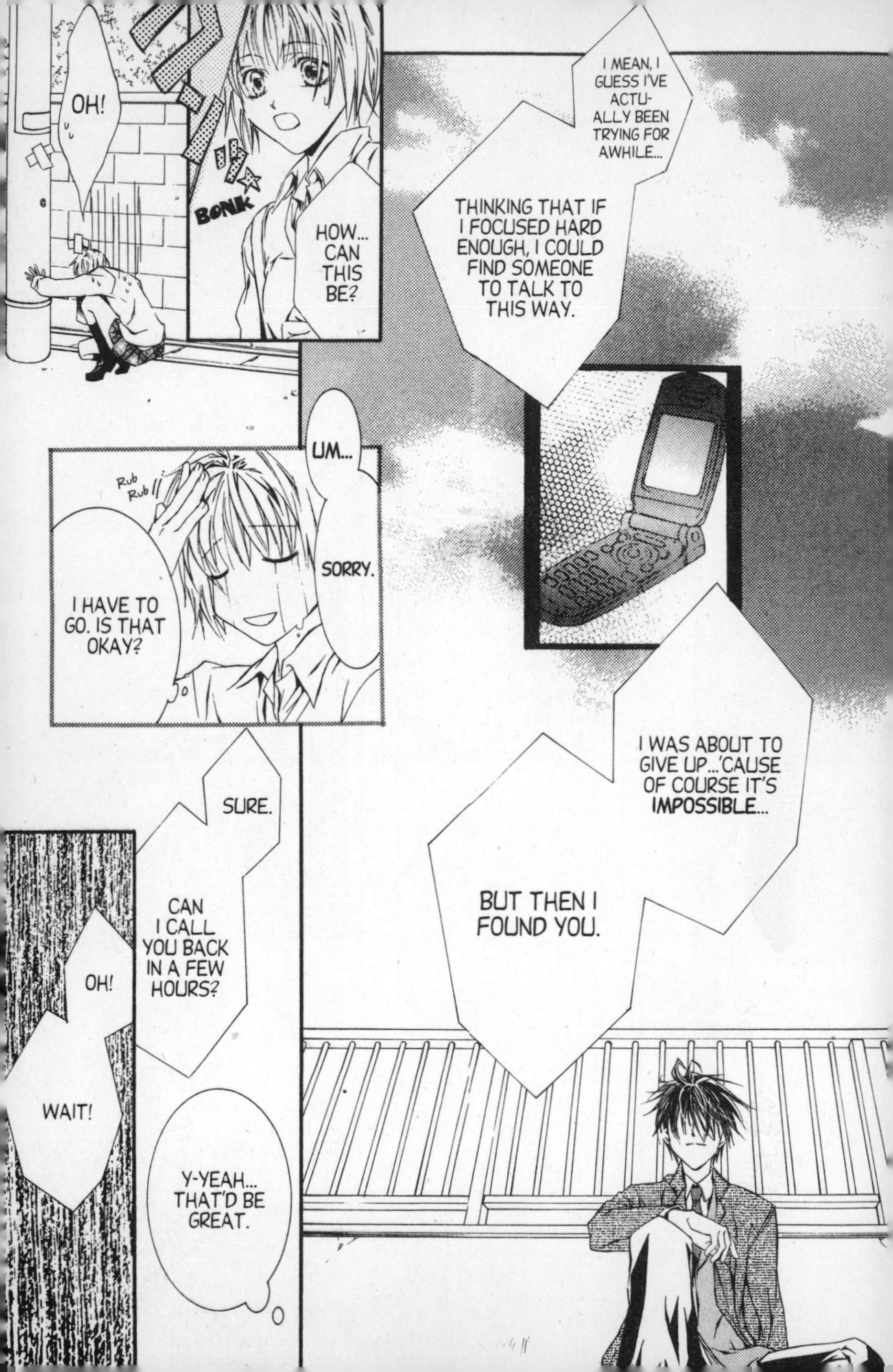
I MEAN, I GUESS I'VE ACTU-ALLY BEEN TRYING FOR AWHILE...
THINKING THAT IF I FOCUSED HARD ENOUGH, I COULD FIND SOMEONE TO TALK TO THIS WAY.
I WAS ABOUT TO GIVE UP...'CAUSE OF COURSE IT'S **IMPOSSIBLE**...
BUT THEN I FOUND YOU.
BONK
HOW... CAN THIS BE?
OH!
UM...
SORRY.
Rub Rub
I HAVE TO GO. IS THAT OKAY?
SURE.
CAN I CALL YOU BACK IN A FEW HOURS?
OH!
WAIT!
Y-YEAH... THAT'D BE GREAT.

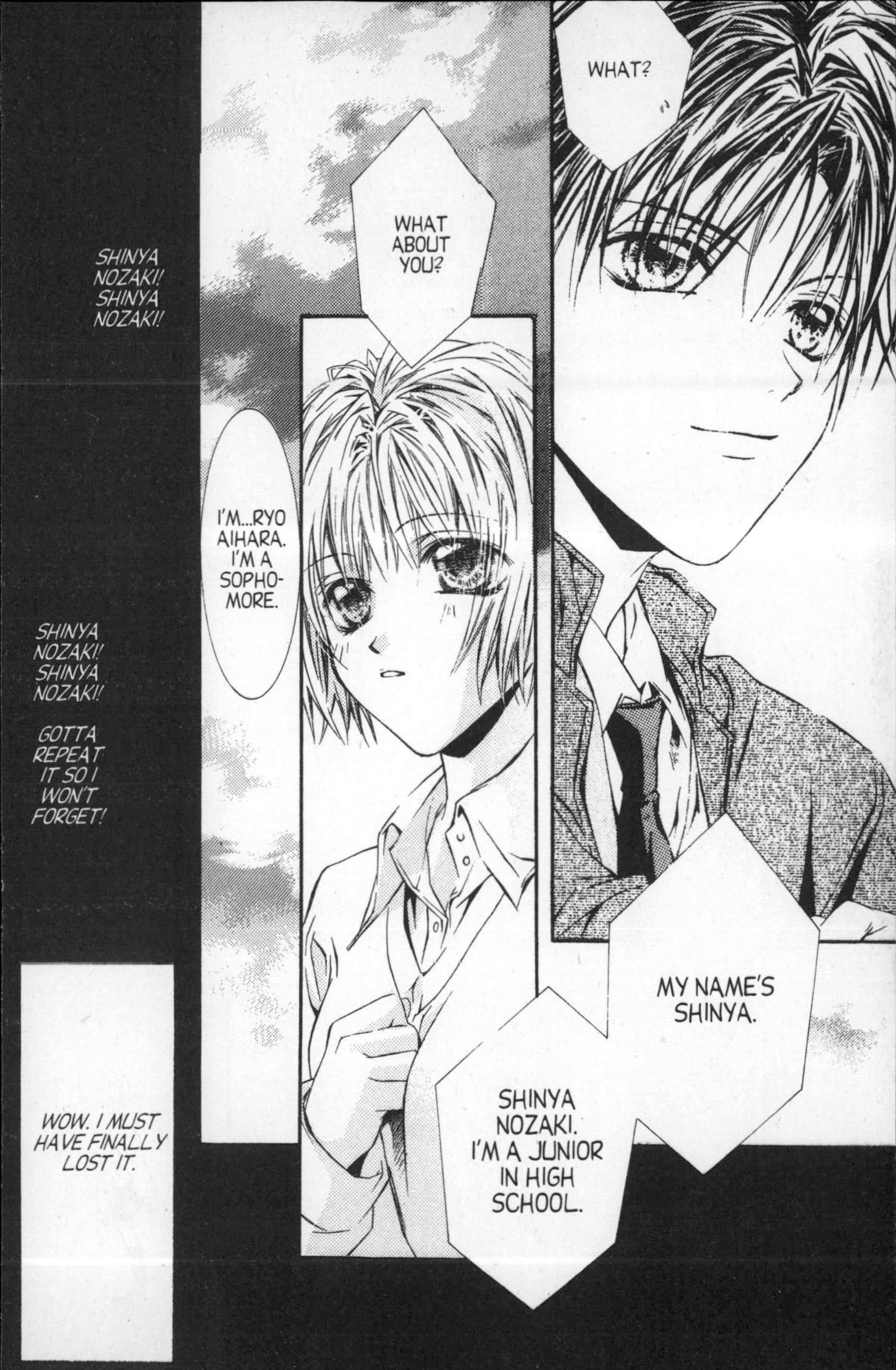
WHAT?
WHAT ABOUT YOU?
MY NAME'S SHINYA.
SHINYA NOZAKI. I'M A JUNIOR IN HIGH SCHOOL.
I'M...RYO AIHARA. I'M A SOPHO-MORE.
SHINYA NOZAKI! SHINYA NOZAKI!
SHINYA NOZAKI! SHINYA NOZAKI!
GOTTA REPEAT IT SO I WON'T FORGET!
WOW. I MUST HAVE FINALLY LOST IT.

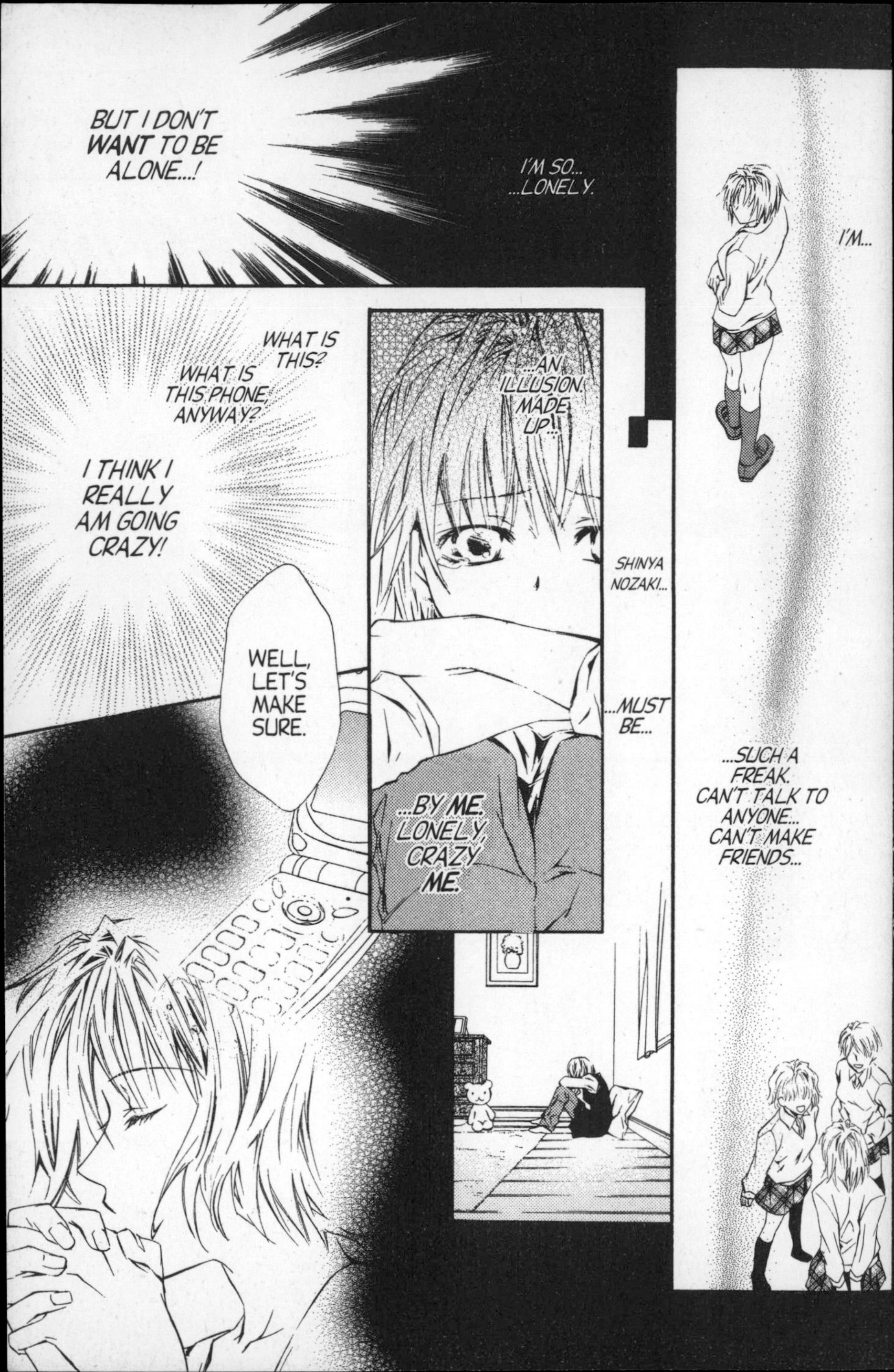
I'M...
...SUCH A FREAK. CAN'T TALK TO ANYONE... CAN'T MAKE FRIENDS...
I'M SO... ...LONELY.
BUT I DON'T WANT TO BE ALONE...!
SHINYA NOZAKI...
...MUST BE...
...AN ILLUSION. MADE UP!...
...BY ME. LONELY, CRAZY ME.
WHAT IS THIS?
WHAT IS THIS PHONE, ANYWAY?
I THINK I REALLY AM GOING CRAZY!
WELL, LET'S MAKE SURE.

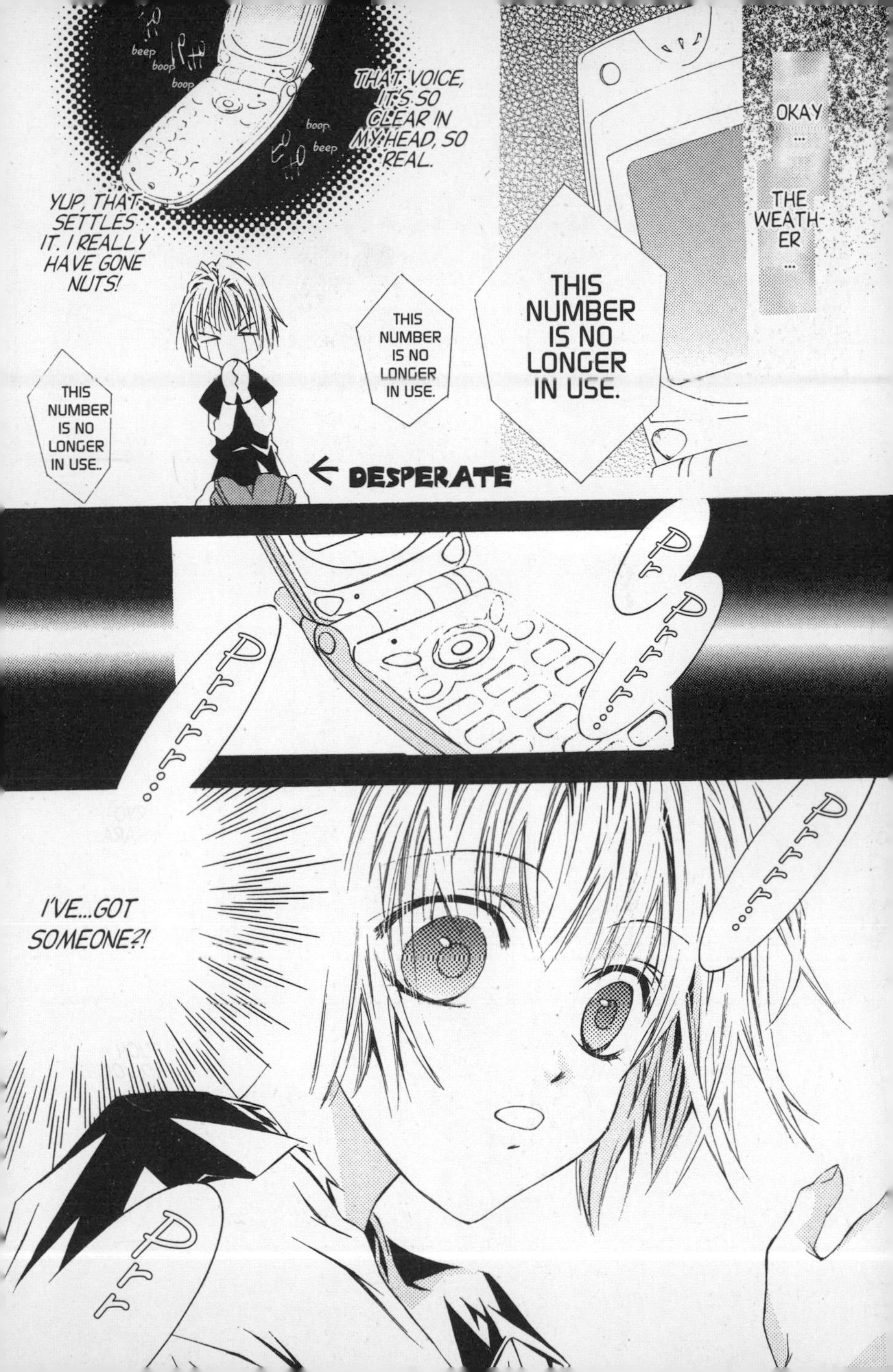
OKAY ... THE WEATHER ...
THIS NUMBER IS NO LONGER IN USE.
THAT VOICE, IT'S SO CLEAR IN MY HEAD, SO REAL.
beep boop boop
boop beep
YUP, THAT SETTLES IT. I REALLY HAVE GONE NUTS!
THIS NUMBER IS NO LONGER IN USE.
THIS NUMBER IS NO LONGER IN USE..
← DESPERATE
Prr
Prrrrrr...
Prrrrrr...
Prrrrr...
I'VE...GOT SOMEONE?!
Prrr

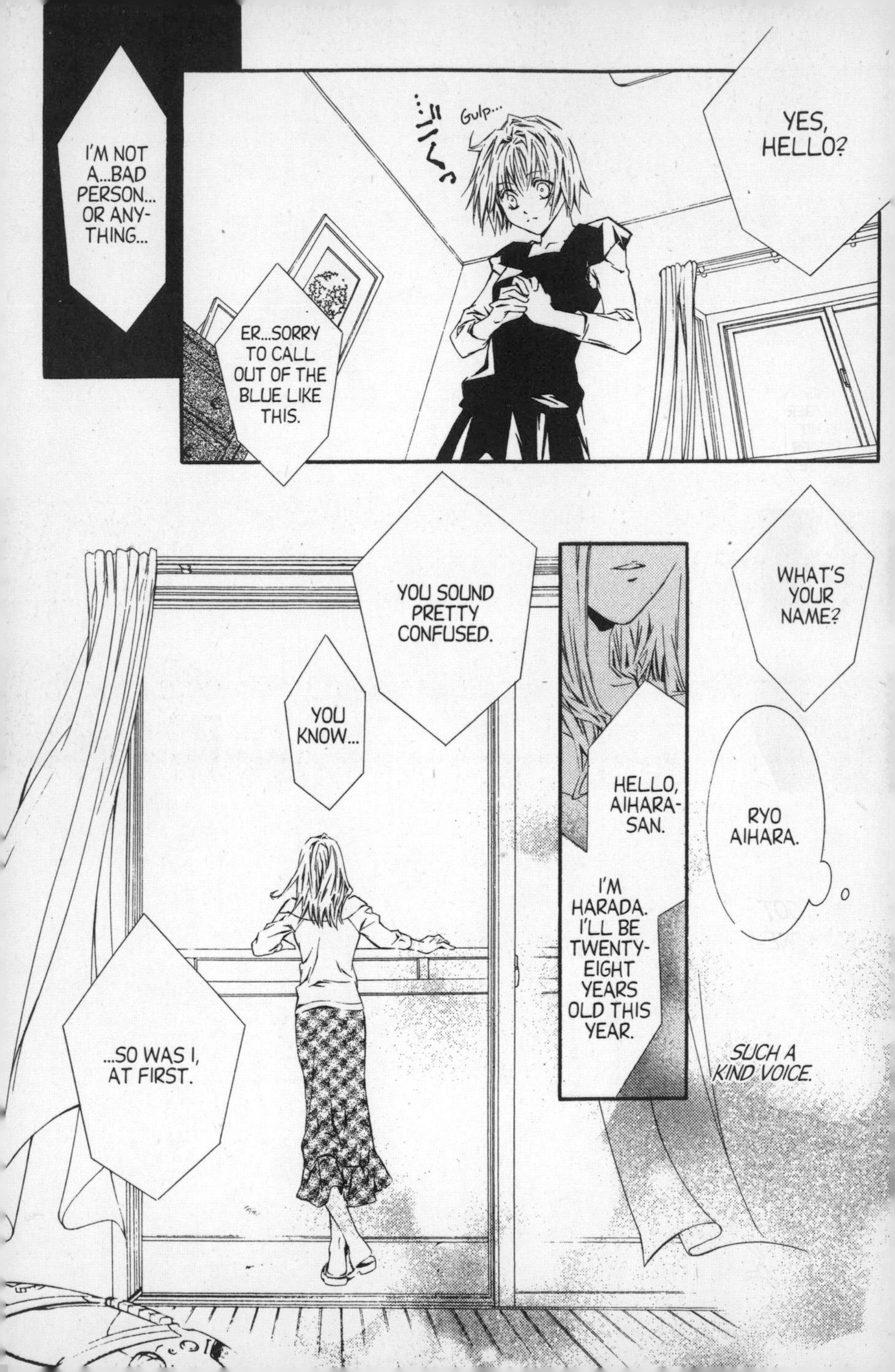
YES, HELLO?
Gulp...
ER...SORRY TO CALL OUT OF THE BLUE LIKE THIS.
I'M NOT A...BAD PERSON... OR ANYTHING...
WHAT'S YOUR NAME?
RYO AIHARA.
SUCH A KIND VOICE.
HELLO, AIHARA-SAN.
I'M HARADA. I'LL BE TWENTY-EIGHT YEARS OLD THIS YEAR.
YOU SOUND PRETTY CONFUSED.
YOU KNOW...
...SO WAS I, AT FIRST.

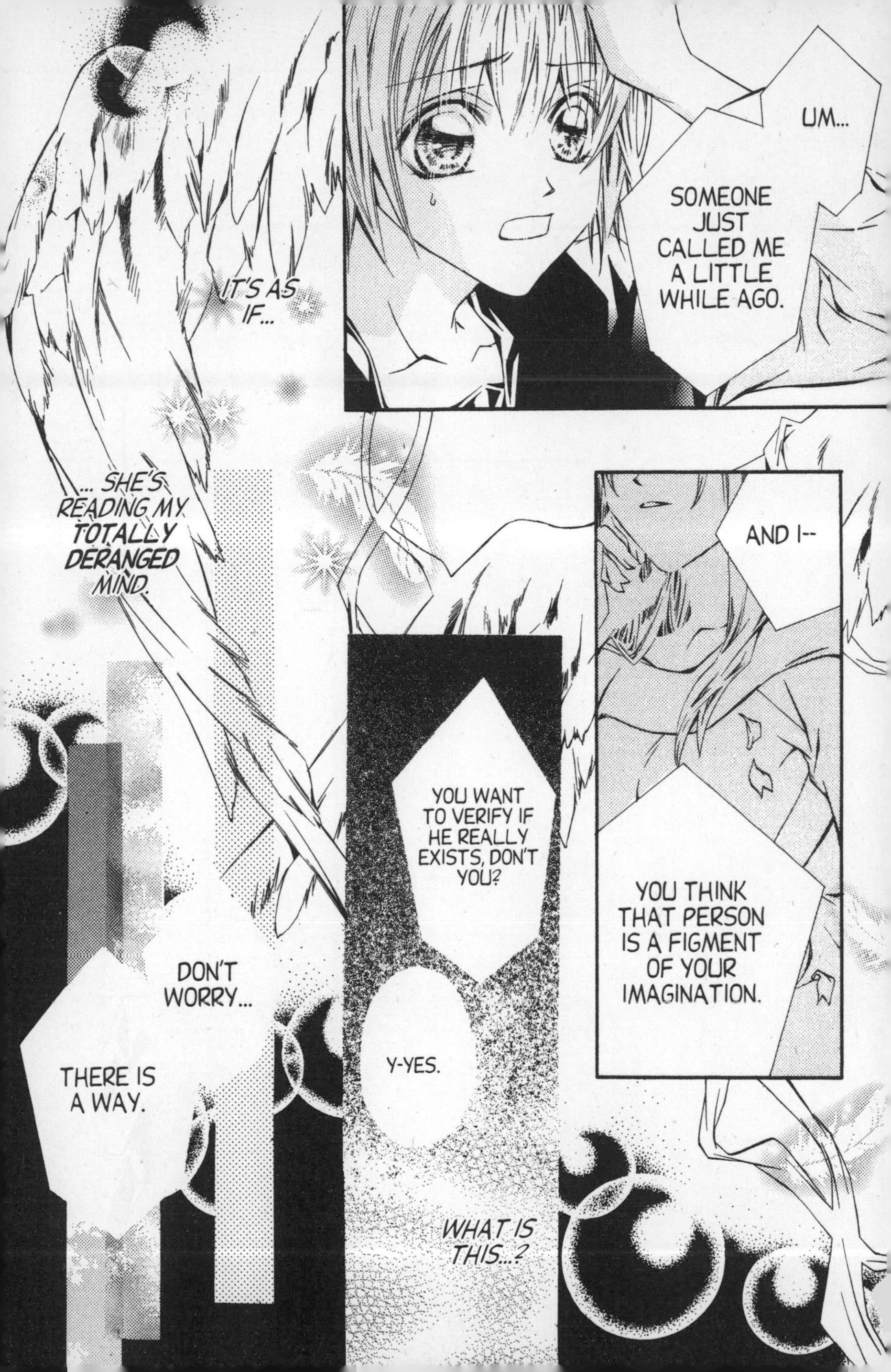
UM...
SOMEONE JUST CALLED ME A LITTLE WHILE AGO.
IT'S AS IF...
...SHE'S READING MY TOTALLY DERANGED MIND.
AND I--
YOU THINK THAT PERSON IS A FIGMENT OF YOUR IMAGINATION.
YOU WANT TO VERIFY IF HE REALLY EXISTS, DON'T YOU?
Y-YES.
WHAT IS THIS...?
DON'T WORRY...
THERE IS A WAY.

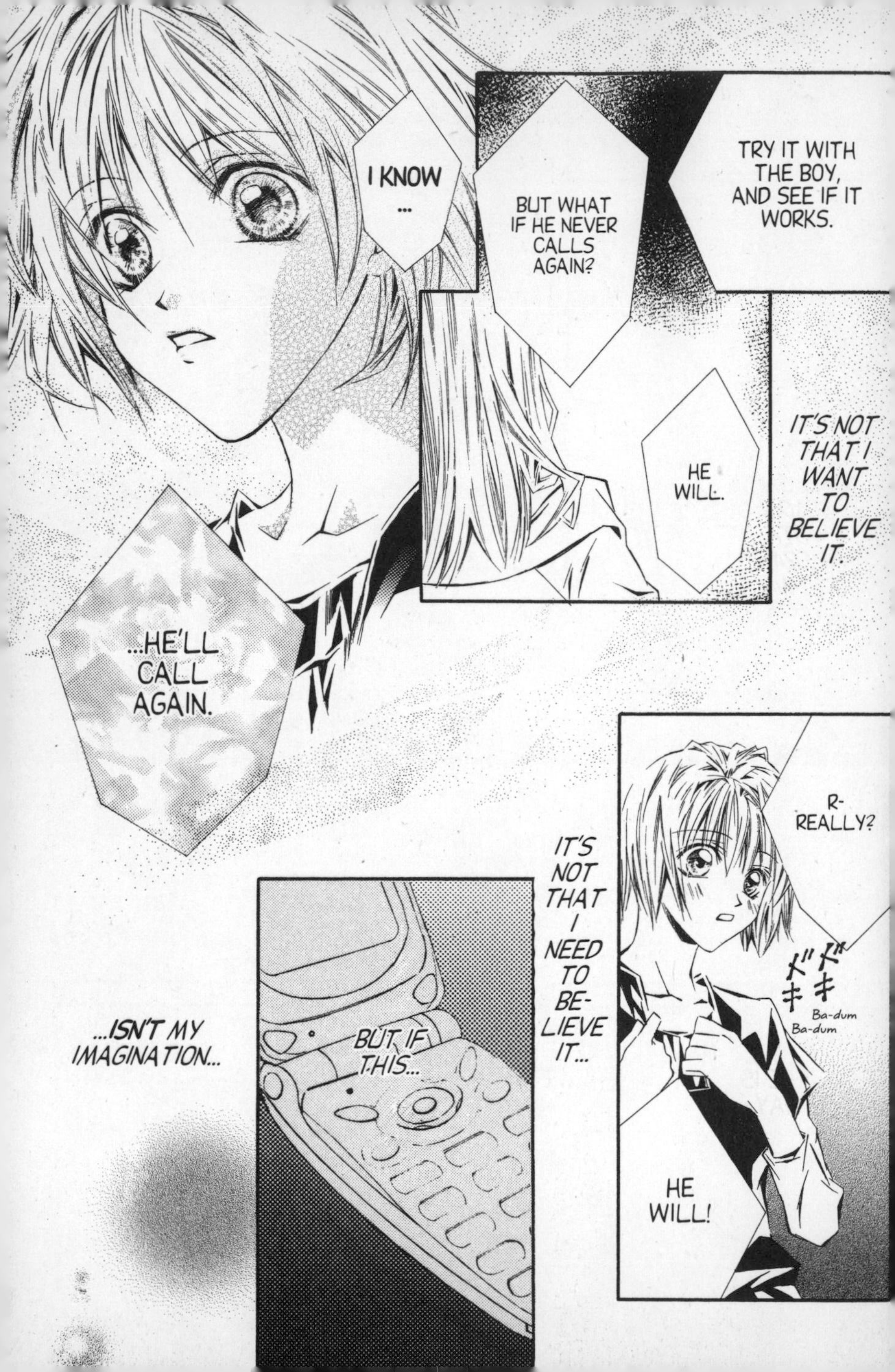
TRY IT WITH THE BOY, AND SEE IF IT WORKS.
BUT WHAT IF HE NEVER CALLS AGAIN?
HE WILL.
IT'S NOT THAT I WANT TO BELIEVE IT.
I KNOW ...
...HE'LL CALL AGAIN.
R-REALLY?
Ba-dum Ba-dum
HE WILL!
IT'S NOT THAT I NEED TO BE-LIEVE IT...
BUT IF THIS...
...ISN'T MY IMAGINATION...

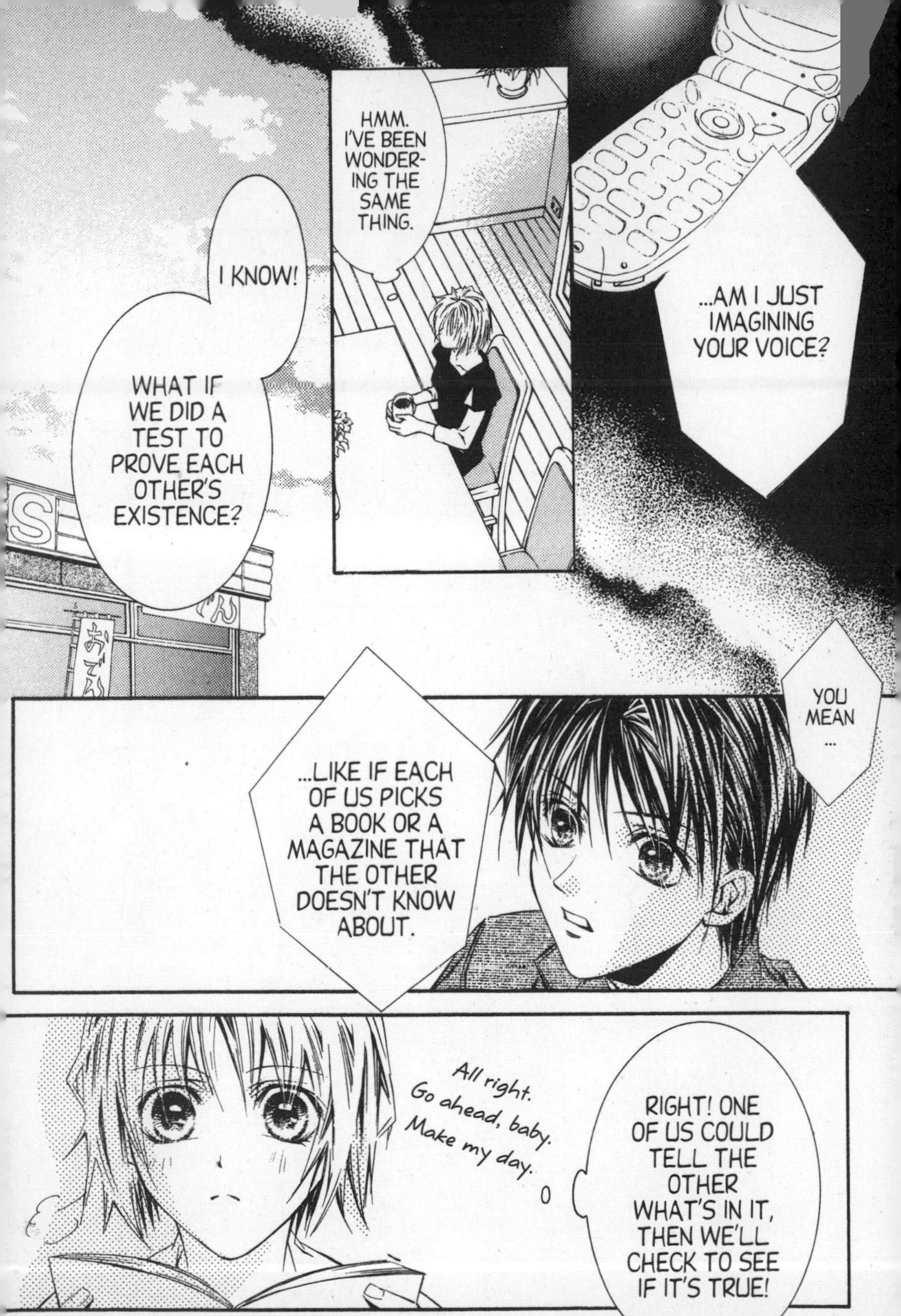
...AM I JUST IMAGINING YOUR VOICE?
HMM. I'VE BEEN WONDERING THE SAME THING.
I KNOW!
WHAT IF WE DID A TEST TO PROVE EACH OTHER'S EXISTENCE?
YOU MEAN ...
...LIKE IF EACH OF US PICKS A BOOK OR A MAGAZINE THAT THE OTHER DOESN'T KNOW ABOUT.
RIGHT! ONE OF US COULD TELL THE OTHER WHAT'S IN IT, THEN WE'LL CHECK TO SEE IF IT'S TRUE!
All right. Go ahead, baby. Make my day.

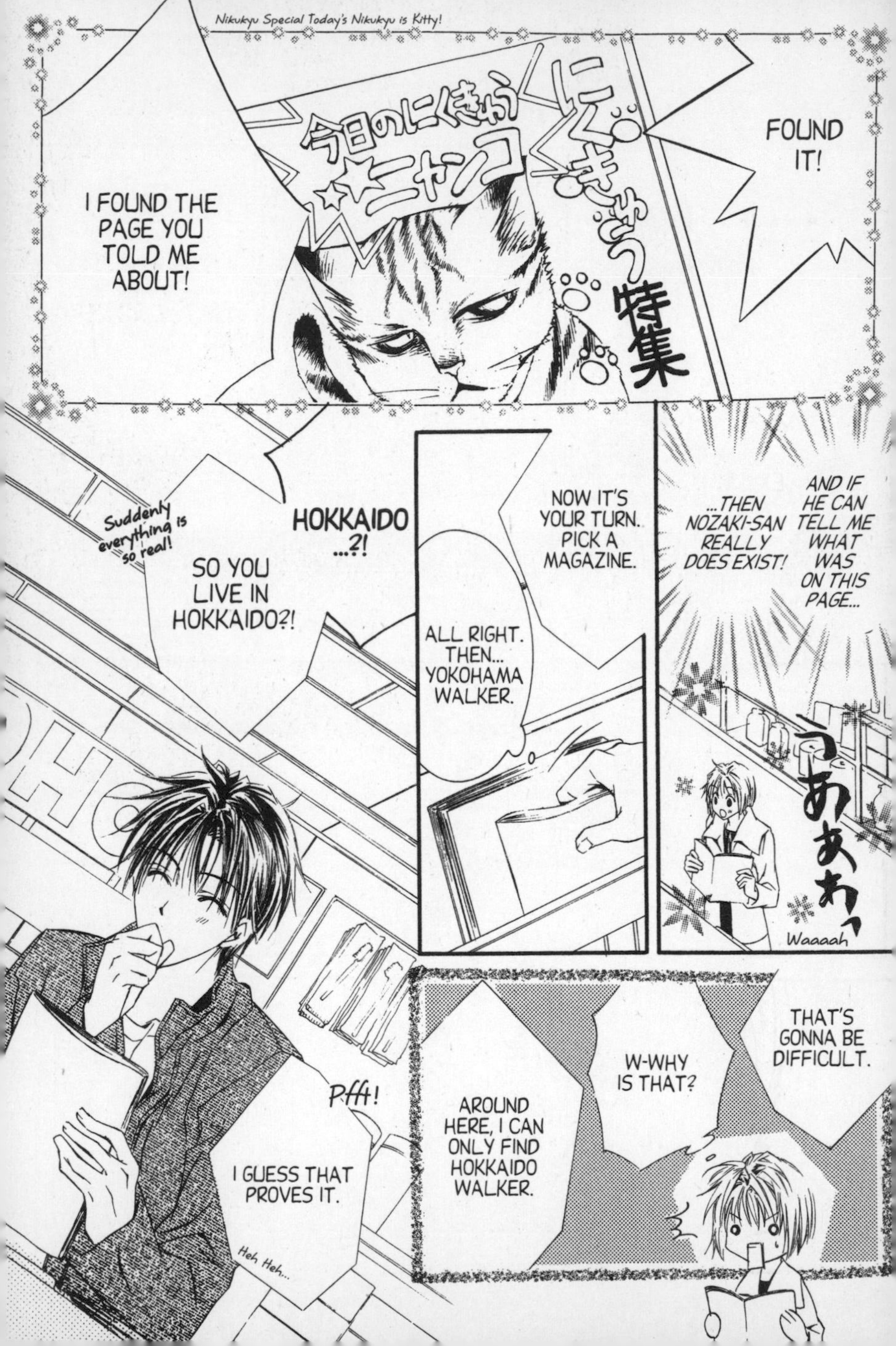
Nikukyu Special Today's Nikukyu is Kitty!
FOUND IT!
今日のにくきゅう
☆ニャンコにくきゅう特集
I FOUND THE PAGE YOU TOLD ME ABOUT!
AND IF HE CAN TELL ME WHAT WAS ON THIS PAGE...
...THEN NOZAKI-SAN REALLY DOES EXIST!
うああわっ
Waaaah
NOW IT'S YOUR TURN. PICK A MAGAZINE.
ALL RIGHT. THEN... YOKOHAMA WALKER.
THAT'S GONNA BE DIFFICULT.
W-WHY IS THAT?
AROUND HERE, I CAN ONLY FIND HOKKAIDO WALKER.
HOKKAIDO ...?!
Suddenly everything is so real!
SO YOU LIVE IN HOKKAIDO?!
Pfft!
I GUESS THAT PROVES IT.
Heh Heh...

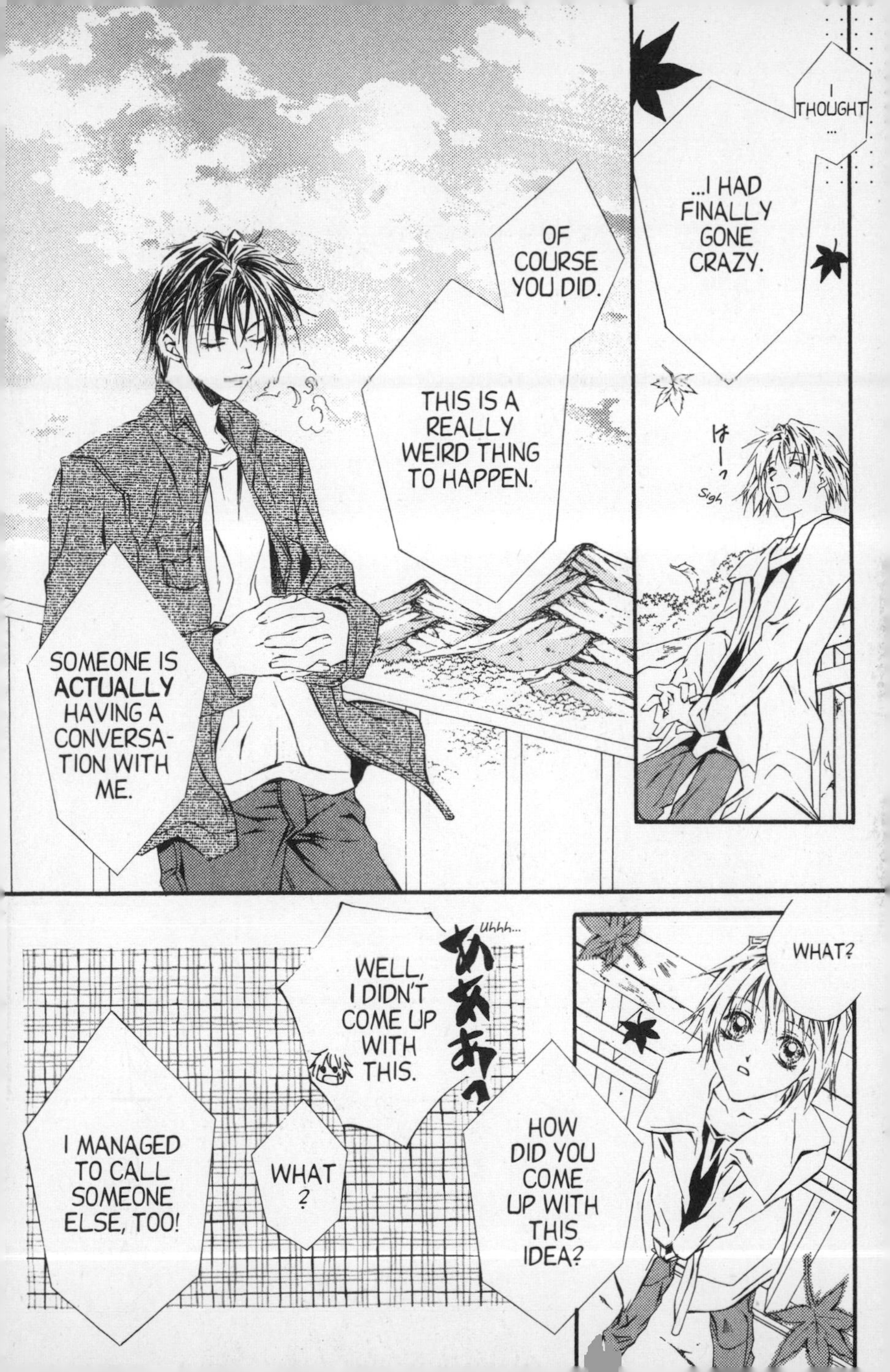

I THOUGHT ...
...I HAD FINALLY GONE CRAZY.
はーっ
Sigh
OF COURSE YOU DID.
THIS IS A REALLY WEIRD THING TO HAPPEN.
SOMEONE IS **ACTUALLY** HAVING A CONVERSA-TION WITH ME.
WHAT?
HOW DID YOU COME UP WITH THIS IDEA?
あああっ
Uhhh...
WELL, I DIDN'T COME UP WITH THIS.
WHAT?
I MANAGED TO CALL SOMEONE ELSE, TOO!

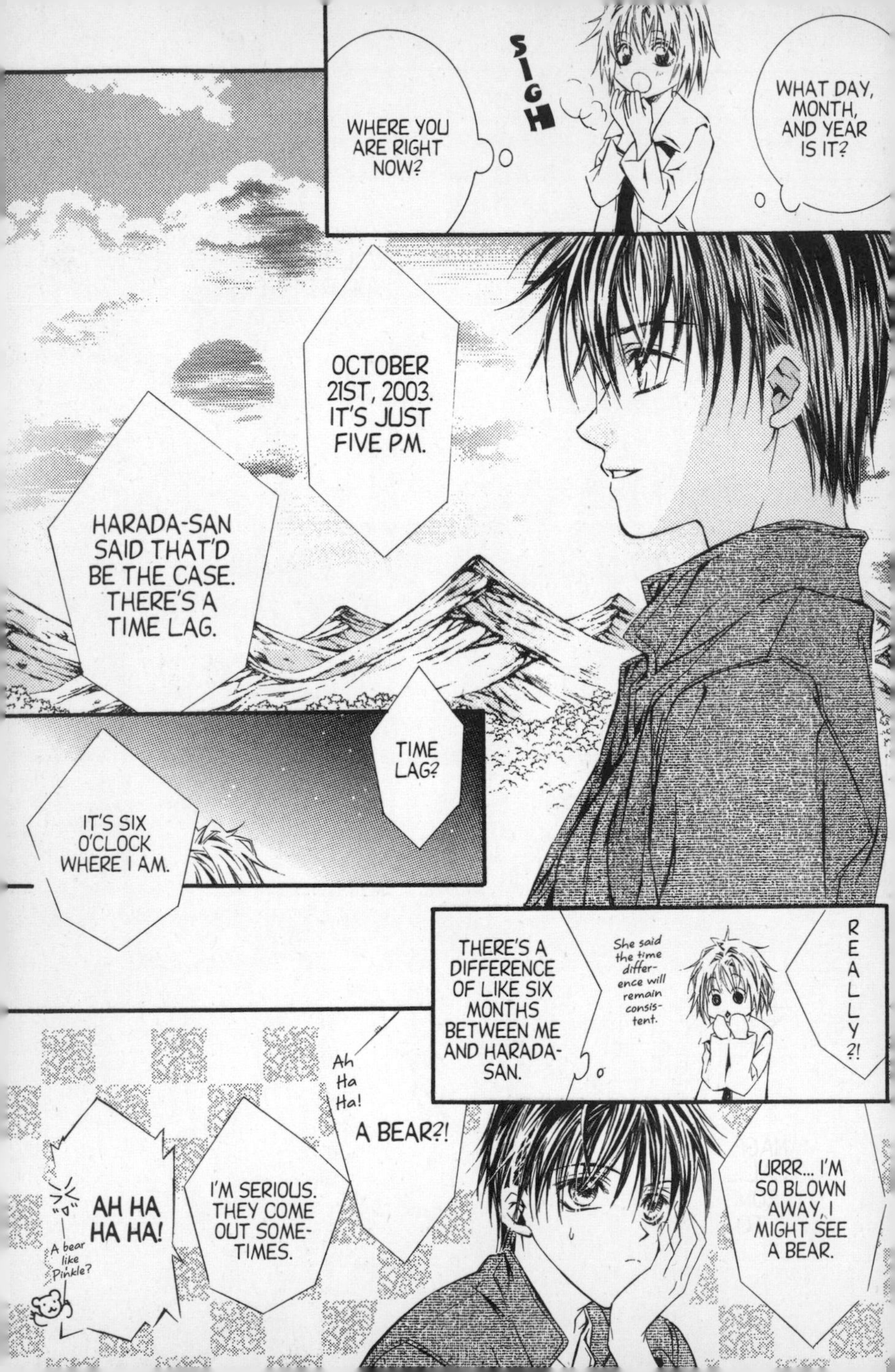
WHAT DAY, MONTH, AND YEAR IS IT?
SIGH
WHERE YOU ARE RIGHT NOW?
OCTOBER 21ST, 2003. IT'S JUST FIVE PM.
HARADA-SAN SAID THAT'D BE THE CASE. THERE'S A TIME LAG.
TIME LAG?
IT'S SIX O'CLOCK WHERE I AM.
REALLY?!
She said the time difference will remain consistent.
THERE'S A DIFFERENCE OF LIKE SIX MONTHS BETWEEN ME AND HARADA-SAN.
URRR... I'M SO BLOWN AWAY, I MIGHT SEE A BEAR.
A BEAR?!
Ah Ha Ha!
I'M SERIOUS. THEY COME OUT SOMETIMES.
AH HA HA HA!
A bear like Pinkle?

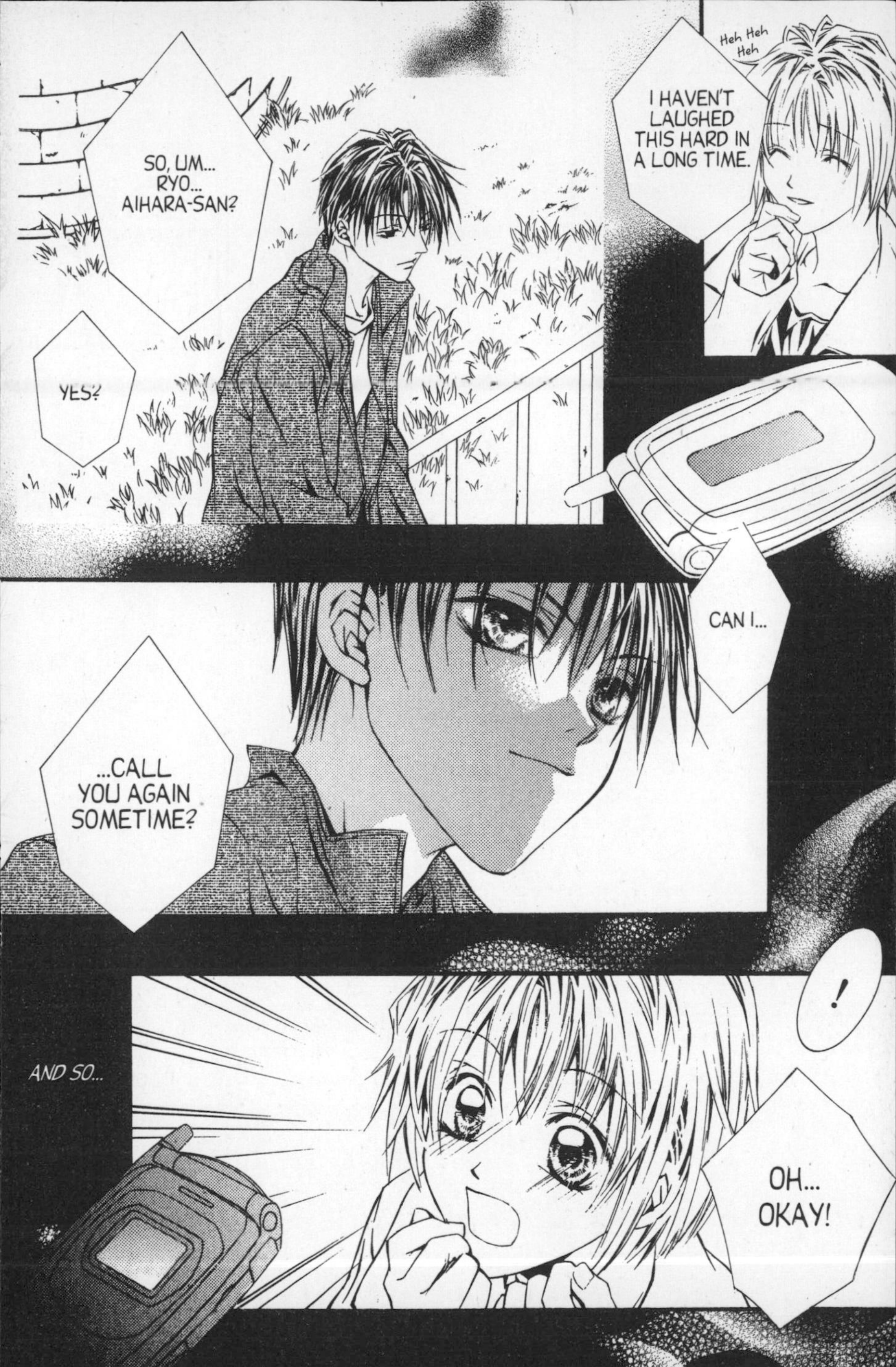
Heh Heh Heh
I HAVEN'T LAUGHED THIS HARD IN A LONG TIME.
SO, UM... RYO... AIHARA-SAN?
YES?
CAN I...
...CALL YOU AGAIN SOMETIME?
!
OH... OKAY!
AND SO...

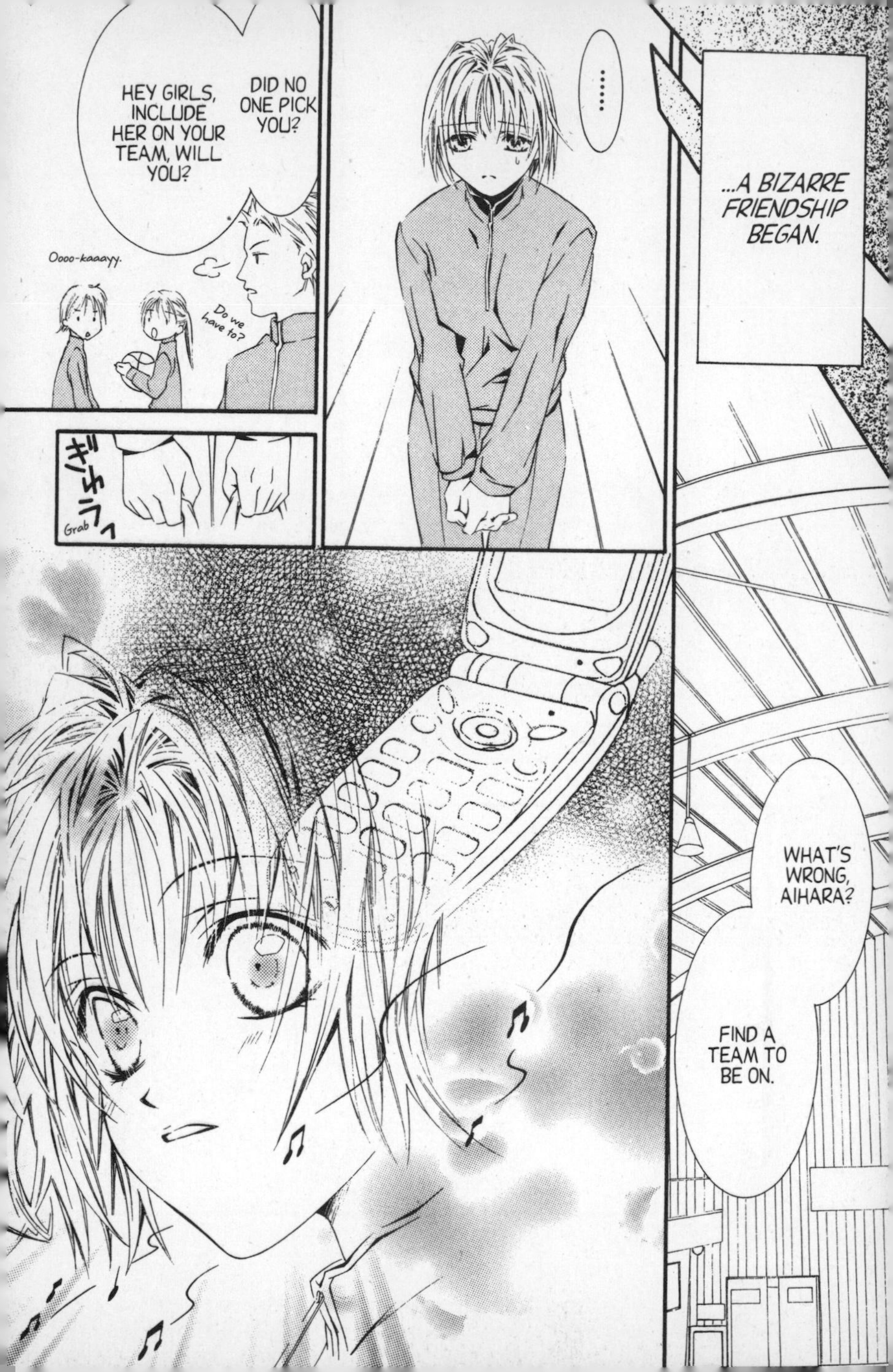
...A BIZARRE FRIENDSHIP BEGAN.
WHAT'S WRONG, AIHARA?
FIND A TEAM TO BE ON.
......
DID NO ONE PICK YOU?
HEY GIRLS, INCLUDE HER ON YOUR TEAM, WILL YOU?
Do we have to?
Oooo-kaaayy.
Grab

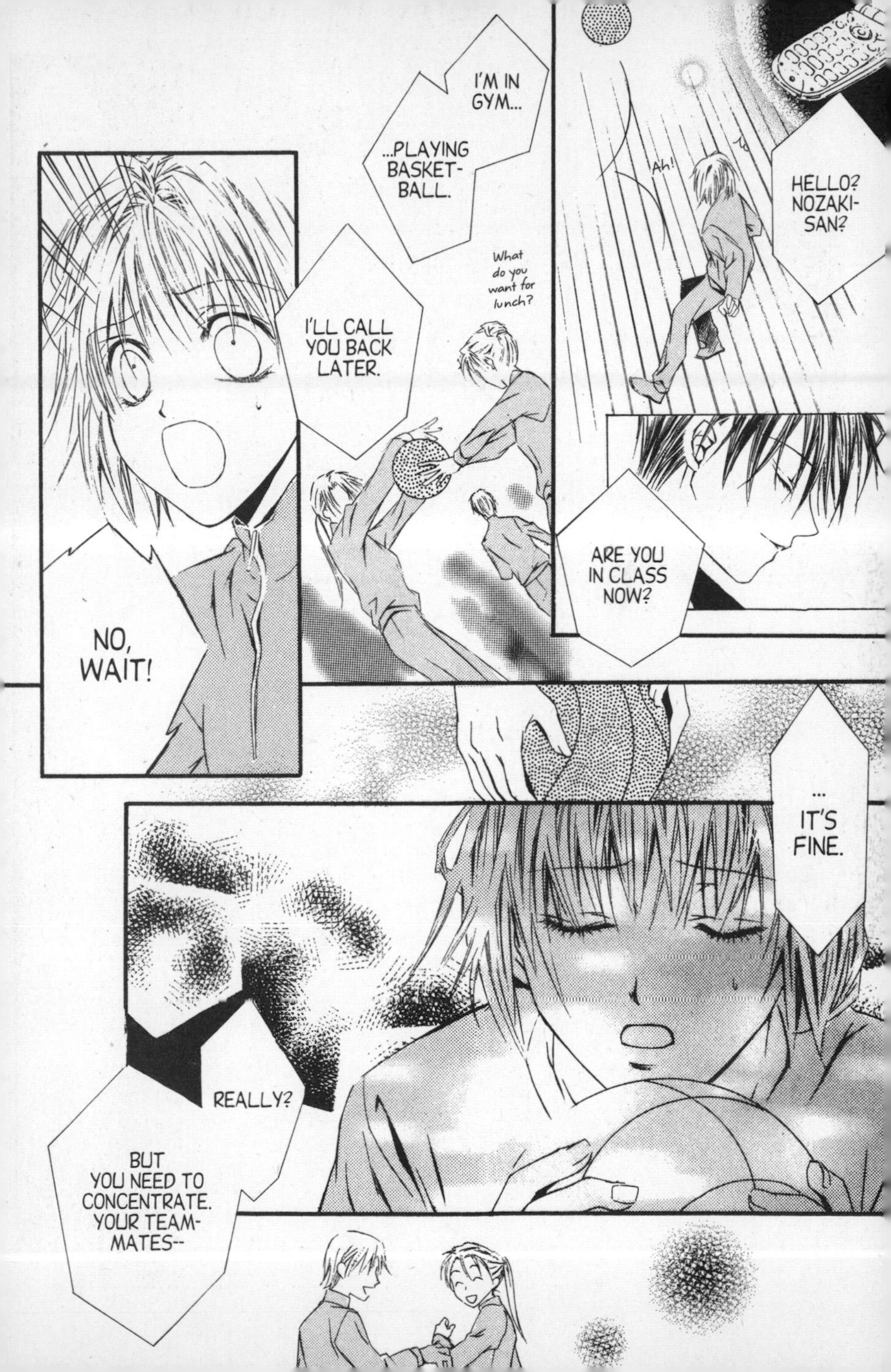
HELLO? NOZAKI-SAN?
Ah!
ARE YOU IN CLASS NOW?
I'M IN GYM...
...PLAYING BASKET-BALL.
What do you want for lunch?
I'LL CALL YOU BACK LATER.
NO, WAIT!
... IT'S FINE.
REALLY?
BUT YOU NEED TO CONCENTRATE. YOUR TEAM-MATES--

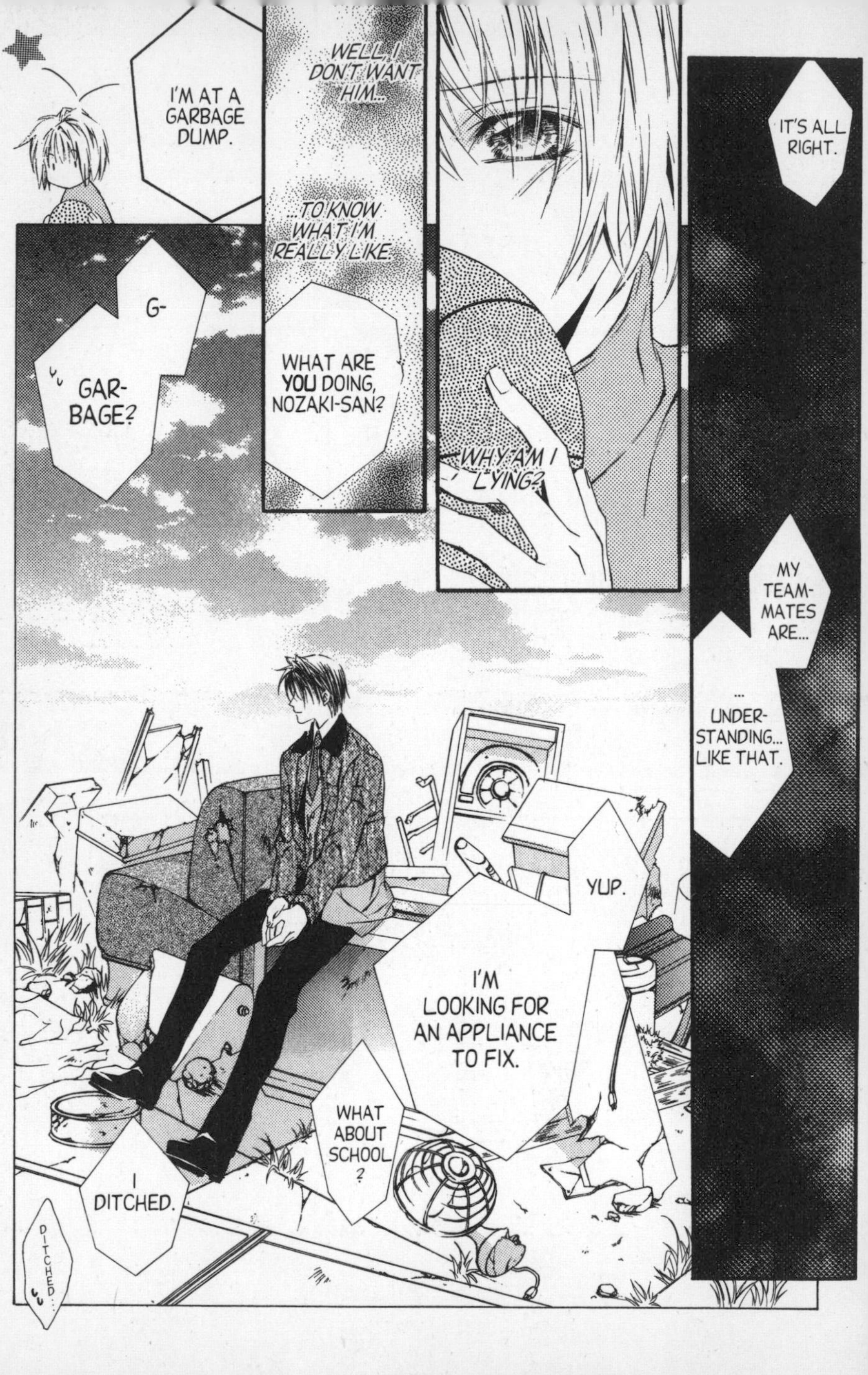
IT'S ALL RIGHT.
MY TEAMMATES ARE...
... UNDERSTANDING... LIKE THAT.
WHY AM I LYING?
WELL, I DON'T WANT HIM...
...TO KNOW WHAT I'M REALLY LIKE.
WHAT ARE YOU DOING, NOZAKI-SAN?
I'M AT A GARBAGE DUMP.
G-
GAR-BAGE?
YUP.
I'M LOOKING FOR AN APPLIANCE TO FIX.
WHAT ABOUT SCHOOL?
I DITCHED.
DITCHED...

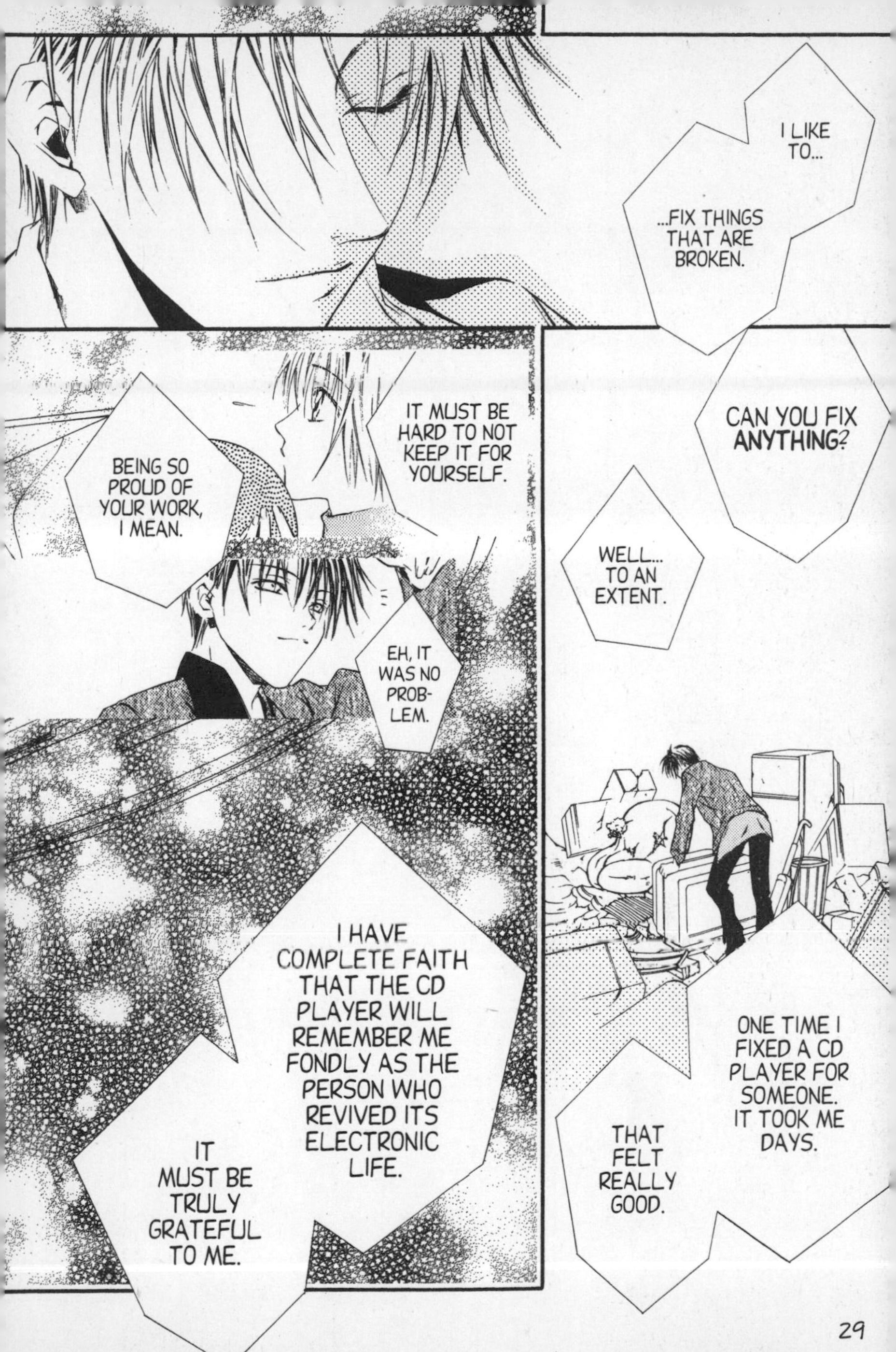
I LIKE TO...
...FIX THINGS THAT ARE BROKEN.
CAN YOU FIX **ANYTHING**?
WELL... TO AN EXTENT.
ONE TIME I FIXED A CD PLAYER FOR SOMEONE. IT TOOK ME DAYS.
THAT FELT REALLY GOOD.
IT MUST BE HARD TO NOT KEEP IT FOR YOURSELF.
BEING SO PROUD OF YOUR WORK, I MEAN.
EH, IT WAS NO PROB-LEM.
I HAVE COMPLETE FAITH THAT THE CD PLAYER WILL REMEMBER ME FONDLY AS THE PERSON WHO REVIVED ITS ELECTRONIC LIFE.
IT MUST BE TRULY GRATEFUL TO ME.

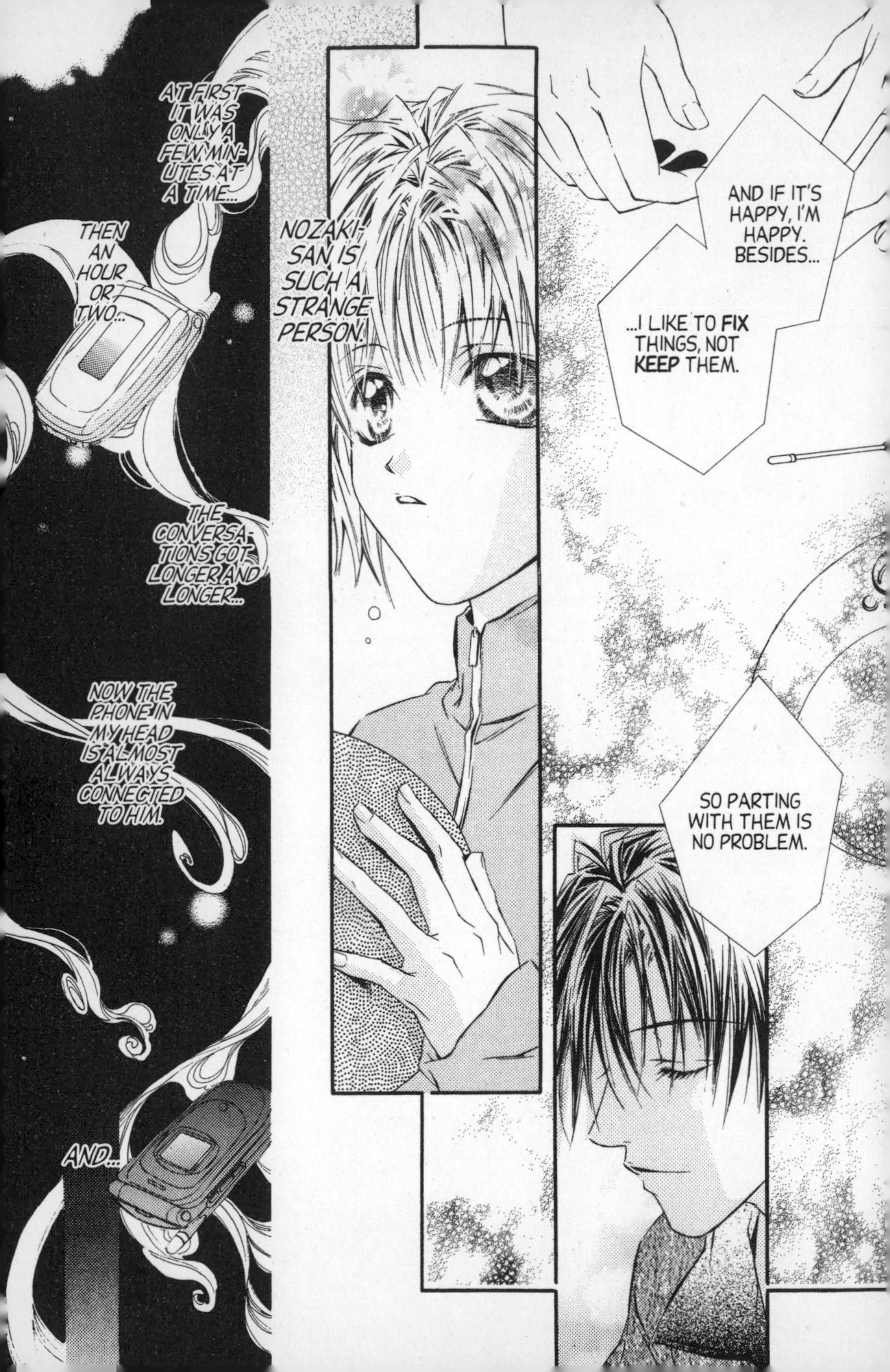
AND IF IT'S HAPPY, I'M HAPPY. BESIDES...
...I LIKE TO FIX THINGS, NOT KEEP THEM.
SO PARTING WITH THEM IS NO PROBLEM.
NOZAKI-SAN IS SUCH A STRANGE PERSON!
AT FIRST IT WAS ONLY A FEW MINUTES AT A TIME...
THEN AN HOUR OR TWO...
THE CONVERSATIONS GOT LONGER AND LONGER...
NOW THE PHONE IN MY HEAD IS ALMOST ALWAYS CONNECTED TO HIM.
AND...

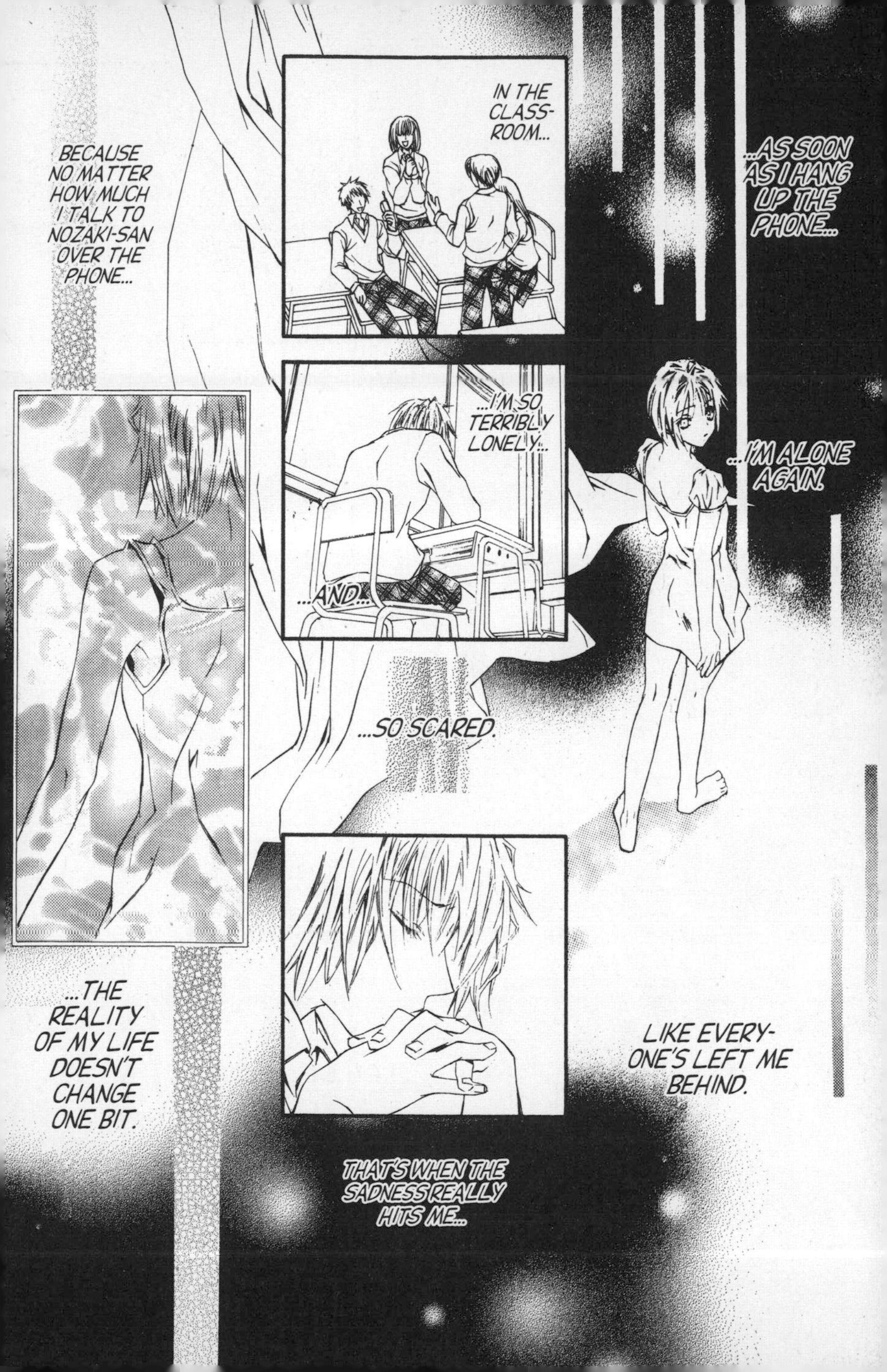
...AS SOON AS I HANG UP THE PHONE...
...I'M ALONE AGAIN.
LIKE EVERY-ONE'S LEFT ME BEHIND.
THAT'S WHEN THE SADNESS REALLY HITS ME...
IN THE CLASS-ROOM...
...I'M SO TERRIBLY LONELY...
...AND...
...SO SCARED.
BECAUSE NO MATTER HOW MUCH I TALK TO NOZAKI-SAN OVER THE PHONE...
...THE REALITY OF MY LIFE DOESN'T CHANGE ONE BIT.

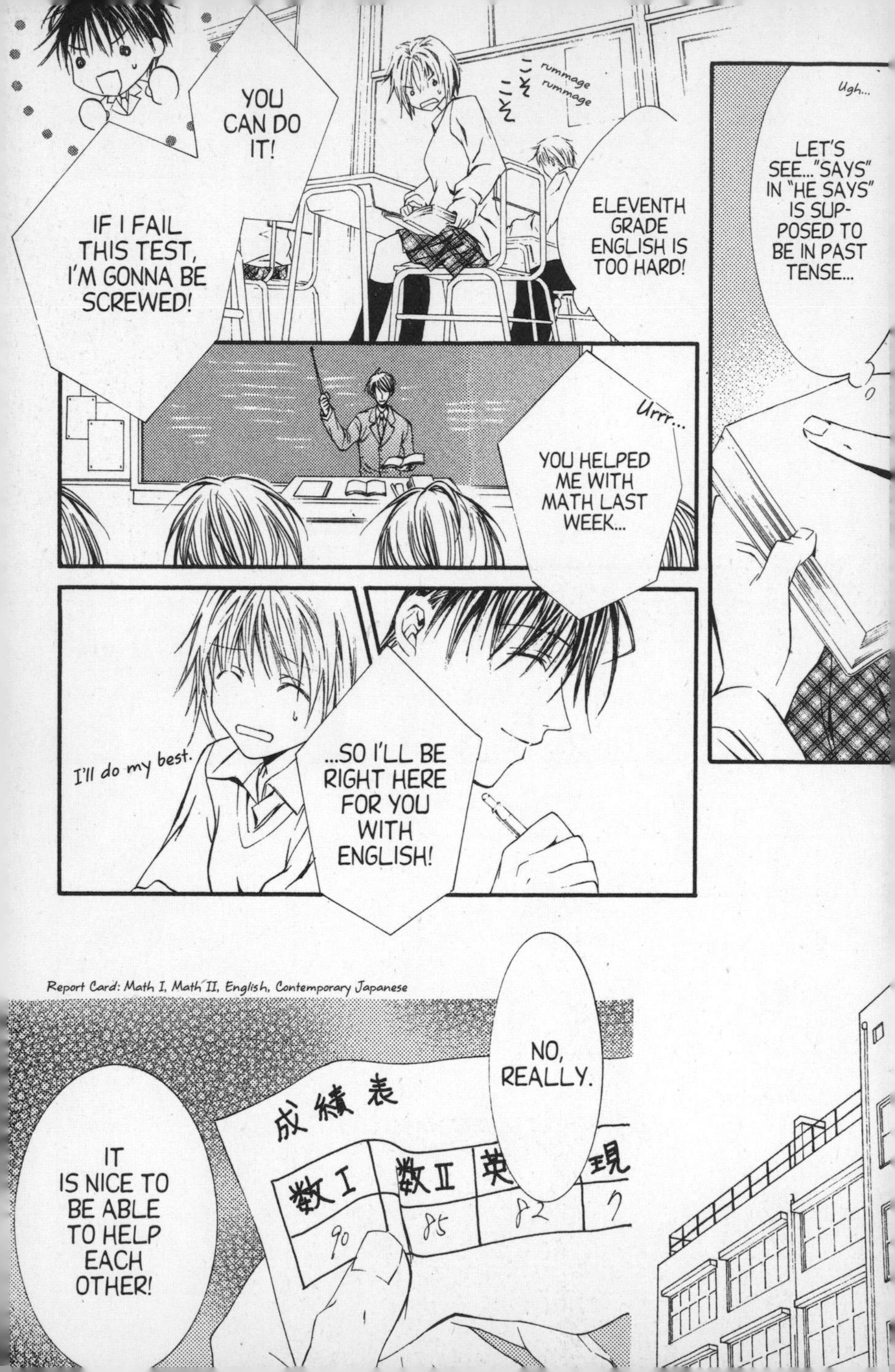
Ugh...
LET'S SEE..."SAYS" IN "HE SAYS" IS SUP-POSED TO BE IN PAST TENSE...
こそこそ
rummage rummage
ELEVENTH GRADE ENGLISH IS TOO HARD!
YOU CAN DO IT!
IF I FAIL THIS TEST, I'M GONNA BE SCREWED!
Urrr...
YOU HELPED ME WITH MATH LAST WEEK...
...SO I'LL BE RIGHT HERE FOR YOU WITH ENGLISH!
I'll do my best.
Report Card: Math I, Math II, English, Contemporary Japanese
NO, REALLY.
成績表
数I
数II
英
現
90
85
82
IT IS NICE TO BE ABLE TO HELP EACH OTHER!

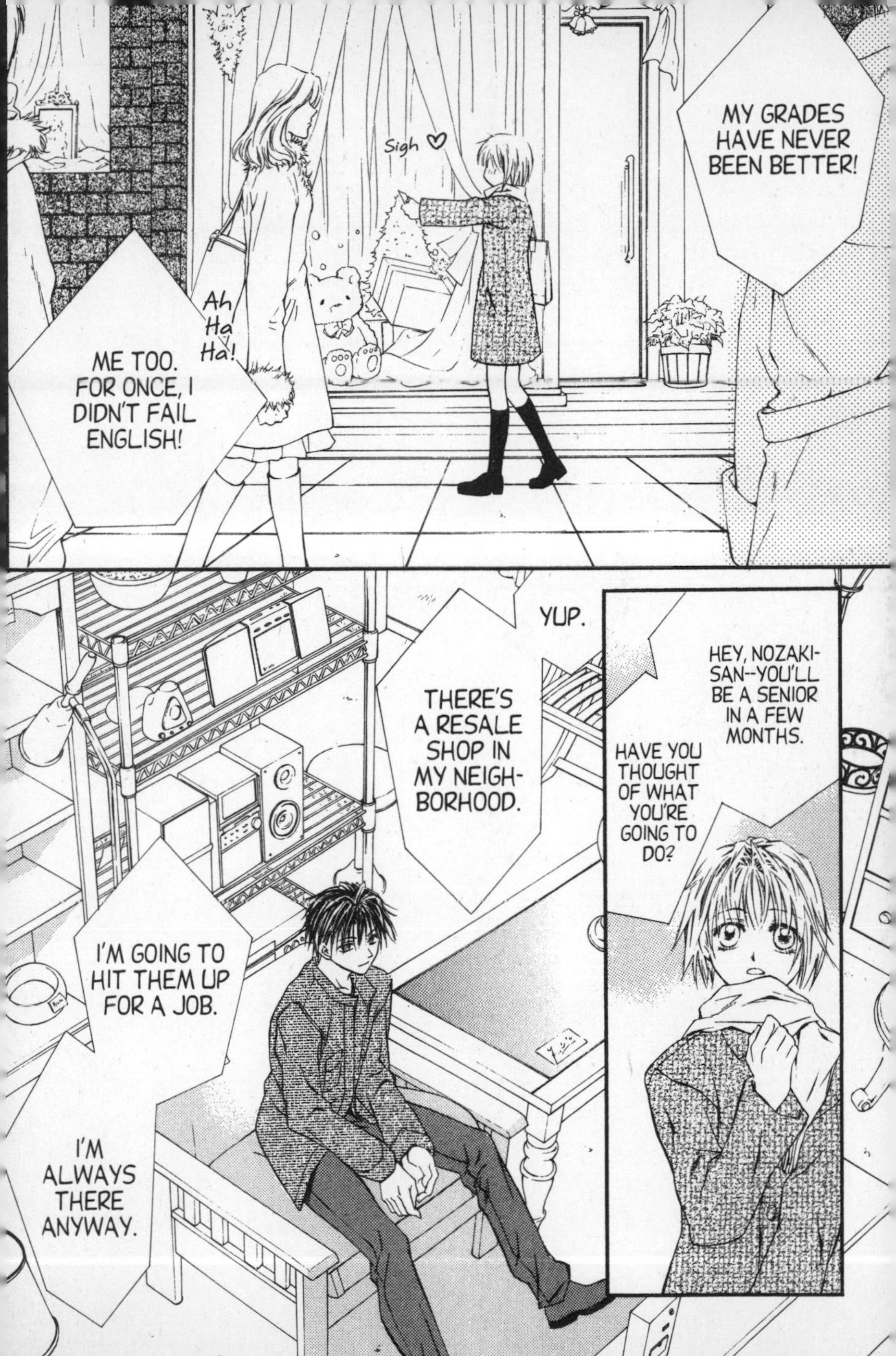
MY GRADES HAVE NEVER BEEN BETTER!
Sigh ♡
Ah Ha Ha!
ME TOO. FOR ONCE, I DIDN'T FAIL ENGLISH!
HEY, NOZAKI-SAN--YOU'LL BE A SENIOR IN A FEW MONTHS.
HAVE YOU THOUGHT OF WHAT YOU'RE GOING TO DO?
YUP.
THERE'S A RESALE SHOP IN MY NEIGHBORHOOD.
I'M GOING TO HIT THEM UP FOR A JOB.
I'M ALWAYS THERE ANYWAY.

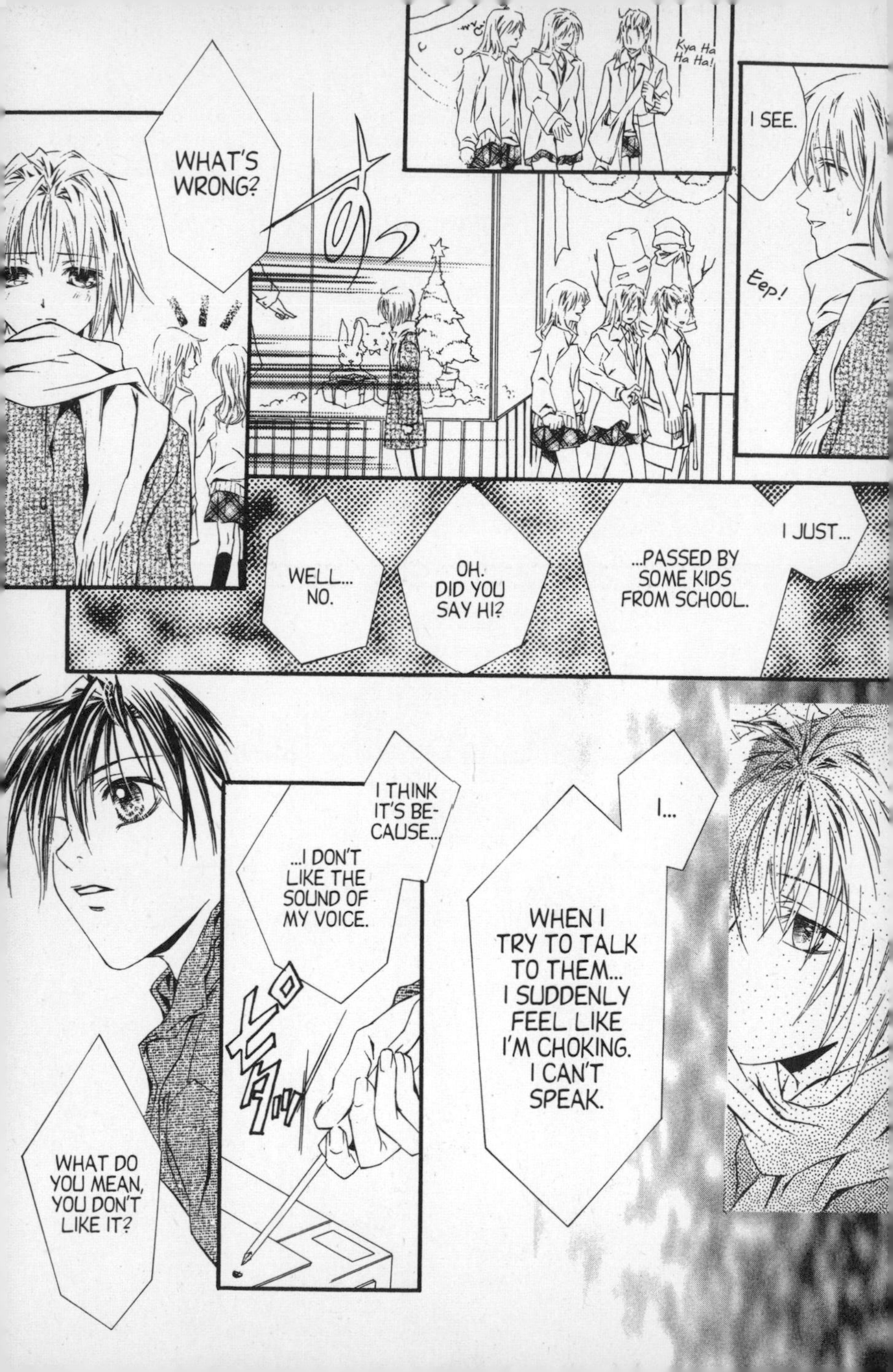
I SEE.
Eep!
Kya Ha Ha Ha!
WHAT'S WRONG?
I JUST...
...PASSED BY SOME KIDS FROM SCHOOL.
OH. DID YOU SAY HI?
WELL... NO.
I...
WHEN I TRY TO TALK TO THEM... I SUDDENLY FEEL LIKE I'M CHOKING. I CAN'T SPEAK.
I THINK IT'S BE- CAUSE...
...I DON'T LIKE THE SOUND OF MY VOICE.
WHAT DO YOU MEAN, YOU DON'T LIKE IT?

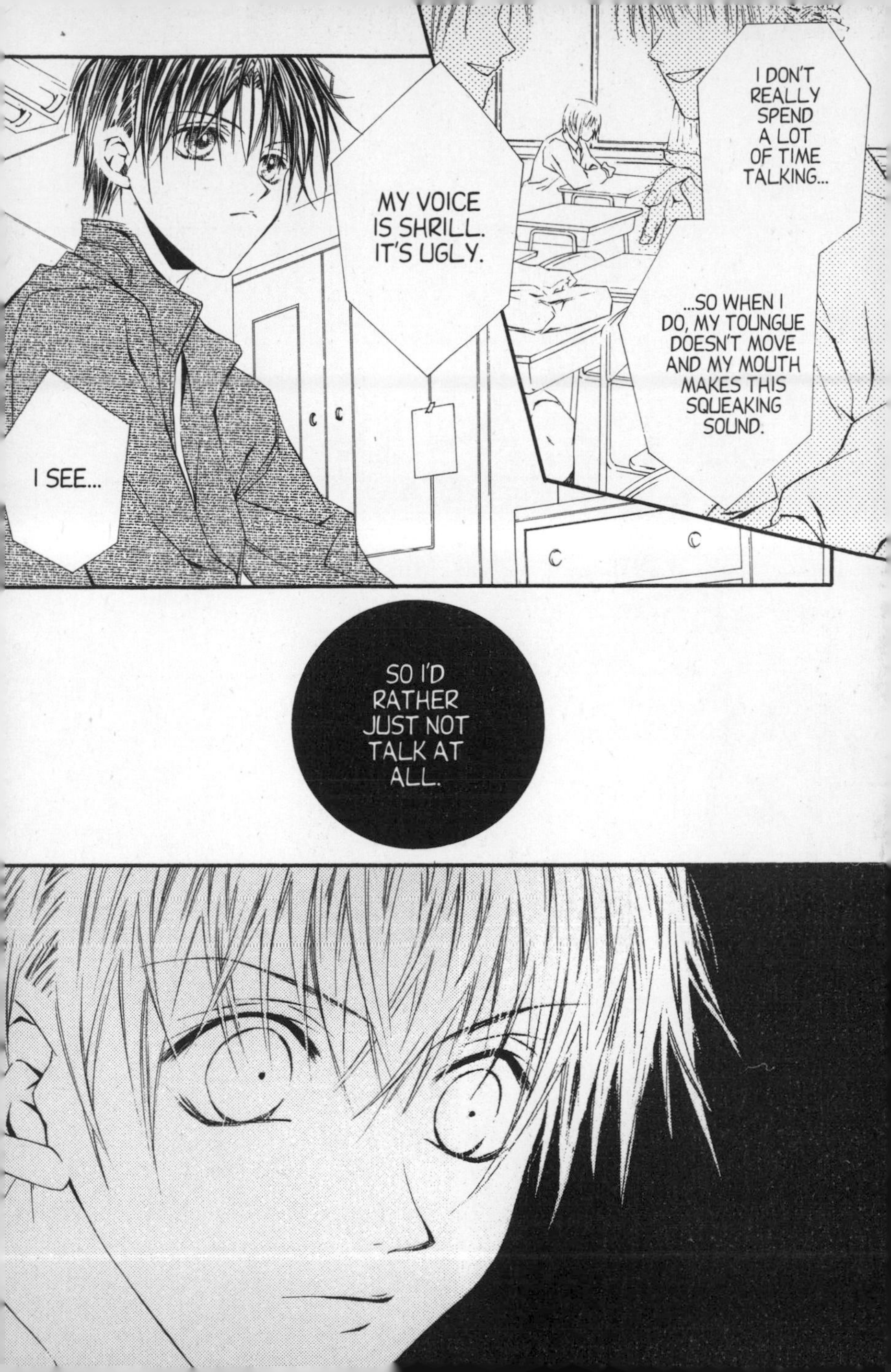
I DON'T REALLY SPEND A LOT OF TIME TALKING...
...SO WHEN I DO, MY TOUNGUE DOESN'T MOVE AND MY MOUTH MAKES THIS SQUEAKING SOUND.
MY VOICE IS SHRILL. IT'S UGLY.
I SEE...
SO I'D RATHER JUST NOT TALK AT ALL.

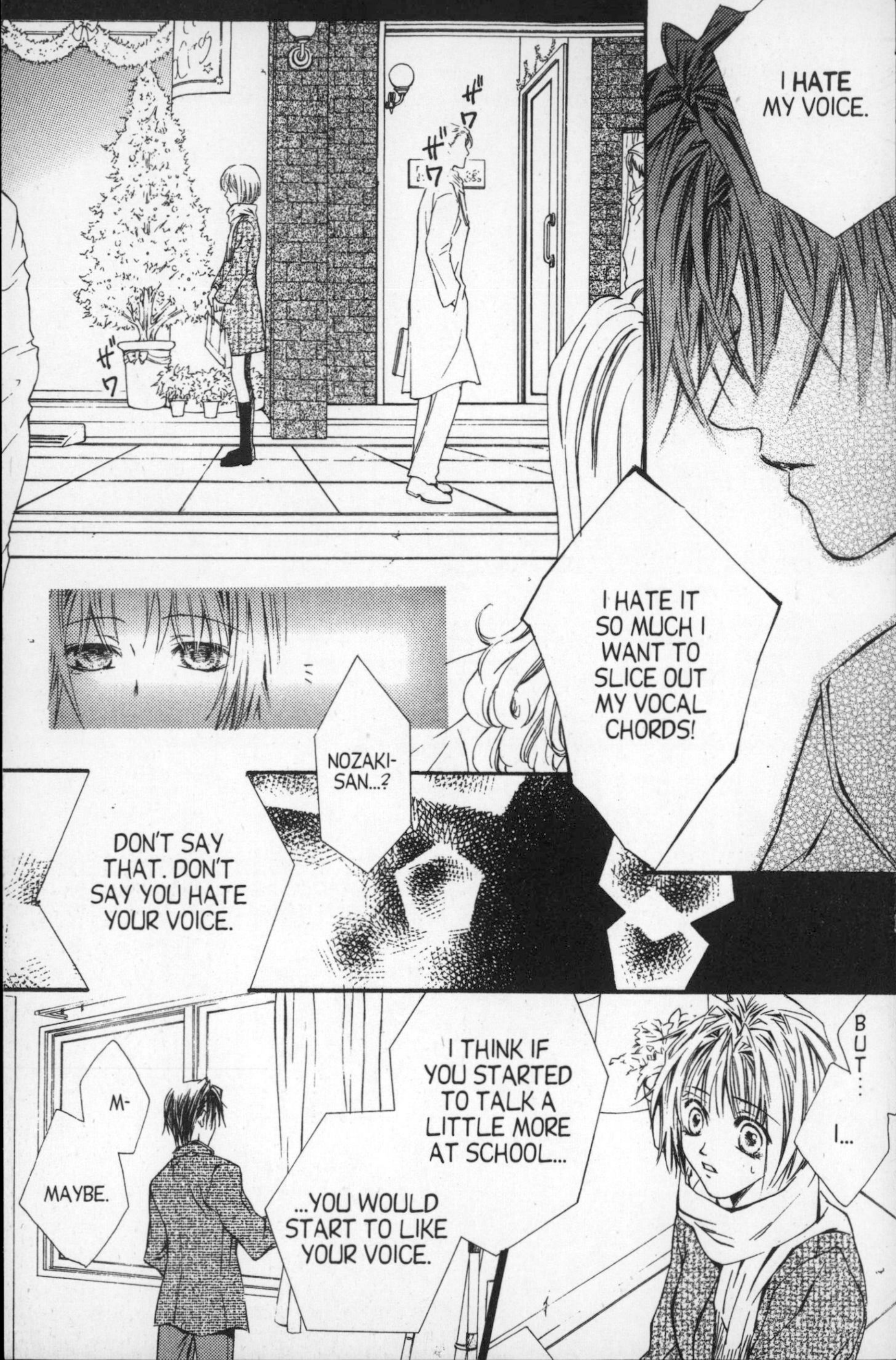

I HATE MY VOICE.
I HATE IT SO MUCH I WANT TO SLICE OUT MY VOCAL CHORDS!
ザワ
ザワ
ザワ
NOZAKI-SAN...?
DON'T SAY THAT. DON'T SAY YOU HATE YOUR VOICE.
BUT...
I...
I THINK IF YOU STARTED TO TALK A LITTLE MORE AT SCHOOL...
...YOU WOULD START TO LIKE YOUR VOICE.
M-
MAYBE.

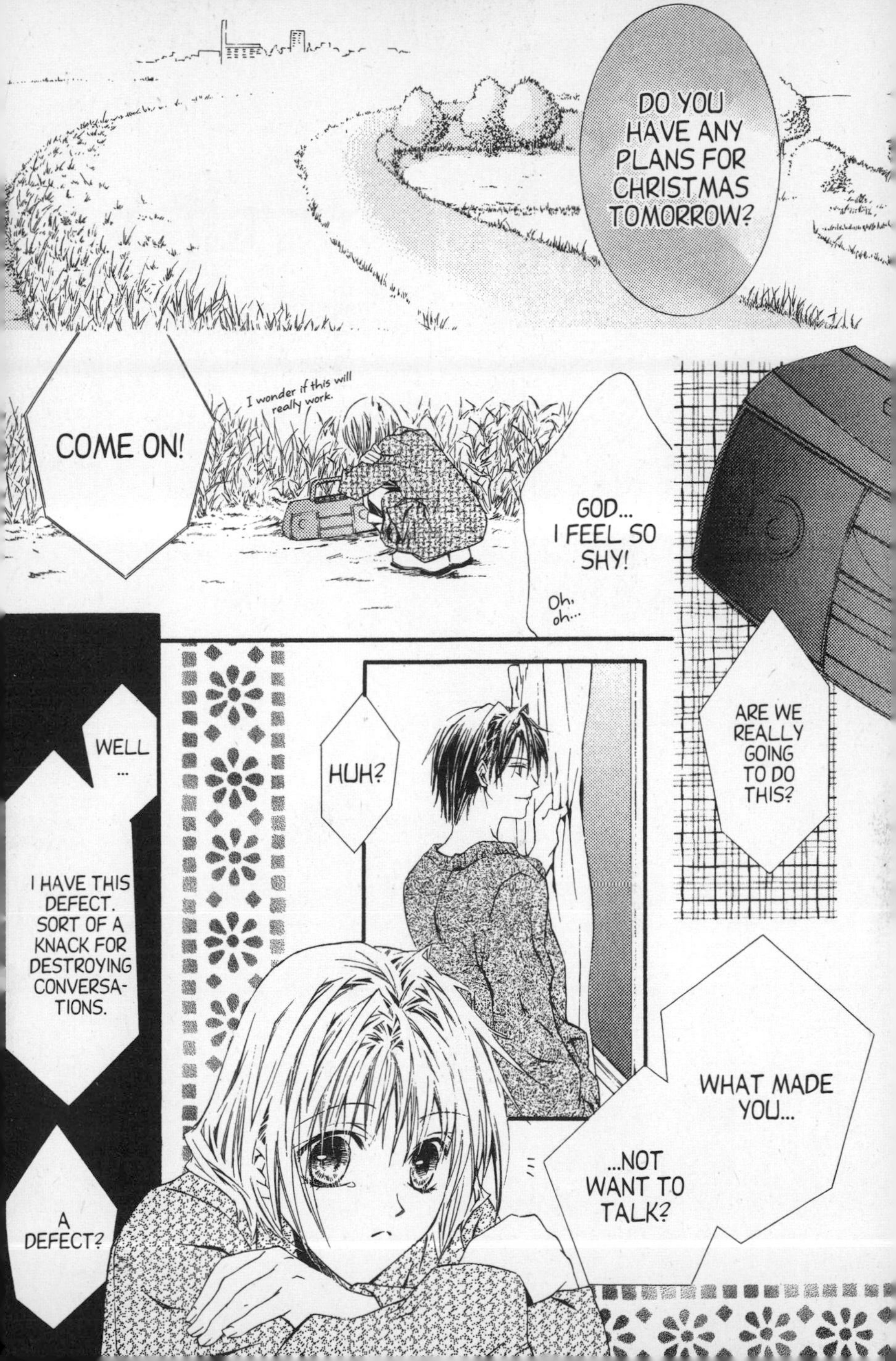
DO YOU HAVE ANY PLANS FOR CHRISTMAS TOMORROW?
ARE WE REALLY GOING TO DO THIS?
GOD... I FEEL SO SHY!
Oh, oh...
I wonder if this will really work.
COME ON!
WHAT MADE YOU...
...NOT WANT TO TALK?
HUH?
WELL ...
I HAVE THIS DEFECT. SORT OF A KNACK FOR DESTROYING CONVERSA-TIONS.
A DEFECT?

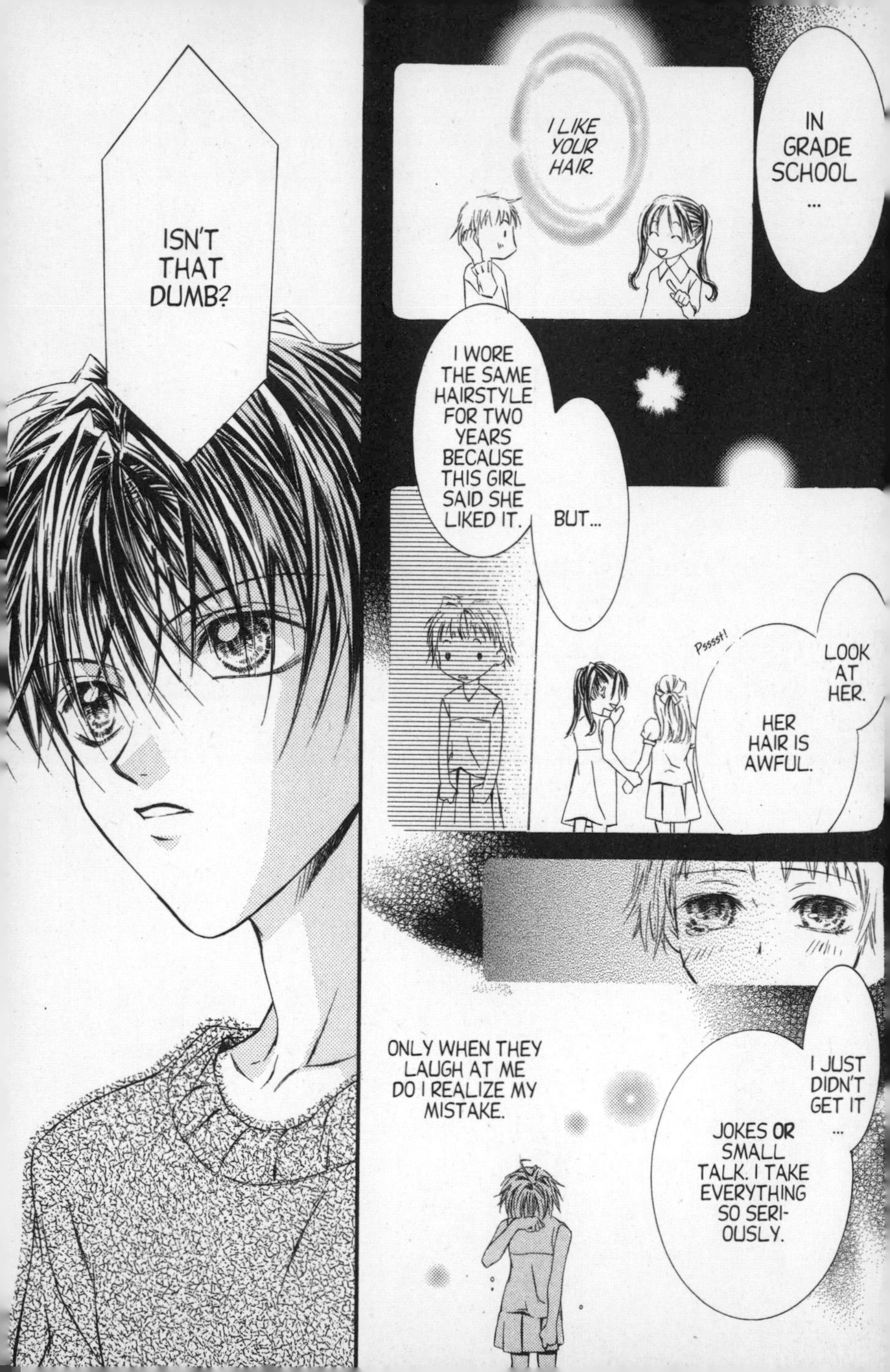

IN GRADE SCHOOL...
I LIKE YOUR HAIR.
I WORE THE SAME HAIRSTYLE FOR TWO YEARS BECAUSE THIS GIRL SAID SHE LIKED IT.
BUT...
Psssst!
LOOK AT HER.
HER HAIR IS AWFUL.
I JUST DIDN'T GET IT...
JOKES OR SMALL TALK. I TAKE EVERYTHING SO SERI-OUSLY.
ONLY WHEN THEY LAUGH AT ME DO I REALIZE MY MISTAKE.
ISN'T THAT DUMB?

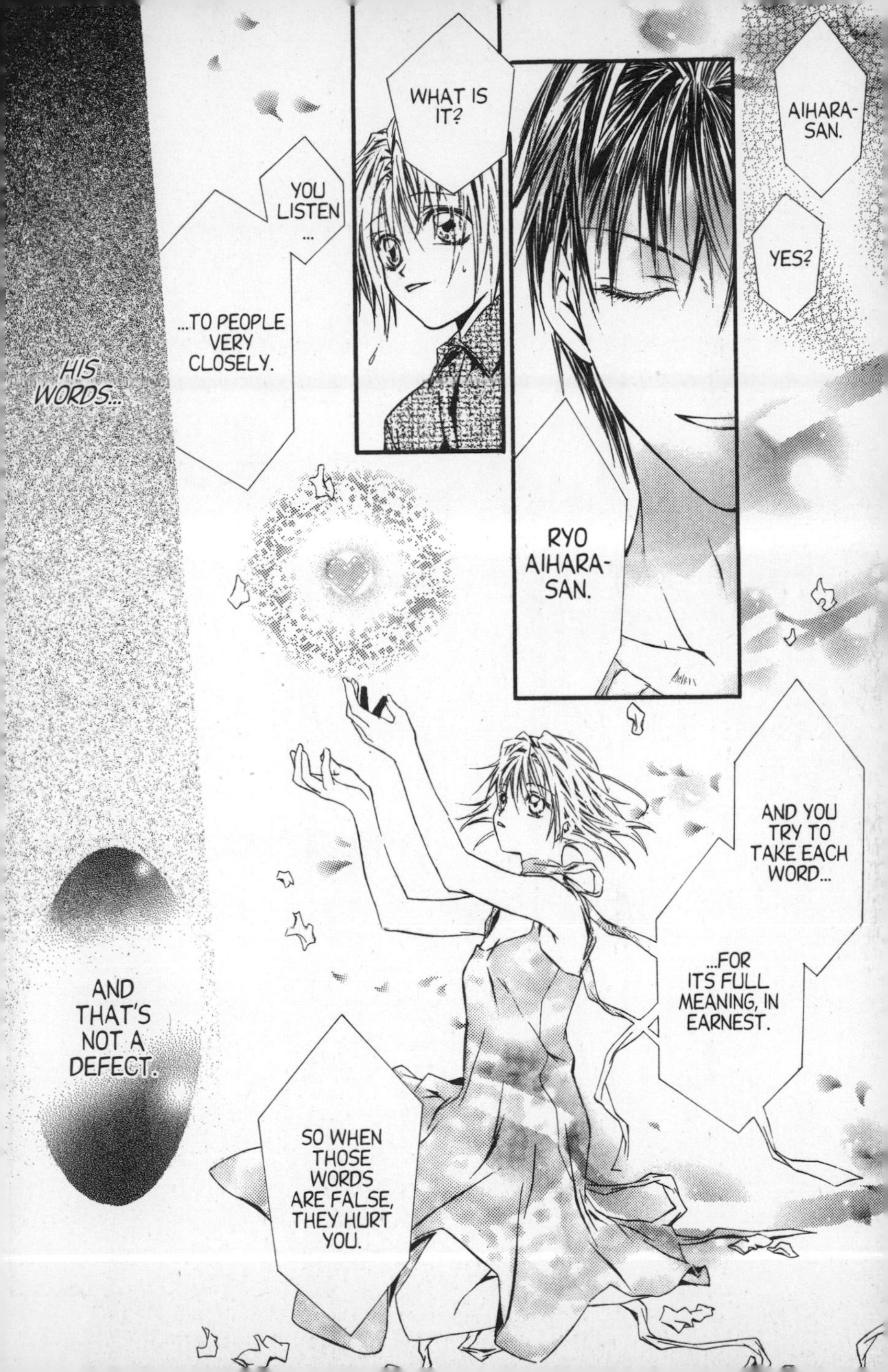
AIHARA-SAN.
YES?
WHAT IS IT?
RYO AIHARA-SAN.
YOU LISTEN ...
...TO PEOPLE VERY CLOSELY.
HIS WORDS...
AND YOU TRY TO TAKE EACH WORD...
...FOR ITS FULL MEANING, IN EARNEST.
SO WHEN THOSE WORDS ARE FALSE, THEY HURT YOU.
AND THAT'S NOT A DEFECT.

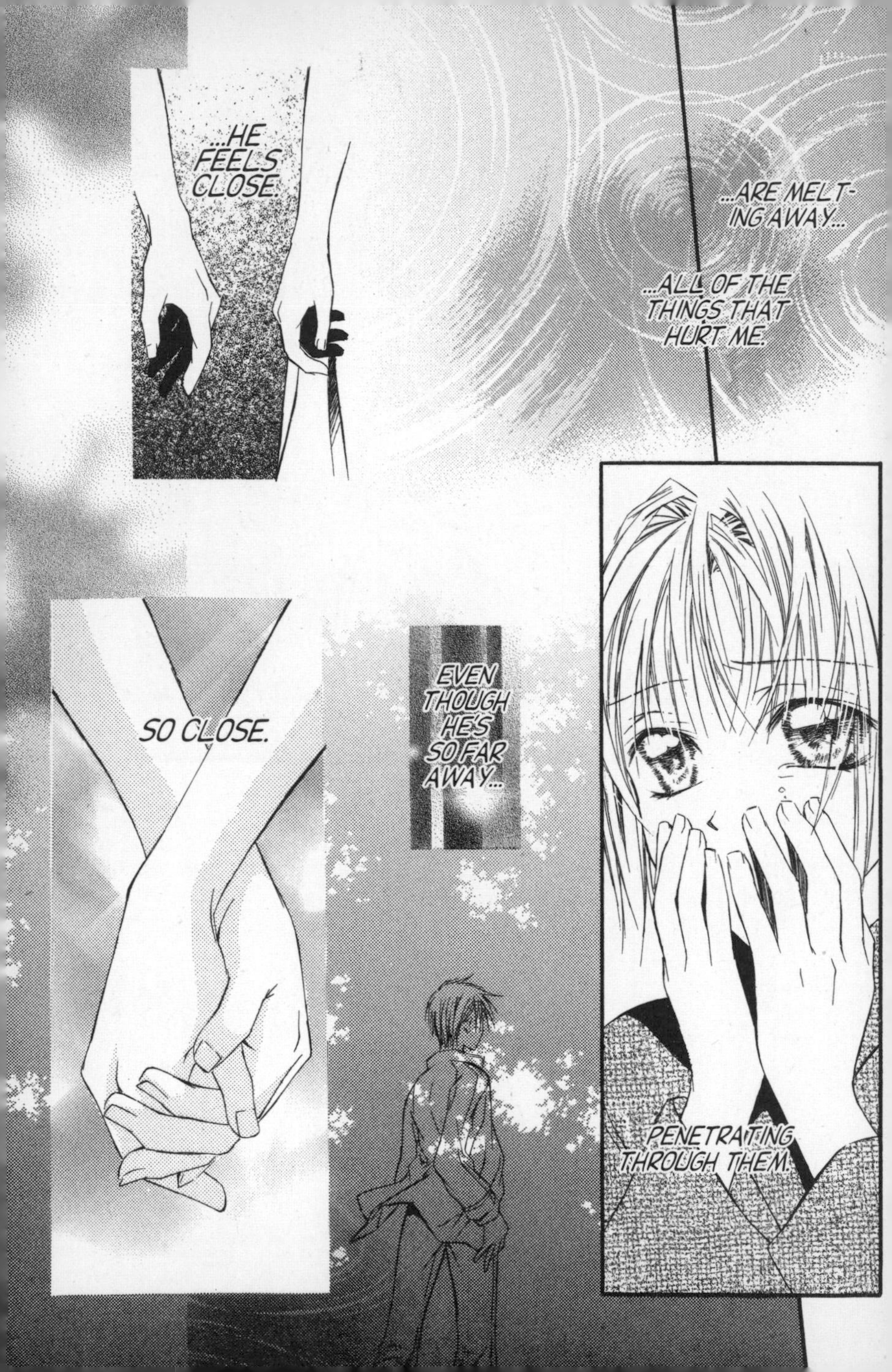
...ARE MELT-ING AWAY...
...ALL OF THE THINGS THAT HURT ME.
...HE FEELS CLOSE.
PENETRATING THROUGH THEM.
EVEN THOUGH HE'S SO FAR AWAY...
SO CLOSE.

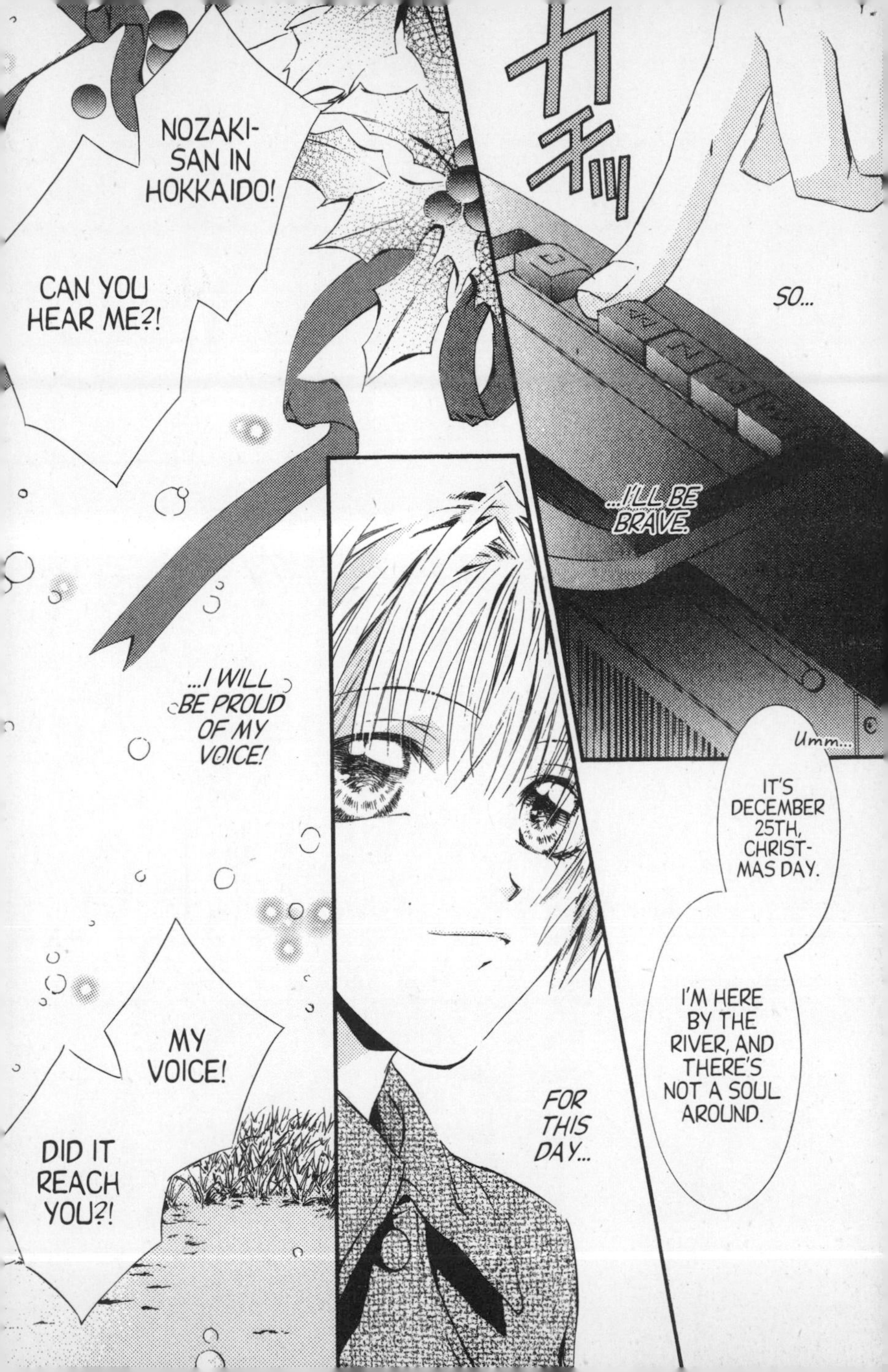
カチッ
SO...
...I'LL BE BRAVE.
Umm...
IT'S DECEMBER 25TH, CHRIST-MAS DAY.
I'M HERE BY THE RIVER, AND THERE'S NOT A SOUL AROUND.
FOR THIS DAY...
NOZAKI-SAN IN HOKKAIDO!
CAN YOU HEAR ME?!
...I WILL BE PROUD OF MY VOICE!
MY VOICE!
DID IT REACH YOU?!

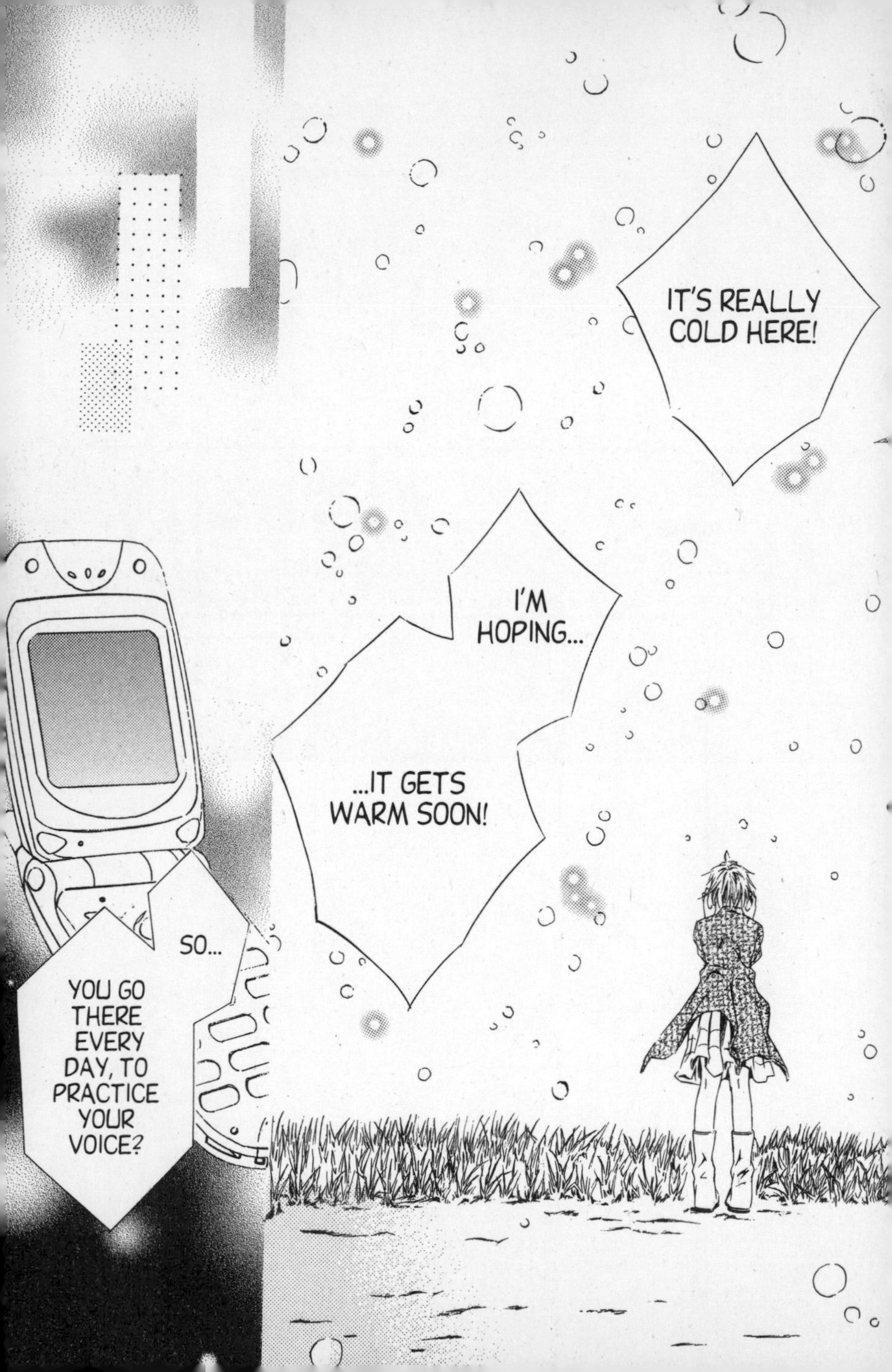
IT'S REALLY COLD HERE!
I'M HOPING...
...IT GETS WARM SOON!
SO...
YOU GO THERE EVERY DAY, TO PRACTICE YOUR VOICE?

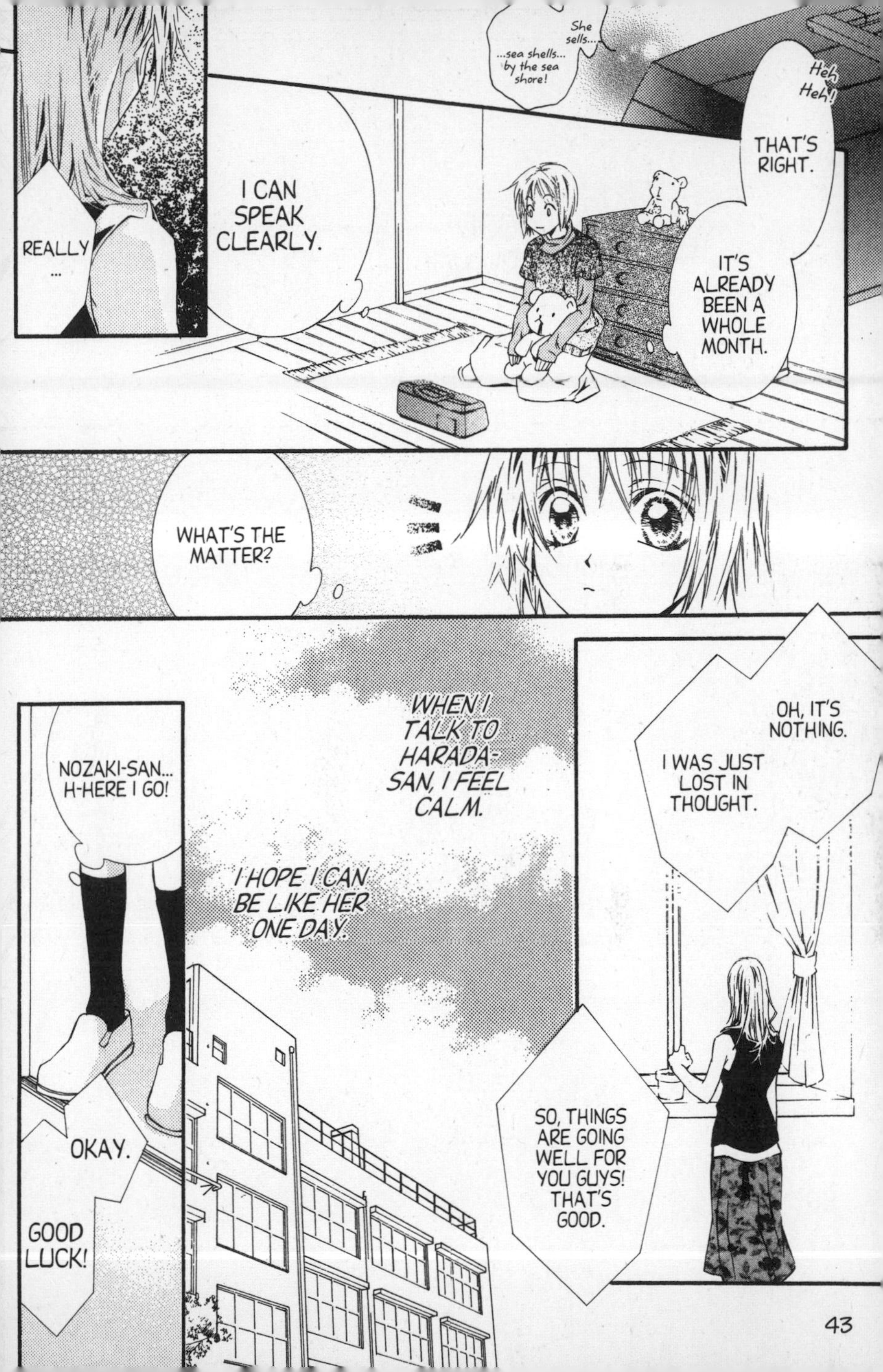

She sells... ...sea shells... by the sea shore!
Heh Heh!
THAT'S RIGHT.
IT'S ALREADY BEEN A WHOLE MONTH.
I CAN SPEAK CLEARLY.
REALLY ...
WHAT'S THE MATTER?
OH, IT'S NOTHING.
I WAS JUST LOST IN THOUGHT.
SO, THINGS ARE GOING WELL FOR YOU GUYS! THAT'S GOOD.
WHEN I TALK TO HARADA-SAN, I FEEL CALM.
I HOPE I CAN BE LIKE HER ONE DAY.
NOZAKI-SAN... H-HERE I GO!
OKAY.
GOOD LUCK!

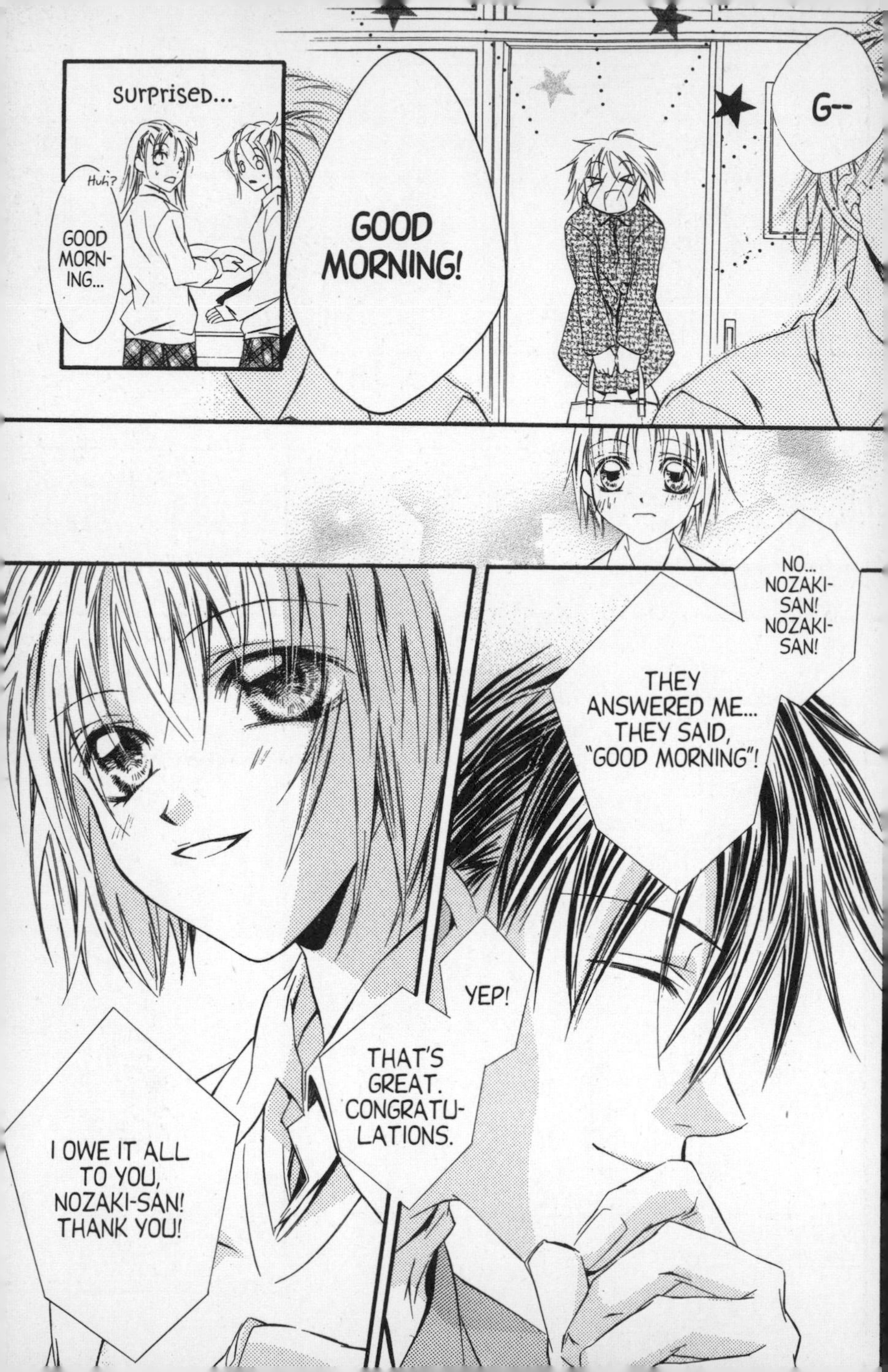
G--
GOOD MORNING!
Surprised...
Huh?
GOOD MORNING...
NO... NOZAKI-SAN! NOZAKI-SAN!
THEY ANSWERED ME... THEY SAID, "GOOD MORNING"!
THAT'S GREAT. CONGRATULATIONS.
YEP!
I OWE IT ALL TO YOU, NOZAKI-SAN! THANK YOU!

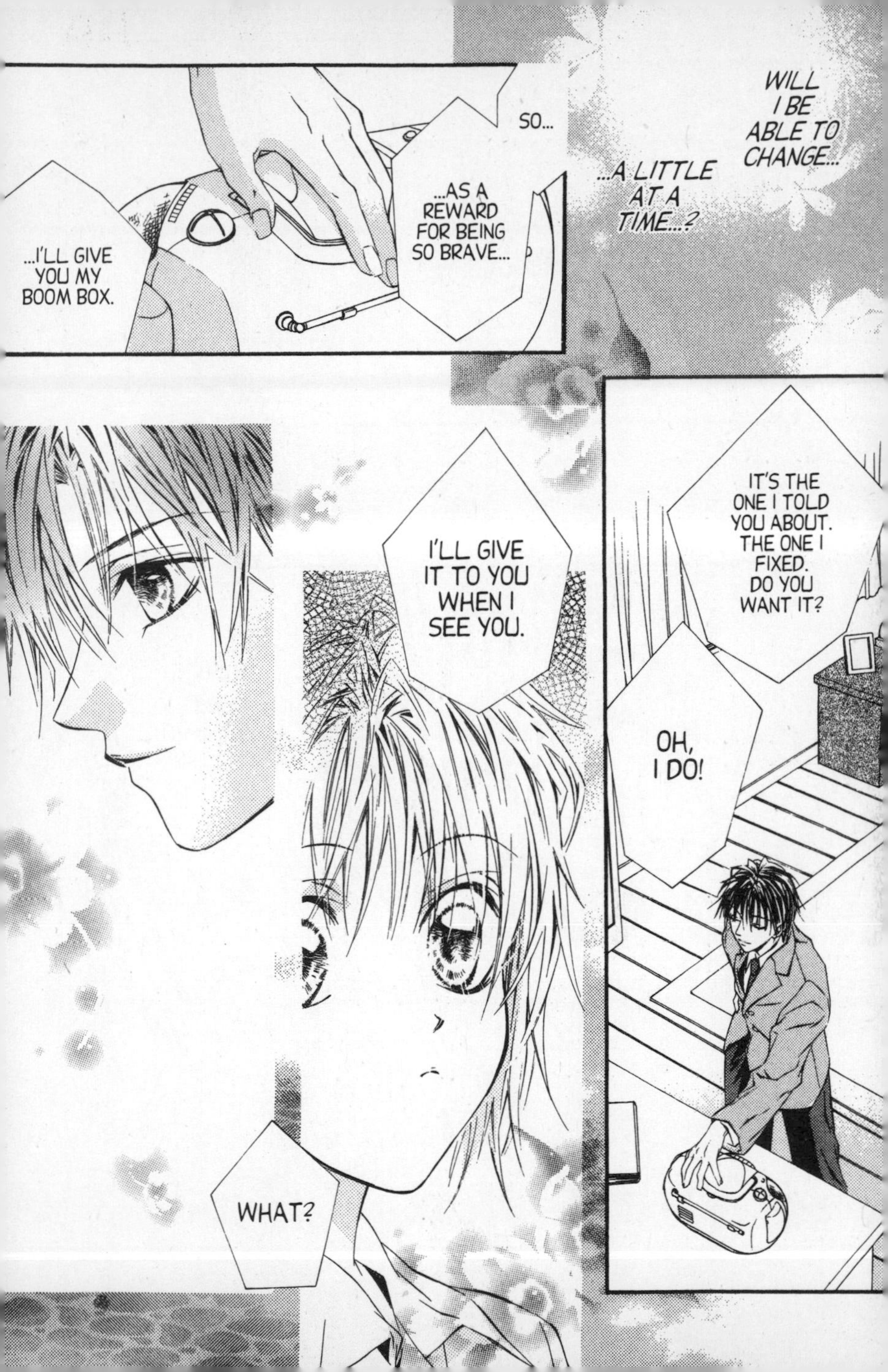
WILL I BE ABLE TO CHANGE...
...A LITTLE AT A TIME...?
SO...
...AS A REWARD FOR BEING SO BRAVE...
...I'LL GIVE YOU MY BOOM BOX.
IT'S THE ONE I TOLD YOU ABOUT. THE ONE I FIXED. DO YOU WANT IT?
OH, I DO!
I'LL GIVE IT TO YOU WHEN I SEE YOU.
WHAT?

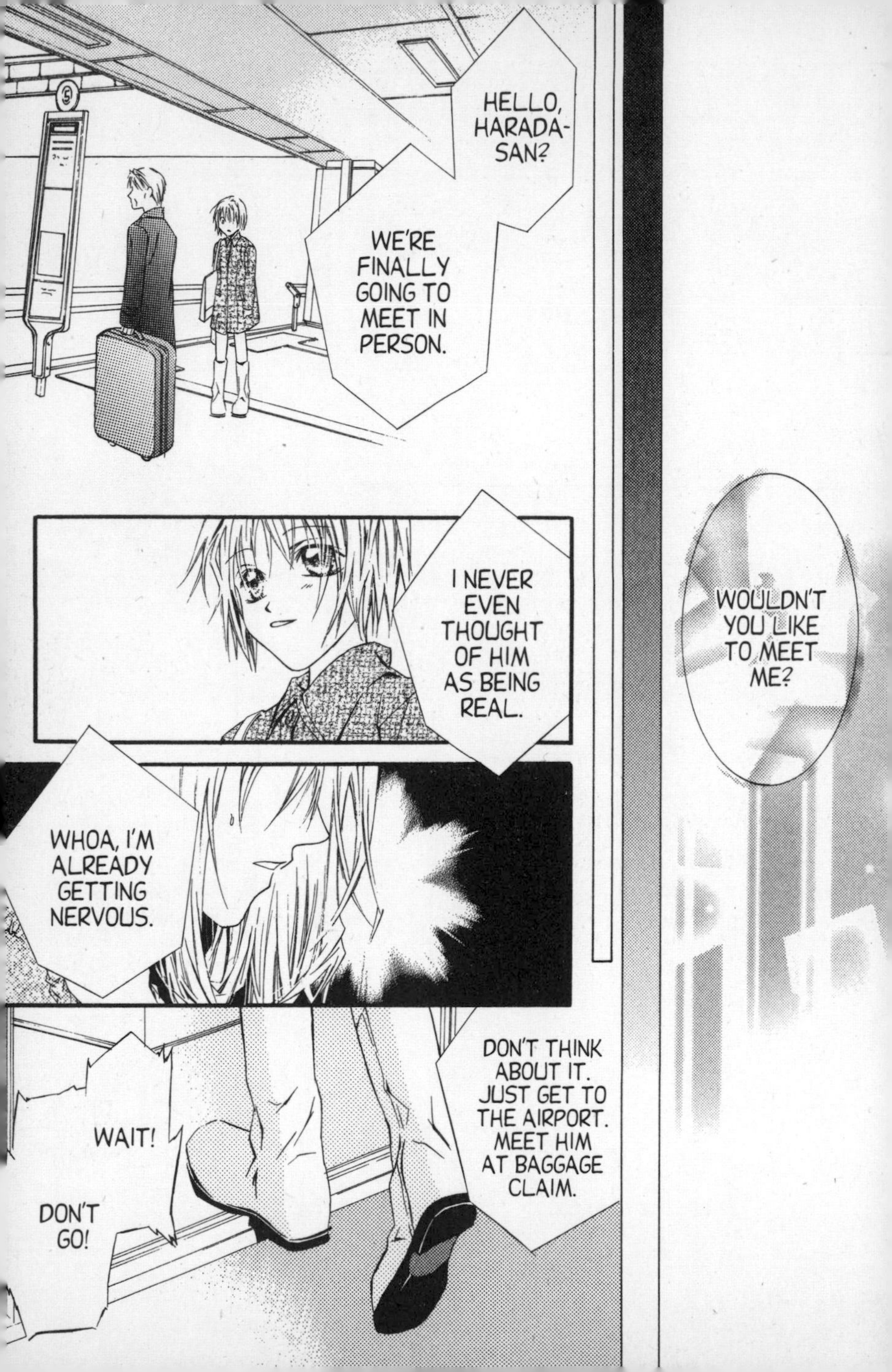
WOULDN'T YOU LIKE TO MEET ME?
HELLO, HARADA-SAN?
WE'RE FINALLY GOING TO MEET IN PERSON.
I NEVER EVEN THOUGHT OF HIM AS BEING REAL.
WHOA, I'M ALREADY GETTING NERVOUS.
DON'T THINK ABOUT IT. JUST GET TO THE AIRPORT. MEET HIM AT BAGGAGE CLAIM.
WAIT!
DON'T GO!

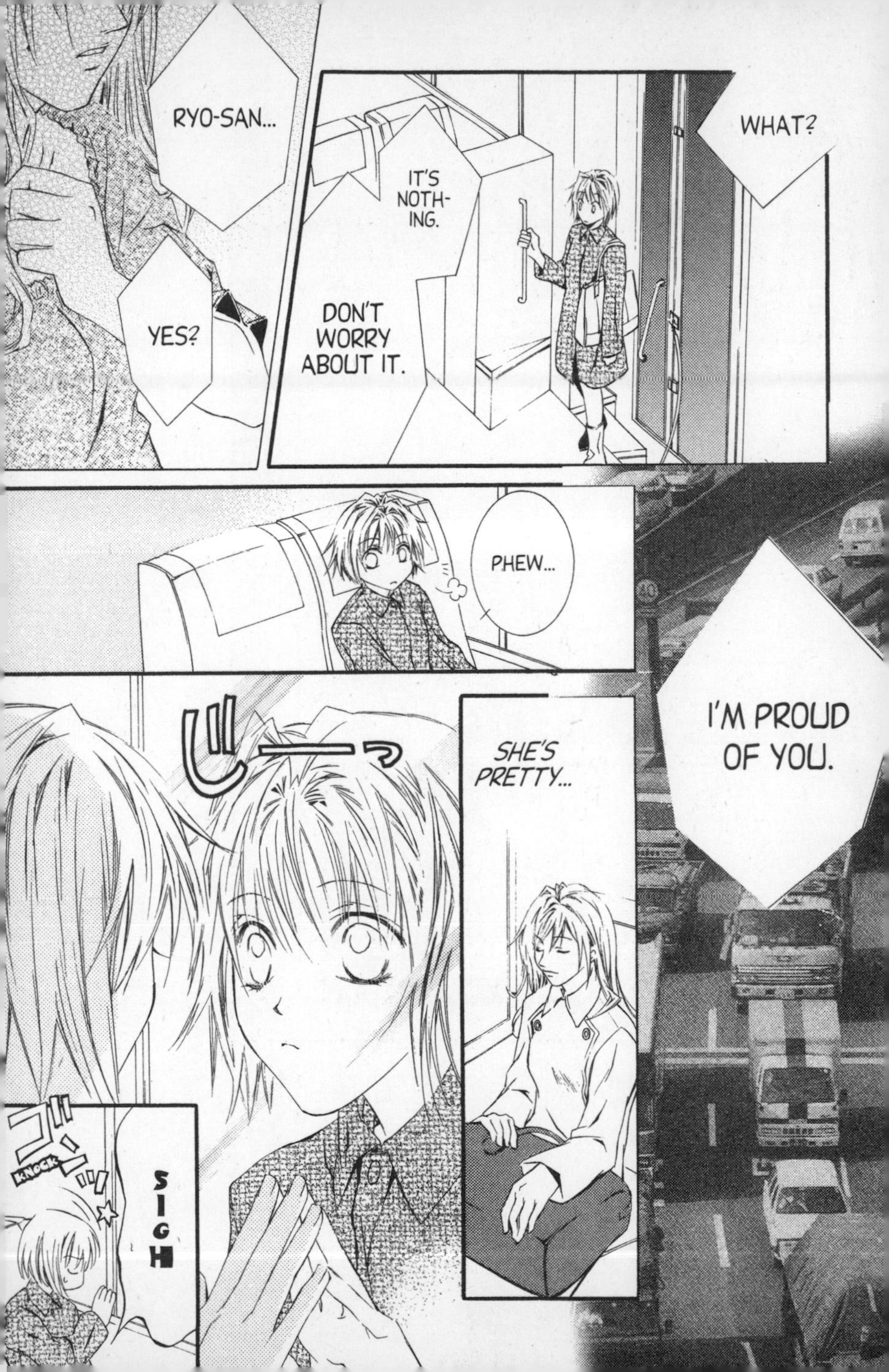
WHAT?
IT'S NOTH-ING.
DON'T WORRY ABOUT IT.
RYO-SAN...
YES?
I'M PROUD OF YOU.
PHEW...
SHE'S PRETTY...
じーっ
ゴン
KNOCK
SIGH

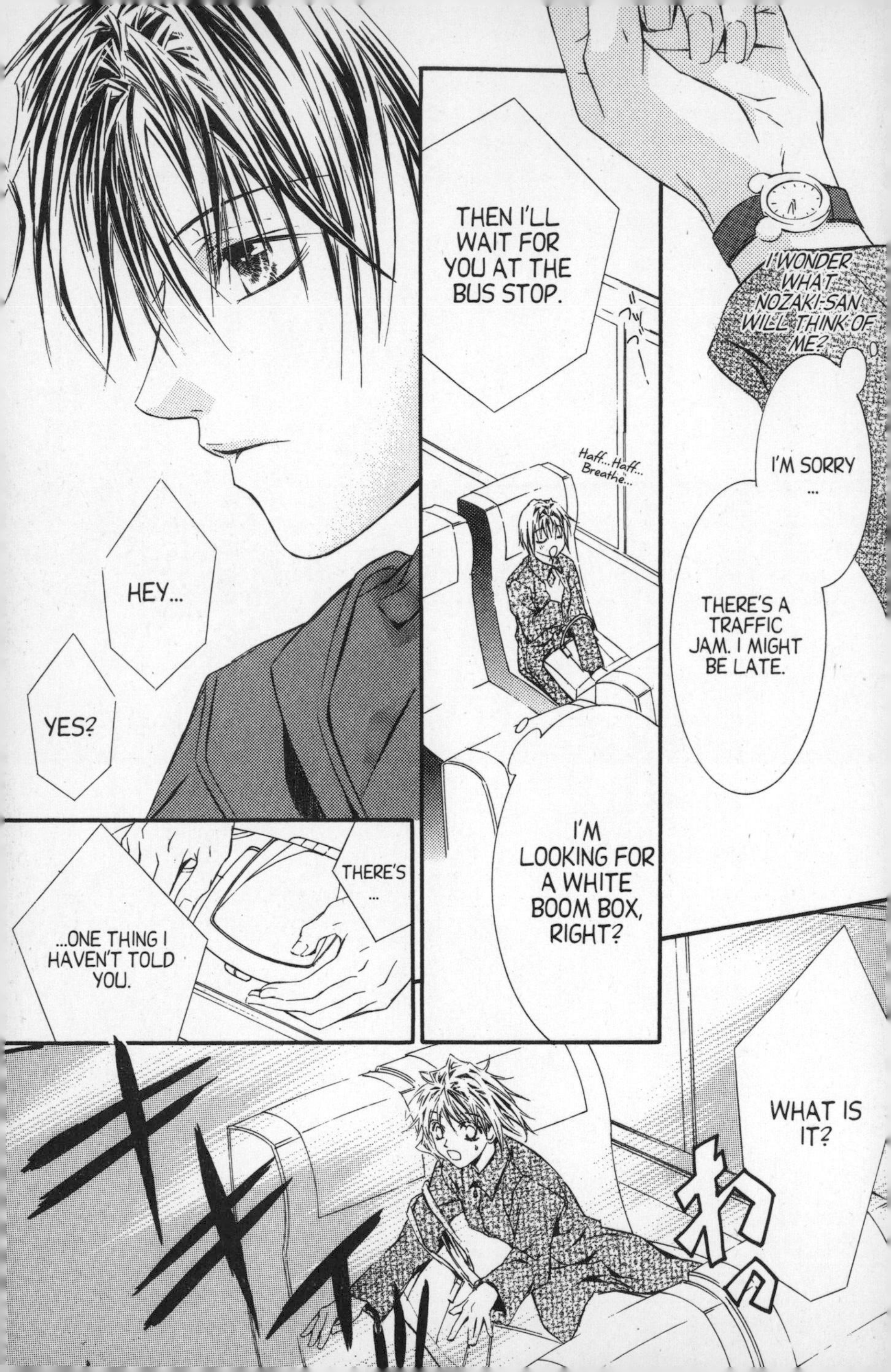
I WONDER WHAT NOZAKI-SAN WILL THINK OF ME?
I'M SORRY ...
THERE'S A TRAFFIC JAM. I MIGHT BE LATE.
THEN I'LL WAIT FOR YOU AT THE BUS STOP.
Haff...Haff... Breathe...
I'M LOOKING FOR A WHITE BOOM BOX, RIGHT?
HEY...
YES?
THERE'S ...
...ONE THING I HAVEN'T TOLD YOU.
WHAT IS IT?

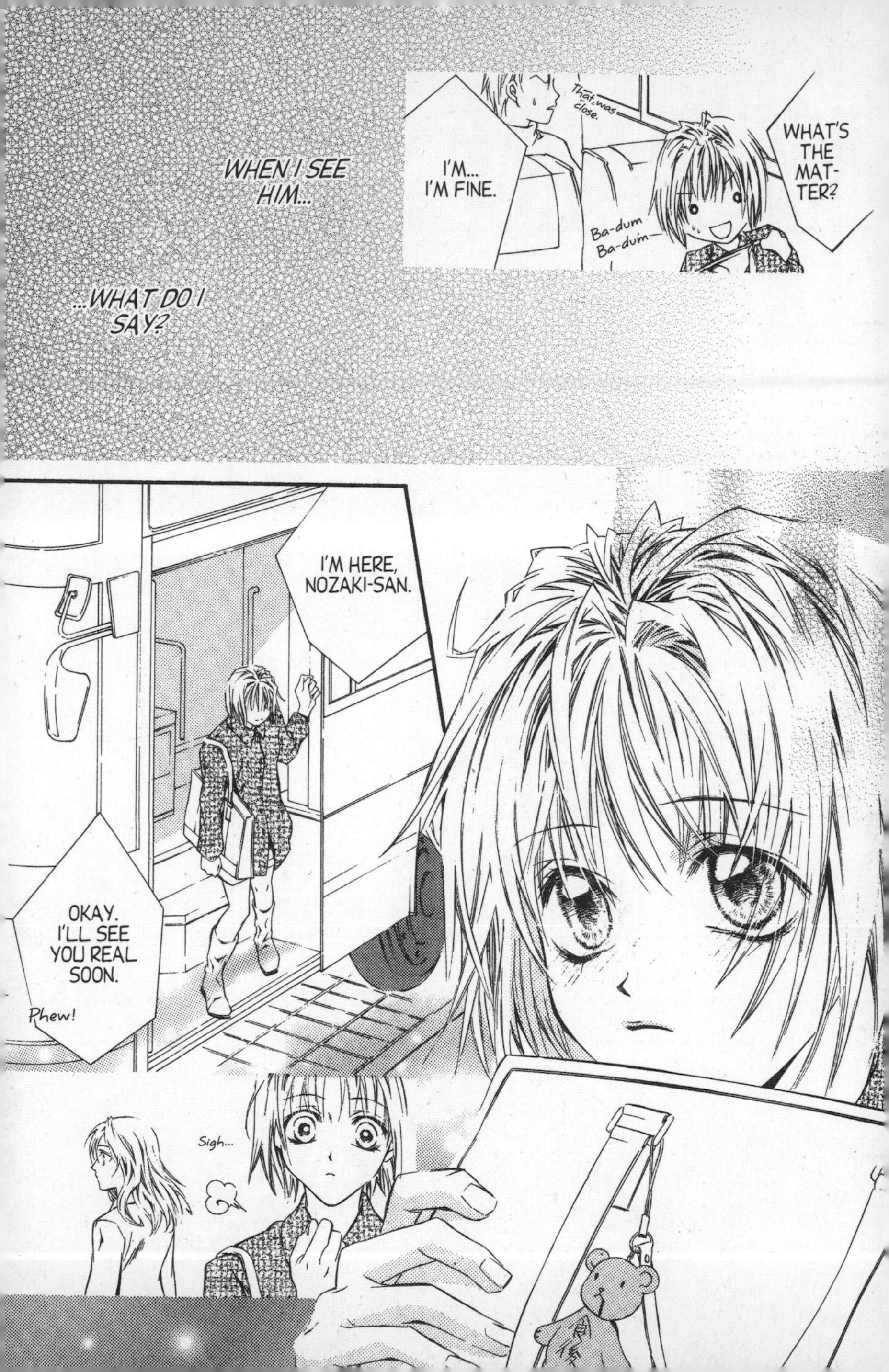
WHAT'S THE MAT-TER?
That was close.
I'M... I'M FINE.
Ba-dum Ba-dum
WHEN I SEE HIM...
...WHAT DO I SAY?
I'M HERE, NOZAKI-SAN.
OKAY. I'LL SEE YOU REAL SOON.
Phew!
Sigh...

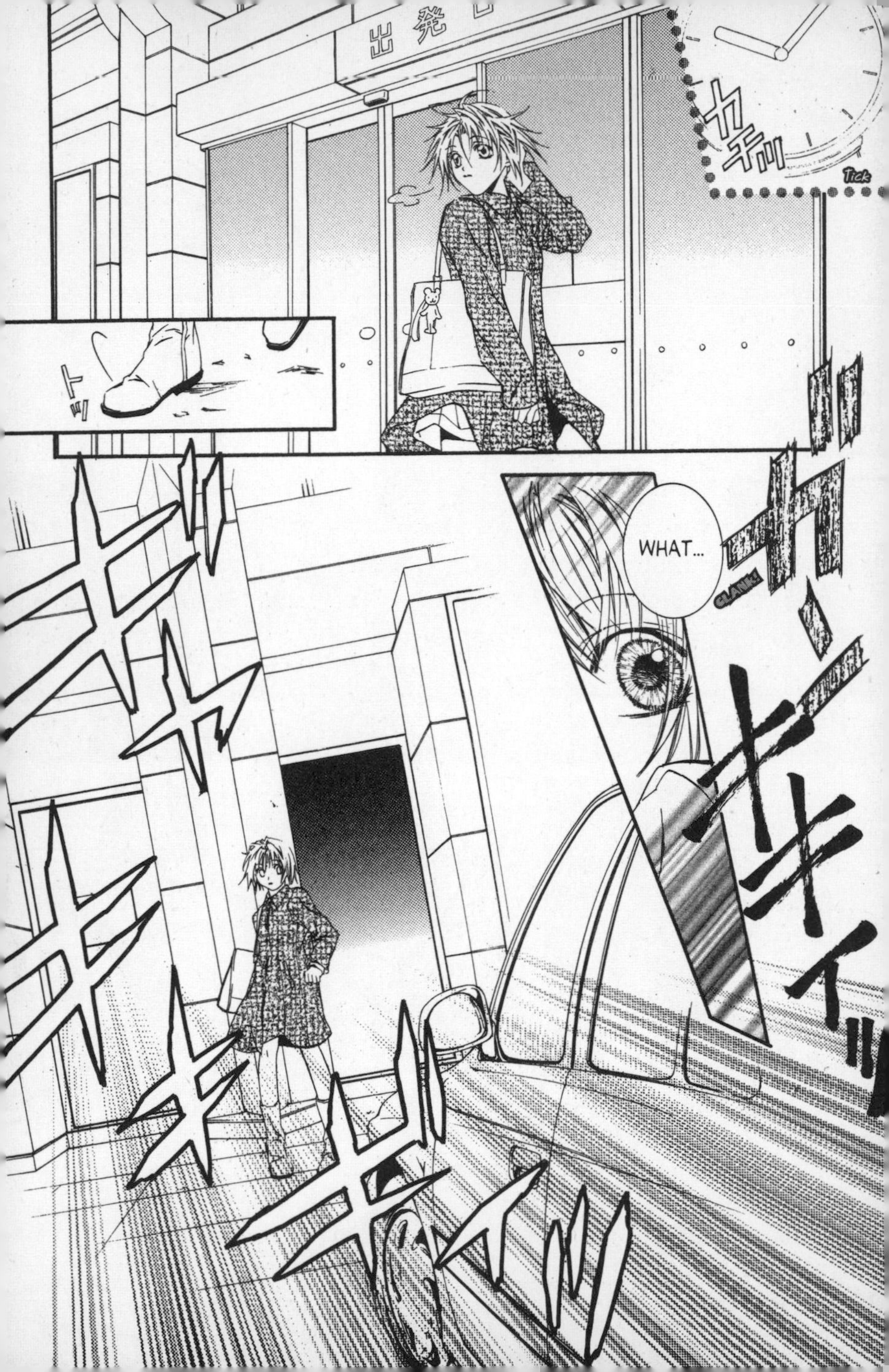
Tick
WHAT...
CLANK!

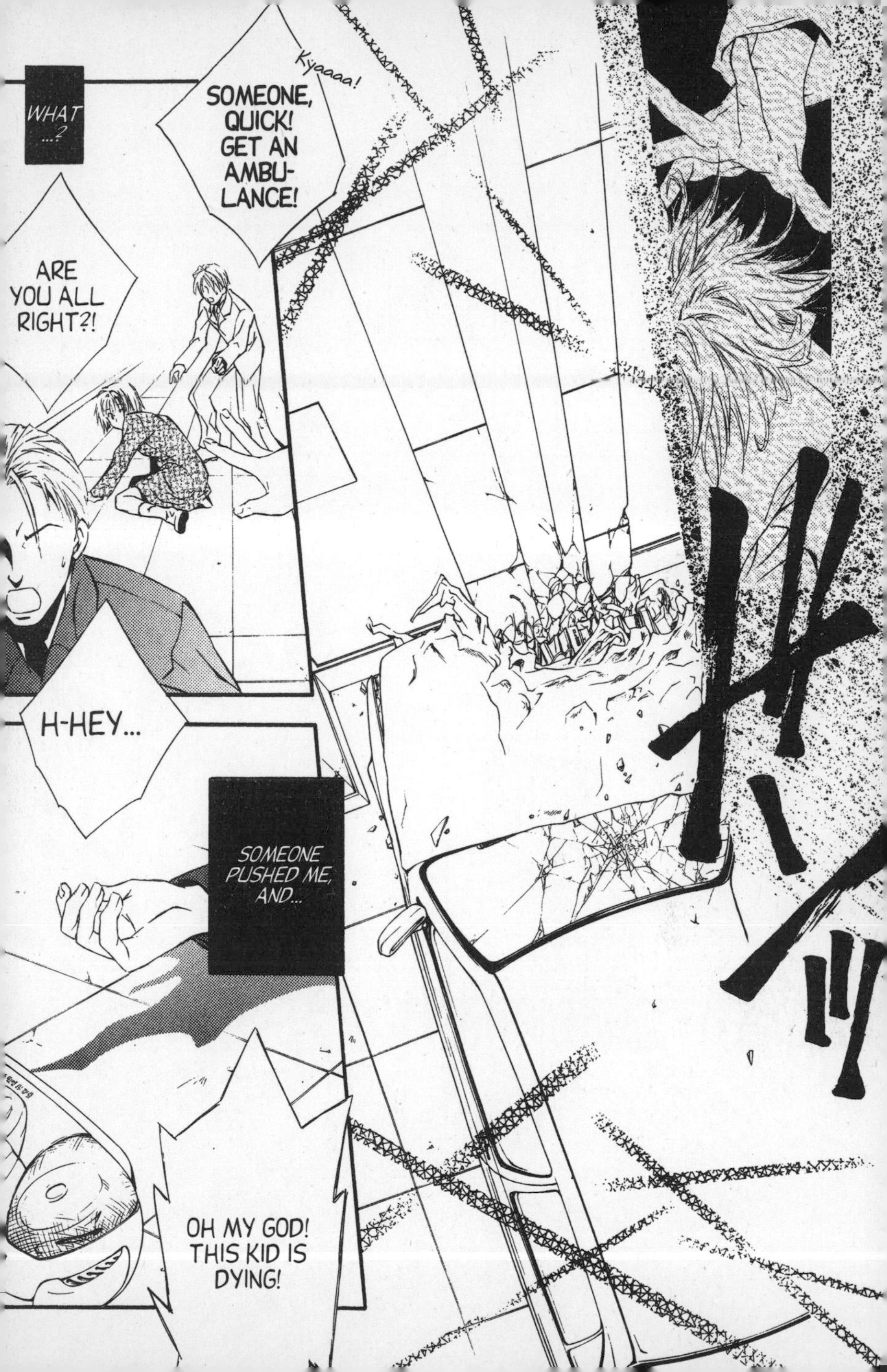
Kyaaaa!
SOMEONE, QUICK! GET AN AMBULANCE!
WHAT ...?
ARE YOU ALL RIGHT?!
H-HEY...
SOMEONE PUSHED ME, AND...
OH MY GOD! THIS KID IS DYING!

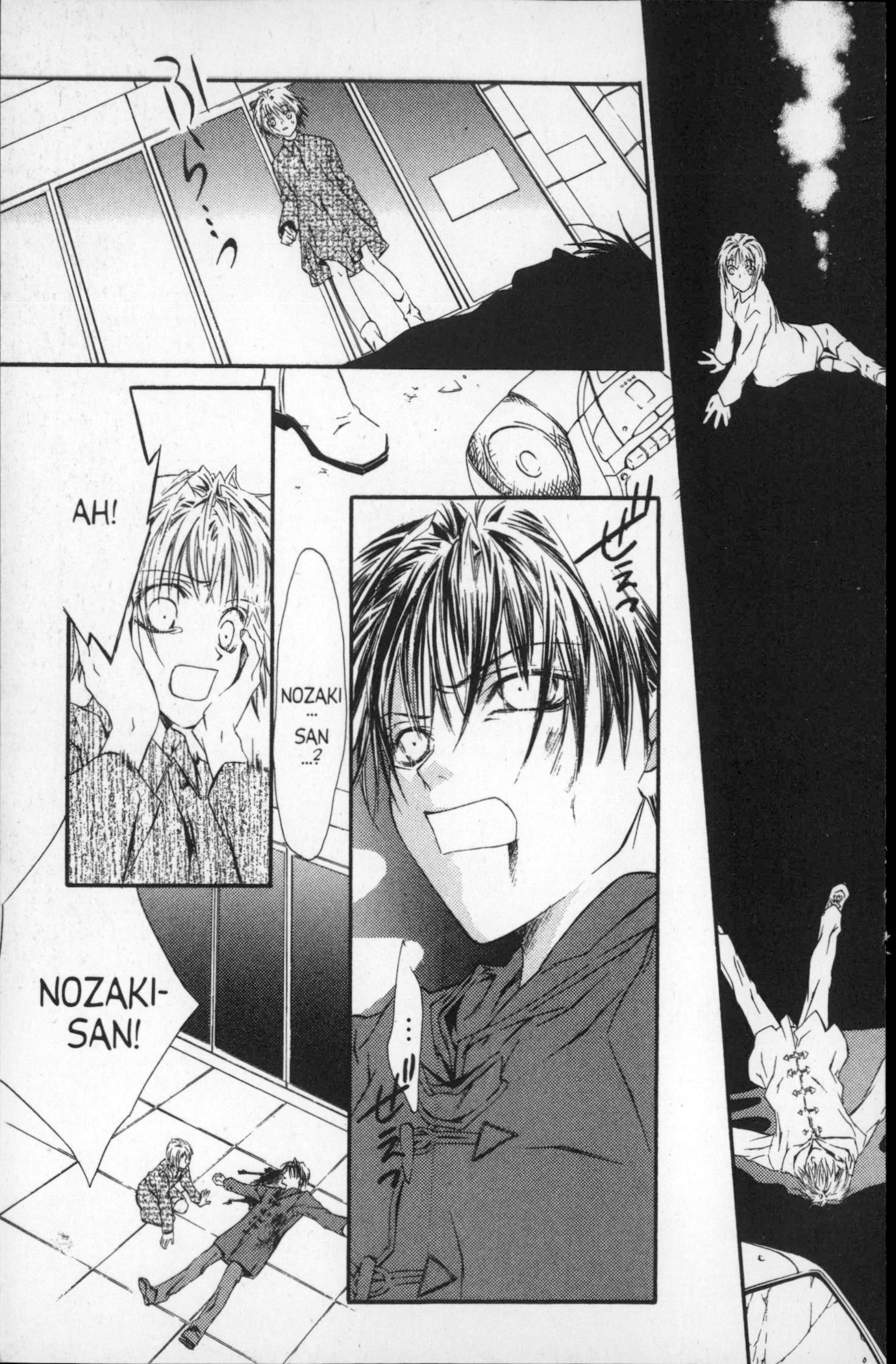

ふら…っ
AH!
NOZAKI ... SAN ...?
...
NOZAKI-SAN!

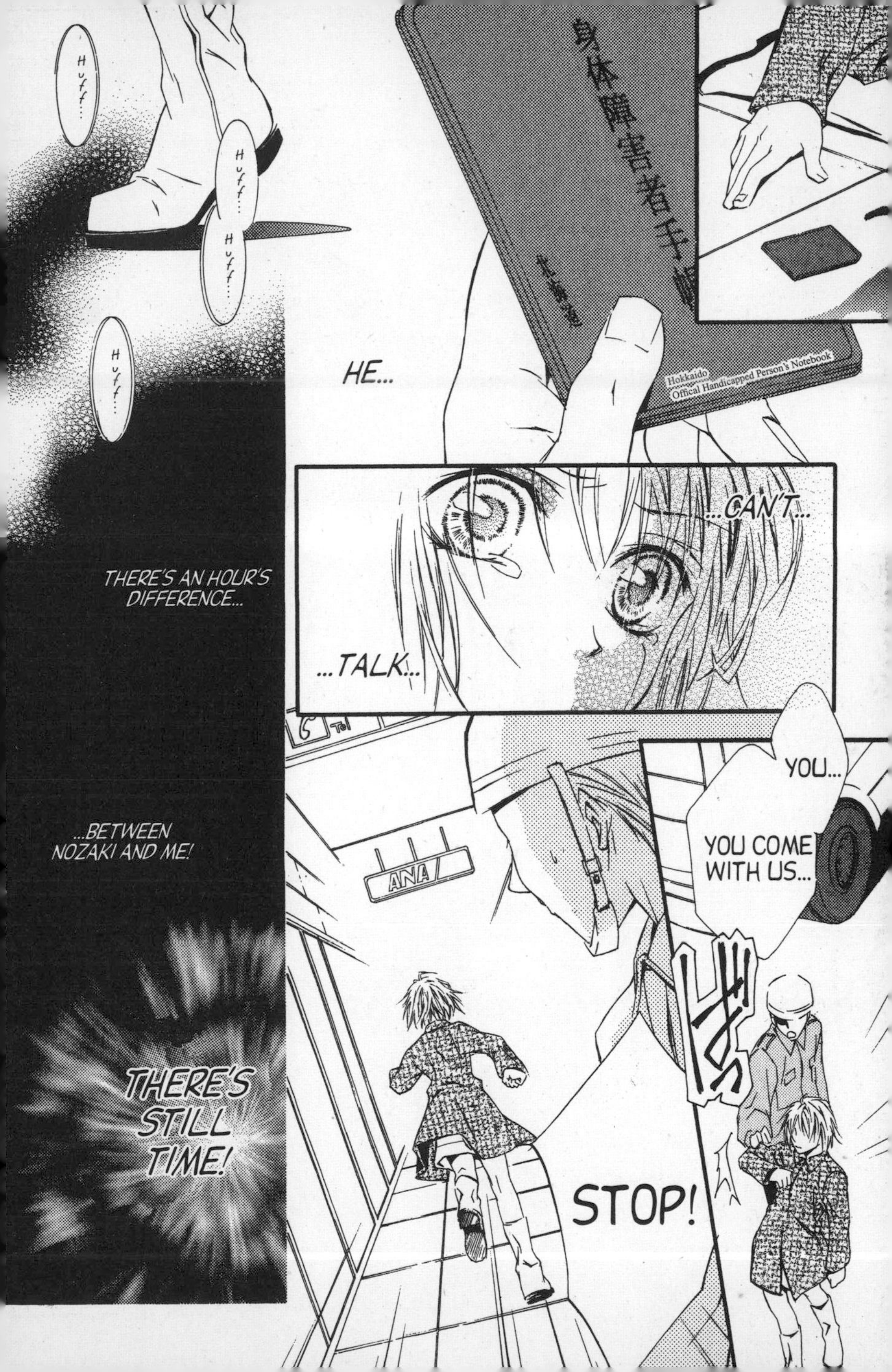
身体障害者手
Hokkaido
Offical Handicapped Person's Notebook
HE...
...CAN'T...
...TALK...
YOU...
YOU COME WITH US...
ANA
STOP!
Huff...
Huff...
Huff...
Huff...
THERE'S AN HOUR'S DIFFERENCE...
...BETWEEN NOZAKI AND ME!
THERE'S STILL TIME!

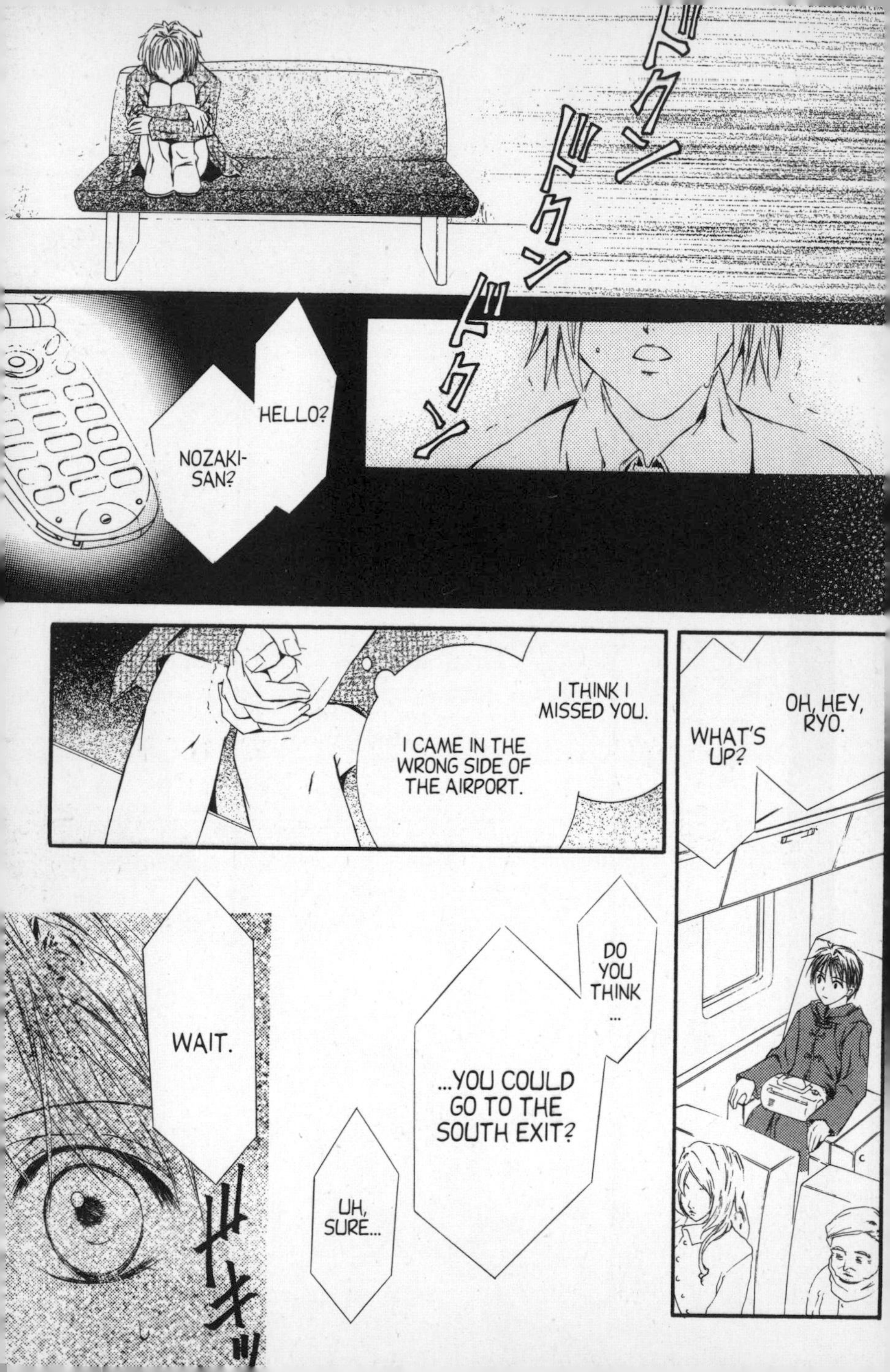

ドクン
ドクン
ドクン
HELLO?
NOZAKI-SAN?
OH, HEY, RYO.
WHAT'S UP?
I THINK I MISSED YOU.
I CAME IN THE WRONG SIDE OF THE AIRPORT.
DO YOU THINK ...
...YOU COULD GO TO THE SOUTH EXIT?
UH, SURE...
WAIT.

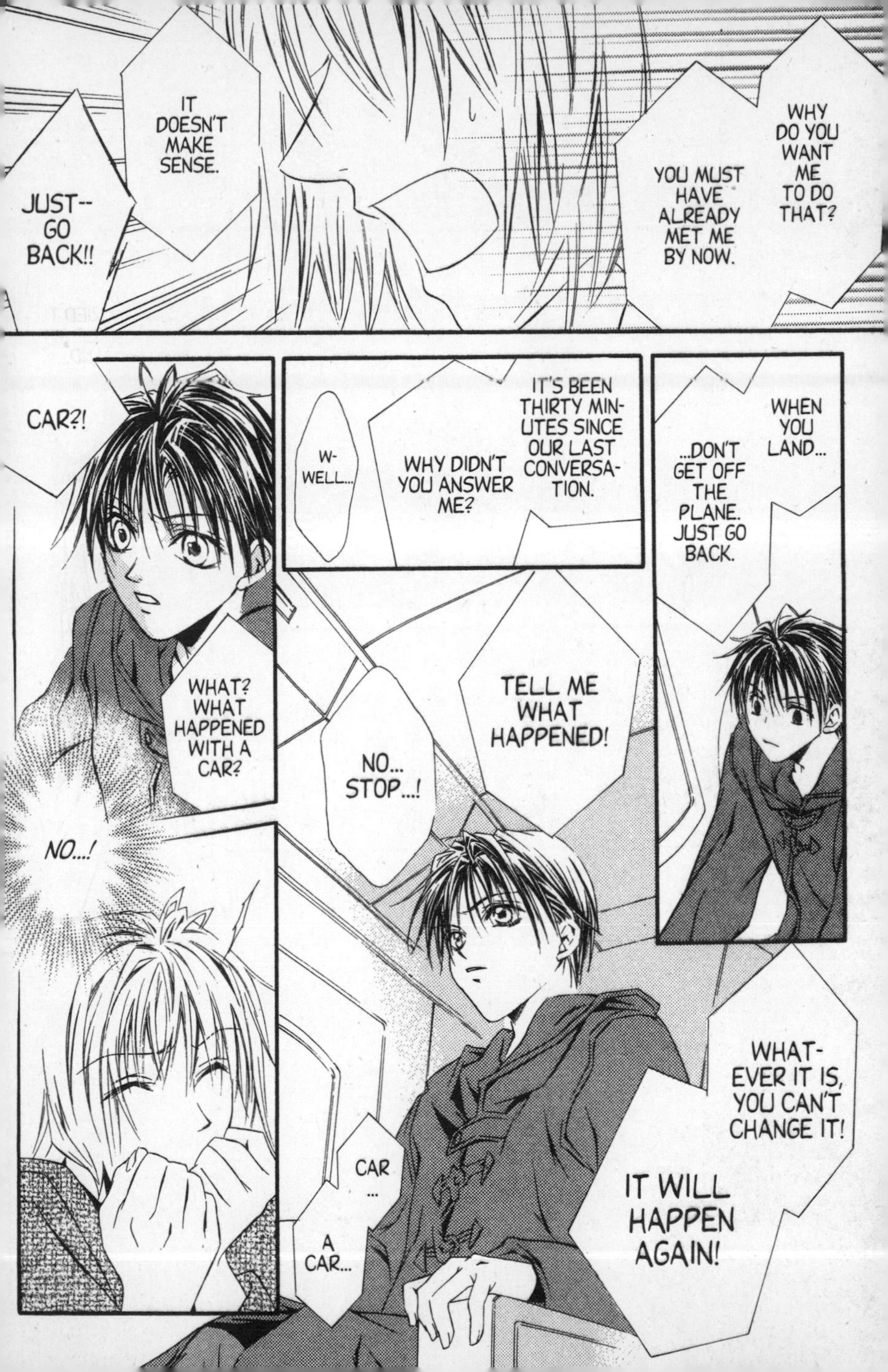
WHY DO YOU WANT ME TO DO THAT?
YOU MUST HAVE ALREADY MET ME BY NOW.
IT DOESN'T MAKE SENSE.
JUST-- GO BACK!!
WHEN YOU LAND...
...DON'T GET OFF THE PLANE. JUST GO BACK.
IT'S BEEN THIRTY MIN-UTES SINCE OUR LAST CONVERSA-TION.
WHY DIDN'T YOU ANSWER ME?
W-WELL...
TELL ME WHAT HAPPENED!
NO... STOP...!
CAR?!
WHAT? WHAT HAPPENED WITH A CAR?
WHAT-EVER IT IS, YOU CAN'T CHANGE IT!
IT WILL HAPPEN AGAIN!
CAR ...
A CAR...
NO...!

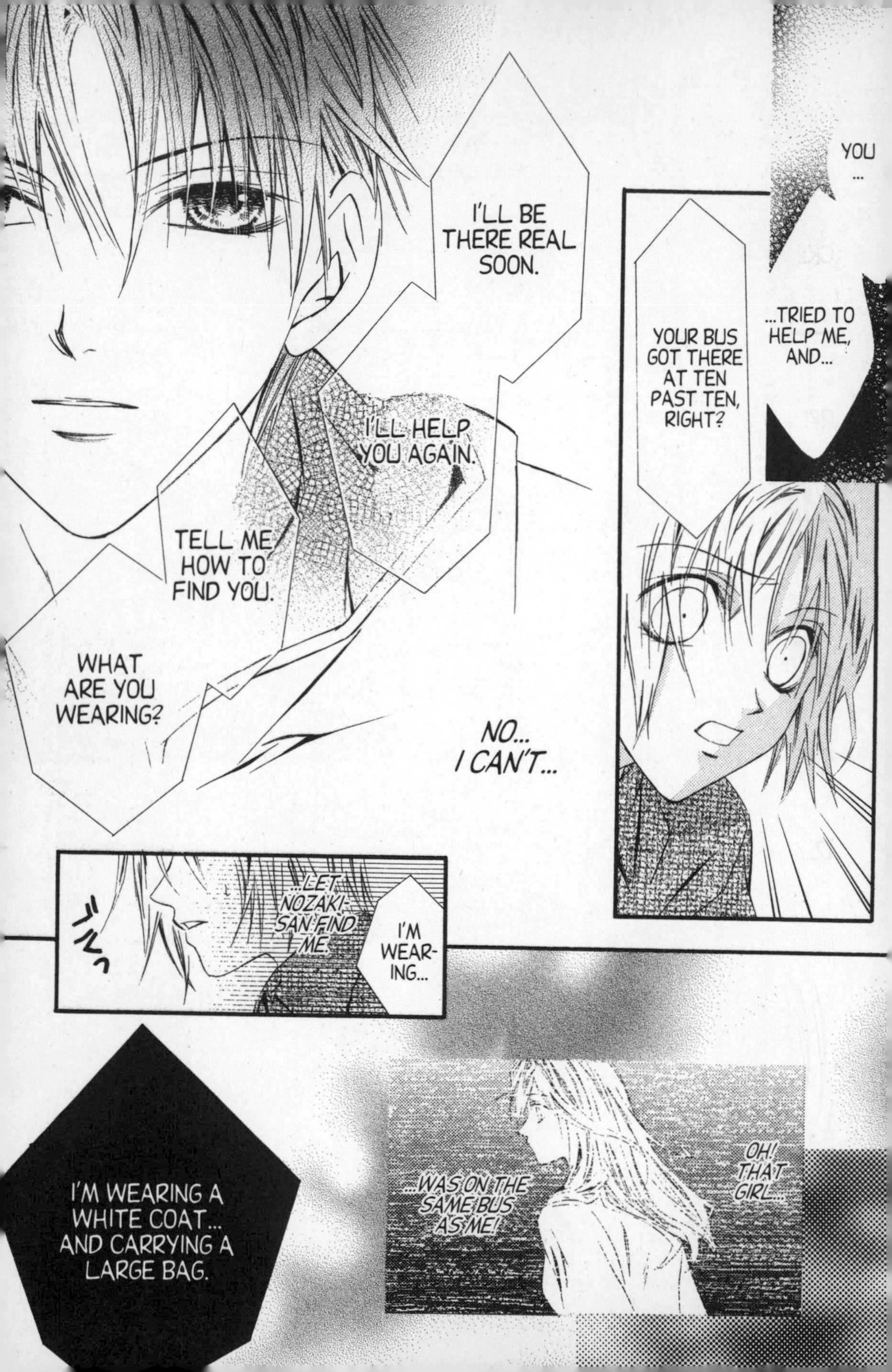
YOU ...
...TRIED TO HELP ME, AND...
YOUR BUS GOT THERE AT TEN PAST TEN, RIGHT?
I'LL BE THERE REAL SOON.
I'LL HELP YOU AGAIN.
TELL ME HOW TO FIND YOU.
WHAT ARE YOU WEARING?
NO... I CAN'T...
I'M WEARING...
...LET NOZAKI-SAN FIND ME.
OH! THAT GIRL...
...WAS ON THE SAME BUS AS ME!
I'M WEARING A WHITE COAT... AND CARRYING A LARGE BAG.

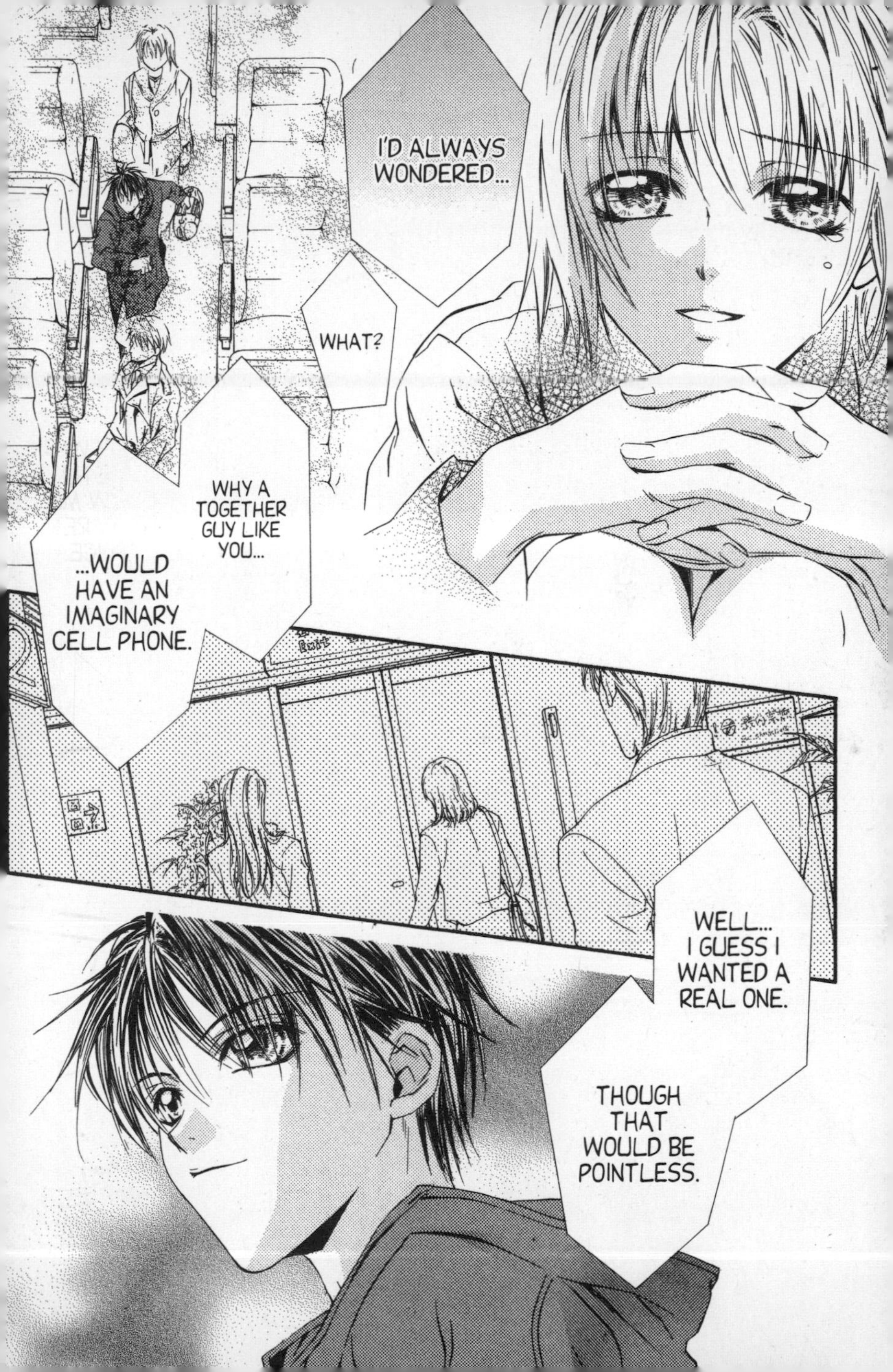
I'D ALWAYS WONDERED...
WHAT?
WHY A TOGETHER GUY LIKE YOU...
...WOULD HAVE AN IMAGINARY CELL PHONE.
WELL... I GUESS I WANTED A REAL ONE.
THOUGH THAT WOULD BE POINTLESS.

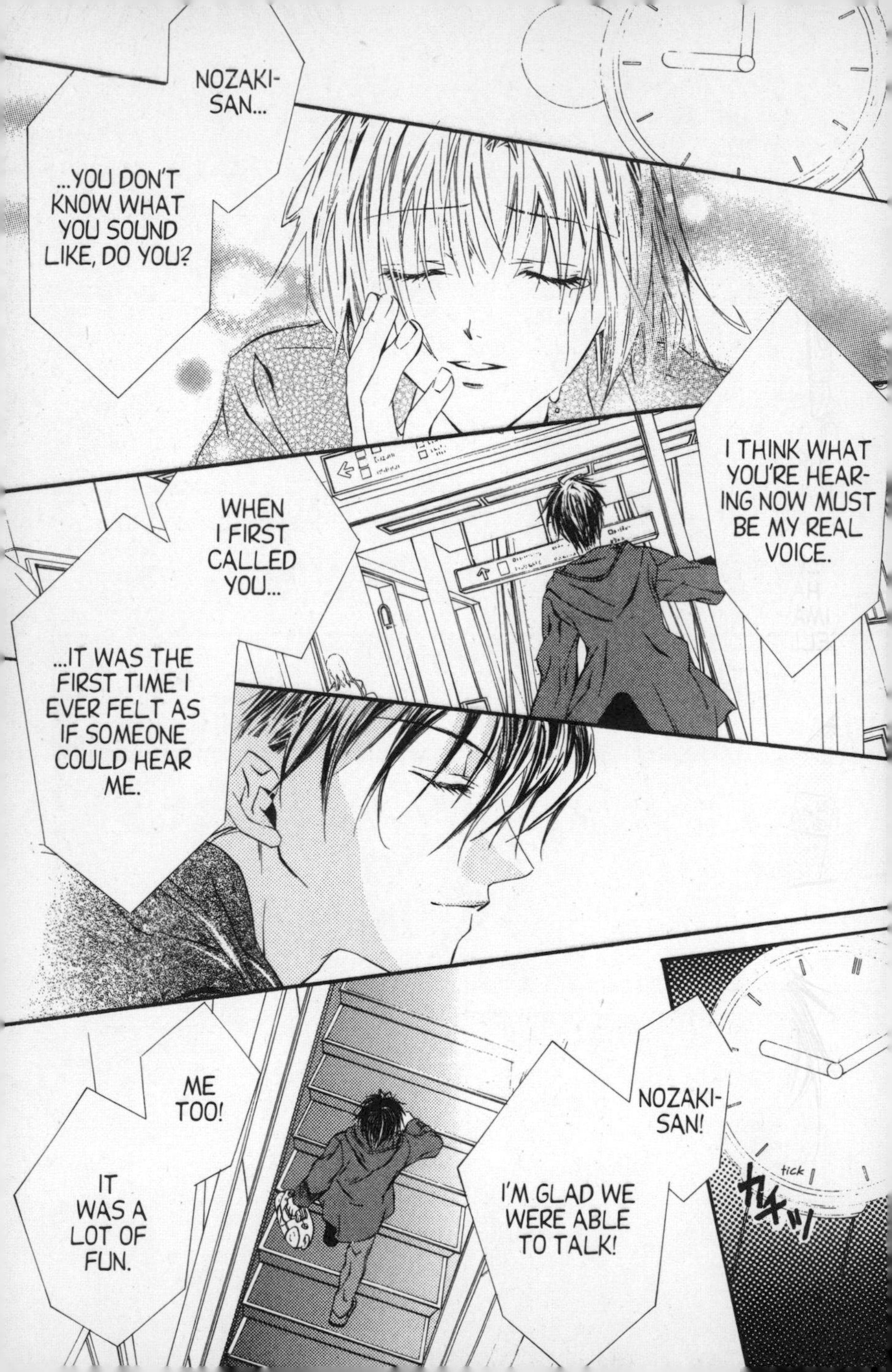
NOZAKI-SAN...
...YOU DON'T KNOW WHAT YOU SOUND LIKE, DO YOU?
I THINK WHAT YOU'RE HEAR-ING NOW MUST BE MY REAL VOICE.
WHEN I FIRST CALLED YOU...
...IT WAS THE FIRST TIME I EVER FELT AS IF SOMEONE COULD HEAR ME.
NOZAKI-SAN!
tick
I'M GLAD WE WERE ABLE TO TALK!
ME TOO!
IT WAS A LOT OF FUN.

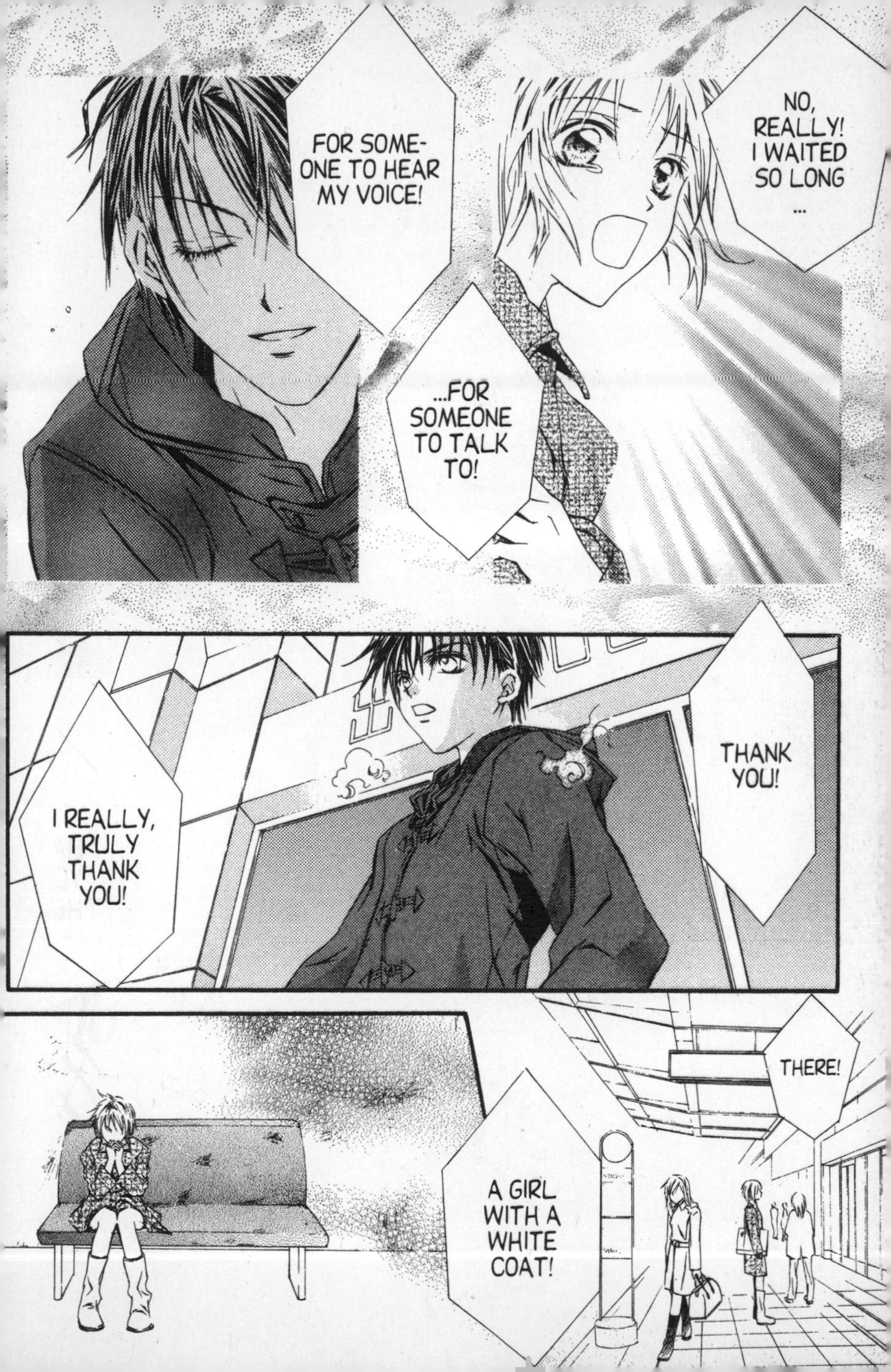
NO, REALLY! I WAITED SO LONG ...
...FOR SOMEONE TO TALK TO!
FOR SOME-ONE TO HEAR MY VOICE!
THANK YOU!
I REALLY, TRULY THANK YOU!
THERE!
A GIRL WITH A WHITE COAT!

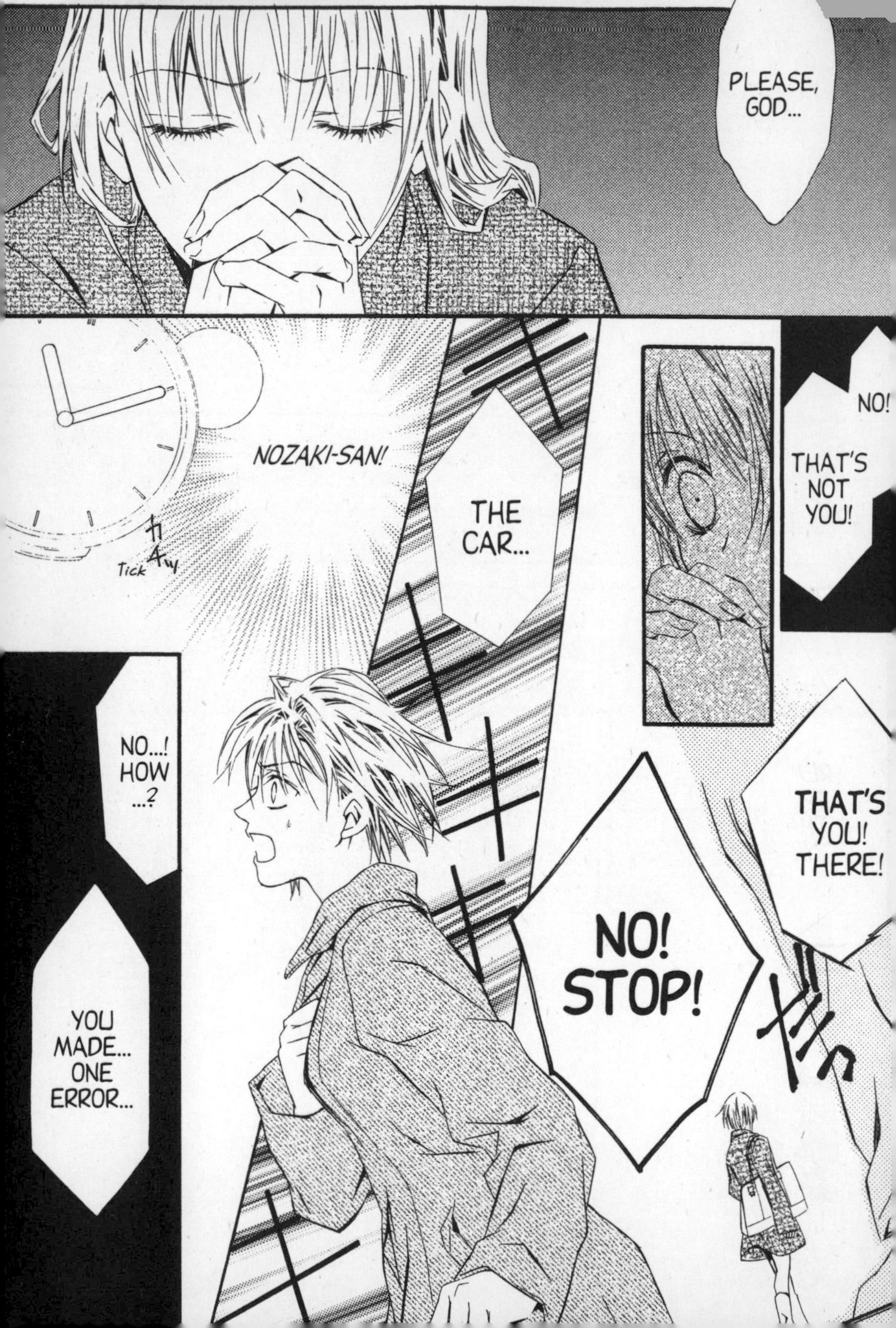
PLEASE, GOD...
NO!
THAT'S NOT YOU!
THE CAR...
NOZAKI-SAN!
Tick
THAT'S YOU! THERE!
NO! STOP!
NO...! HOW ...?
YOU MADE... ONE ERROR...

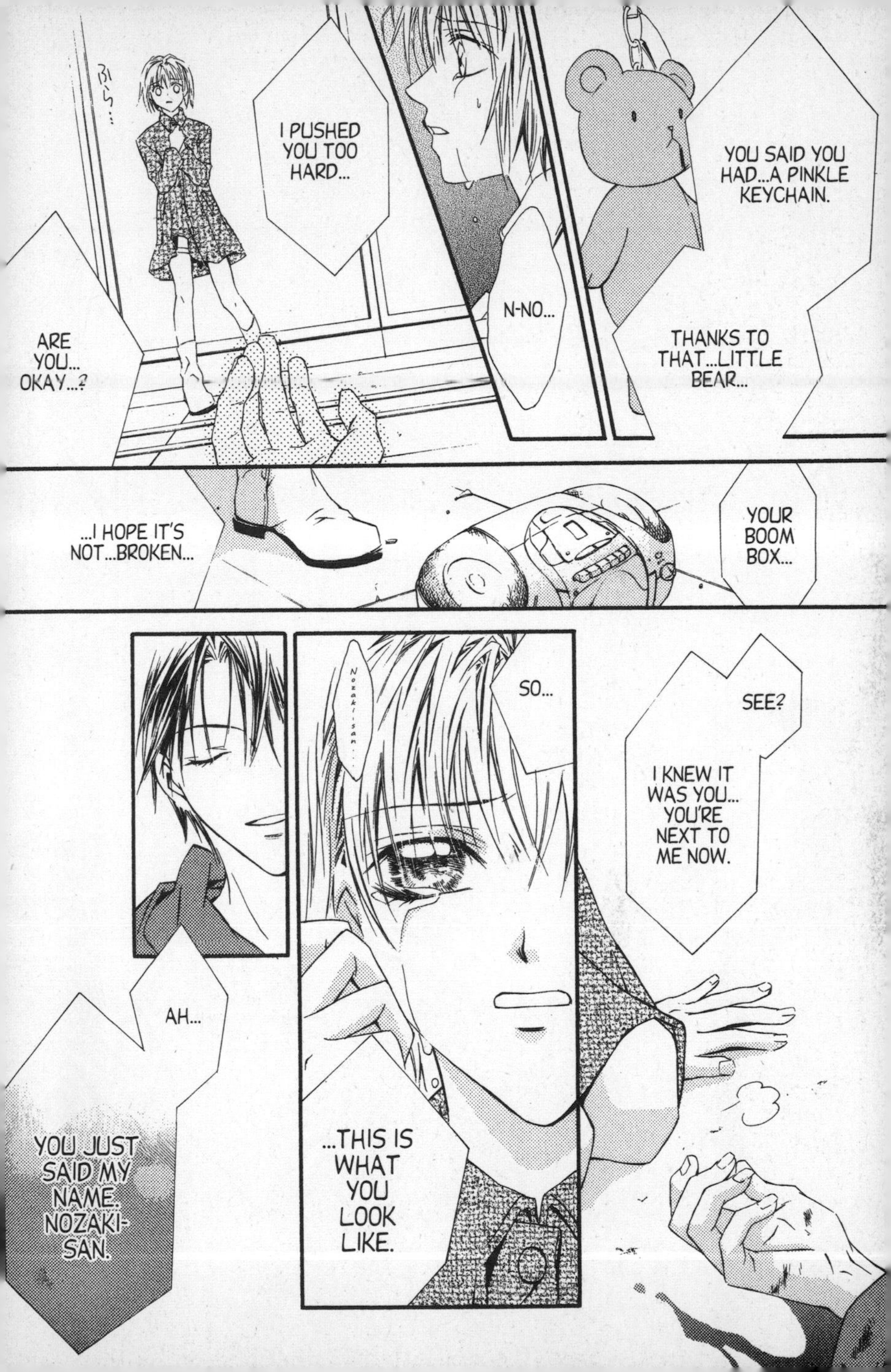
YOU SAID YOU HAD...A PINKLE KEYCHAIN.
THANKS TO THAT...LITTLE BEAR...
I PUSHED YOU TOO HARD...
N-NO...
ふら…
ARE YOU... OKAY...?
YOUR BOOM BOX...
...I HOPE IT'S NOT...BROKEN...
SEE?
I KNEW IT WAS YOU... YOU'RE NEXT TO ME NOW.
SO...
Nozaki-san...
AH...
...THIS IS WHAT YOU LOOK LIKE.
YOU JUST SAID MY NAME. NOZAKI-SAN.

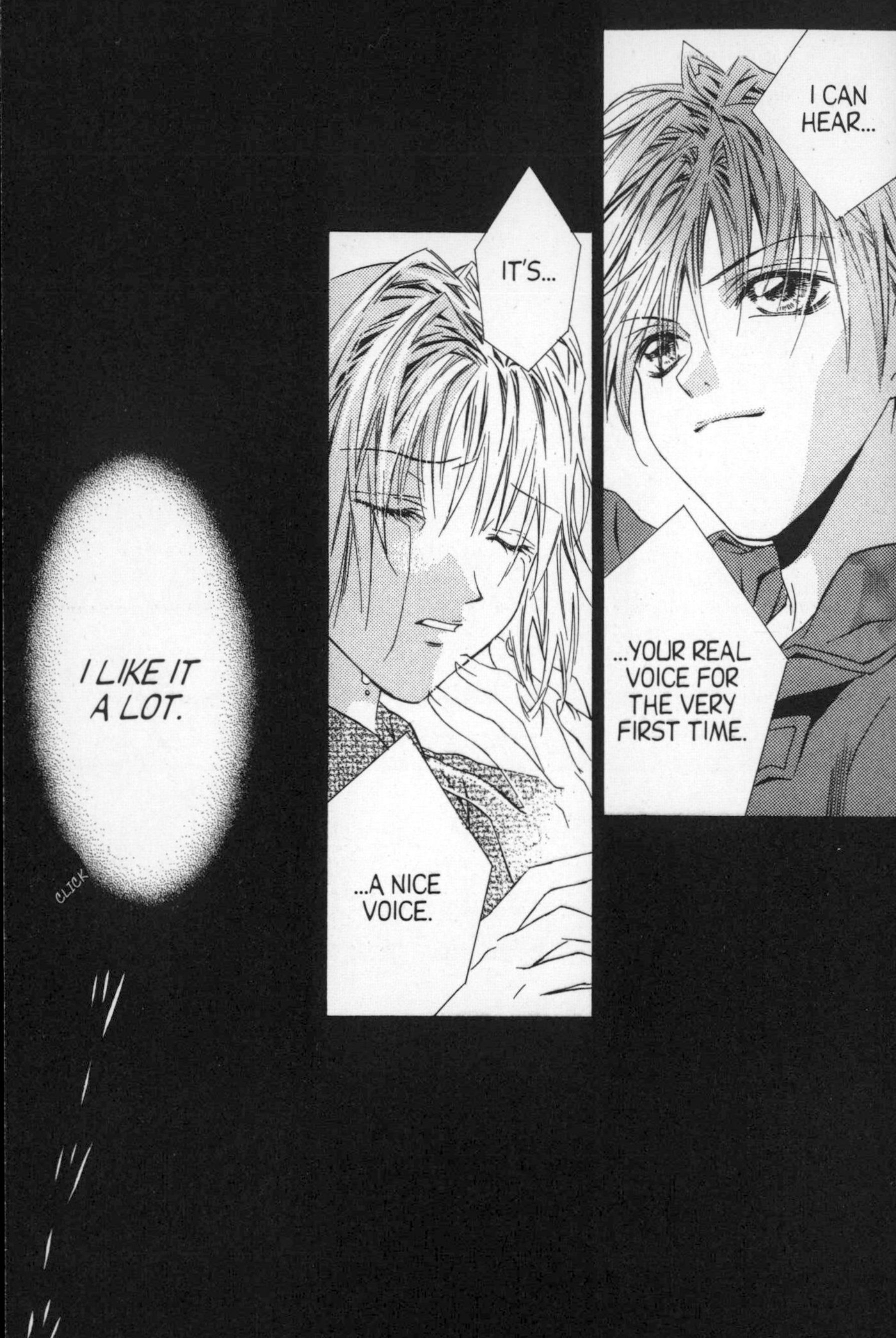
I CAN HEAR...
...YOUR REAL VOICE FOR THE VERY FIRST TIME.
IT'S...
...A NICE VOICE.
I LIKE IT A LOT.
CLICK

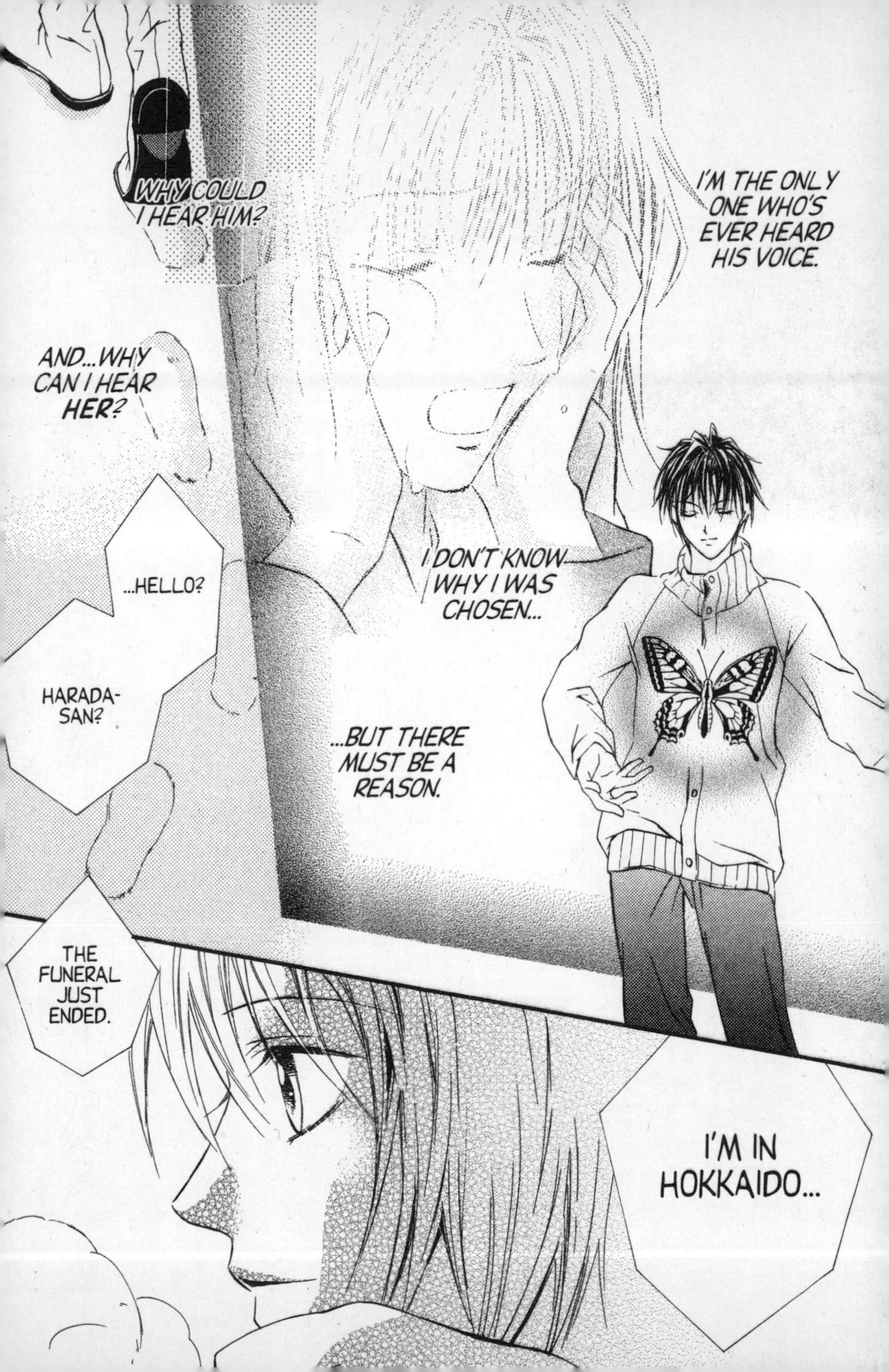
I'M THE ONLY ONE WHO'S EVER HEARD HIS VOICE.
WHY COULD I HEAR HIM?
AND...WHY CAN I HEAR HER?
I DON'T KNOW WHY I WAS CHOSEN...
...BUT THERE MUST BE A REASON.
...HELLO?
HARADA-SAN?
I'M IN HOKKAIDO...
THE FUNERAL JUST ENDED.

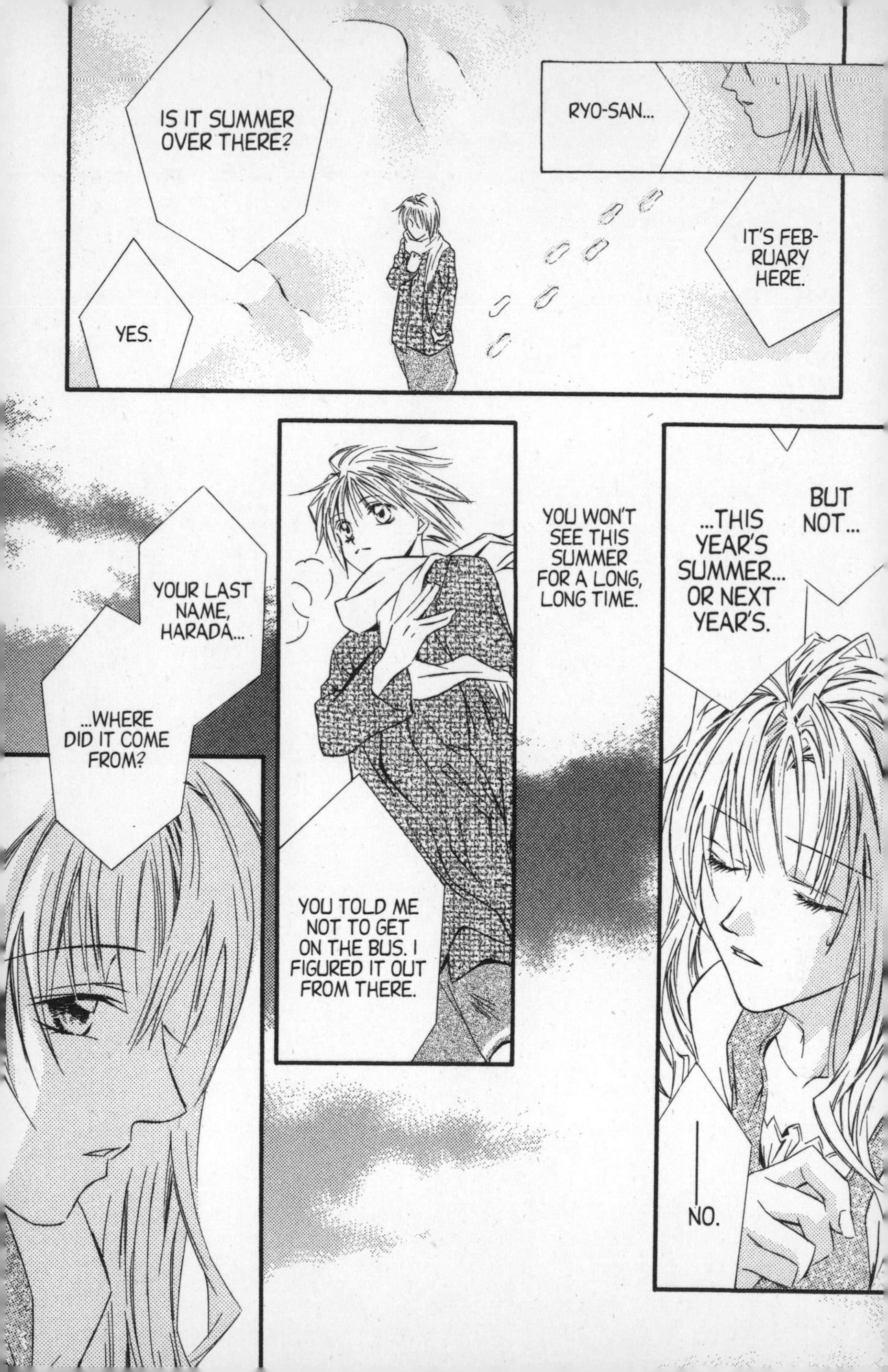
RYO-SAN...
IT'S FEB-RUARY HERE.
IS IT SUMMER OVER THERE?
YES.
YOU WON'T SEE THIS SUMMER FOR A LONG, LONG TIME.
BUT NOT...
...THIS YEAR'S SUMMER... OR NEXT YEAR'S.
NO.
YOUR LAST NAME, HARADA...
...WHERE DID IT COME FROM?
YOU TOLD ME NOT TO GET ON THE BUS. I FIGURED IT OUT FROM THERE.

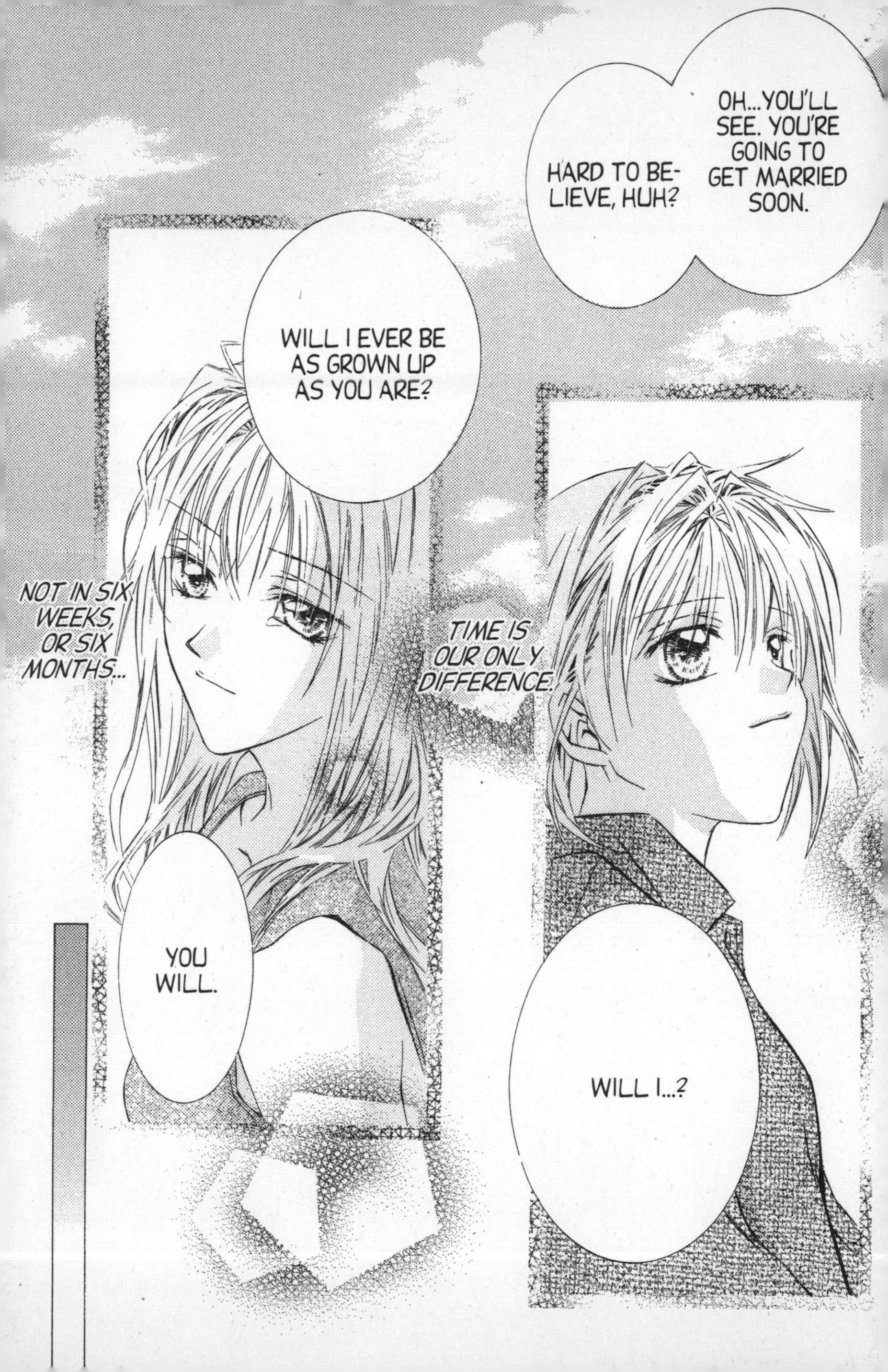

OH... YOU'LL SEE. YOU'RE GOING TO GET MARRIED SOON.
HARD TO BE-LIEVE, HUH?
WILL I EVER BE AS GROWN UP AS YOU ARE?
YOU WILL.
NOT IN SIX WEEKS, OR SIX MONTHS...
TIME IS OUR ONLY DIFFERENCE.
WILL I...?

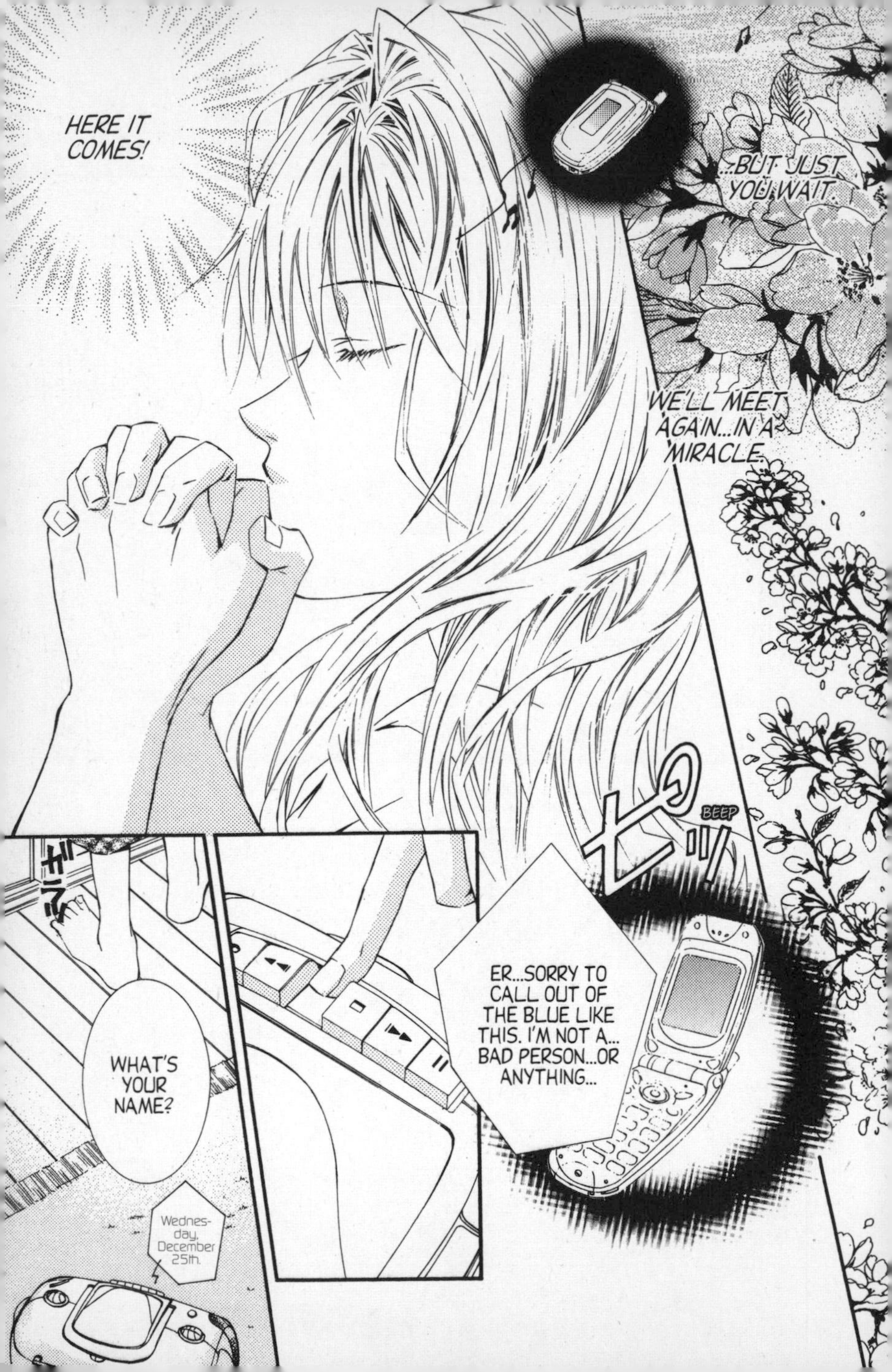
...BUT JUST YOU WAIT.
WE'LL MEET AGAIN...IN A MIRACLE.
HERE IT COMES!
BEEP
ER...SORRY TO CALL OUT OF THE BLUE LIKE THIS. I'M NOT A... BAD PERSON...OR ANYTHING...
WHAT'S YOUR NAME?
Wednes-day, December 25th.

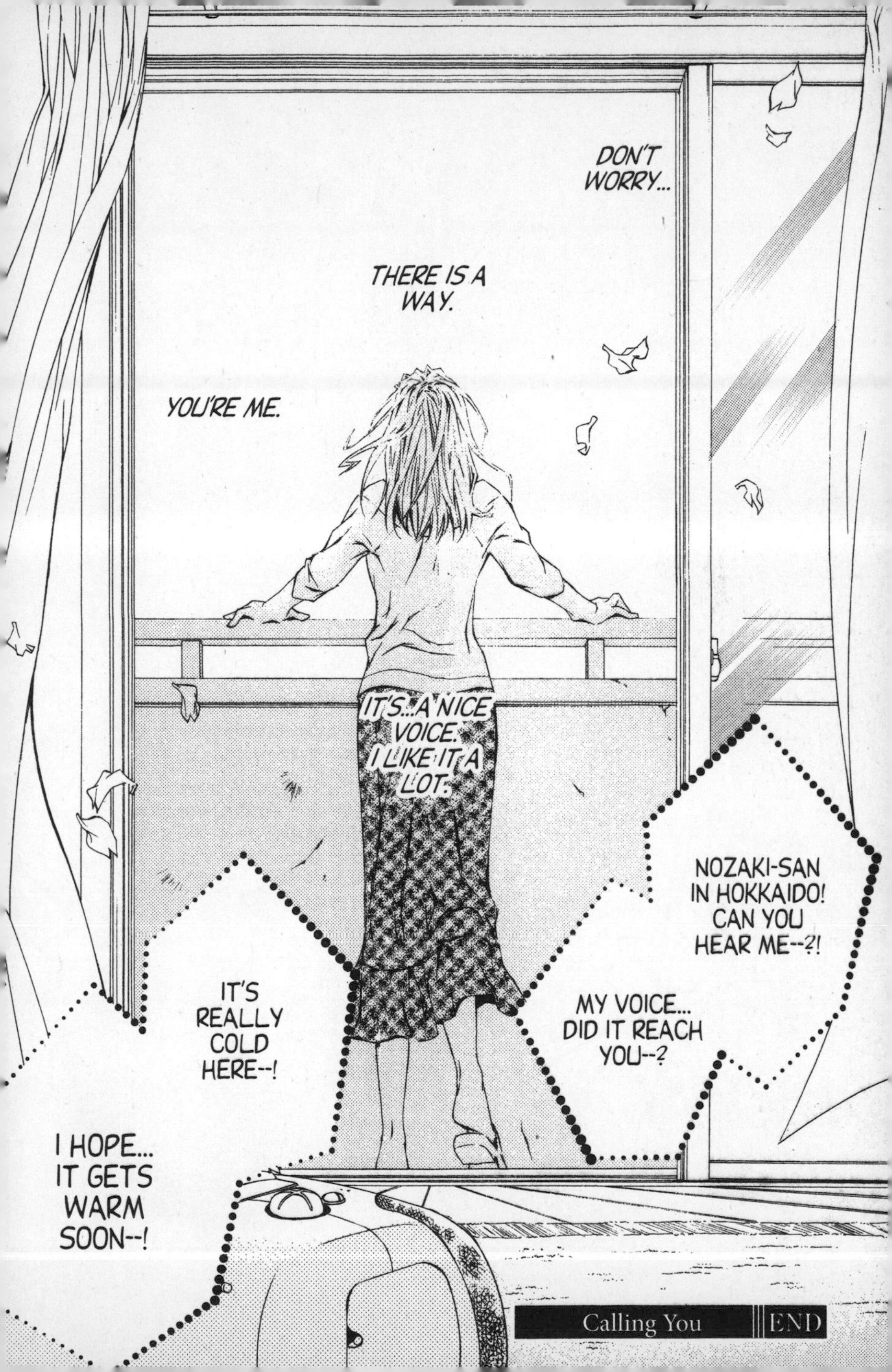
DON'T WORRY...
THERE IS A WAY.
YOU'RE ME.
IT'S...A NICE VOICE. I LIKE IT A LOT.
NOZAKI-SAN IN HOKKAIDO! CAN YOU HEAR ME--?!
MY VOICE... DID IT REACH YOU--?
IT'S REALLY COLD HERE--!
I HOPE... IT GETS WARM SOON--!

Calling You END

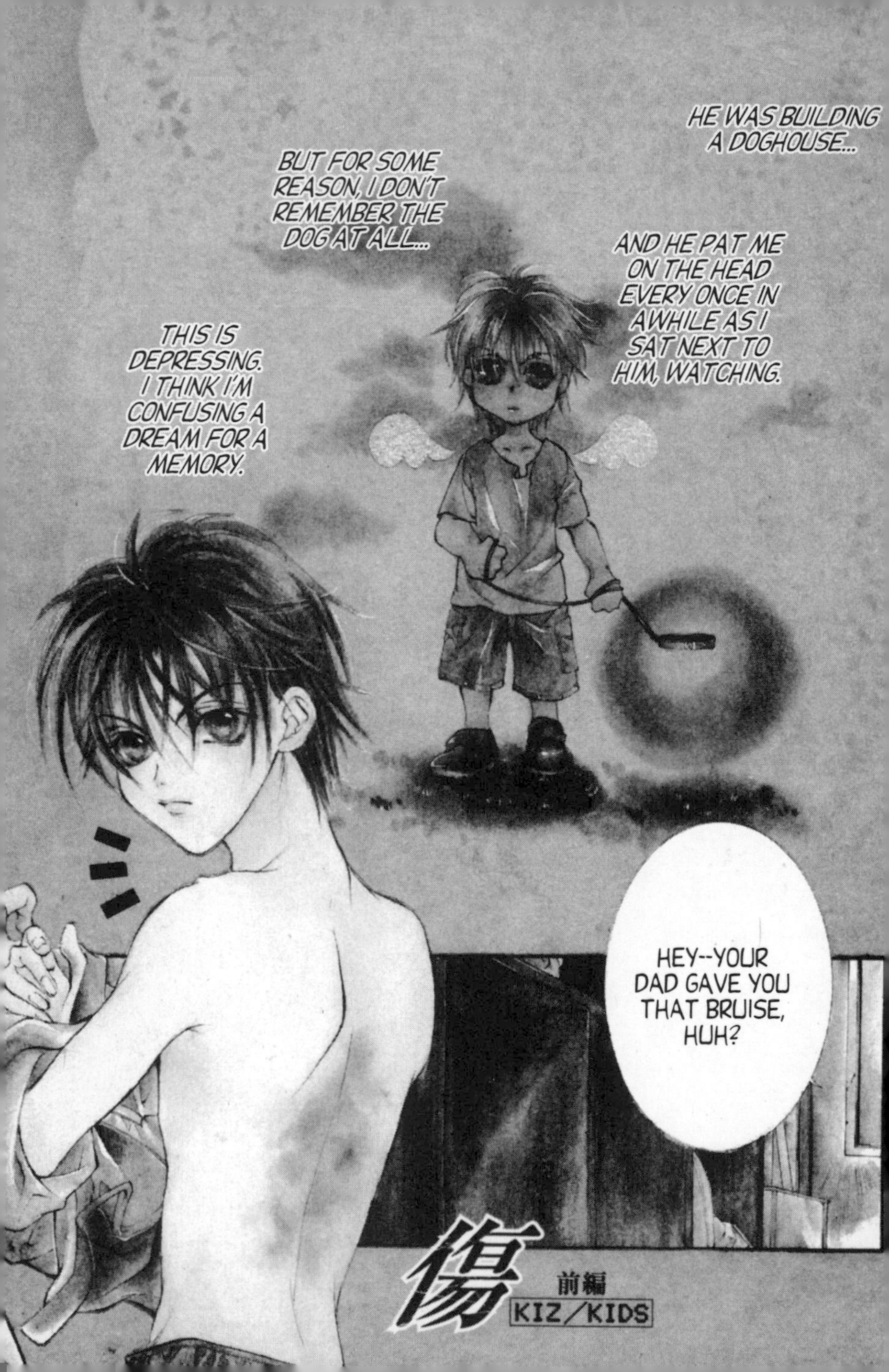
HE WAS BUILDING A DOGHOUSE...
AND HE PAT ME ON THE HEAD EVERY ONCE IN AWHILE AS I SAT NEXT TO HIM, WATCHING.
BUT FOR SOME REASON, I DON'T REMEMBER THE DOG AT ALL...
THIS IS DEPRESSING. I THINK I'M CONFUSING A DREAM FOR A MEMORY.
HEY--YOUR DAD GAVE YOU THAT BRUISE, HUH?
傷
前編
KIZ/KIDS

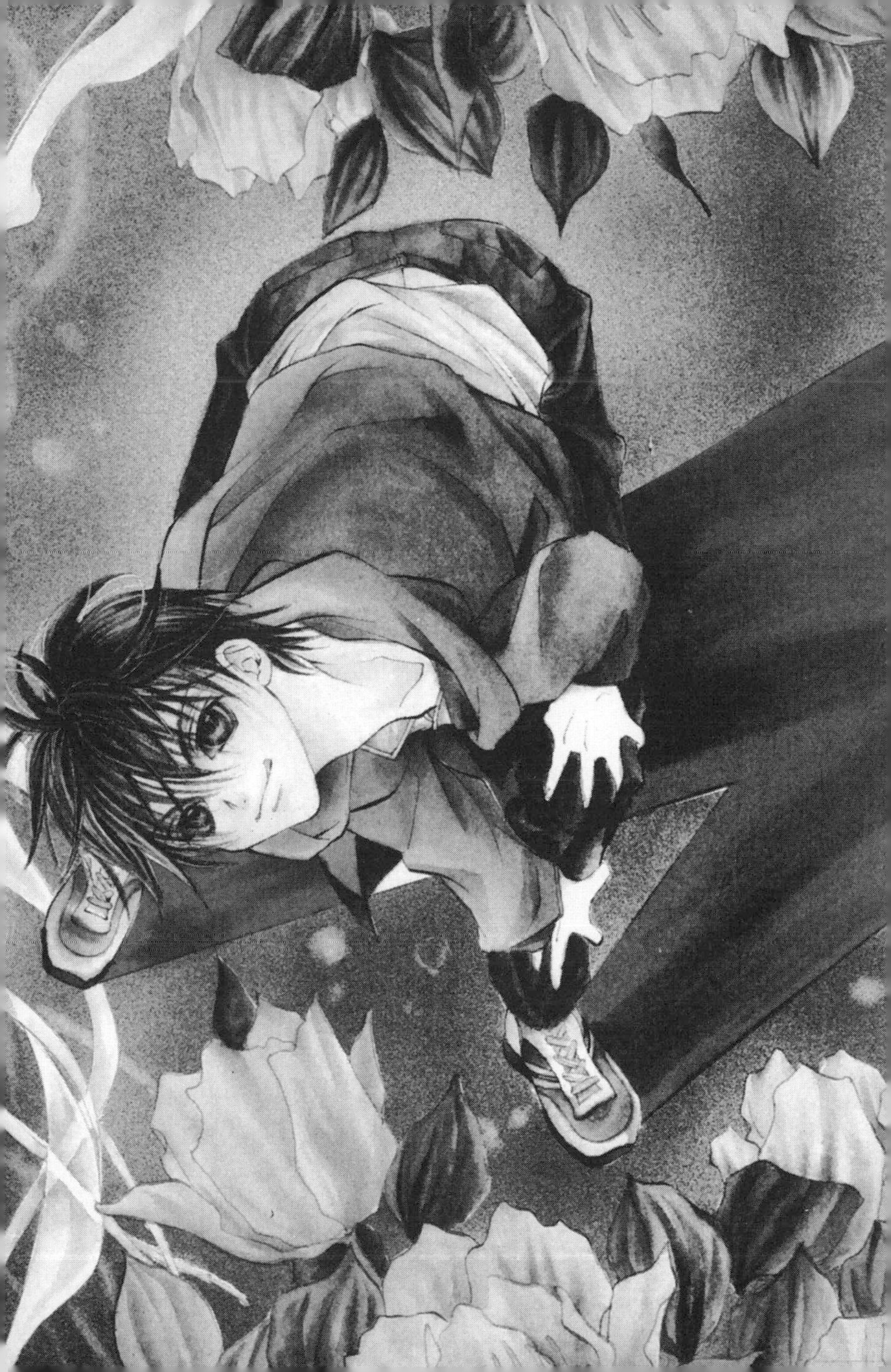

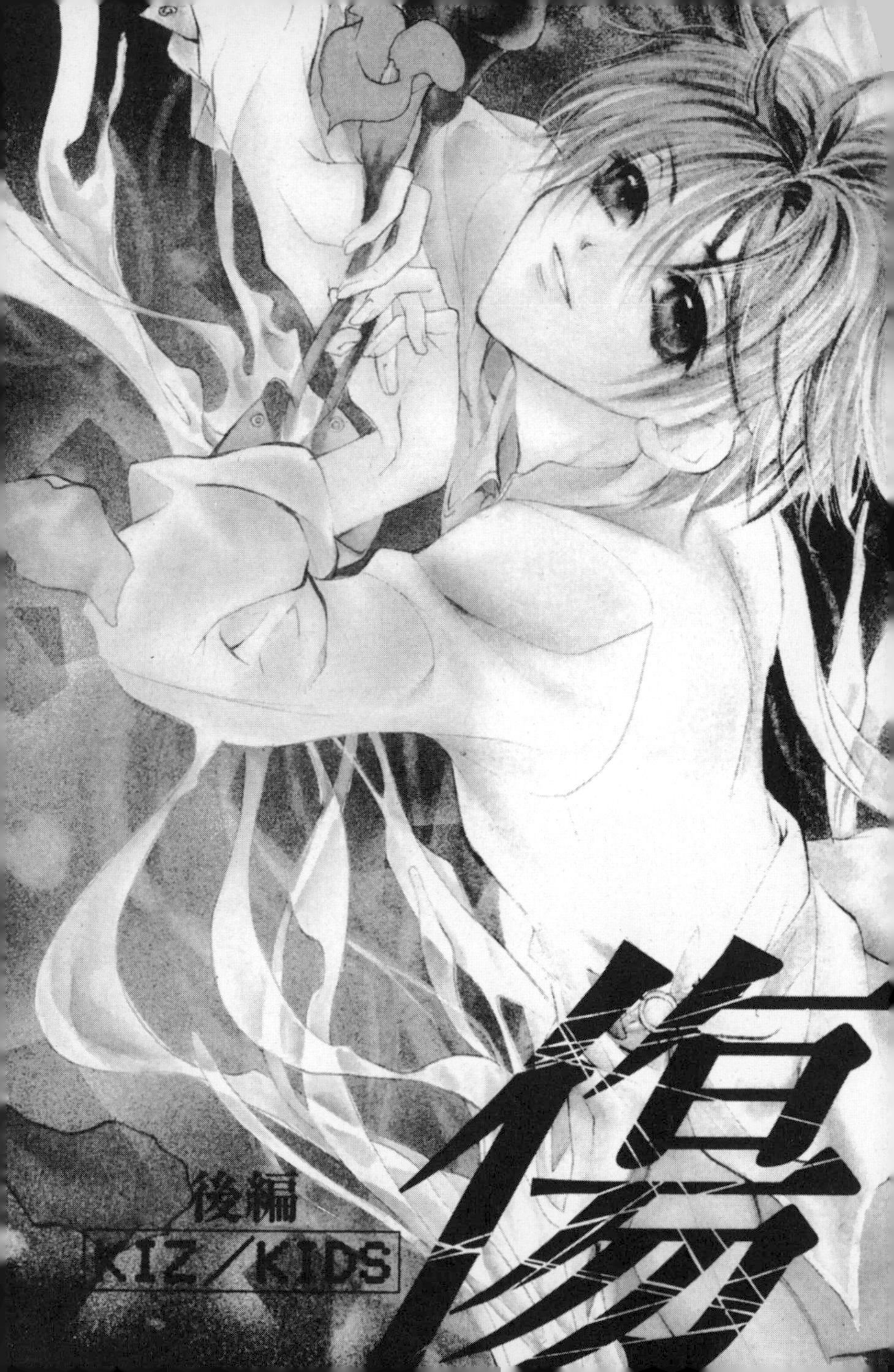
傷
後編
KIZ／KIDS

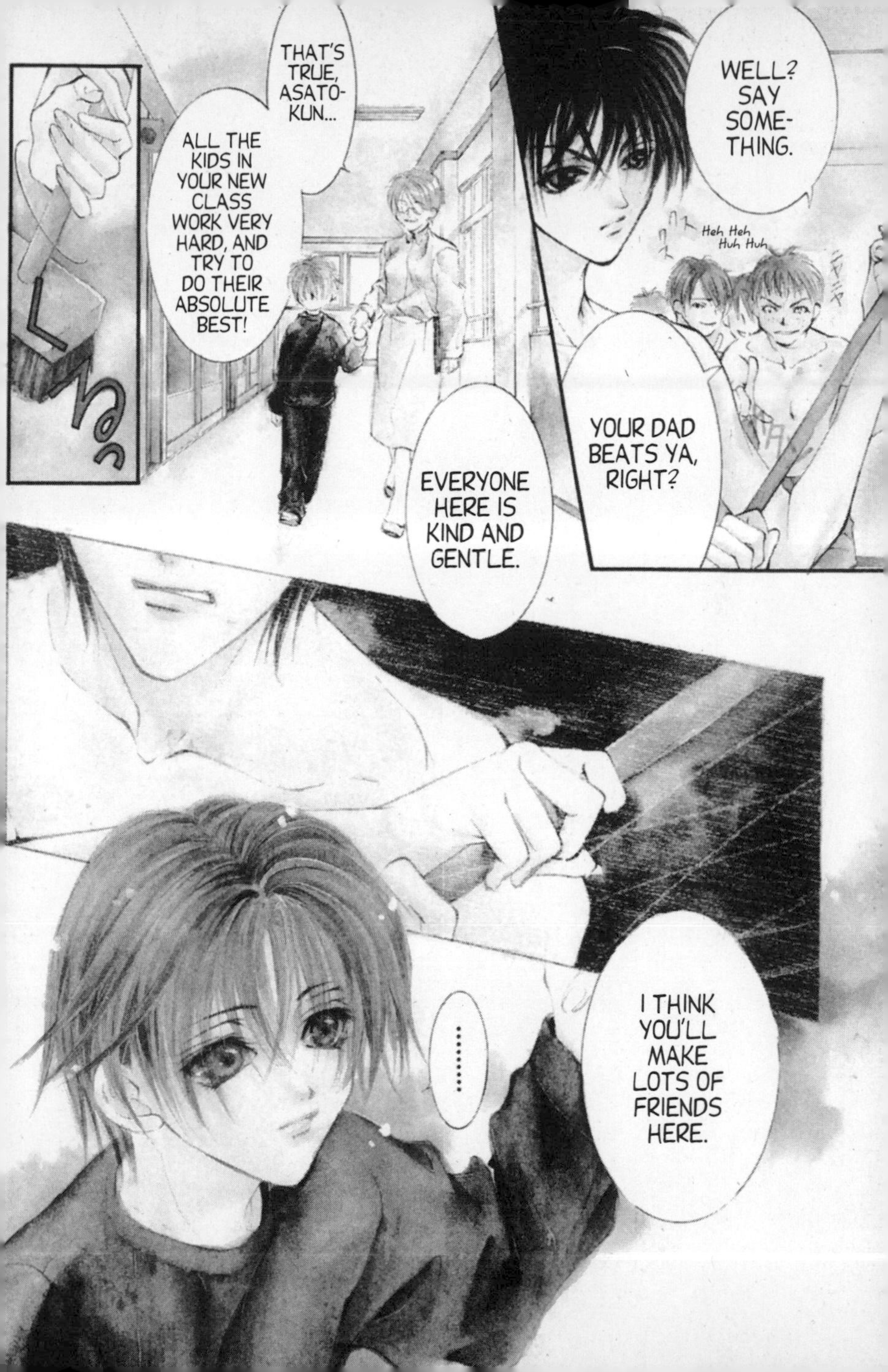
WELL? SAY SOMETHING.
Heh Heh Huh Huh
YOUR DAD BEATS YA, RIGHT?
THAT'S TRUE, ASATO-KUN...
ALL THE KIDS IN YOUR NEW CLASS WORK VERY HARD, AND TRY TO DO THEIR ABSOLUTE BEST!
EVERYONE HERE IS KIND AND GENTLE.
I THINK YOU'LL MAKE LOTS OF FRIENDS HERE.
......

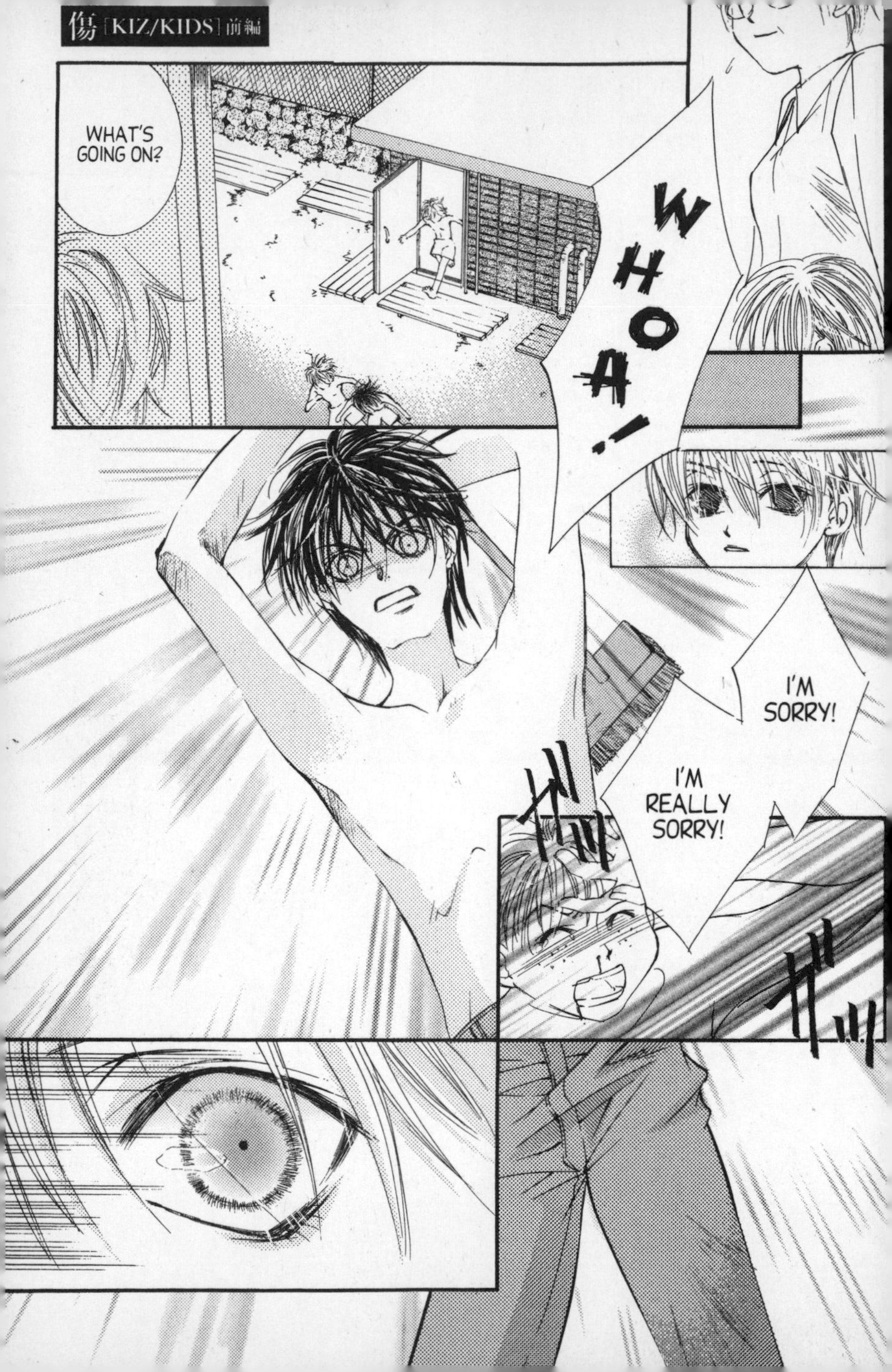
WHAT'S GOING ON?
WHOA!
I'M SORRY!
I'M REALLY SORRY!

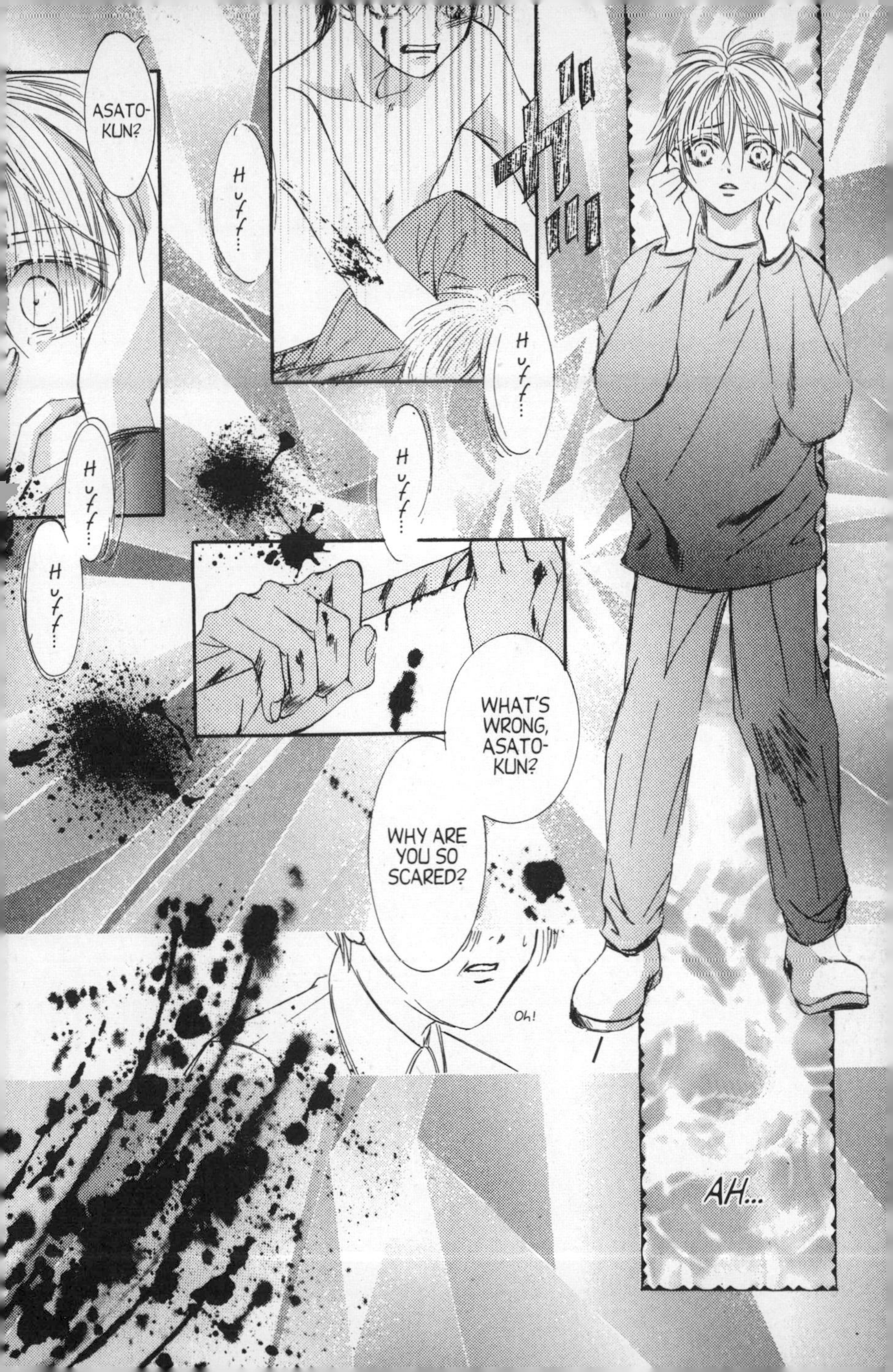
AH...
Huff...
ASATO-KUN?
Huff...
Huff...
Huff...
Huff...
WHAT'S WRONG, ASATO-KUN?
WHY ARE YOU SO SCARED?
Oh!

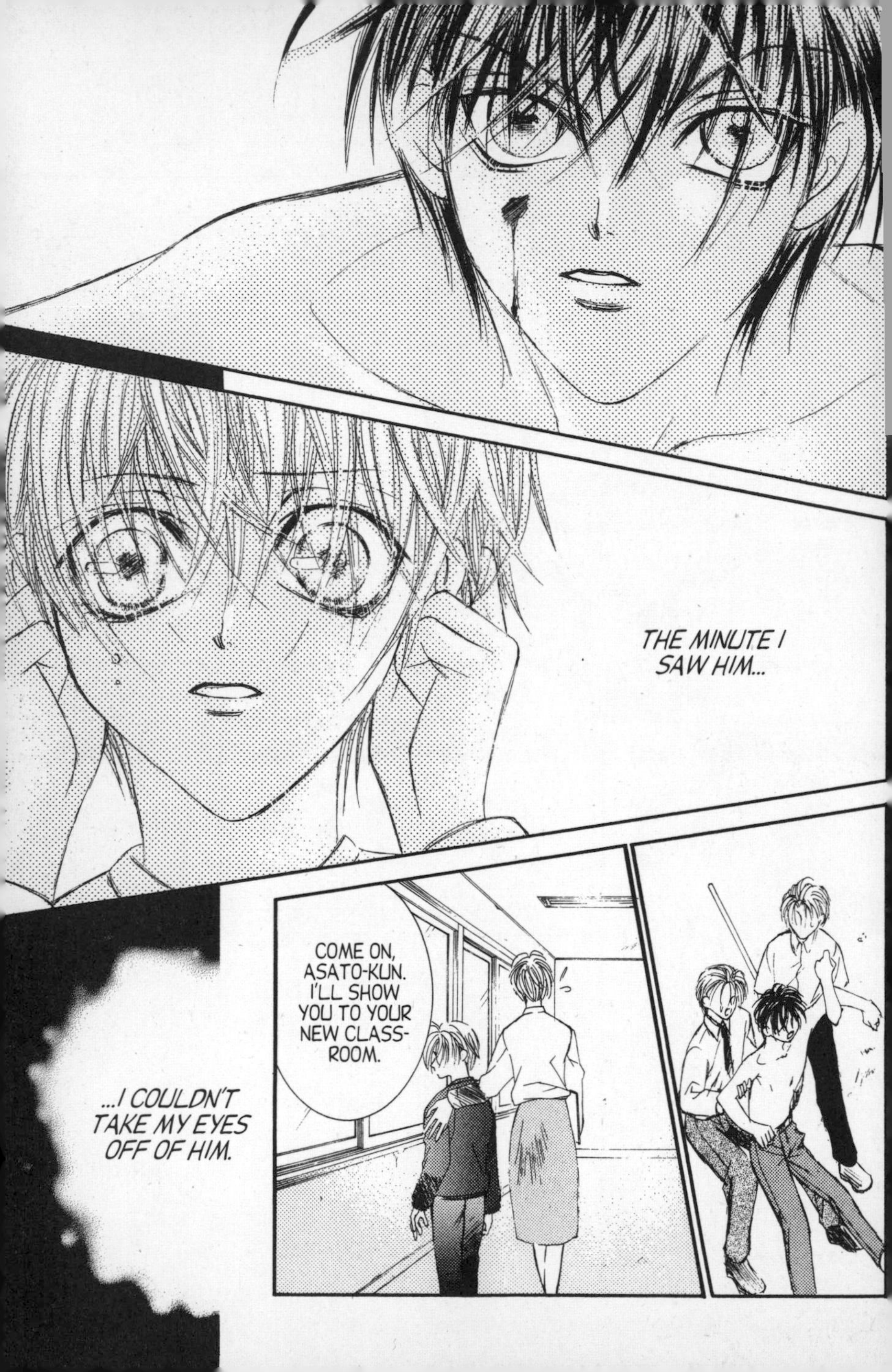
THE MINUTE I SAW HIM...
COME ON, ASATO-KUN. I'LL SHOW YOU TO YOUR NEW CLASSROOM.
...I COULDN'T TAKE MY EYES OFF OF HIM.

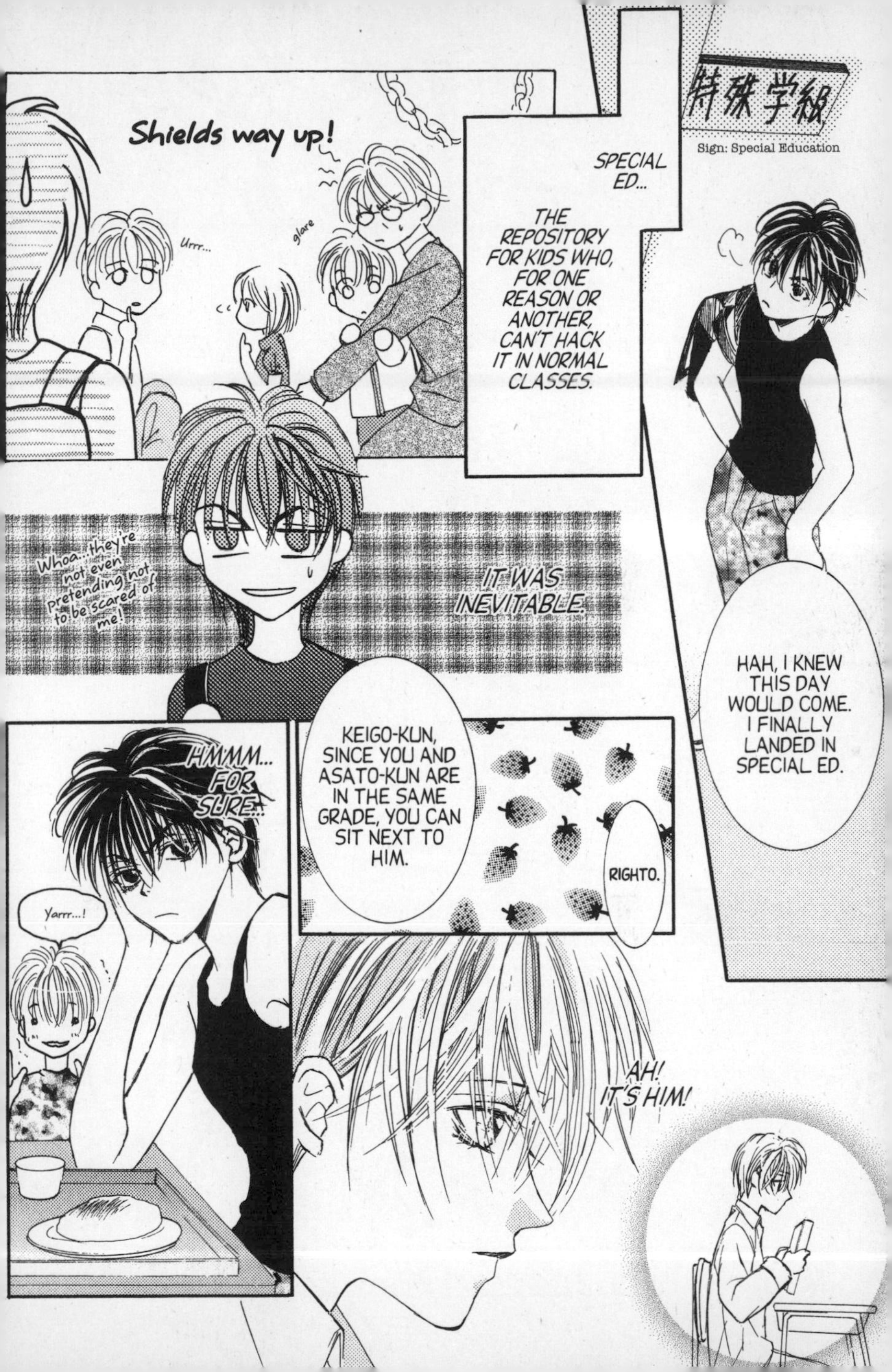
特殊学級
Sign: Special Education
HAH, I KNEW THIS DAY WOULD COME. I FINALLY LANDED IN SPECIAL ED.
SPECIAL ED...
THE REPOSITORY FOR KIDS WHO, FOR ONE REASON OR ANOTHER, CAN'T HACK IT IN NORMAL CLASSES.
glare
Urrr...
Shields way up!
IT WAS INEVITABLE.
Whoa... they're not even pretending not to be scared of me!
RIGHTO.
KEIGO-KUN, SINCE YOU AND ASATO-KUN ARE IN THE SAME GRADE, YOU CAN SIT NEXT TO HIM.
HMMM... FOR SURE...
Yarrr...!
AH! IT'S HIM!

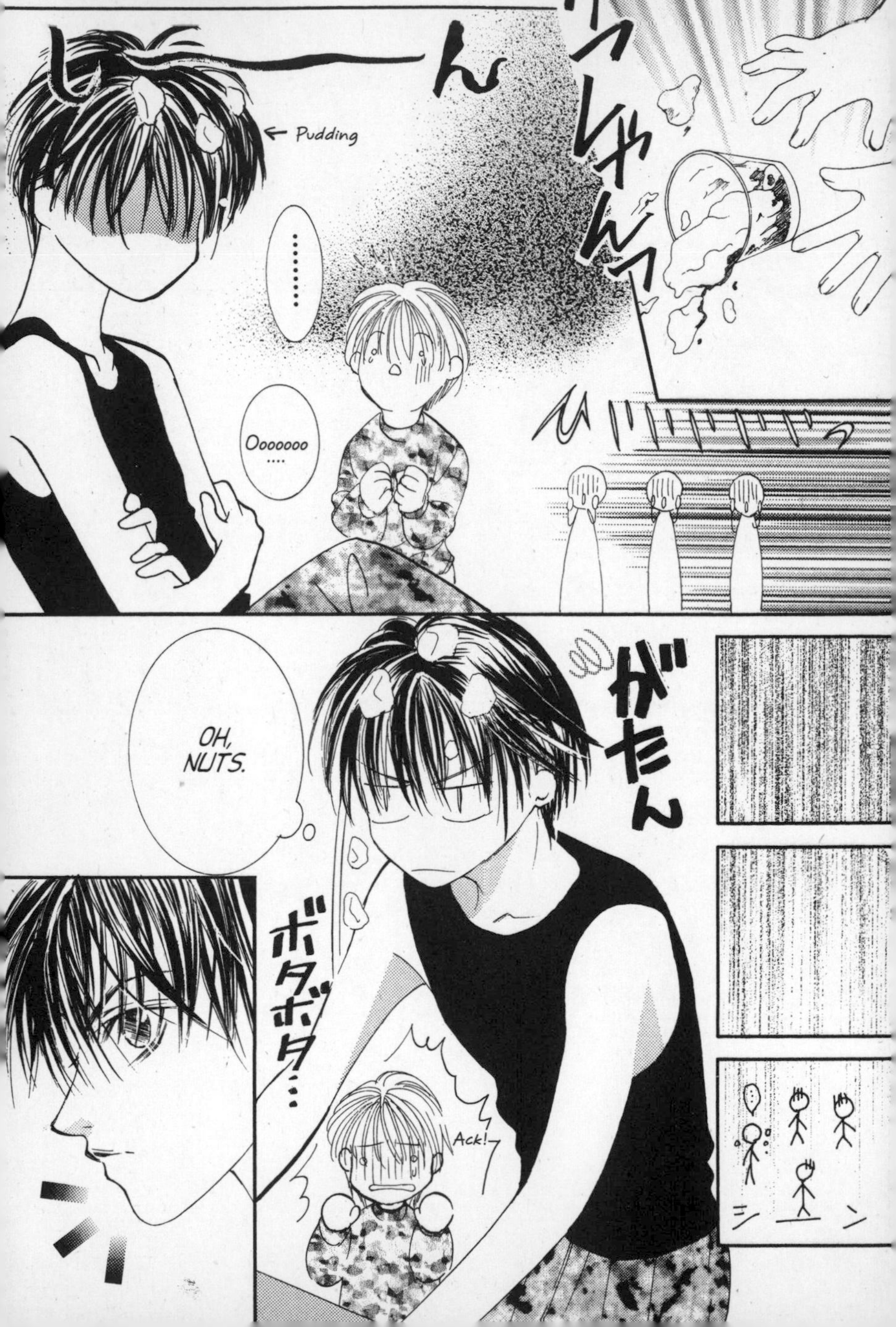
がっしゃんっ
ひッ
しーん
← Pudding
……
Oooooo ....
シーン
がたん
OH, NUTS.
ボタボタ…
Ack!

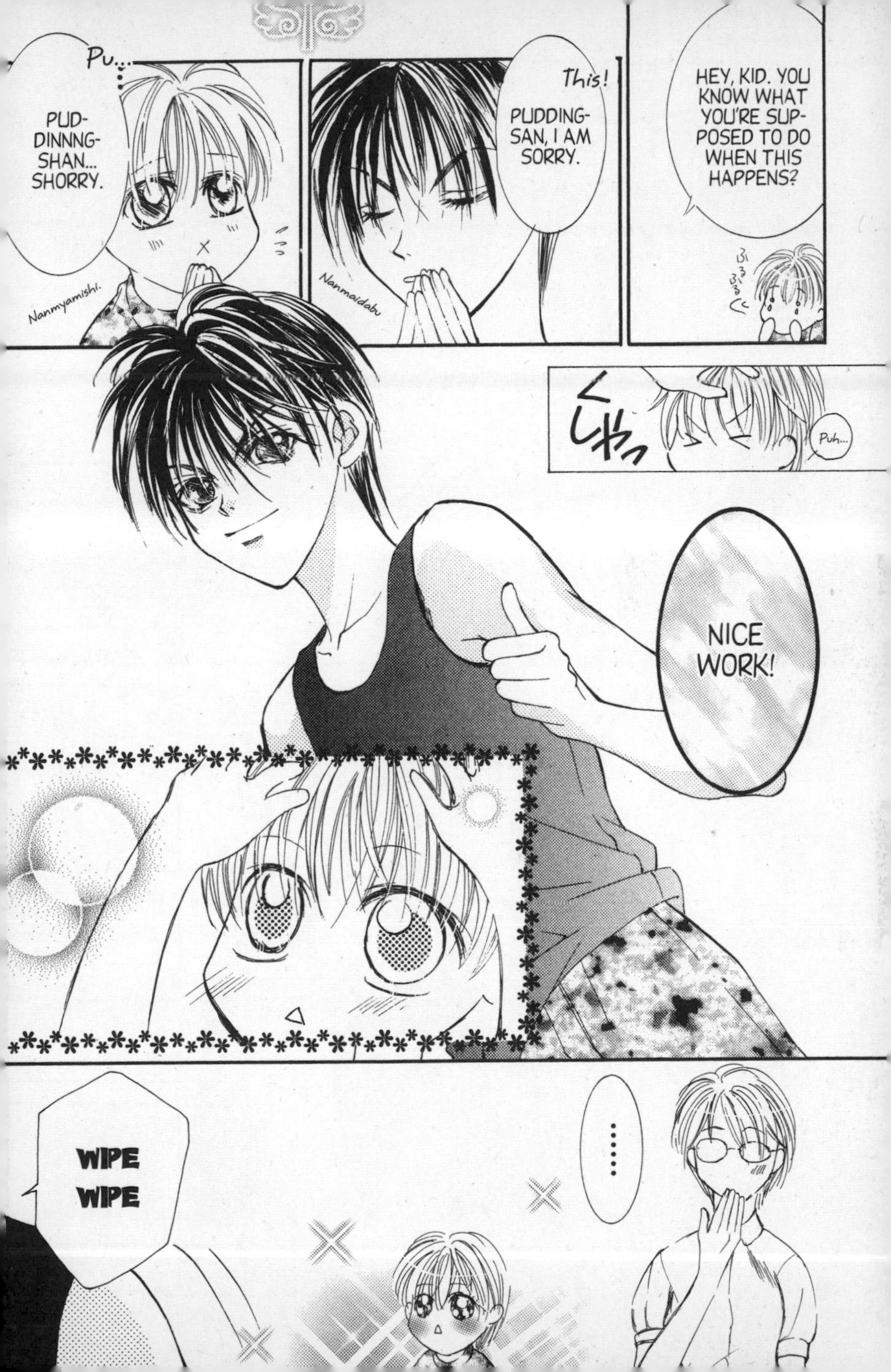
HEY, KID. YOU KNOW WHAT YOU'RE SUP-POSED TO DO WHEN THIS HAPPENS?
ふるふるく
This!
PUDDING-SAN, I AM SORRY.
Nanmaidabu
Pu...
PUD-DINNNG-SHAN... SHORRY.
Nanmyamishi.
くしゃっ
Puh...
NICE WORK!
......
WIPE WIPE

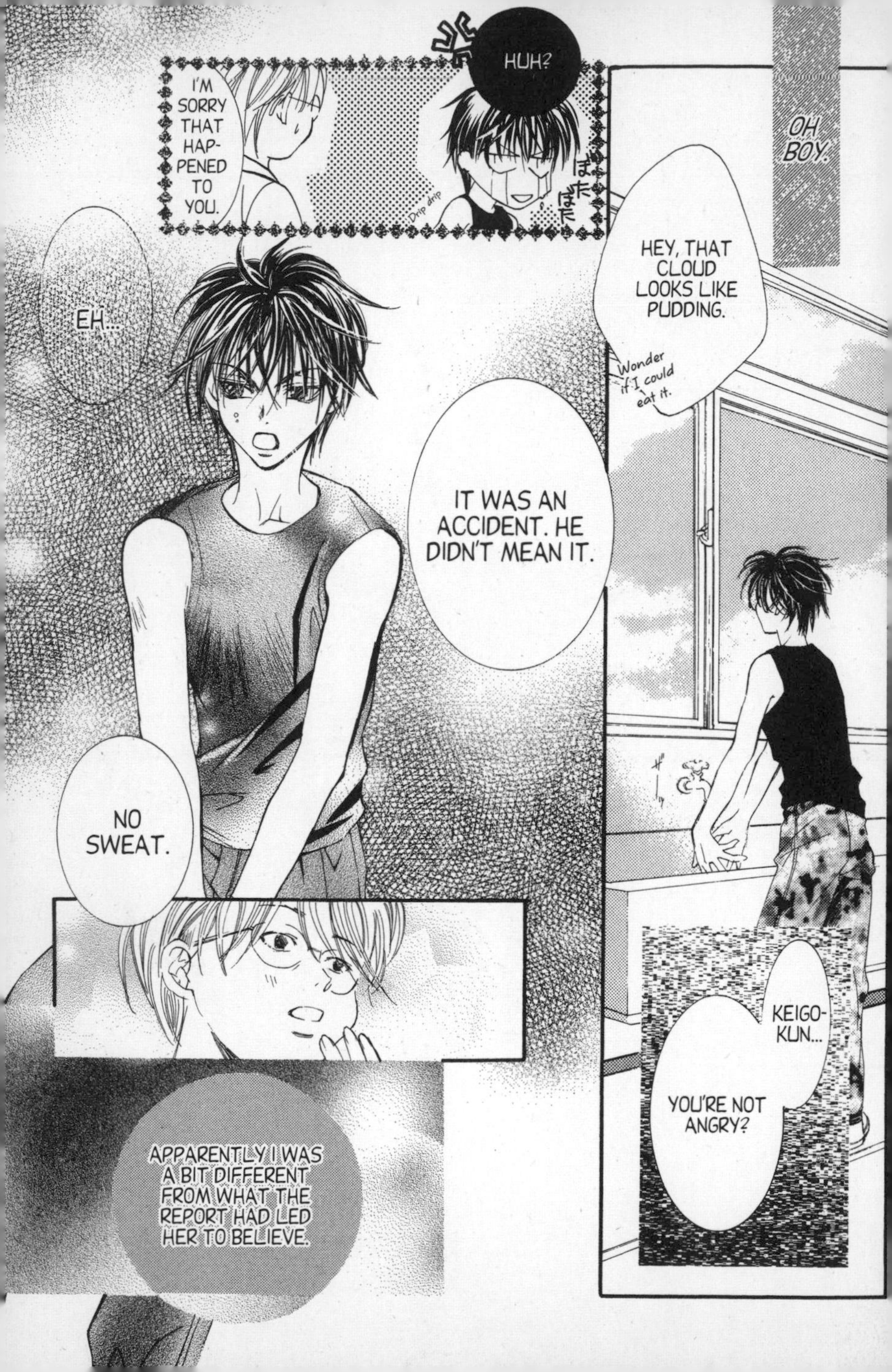
OH BOY.
HEY, THAT CLOUD LOOKS LIKE PUDDING.
Wonder if I could eat it.
KEIGO-KUN...
YOU'RE NOT ANGRY?
HUH?
I'M SORRY THAT HAP-PENED TO YOU.
ぽたぽた
Drip drip
IT WAS AN ACCIDENT. HE DIDN'T MEAN IT.
EH...
NO SWEAT.
APPARENTLY I WAS A BIT DIFFERENT FROM WHAT THE REPORT HAD LED HER TO BELIEVE.

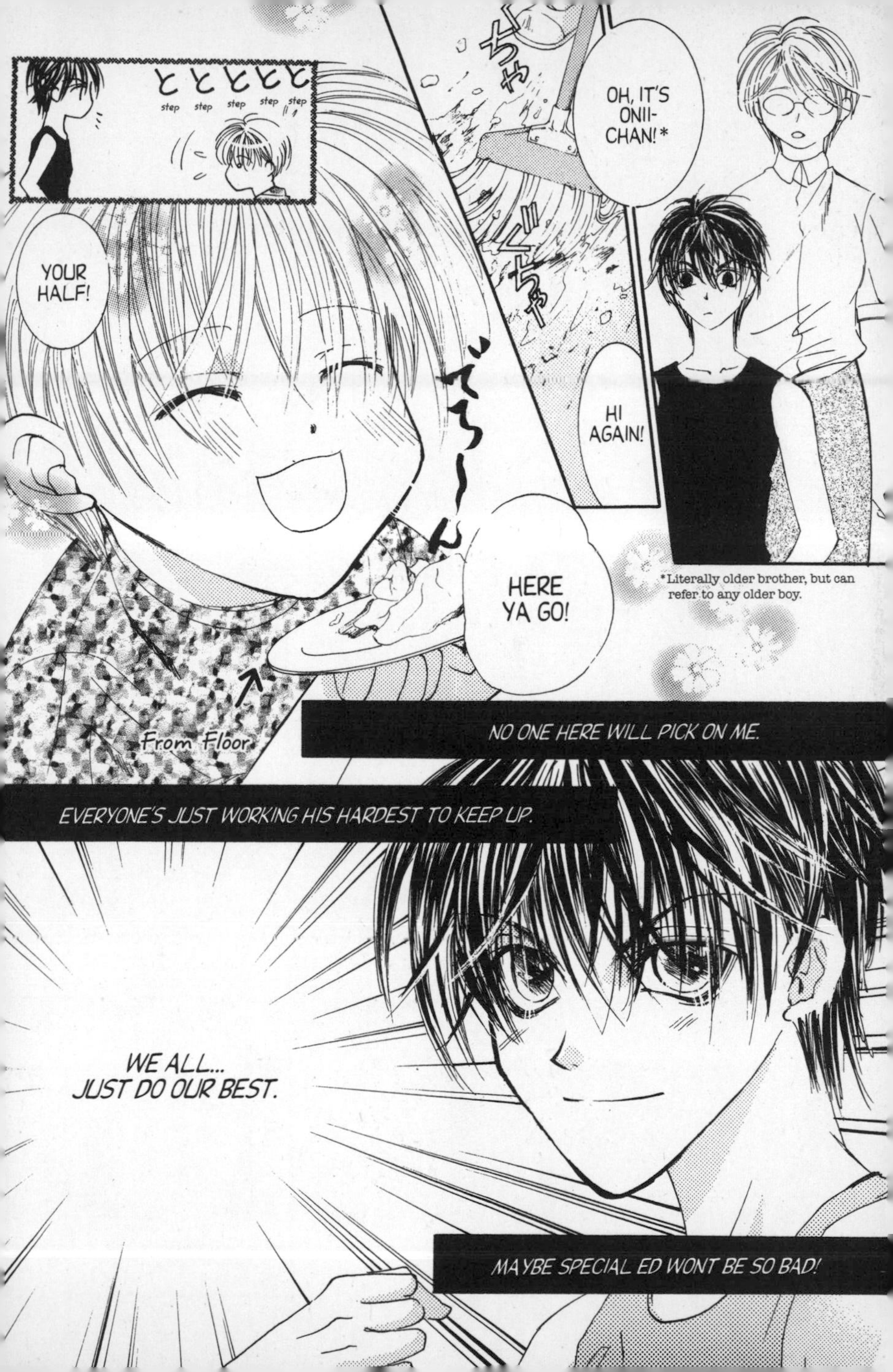
OH, IT'S ONII-CHAN!*
ぐちゃ
HI AGAIN!
*Literally older brother, but can refer to any older boy.
ととととと
step step step step step
YOUR HALF!
でろ~ん
HERE YA GO!
From Floor
NO ONE HERE WILL PICK ON ME.
EVERYONE'S JUST WORKING HIS HARDEST TO KEEP UP.
WE ALL... JUST DO OUR BEST.
MAYBE SPECIAL ED WONT BE SO BAD!

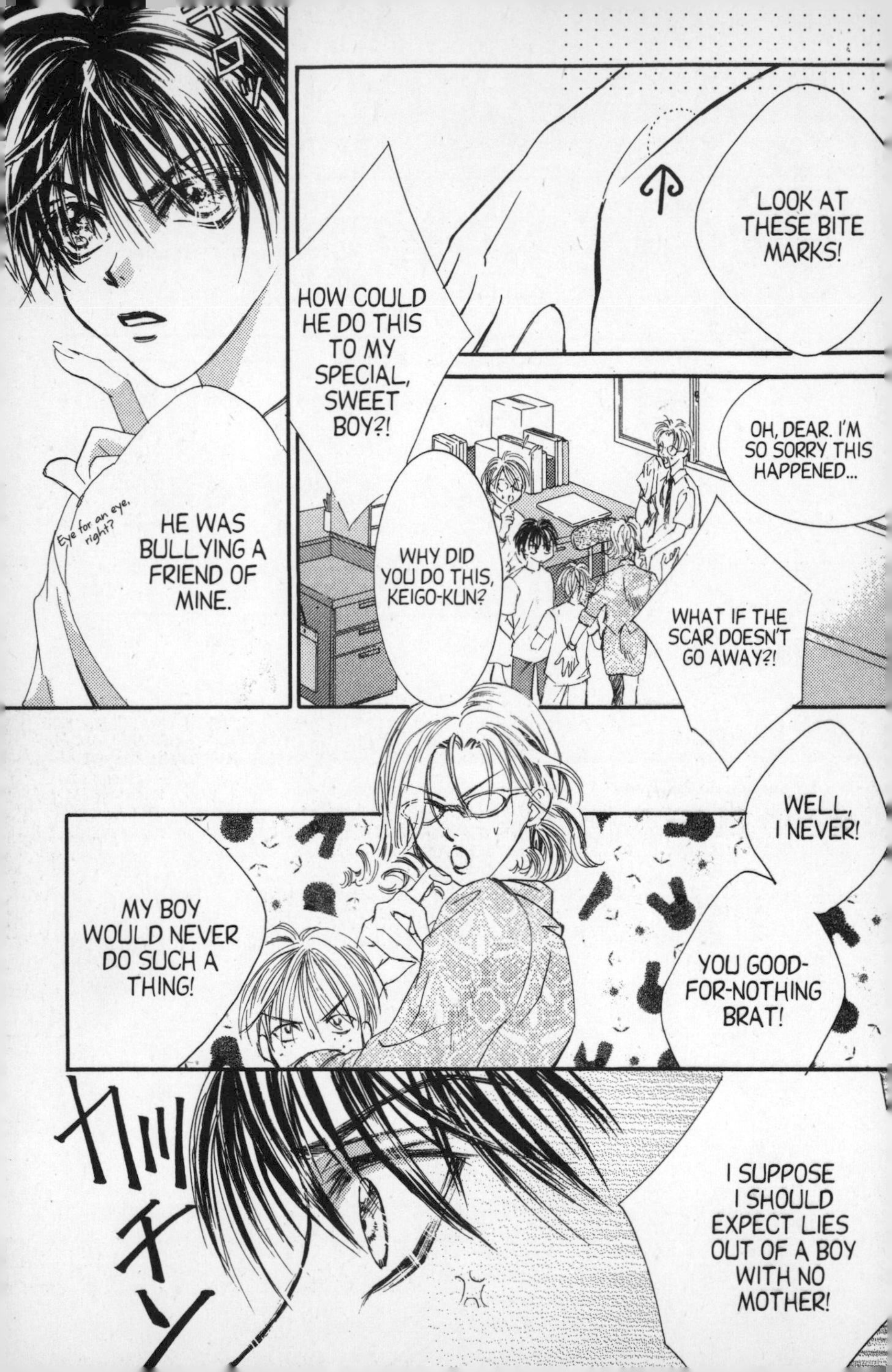
LOOK AT THESE BITE MARKS!
HOW COULD HE DO THIS TO MY SPECIAL, SWEET BOY?!
OH, DEAR. I'M SO SORRY THIS HAPPENED...
WHAT IF THE SCAR DOESN'T GO AWAY?!
WHY DID YOU DO THIS, KEIGO-KUN?
HE WAS BULLYING A FRIEND OF MINE.
Eye for an eye, right?
WELL, I NEVER!
YOU GOOD-FOR-NOTHING BRAT!
MY BOY WOULD NEVER DO SUCH A THING!
I SUPPOSE I SHOULD EXPECT LIES OUT OF A BOY WITH NO MOTHER!

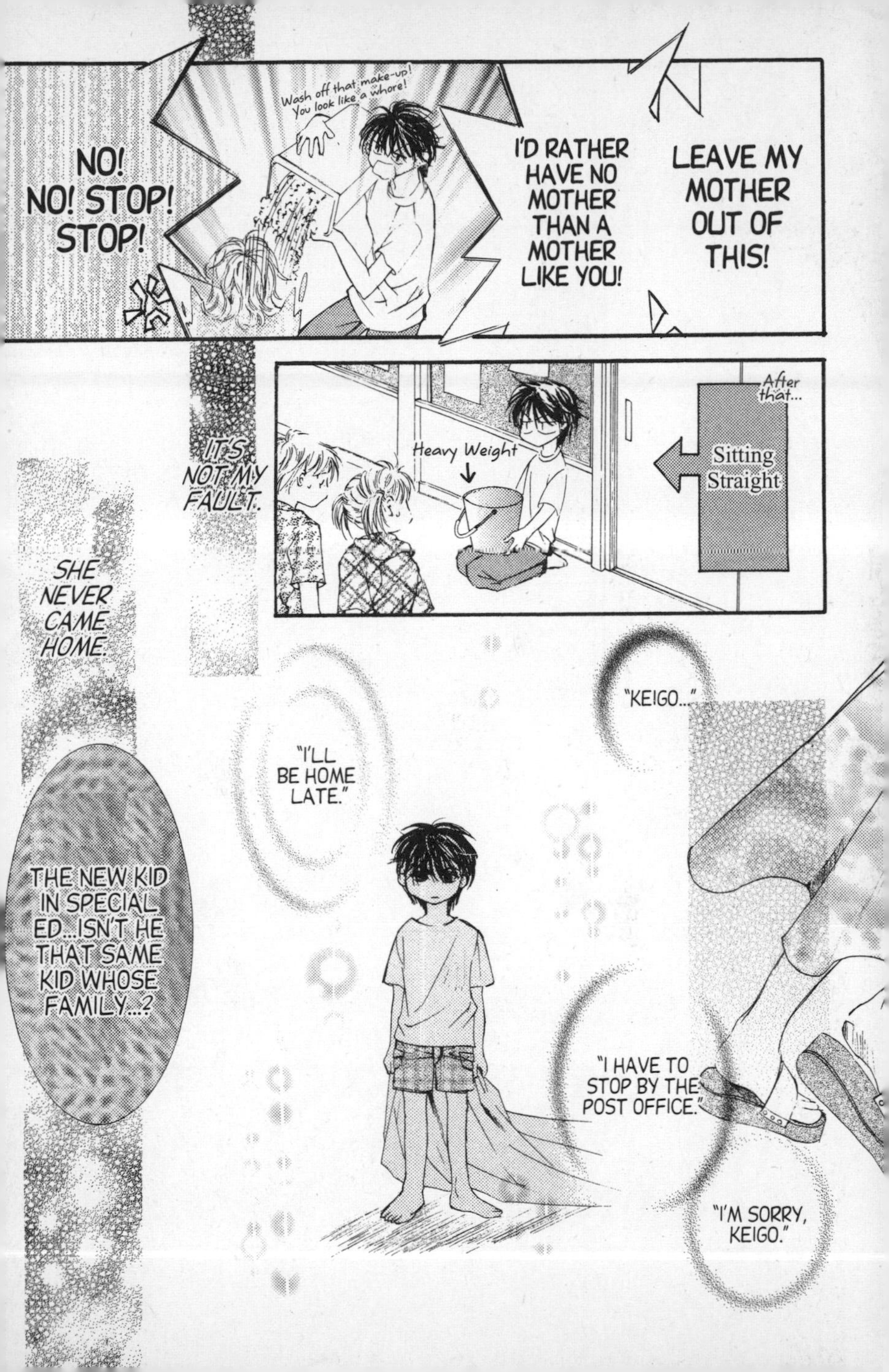
LEAVE MY MOTHER OUT OF THIS!
I'D RATHER HAVE NO MOTHER THAN A MOTHER LIKE YOU!
Wash off that make-up! You look like a whore!
NO! NO! STOP! STOP!
After that...
Sitting Straight
Heavy Weight
IT'S NOT MY FAULT.
SHE NEVER CAME HOME.
"KEIGO..."
"I'LL BE HOME LATE."
"I HAVE TO STOP BY THE POST OFFICE."
"I'M SORRY, KEIGO."
THE NEW KID IN SPECIAL ED...ISN'T HE THAT SAME KID WHOSE FAMILY...?

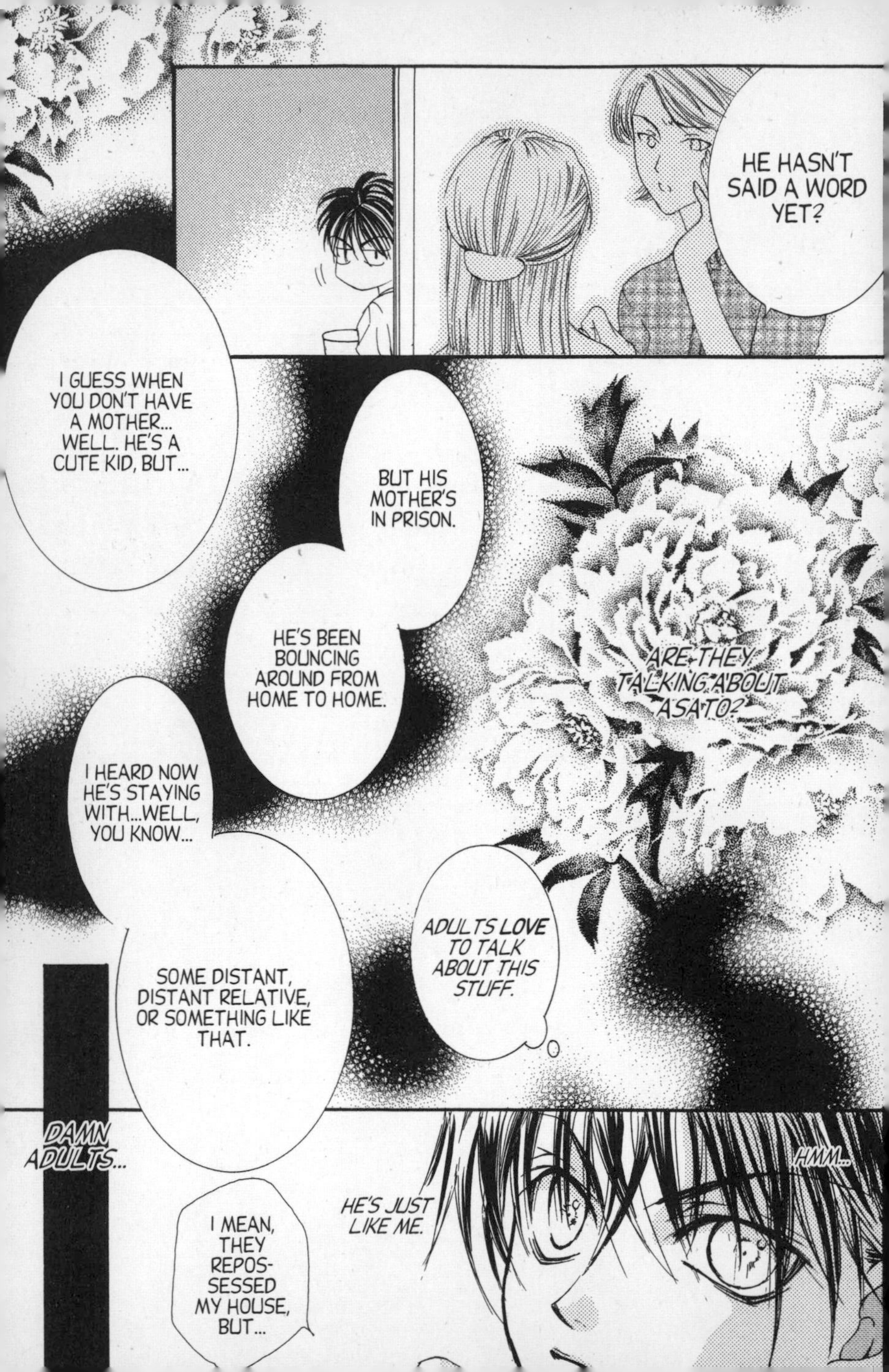

HE HASN'T SAID A WORD YET?
I GUESS WHEN YOU DON'T HAVE A MOTHER... WELL. HE'S A CUTE KID, BUT...
BUT HIS MOTHER'S IN PRISON.
HE'S BEEN BOUNCING AROUND FROM HOME TO HOME.
ARE THEY TALKING ABOUT ASATO?
I HEARD NOW HE'S STAYING WITH...WELL, YOU KNOW...
SOME DISTANT, DISTANT RELATIVE, OR SOMETHING LIKE THAT.
ADULTS **LOVE** TO TALK ABOUT THIS STUFF.
HMM...
HE'S JUST LIKE ME.
I MEAN, THEY REPOS-SESSED MY HOUSE, BUT...
DAMN ADULTS...

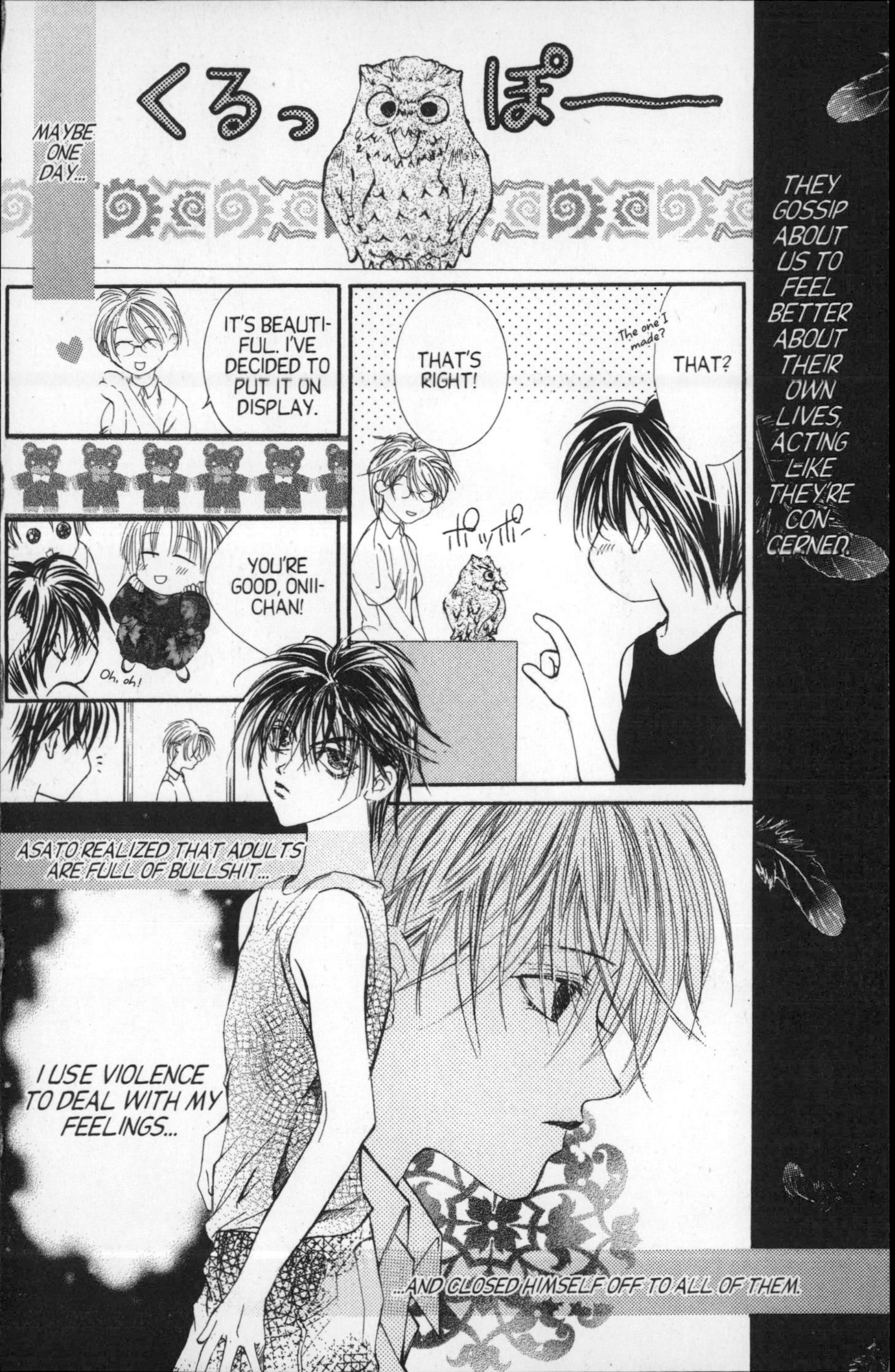
THEY GOSSIP ABOUT US TO FEEL BETTER ABOUT THEIR OWN LIVES, ACTING LIKE THEY'RE CONCERNED.
くるっぽーー
MAYBE ONE DAY...
THAT?
The one I made?
THAT'S RIGHT!
IT'S BEAUTIFUL. I'VE DECIDED TO PUT IT ON DISPLAY.
YOU'RE GOOD, ONII-CHAN!
Oh, oh!
ASATO REALIZED THAT ADULTS ARE FULL OF BULLSHIT...
I USE VIOLENCE TO DEAL WITH MY FEELINGS...
...AND CLOSED HIMSELF OFF TO ALL OF THEM.

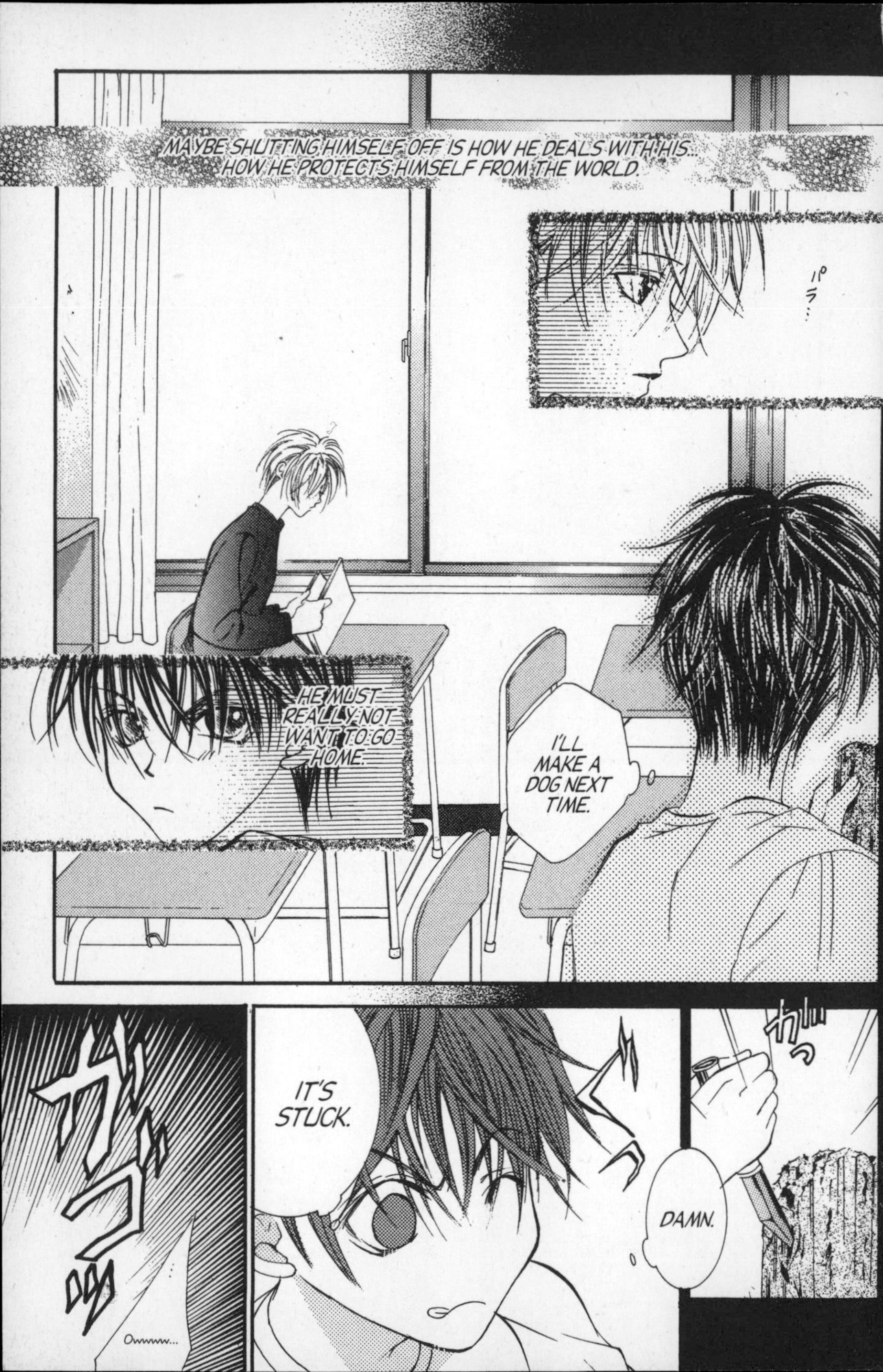
MAYBE SHUTTING HIMSELF OFF IS HOW HE DEALS WITH HIS... HOW HE PROTECTS HIMSELF FROM THE WORLD.
パラ…
I'LL MAKE A DOG NEXT TIME.
HE MUST REALLY NOT WANT TO GO HOME.
DAMN.
IT'S STUCK.
Owwww...

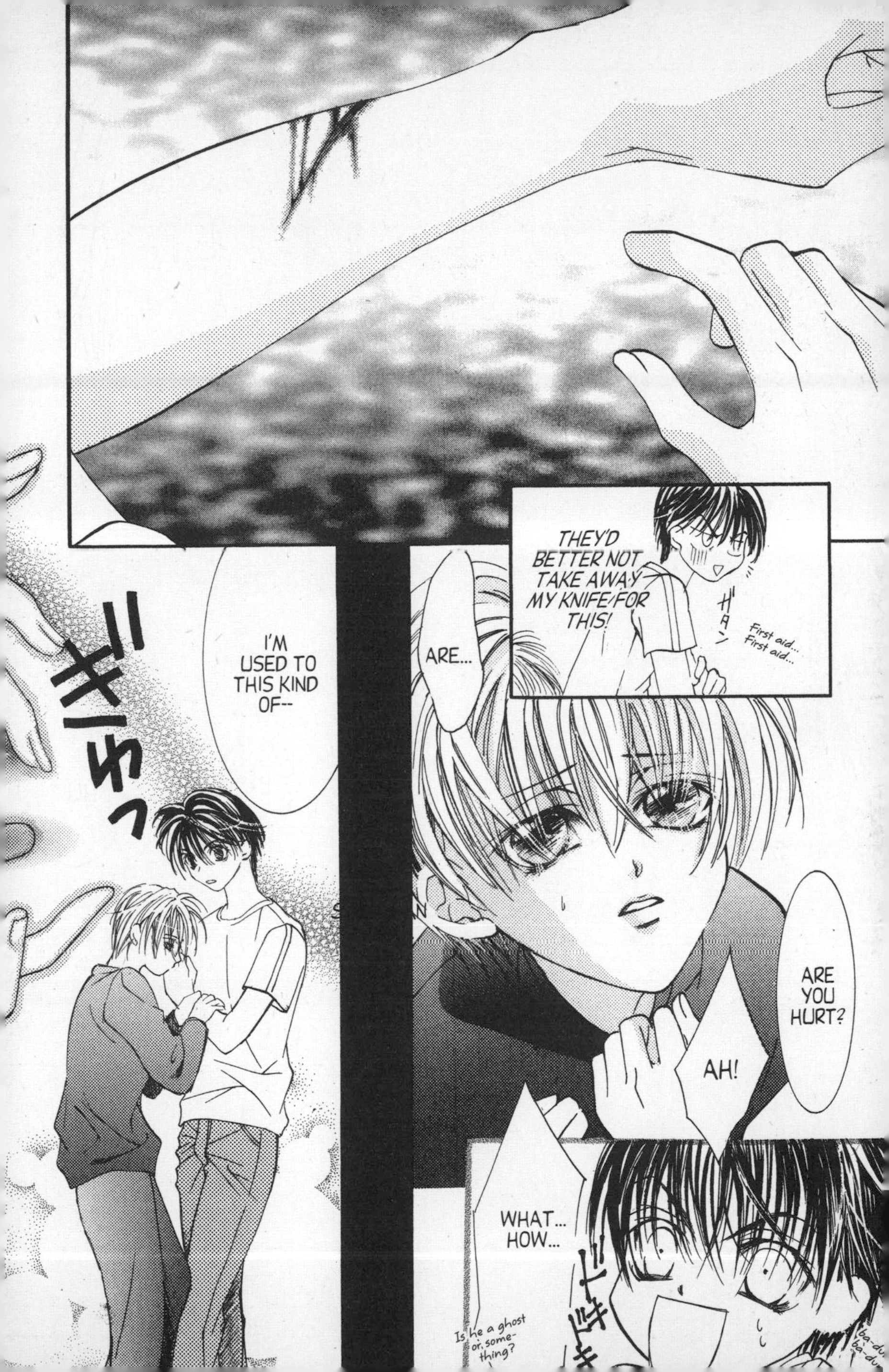
THEY'D BETTER NOT TAKE AWAY MY KNIFE FOR THIS!
ガタン
First aid... First aid...
ARE...
ARE YOU HURT?
AH!
WHAT... HOW...
Is he a ghost or some-thing?
I'M USED TO THIS KIND OF--

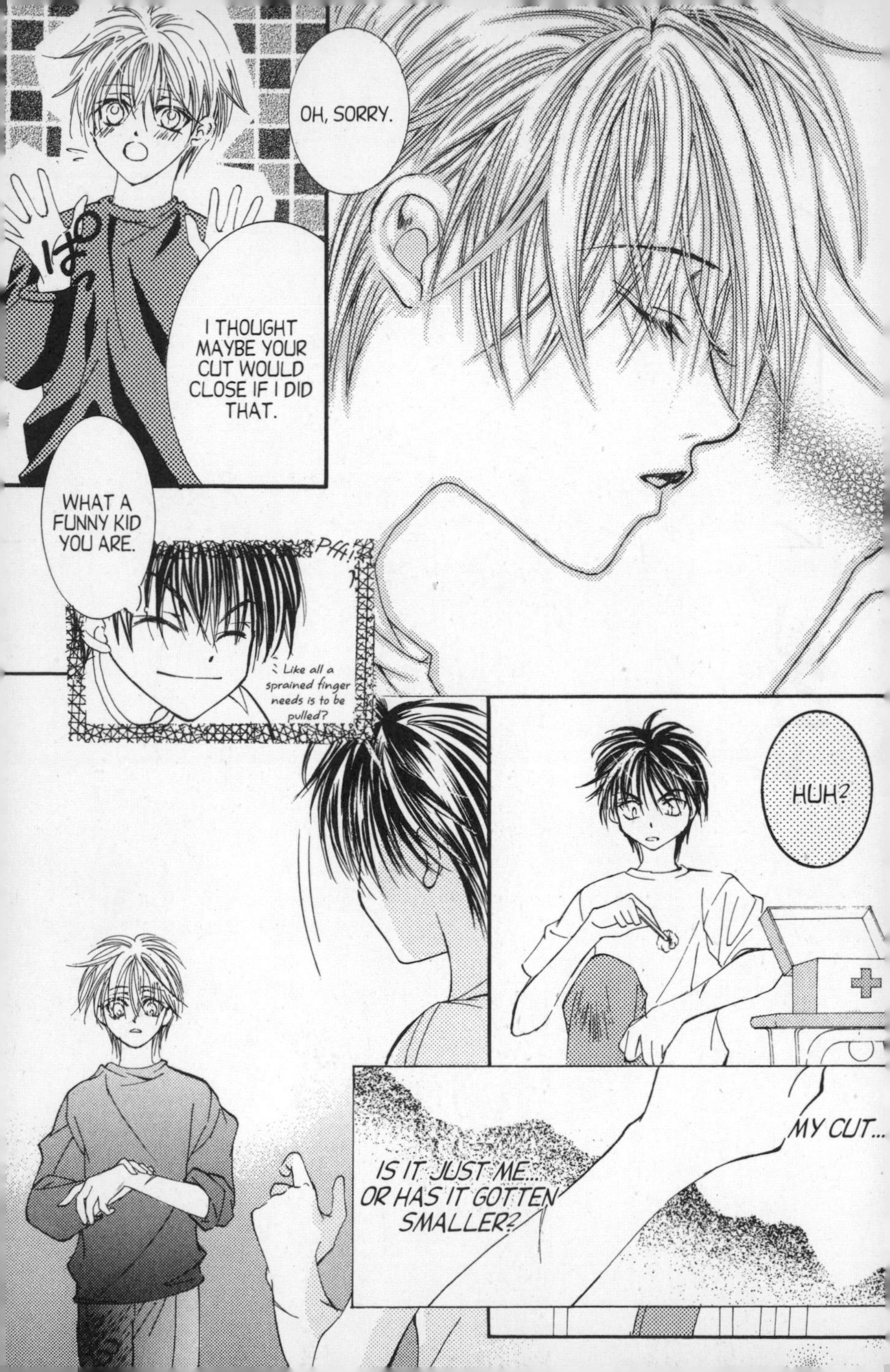
OH, SORRY.
ぱ
I THOUGHT MAYBE YOUR CUT WOULD CLOSE IF I DID THAT.
WHAT A FUNNY KID YOU ARE.
Pff!
Like all a sprained finger needs is to be pulled?
HUH?
MY CUT...
IS IT JUST ME... OR HAS IT GOTTEN SMALLER?

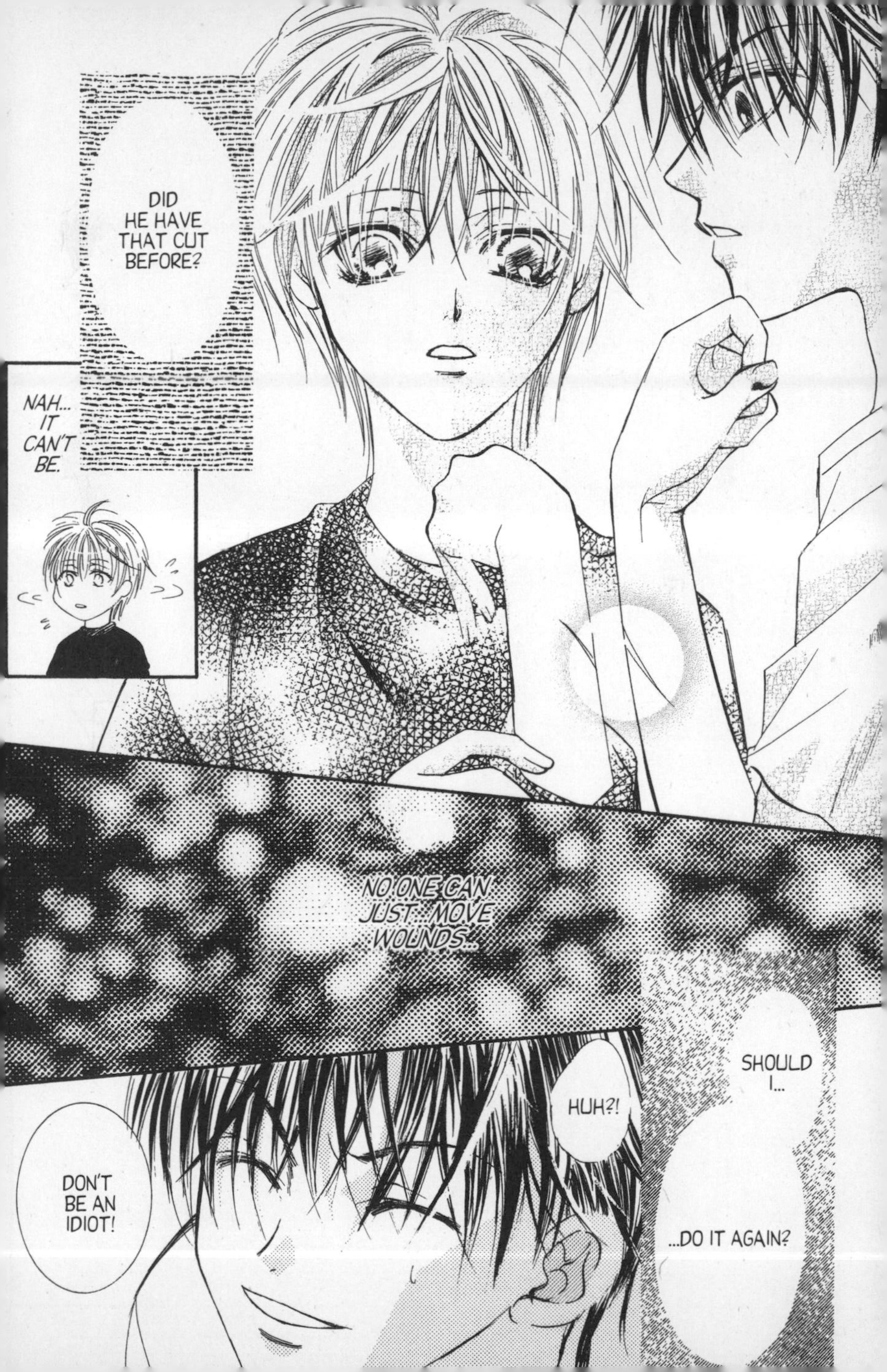
DID HE HAVE THAT CUT BEFORE?
NAH... IT CAN'T BE.
NO ONE CAN JUST MOVE WOUNDS...
SHOULD I...
...DO IT AGAIN?
HUH?!
DON'T BE AN IDIOT!

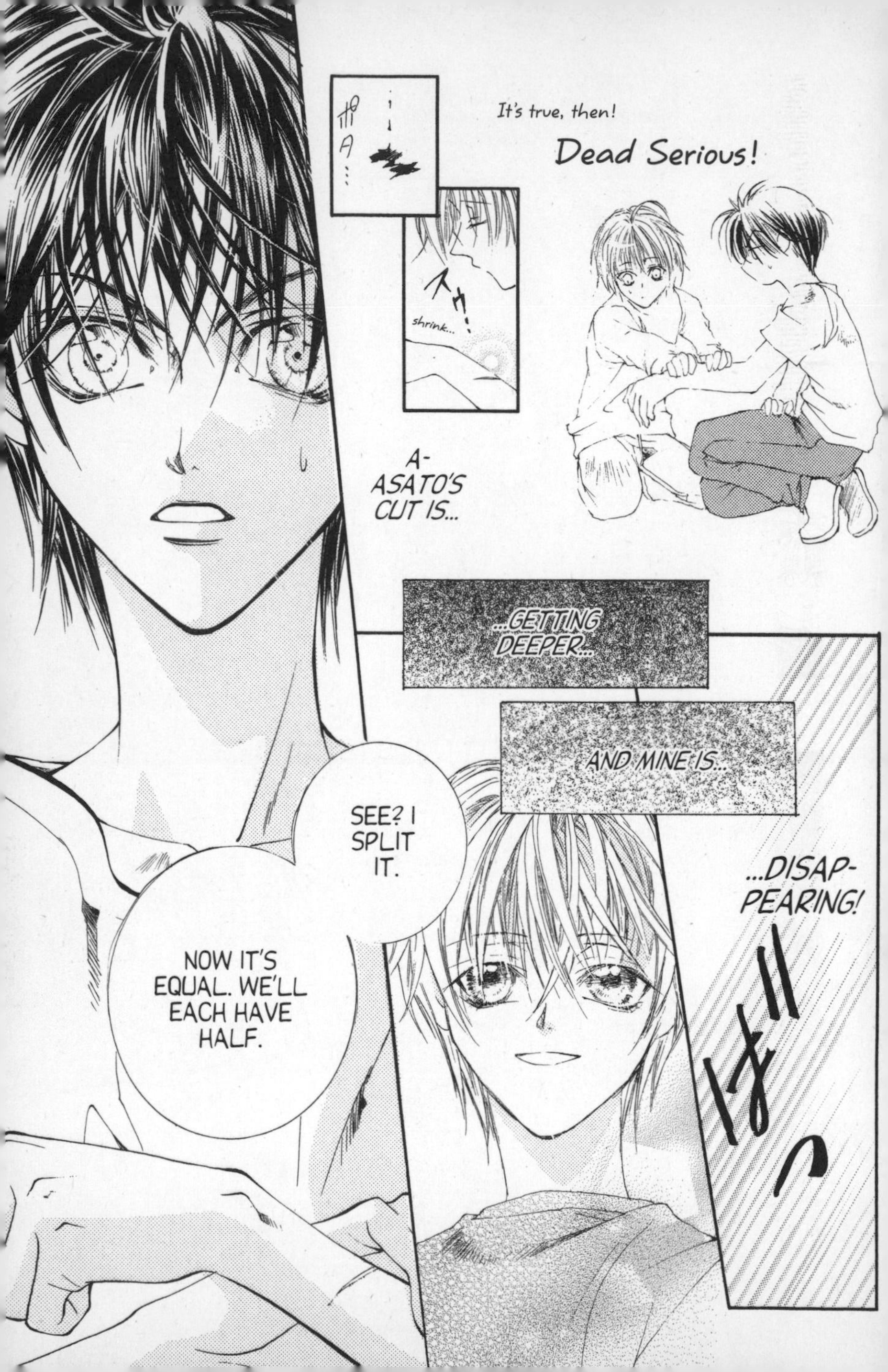
It's true, then!
Dead Serious!
shrink...
A-
ASATO'S
CUT IS...
...GETTING
DEEPER...
AND MINE IS...
...DISAP-
PEARING!
SEE? I
SPLIT
IT.
NOW IT'S
EQUAL. WE'LL
EACH HAVE
HALF.

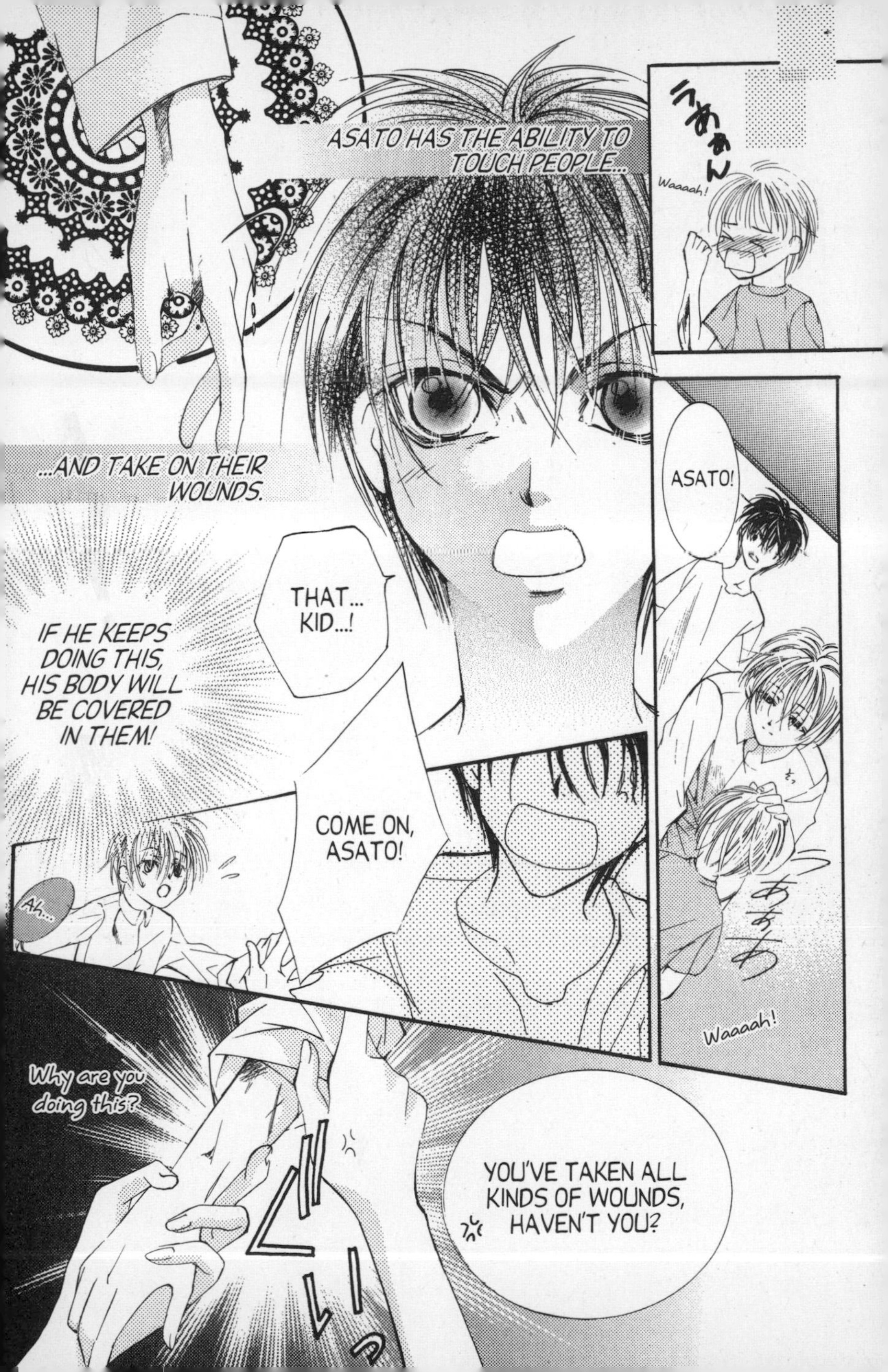
Waaaah!
ASATO HAS THE ABILITY TO TOUCH PEOPLE...
...AND TAKE ON THEIR WOUNDS.
ASATO!
Waaaah!
THAT... KID...!
IF HE KEEPS DOING THIS, HIS BODY WILL BE COVERED IN THEM!
COME ON, ASATO!
Ah...
YOU'VE TAKEN ALL KINDS OF WOUNDS, HAVEN'T YOU?
Why are you doing this?

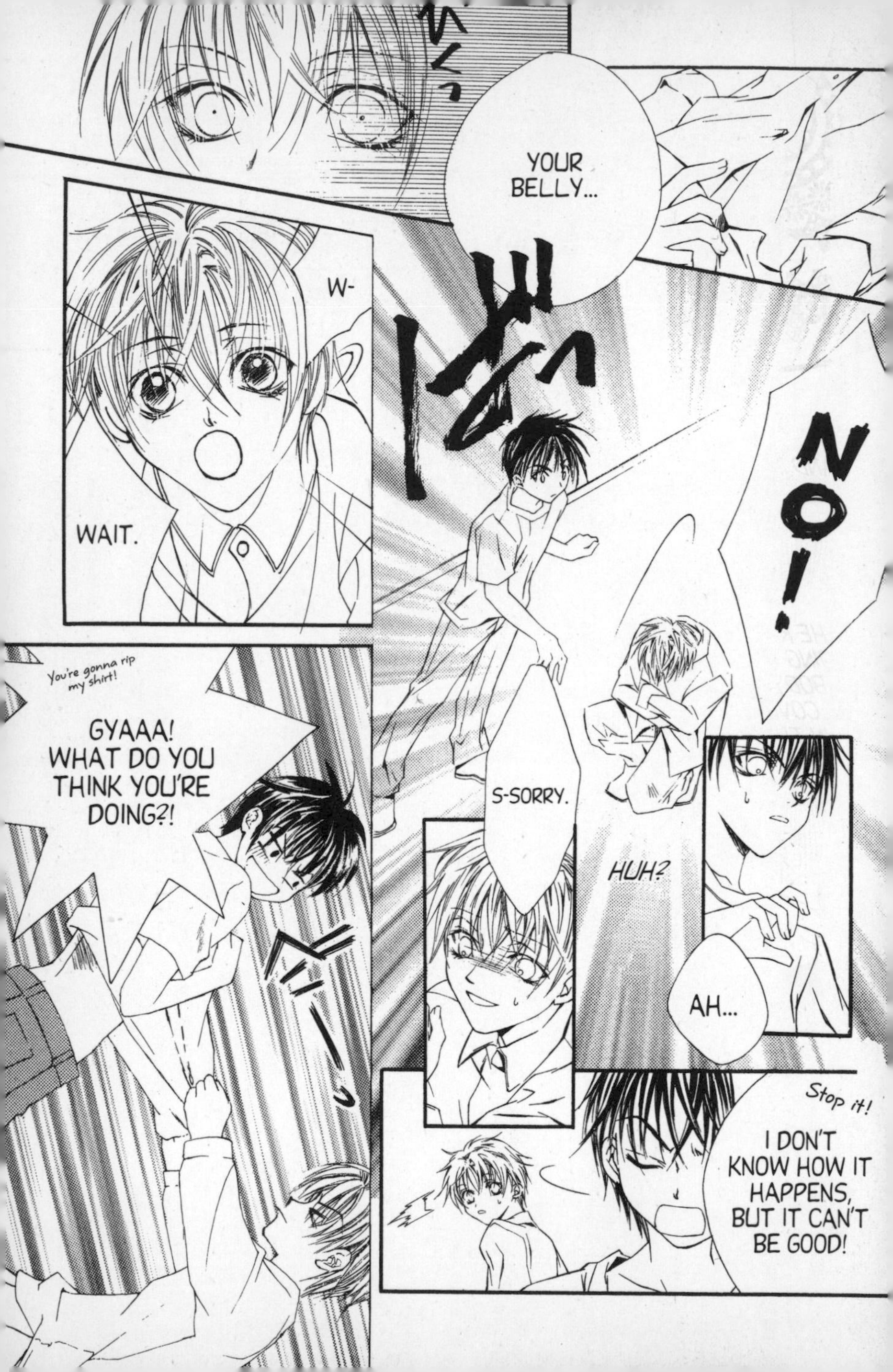
YOUR BELLY...
NO!
W-
WAIT.
AH...
HUH?
S-SORRY.
Stop it!
I DON'T KNOW HOW IT HAPPENS, BUT IT CAN'T BE GOOD!
You're gonna rip my shirt!
GYAAA! WHAT DO YOU THINK YOU'RE DOING?!

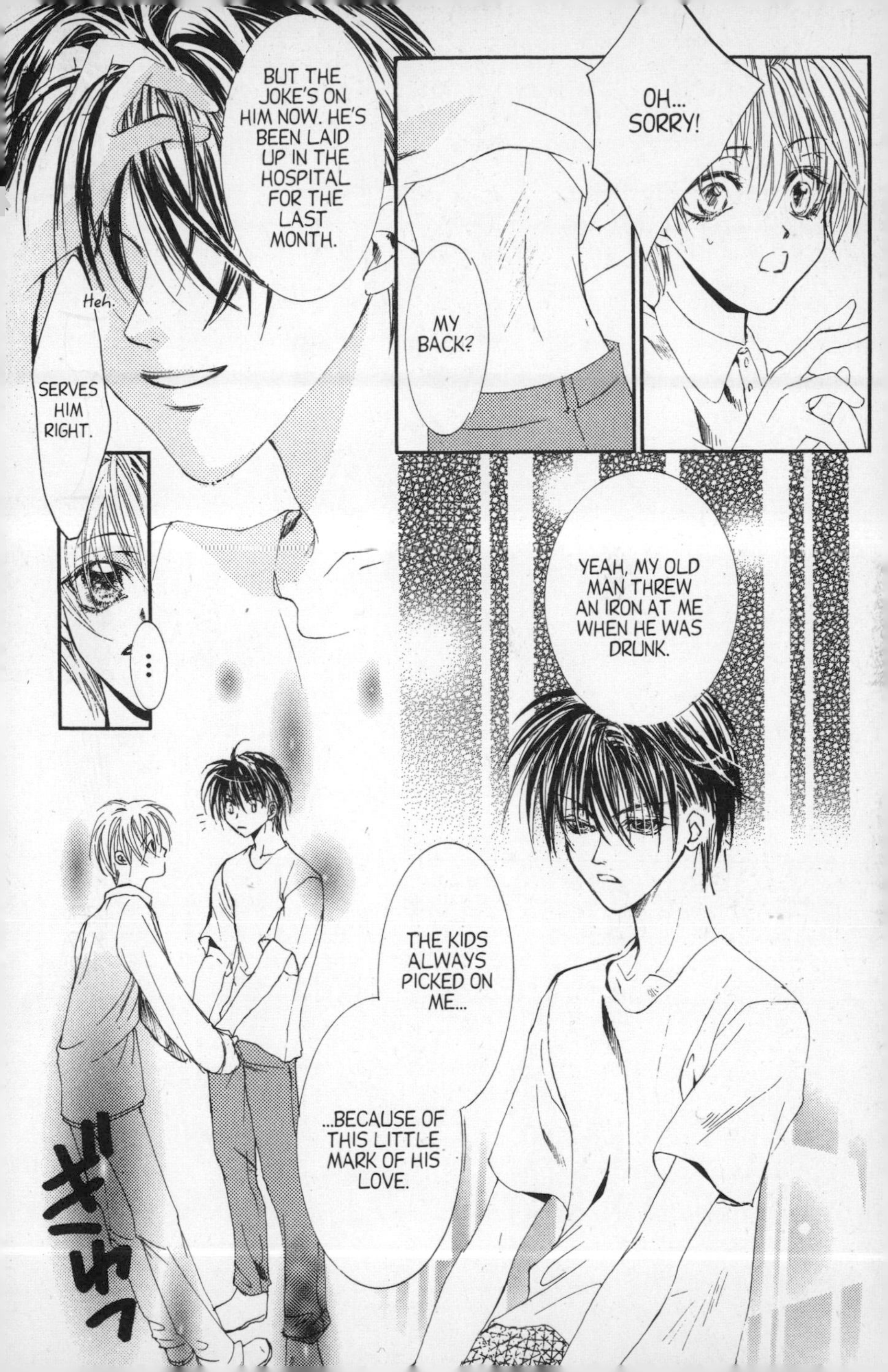
OH... SORRY!
MY BACK?
YEAH, MY OLD MAN THREW AN IRON AT ME WHEN HE WAS DRUNK.
THE KIDS ALWAYS PICKED ON ME...
...BECAUSE OF THIS LITTLE MARK OF HIS LOVE.
BUT THE JOKE'S ON HIM NOW. HE'S BEEN LAID UP IN THE HOSPITAL FOR THE LAST MONTH.
Heh.
SERVES HIM RIGHT.
...

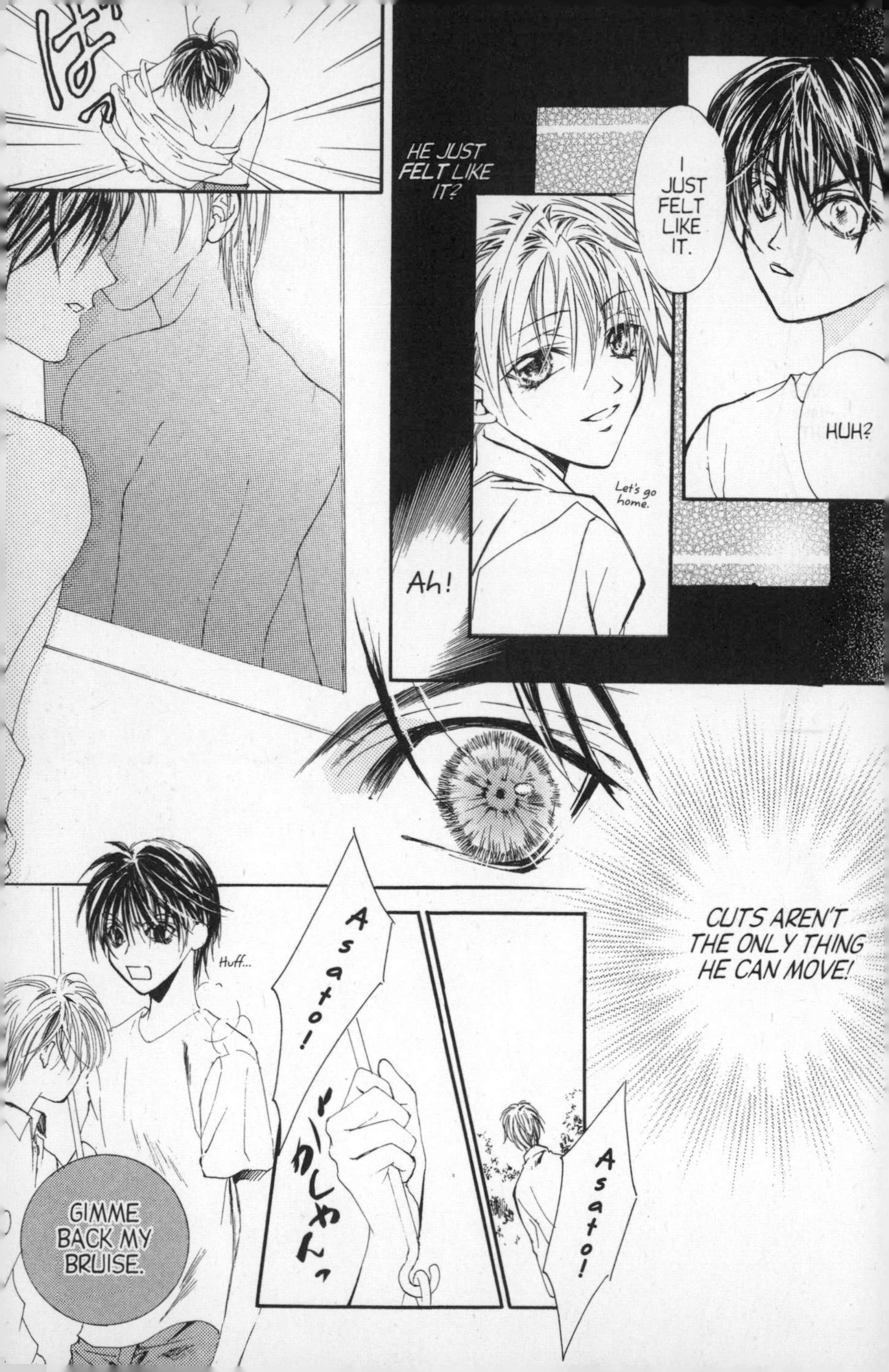

I JUST FELT LIKE IT.
HUH?
Let's go home.
HE JUST FELT LIKE IT?
Ah!
ぱっ
CUTS AREN'T THE ONLY THING HE CAN MOVE!
Asato!
Asato!
がしゃん
Huff...
GIMME BACK MY BRUISE.

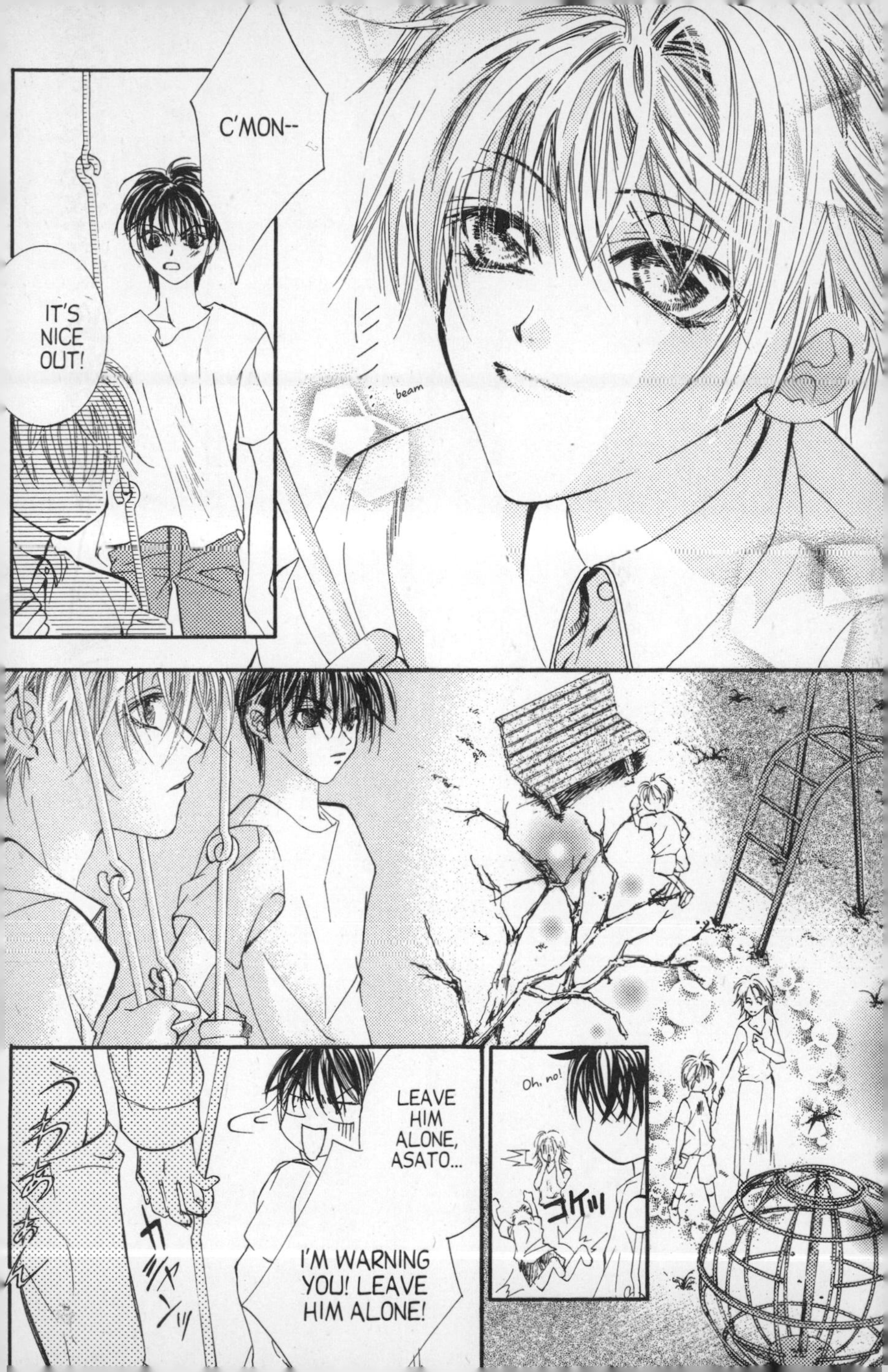
C'MON--
beam
IT'S NICE OUT!
Oh, no!
コケッ
LEAVE HIM ALONE, ASATO...
I'M WARNING YOU! LEAVE HIM ALONE!
カシャンッ

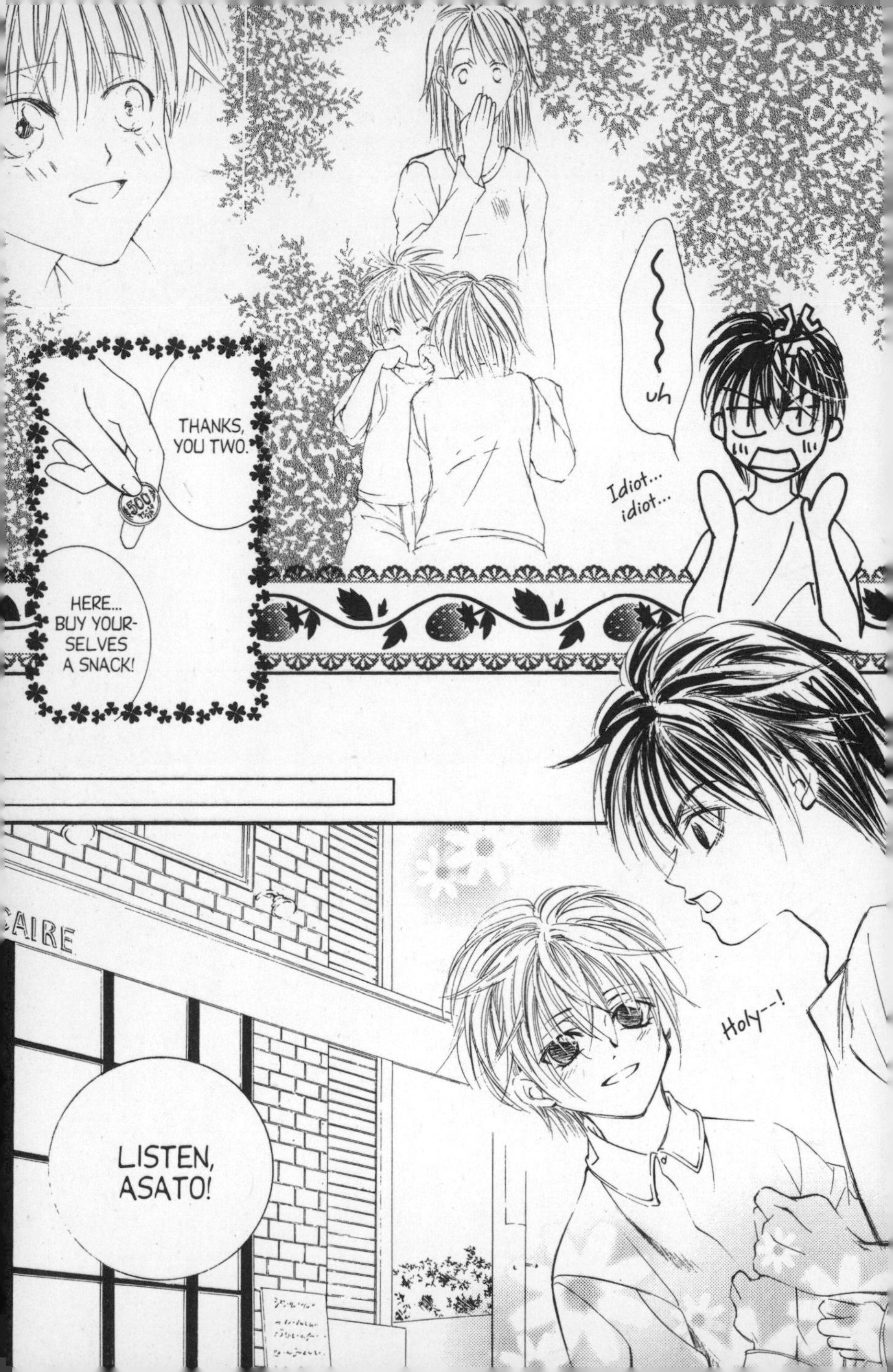

uh
Idiot... idiot...
THANKS, YOU TWO.
HERE... BUY YOUR-SELVES A SNACK!
Holy--!
CAIRE
LISTEN, ASATO!

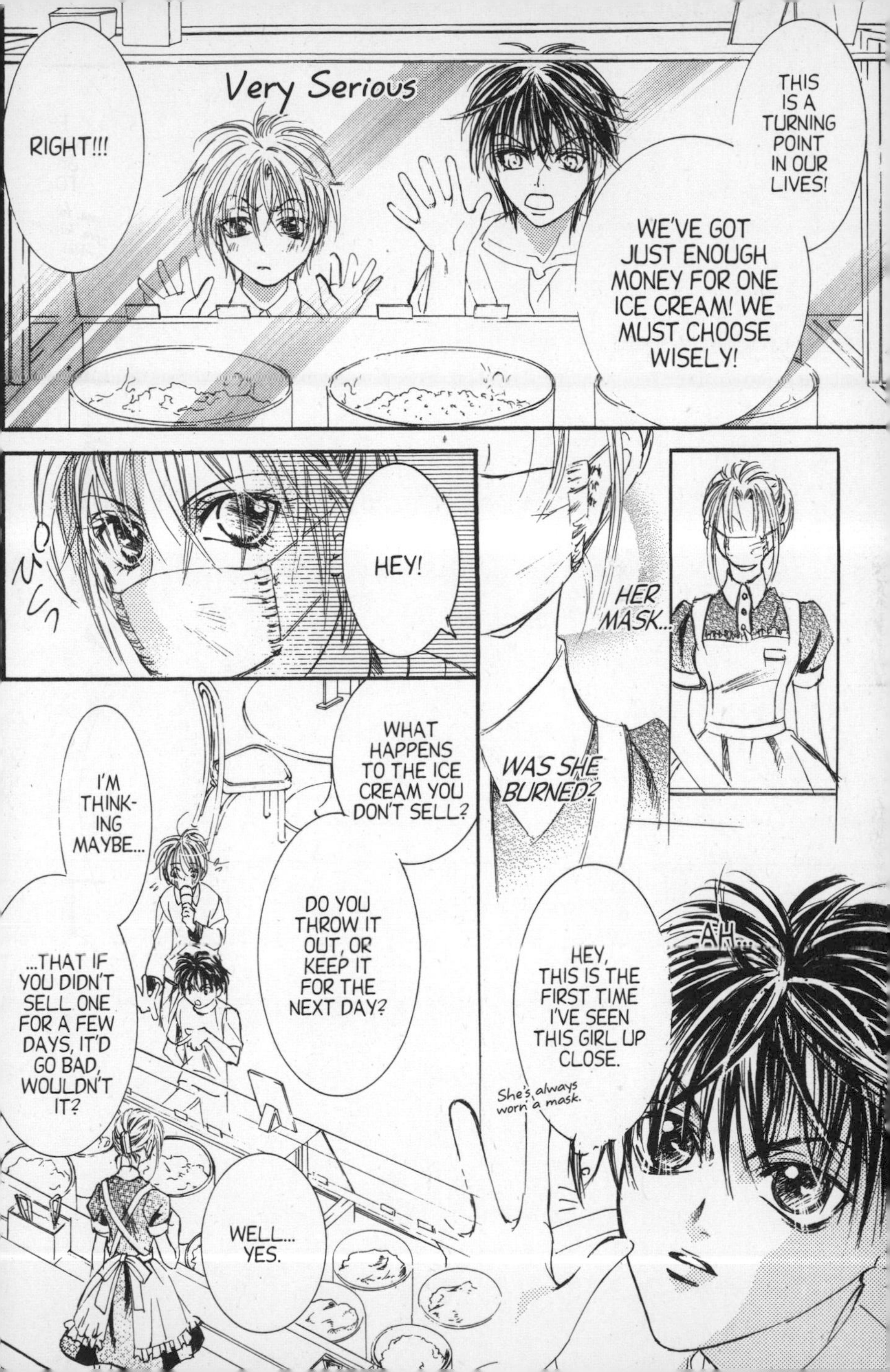
THIS IS A TURNING POINT IN OUR LIVES!
WE'VE GOT JUST ENOUGH MONEY FOR ONE ICE CREAM! WE MUST CHOOSE WISELY!
Very Serious
RIGHT!!!
HER MASK...
WAS SHE BURNED?
HEY!
AH...
HEY, THIS IS THE FIRST TIME I'VE SEEN THIS GIRL UP CLOSE.
She's always worn a mask.
WHAT HAPPENS TO THE ICE CREAM YOU DON'T SELL?
DO YOU THROW IT OUT, OR KEEP IT FOR THE NEXT DAY?
I'M THINKING MAYBE...
...THAT IF YOU DIDN'T SELL ONE FOR A FEW DAYS, IT'D GO BAD, WOULDN'T IT?
WELL... YES.

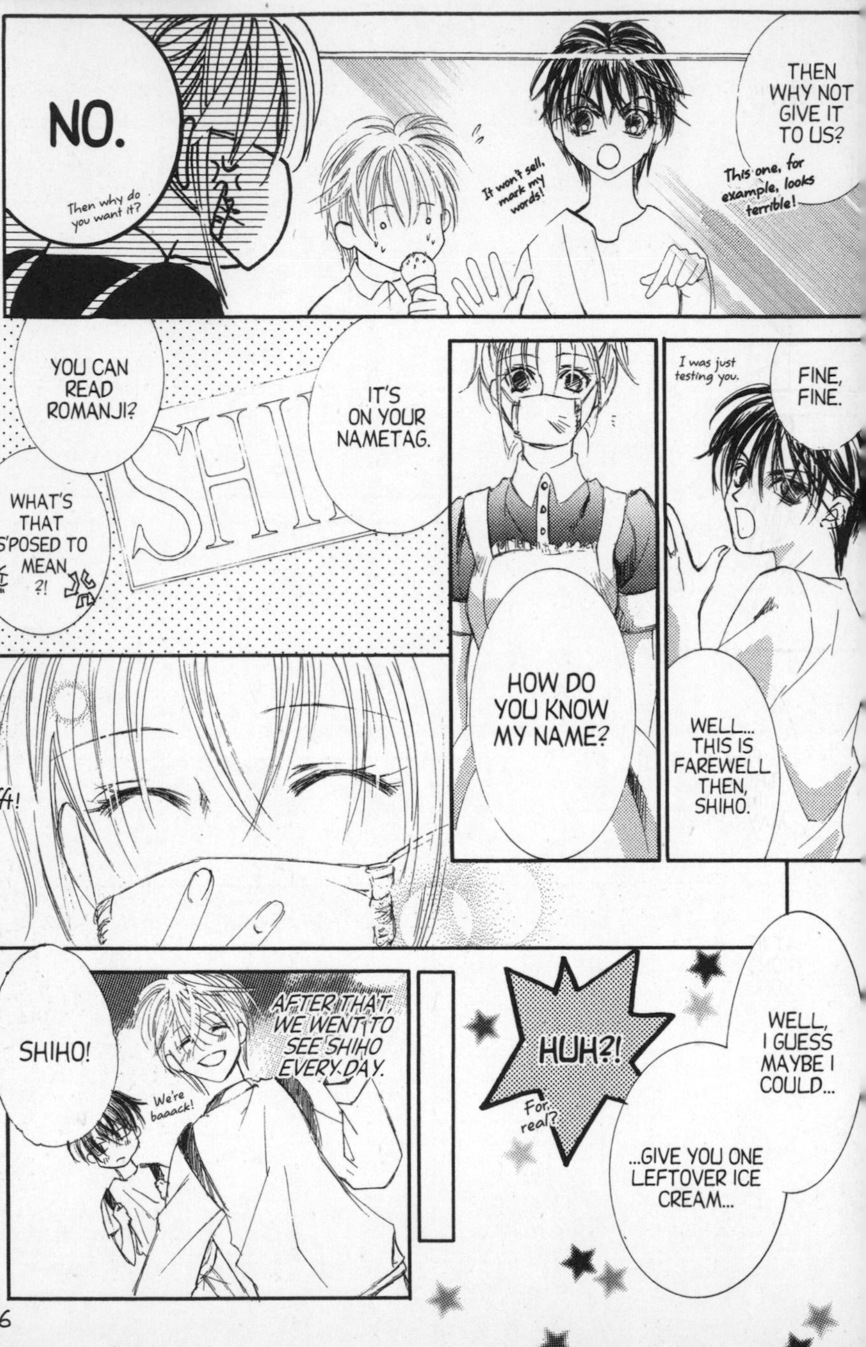
THEN WHY NOT GIVE IT TO US?
This one, for example, looks terrible!
It won't sell, mark my words!
NO.
Then why do you want it?
FINE, FINE.
I was just testing you.
WELL... THIS IS FAREWELL THEN, SHIHO.
HOW DO YOU KNOW MY NAME?
IT'S ON YOUR NAMETAG.
YOU CAN READ ROMANJI?
WHAT'S THAT S'POSED TO MEAN ?!
Pffft!
WELL, I GUESS MAYBE I COULD...
...GIVE YOU ONE LEFTOVER ICE CREAM...
HUH?!
For real?
AFTER THAT WE WENT TO SEE SHIHO EVERY DAY.
SHIHO!
We're baaack!

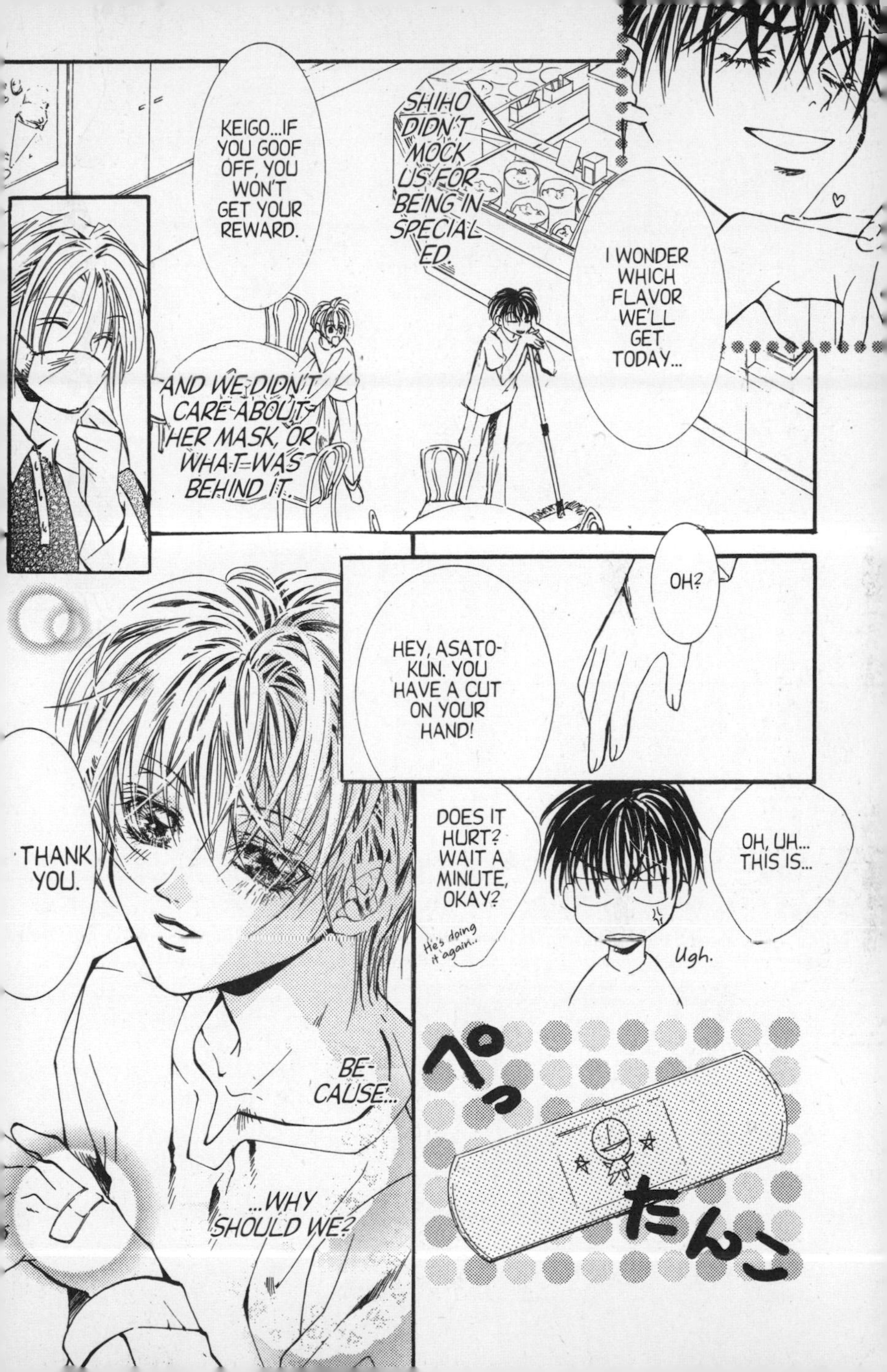
I WONDER WHICH FLAVOR WE'LL GET TODAY...
SHIHO DIDN'T MOCK US FOR BEING IN SPECIAL ED.
KEIGO...IF YOU GOOF OFF, YOU WON'T GET YOUR REWARD.
AND WE DIDN'T CARE ABOUT HER MASK, OR WHAT WAS BEHIND IT.
OH?
HEY, ASATO-KUN. YOU HAVE A CUT ON YOUR HAND!
OH, UH... THIS IS...
Ugh.
DOES IT HURT? WAIT A MINUTE, OKAY?
He's doing it again...
ぺっ
たんこ
THANK YOU.
BE-CAUSE...
...WHY SHOULD WE?

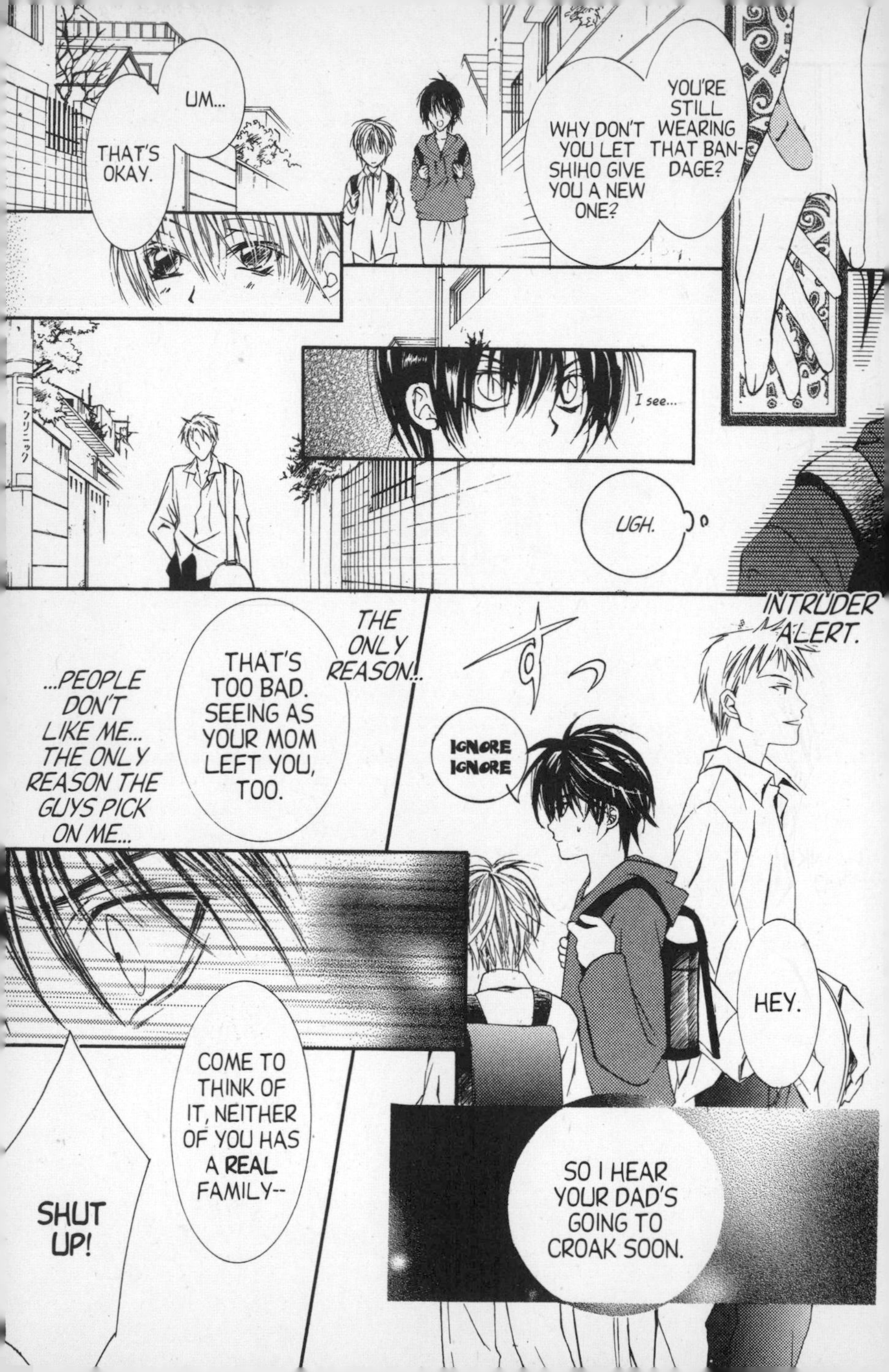
YOU'RE STILL WEARING THAT BAN-DAGE? WHY DON'T YOU LET SHIHO GIVE YOU A NEW ONE?
UM...
THAT'S OKAY.
I see...
UGH.
INTRUDER ALERT.
IGNORE IGNORE
HEY.
SO I HEAR YOUR DAD'S GOING TO CROAK SOON.
THE ONLY REASON...
THAT'S TOO BAD. SEEING AS YOUR MOM LEFT YOU, TOO.
...PEOPLE DON'T LIKE ME... THE ONLY REASON THE GUYS PICK ON ME...
COME TO THINK OF IT, NEITHER OF YOU HAS A REAL FAMILY--
SHUT UP!

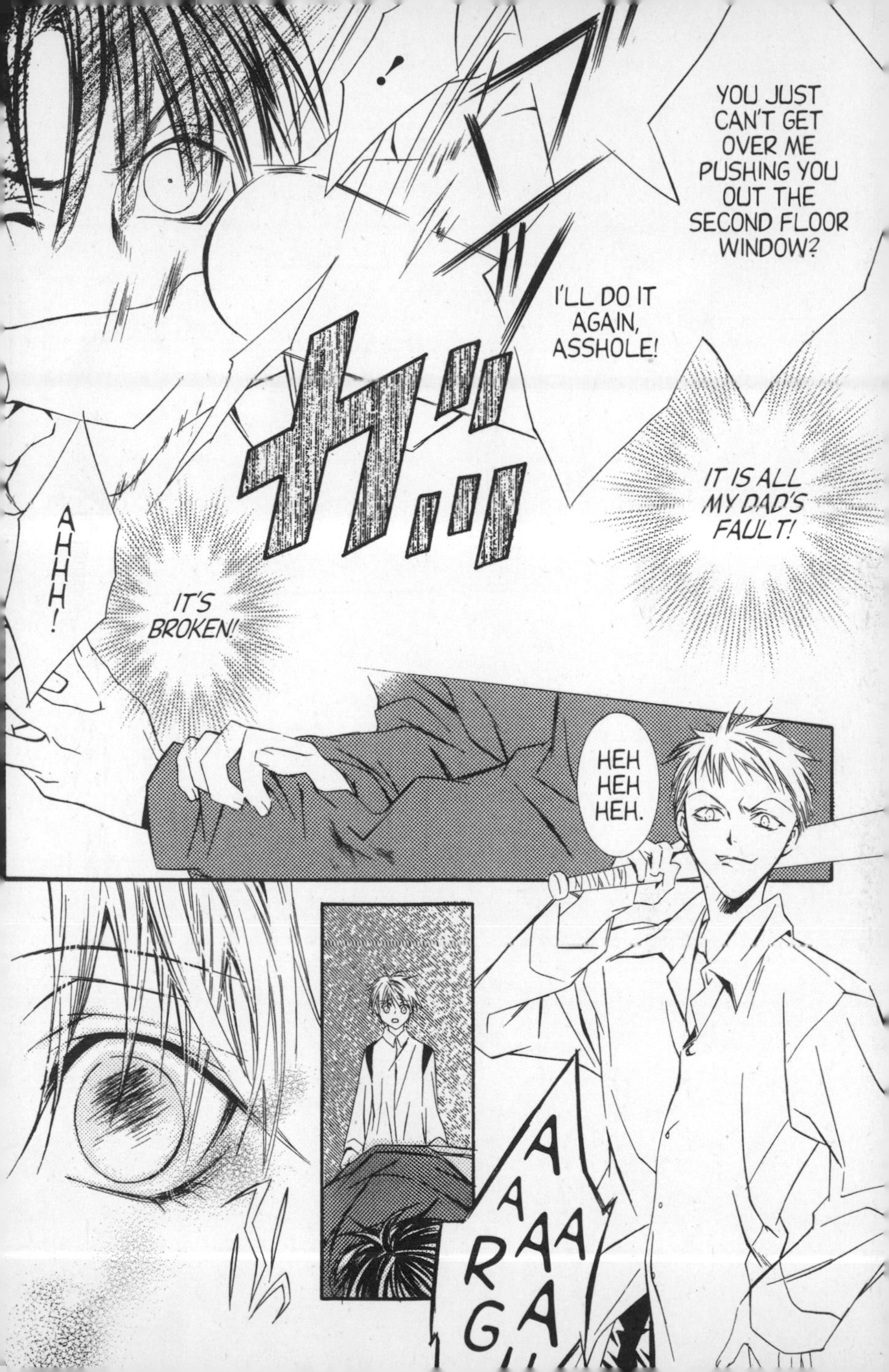
YOU JUST CAN'T GET OVER ME PUSHING YOU OUT THE SECOND FLOOR WINDOW?
I'LL DO IT AGAIN, ASSHOLE!
ガッ!!
IT IS ALL MY DAD'S FAULT!
IT'S BROKEN!
AHHH!
HEH HEH HEH.
AAAAAARG

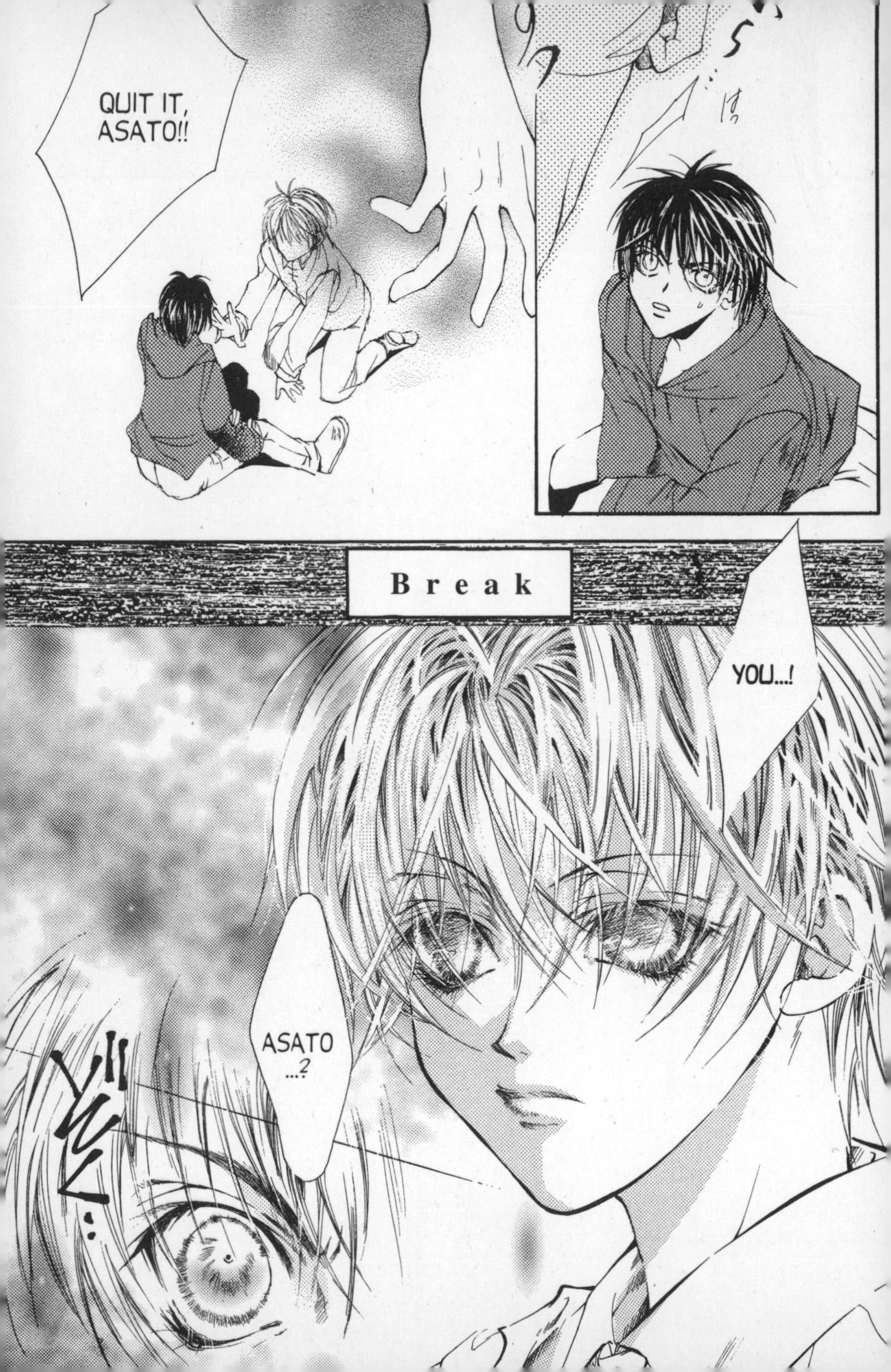
QUIT IT, ASATO!!
Break
YOU...!
ASATO ...?

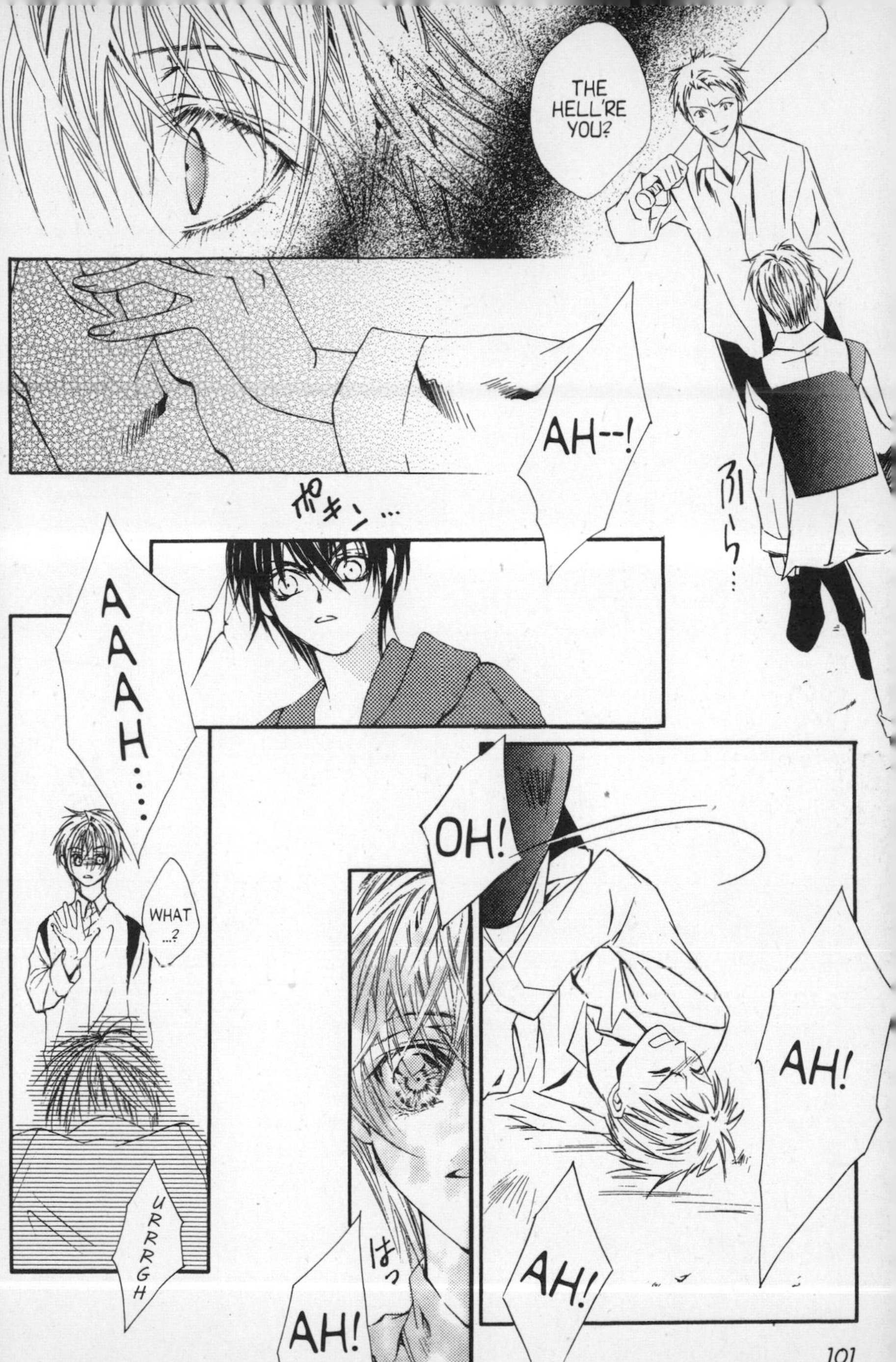
THE HELL'RE YOU?
ぶら…
AH--!
ポキン…
AAAH....
WHAT ...?
URRRGH
OH!
AH!
AH!
はっ
AH!

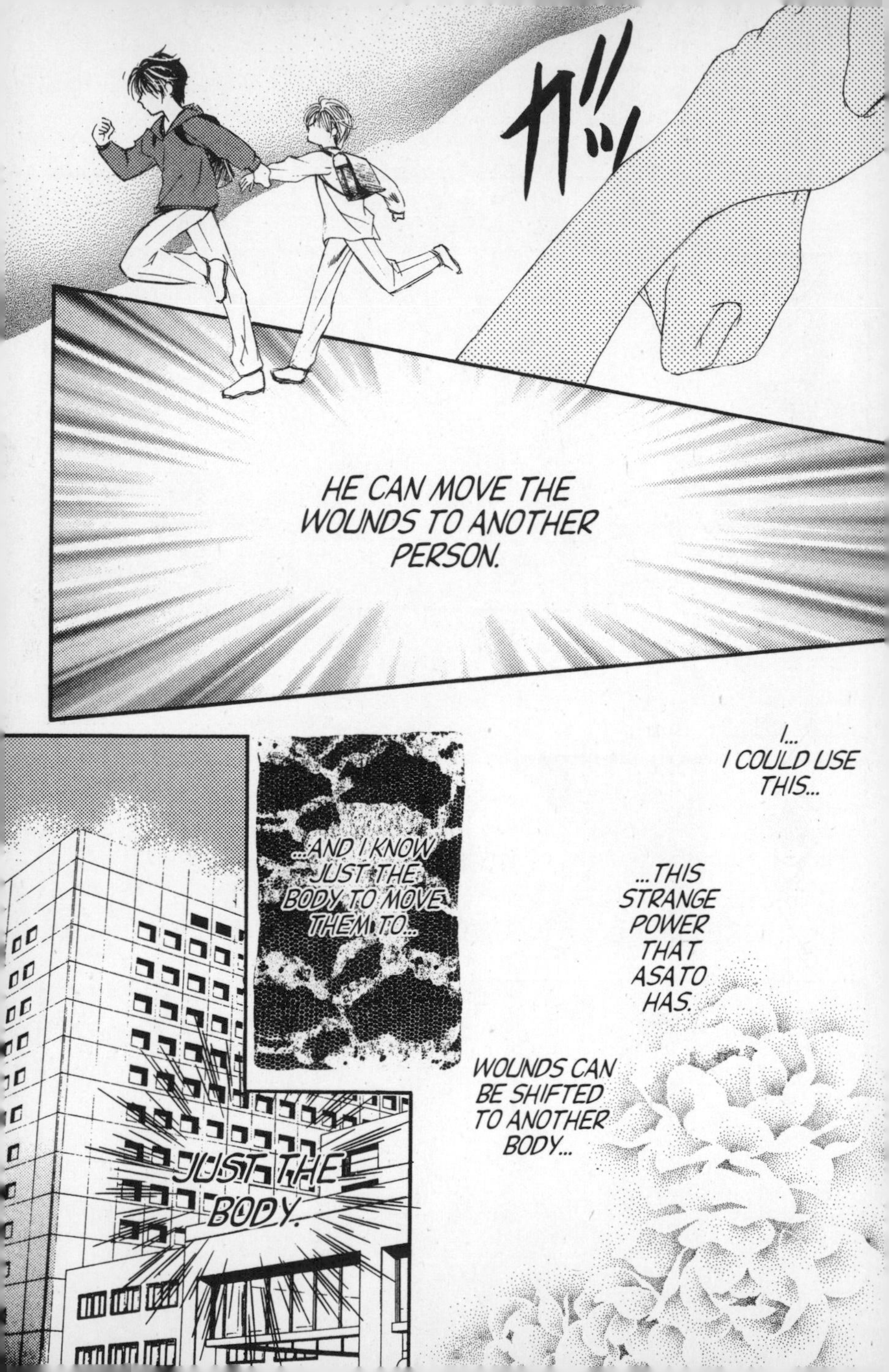
ガッ
HE CAN MOVE THE WOUNDS TO ANOTHER PERSON.
I... I COULD USE THIS...
...THIS STRANGE POWER THAT ASATO HAS.
WOUNDS CAN BE SHIFTED TO ANOTHER BODY...
...AND I KNOW JUST THE BODY TO MOVE THEM TO...
JUST THE BODY.

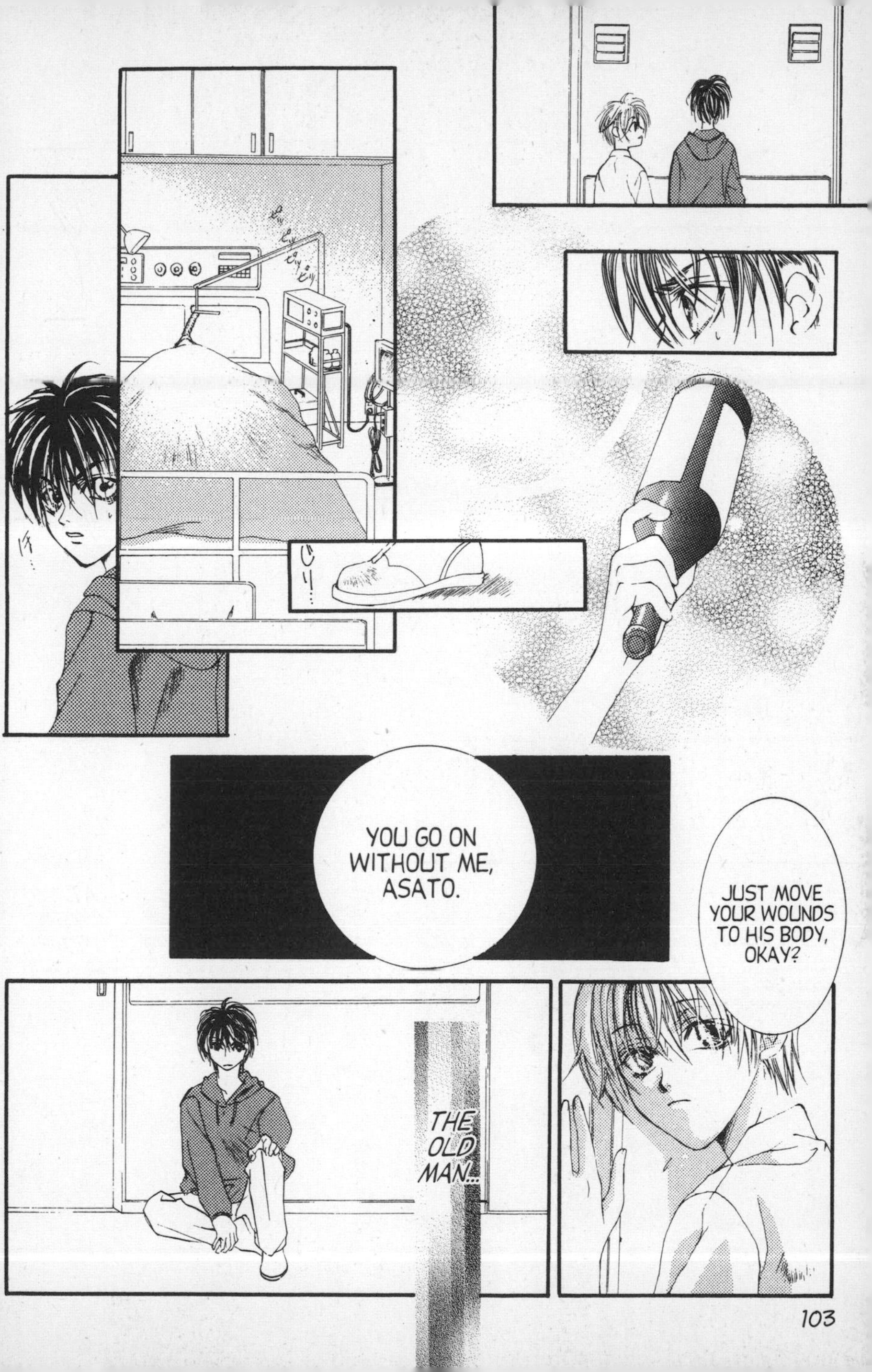
YOU GO ON WITHOUT ME, ASATO.
JUST MOVE YOUR WOUNDS TO HIS BODY, OKAY?
THE OLD MAN...

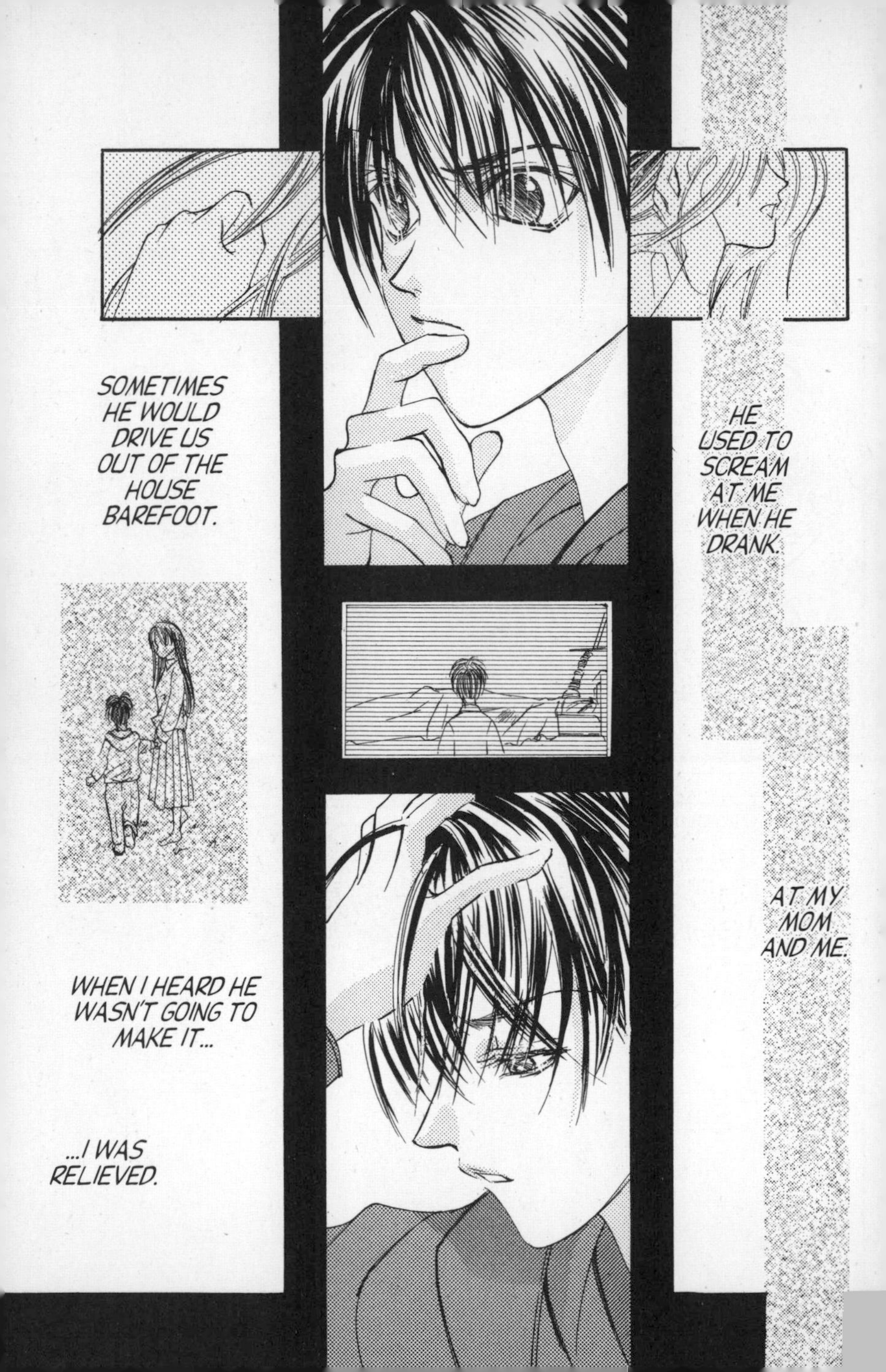
HE USED TO SCREAM AT ME WHEN HE DRANK.
AT MY MOM AND ME.
SOMETIMES HE WOULD DRIVE US OUT OF THE HOUSE BAREFOOT.
WHEN I HEARD HE WASN'T GOING TO MAKE IT...
...I WAS RELIEVED.

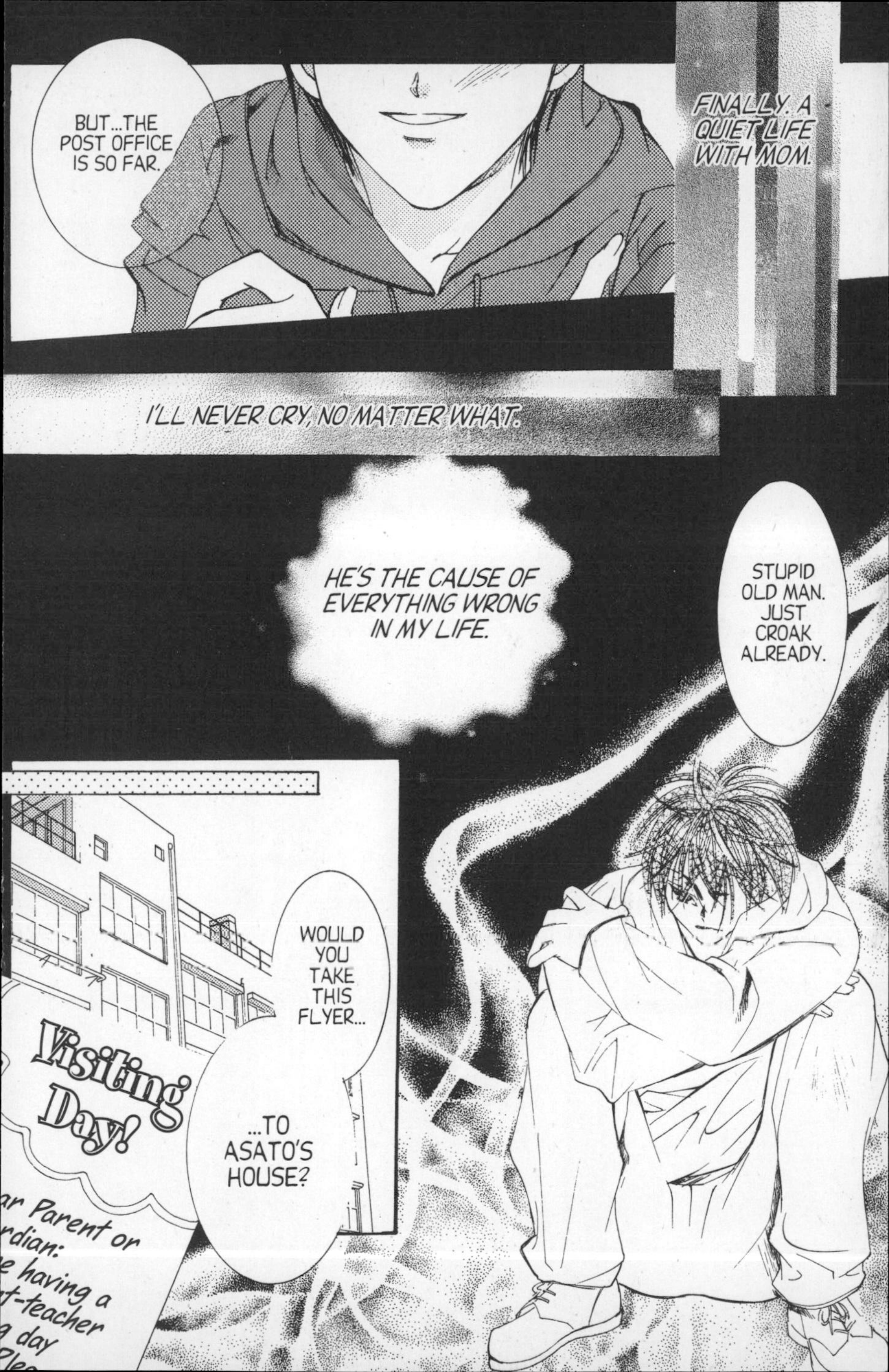
FINALLY. A QUIET LIFE WITH MOM.
BUT...THE POST OFFICE IS SO FAR.
I'LL NEVER CRY, NO MATTER WHAT.
STUPID OLD MAN. JUST CROAK ALREADY.
HE'S THE CAUSE OF EVERYTHING WRONG IN MY LIFE.
WOULD YOU TAKE THIS FLYER...
...TO ASATO'S HOUSE?
Visiting Day!
ar Parent or
rdian:
e having a
t-teacher
g day

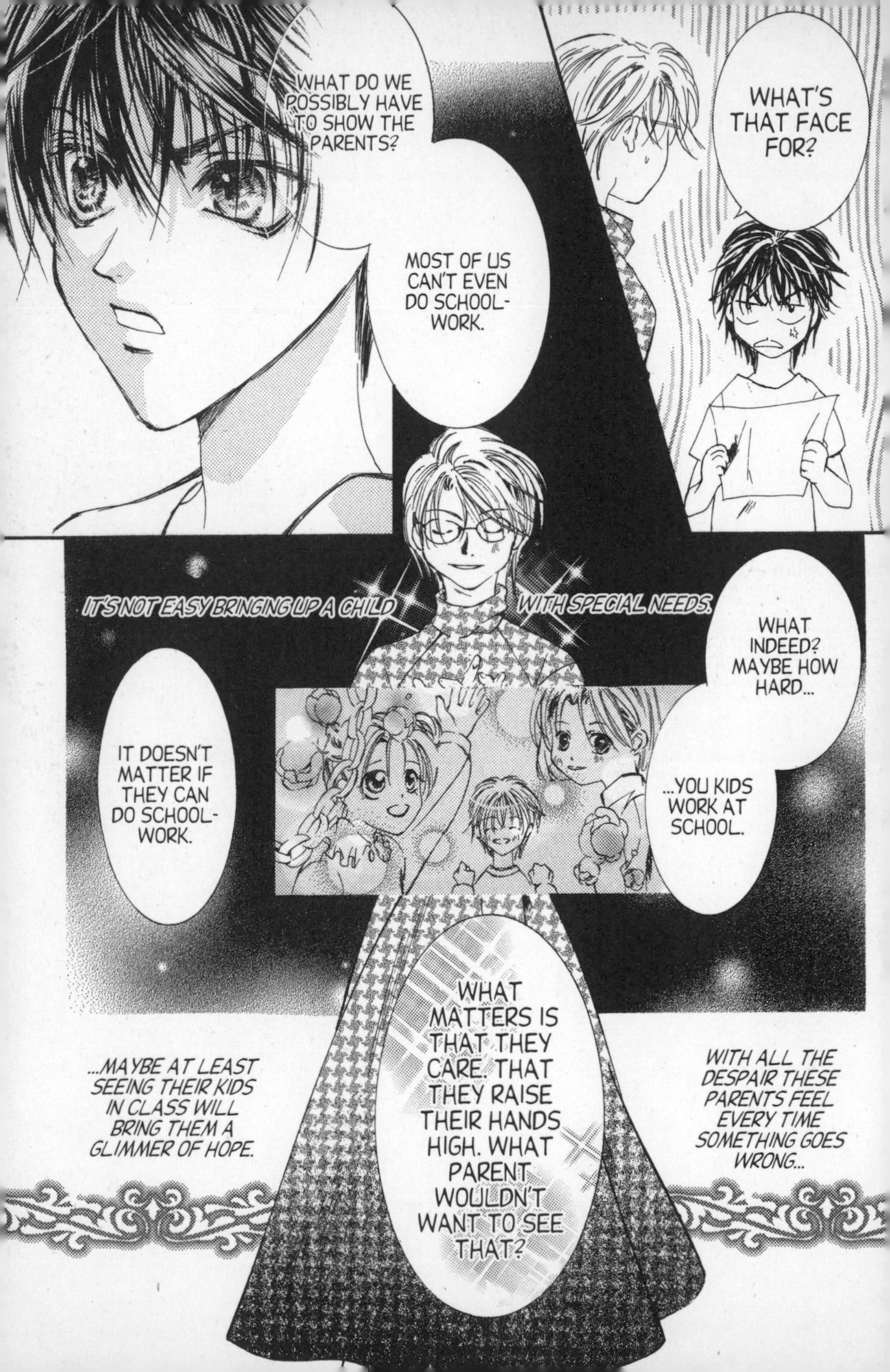
WHAT'S THAT FACE FOR?
WHAT DO WE POSSIBLY HAVE TO SHOW THE PARENTS?
MOST OF US CAN'T EVEN DO SCHOOL-WORK.
IT'S NOT EASY BRINGING UP A CHILD WITH SPECIAL NEEDS.
WHAT INDEED? MAYBE HOW HARD...
...YOU KIDS WORK AT SCHOOL.
IT DOESN'T MATTER IF THEY CAN DO SCHOOL-WORK.
WHAT MATTERS IS THAT THEY CARE. THAT THEY RAISE THEIR HANDS HIGH. WHAT PARENT WOULDN'T WANT TO SEE THAT?
WITH ALL THE DESPAIR THESE PARENTS FEEL EVERY TIME SOMETHING GOES WRONG...
...MAYBE AT LEAST SEEING THEIR KIDS IN CLASS WILL BRING THEM A GLIMMER OF HOPE.

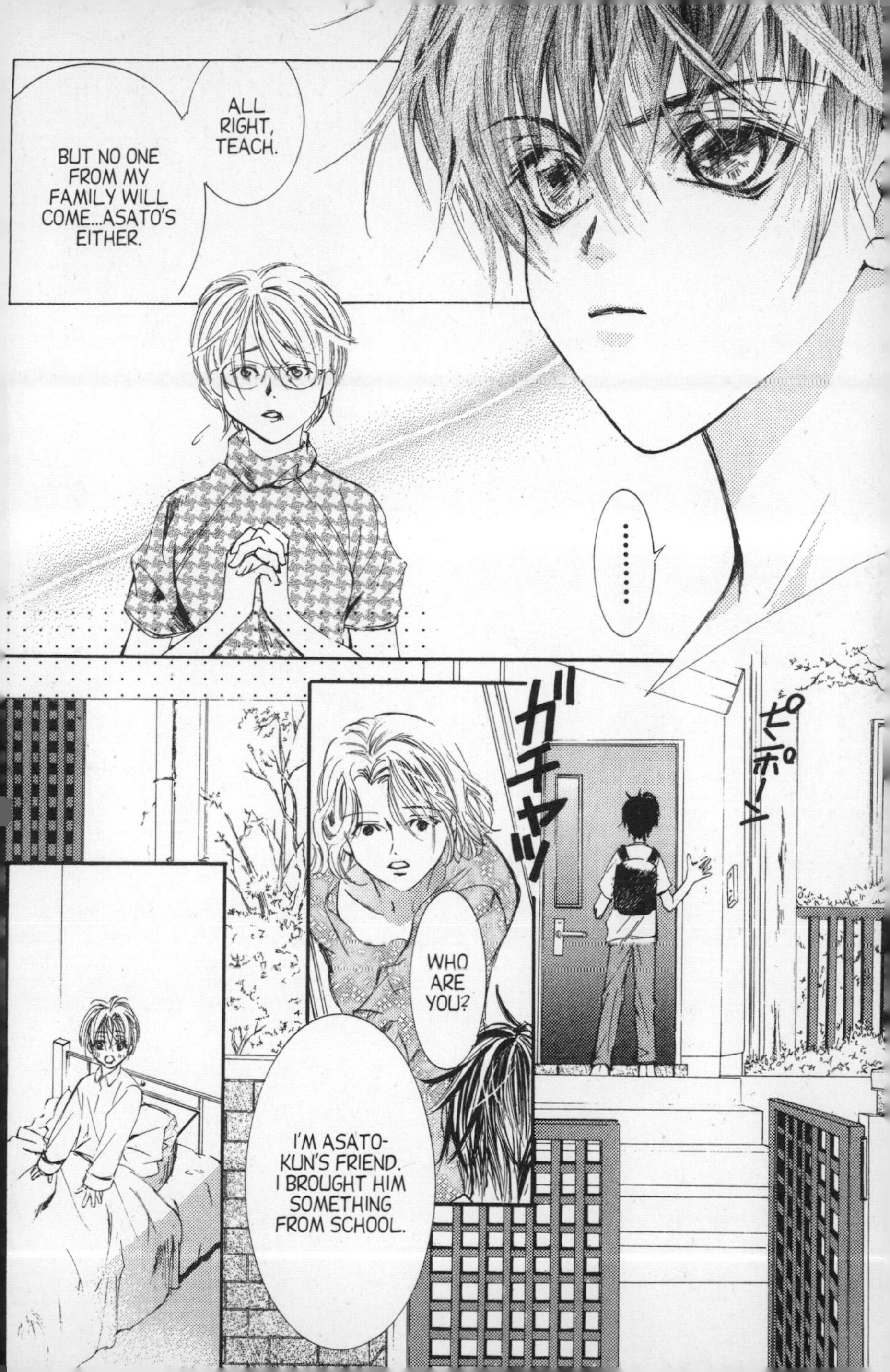

ALL RIGHT, TEACH.
BUT NO ONE FROM MY FAMILY WILL COME...ASATO'S EITHER.
......
ピポーン
ガチャッ
WHO ARE YOU?
I'M ASATO-KUN'S FRIEND. I BROUGHT HIM SOMETHING FROM SCHOOL.

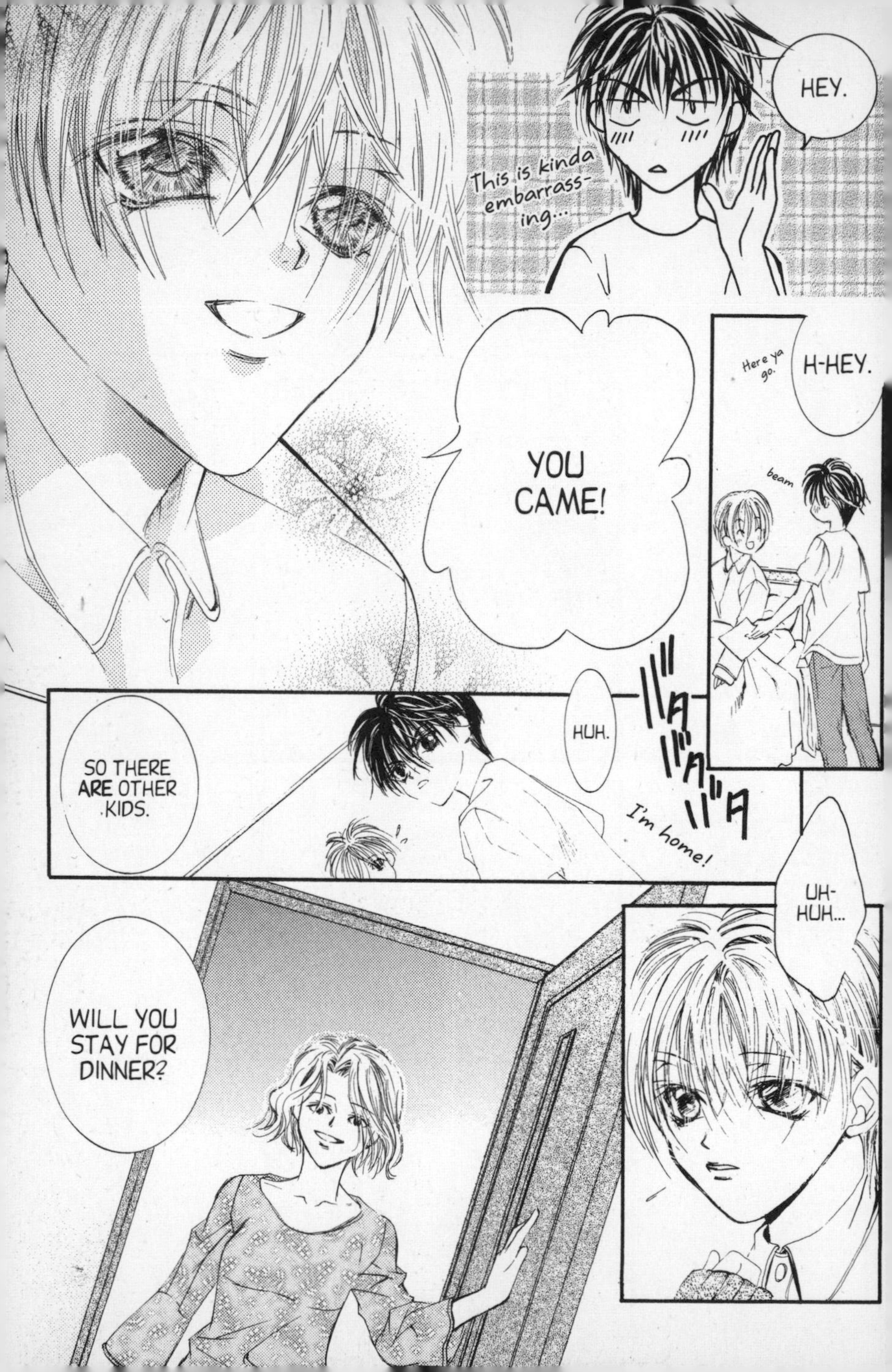
HEY.
This is kinda embarrass-ing...
Here ya go.
H-HEY.
beam
YOU CAME!
バタバタバタ
I'm home!
HUH.
SO THERE ARE OTHER KIDS.
UH-HUH...
WILL YOU STAY FOR DINNER?

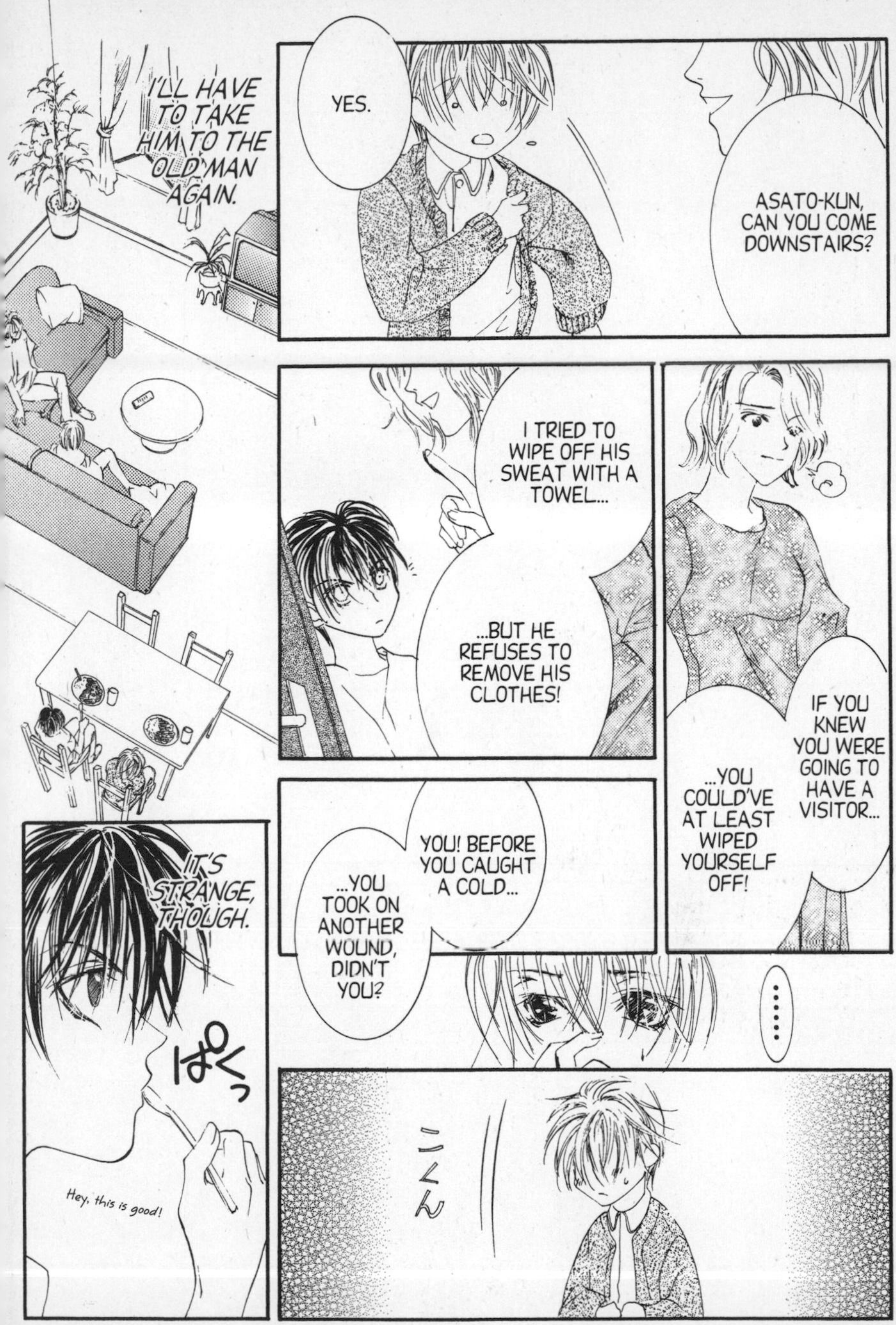
ASATO-KUN, CAN YOU COME DOWNSTAIRS?
YES.
IF YOU KNEW YOU WERE GOING TO HAVE A VISITOR...
...YOU COULD'VE AT LEAST WIPED YOURSELF OFF!
I TRIED TO WIPE OFF HIS SWEAT WITH A TOWEL...
...BUT HE REFUSES TO REMOVE HIS CLOTHES!
......
YOU! BEFORE YOU CAUGHT A COLD...
...YOU TOOK ON ANOTHER WOUND, DIDN'T YOU?
こくん
I'LL HAVE TO TAKE HIM TO THE OLD MAN AGAIN.
IT'S STRANGE, THOUGH.
ぱくっ
Hey, this is good!

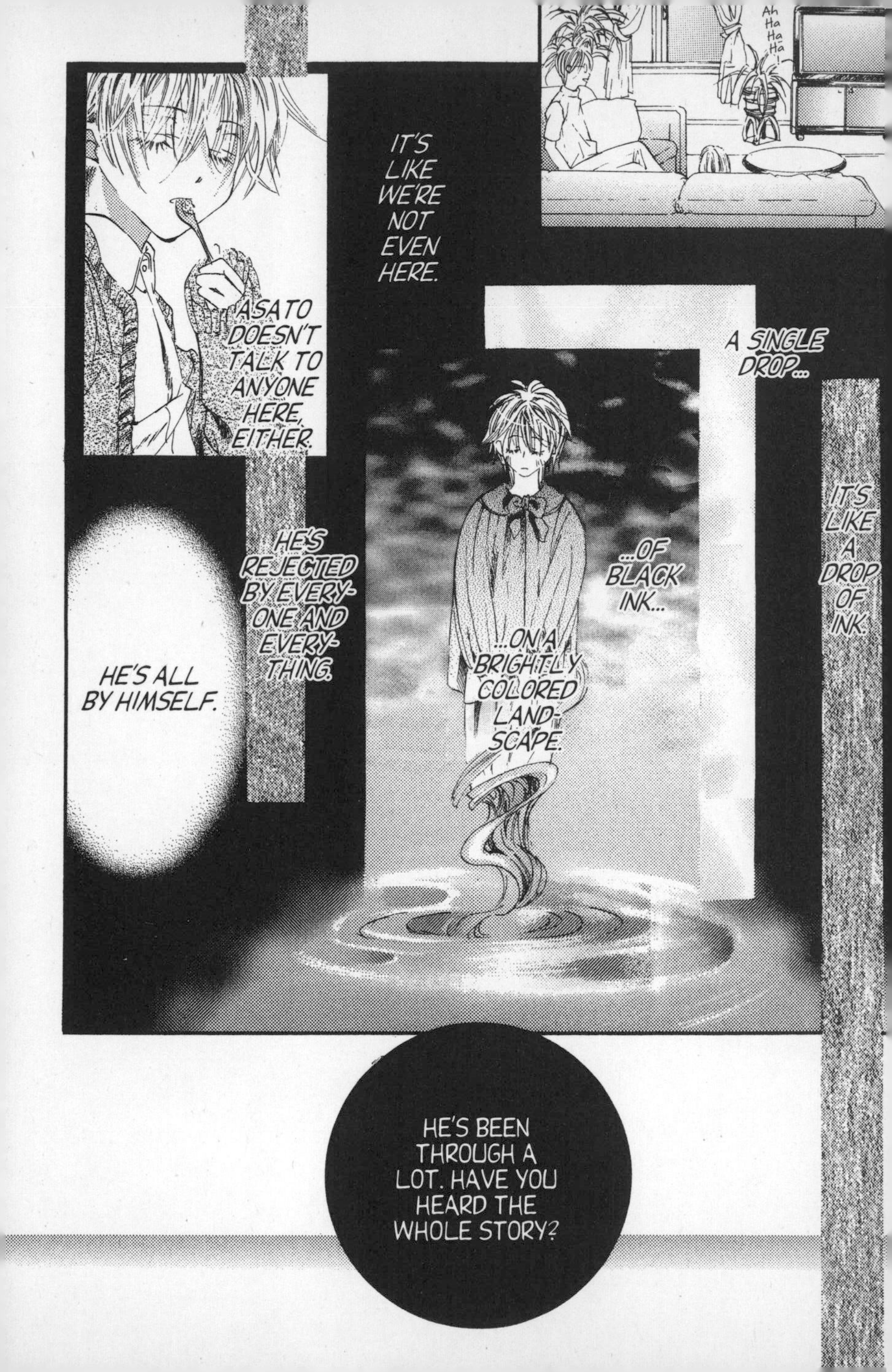
Ah Ha Ha Ha!
IT'S LIKE WE'RE NOT EVEN HERE.
ASATO DOESN'T TALK TO ANYONE HERE, EITHER.
IT'S LIKE A DROP OF INK.
A SINGLE DROP...
...OF BLACK INK...
...ON A BRIGHTLY COLORED LAND-SCAPE.
HE'S REJECTED BY EVERY-ONE AND EVERY-THING.
HE'S ALL BY HIMSELF.
HE'S BEEN THROUGH A LOT. HAVE YOU HEARD THE WHOLE STORY?

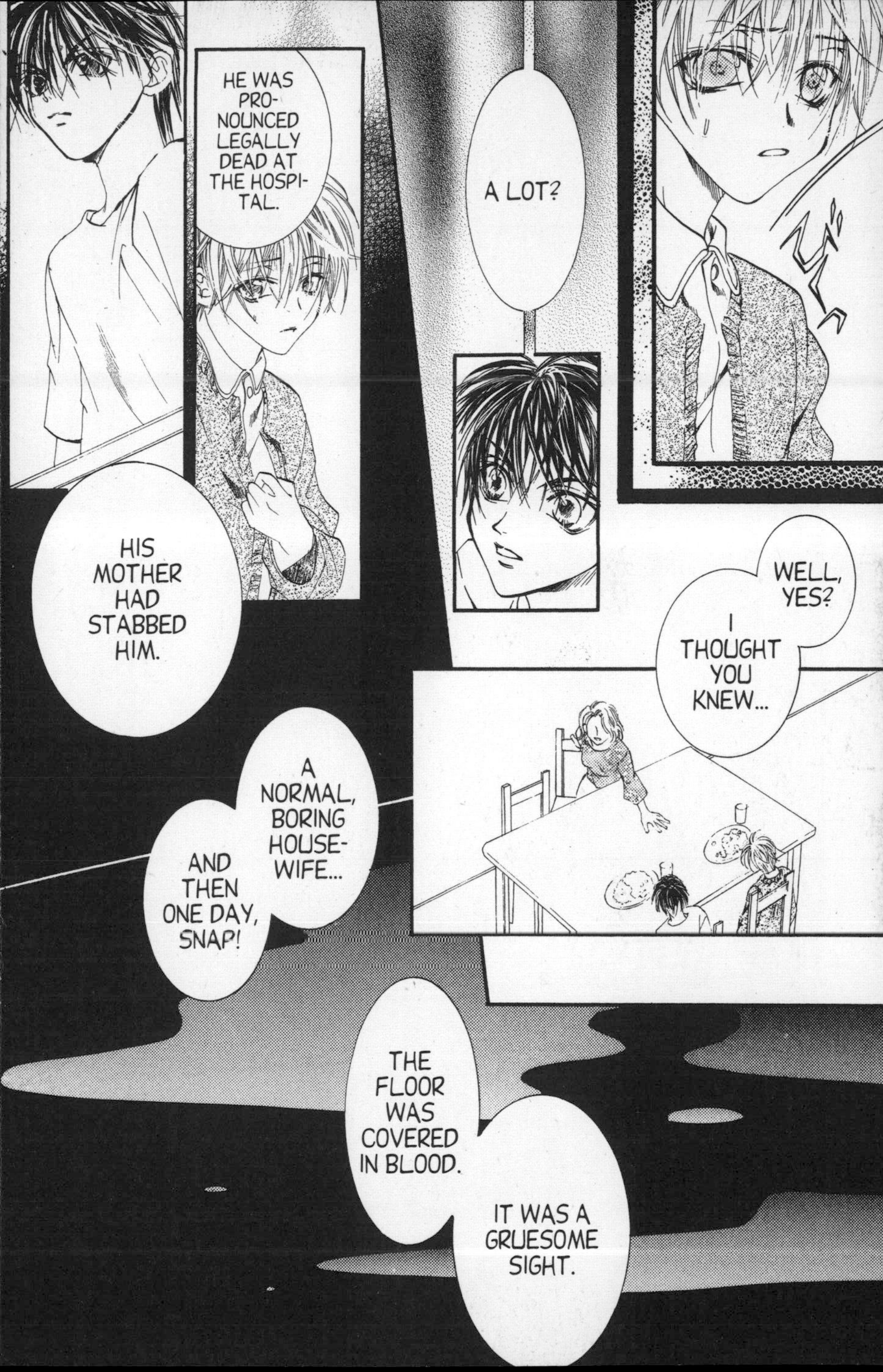
A LOT?
HE WAS PRO-NOUNCED LEGALLY DEAD AT THE HOSPI-TAL.
WELL, YES? I THOUGHT YOU KNEW...
HIS MOTHER HAD STABBED HIM.
A NORMAL, BORING HOUSE-WIFE...
AND THEN ONE DAY, SNAP!
THE FLOOR WAS COVERED IN BLOOD.
IT WAS A GRUESOME SIGHT.

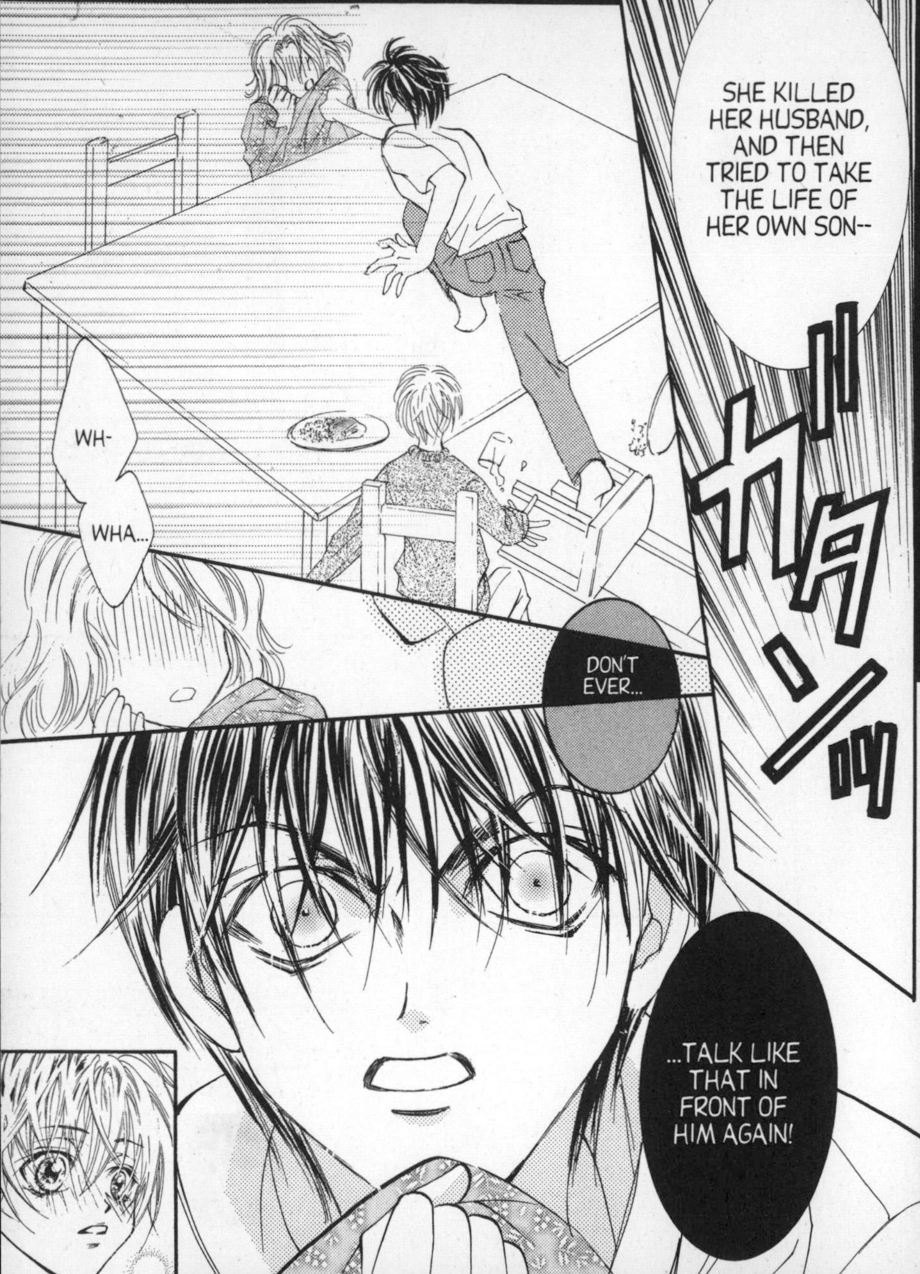
SHE KILLED HER HUSBAND, AND THEN TRIED TO TAKE THE LIFE OF HER OWN SON--
ガタンッ
WH-
WHA...
DON'T EVER...
...TALK LIKE THAT IN FRONT OF HIM AGAIN!

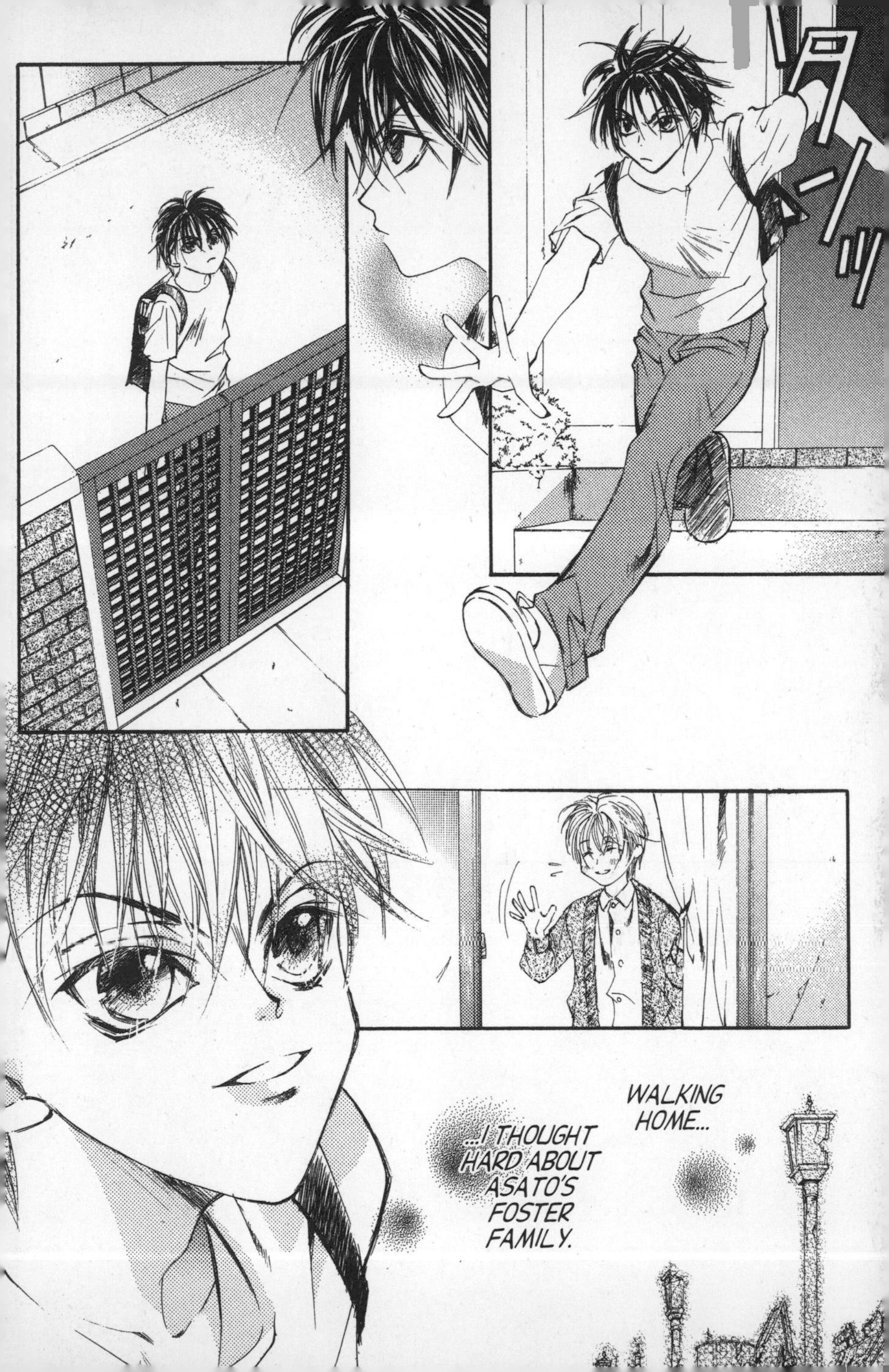
WALKING HOME...
...I THOUGHT HARD ABOUT ASATO'S FOSTER FAMILY.

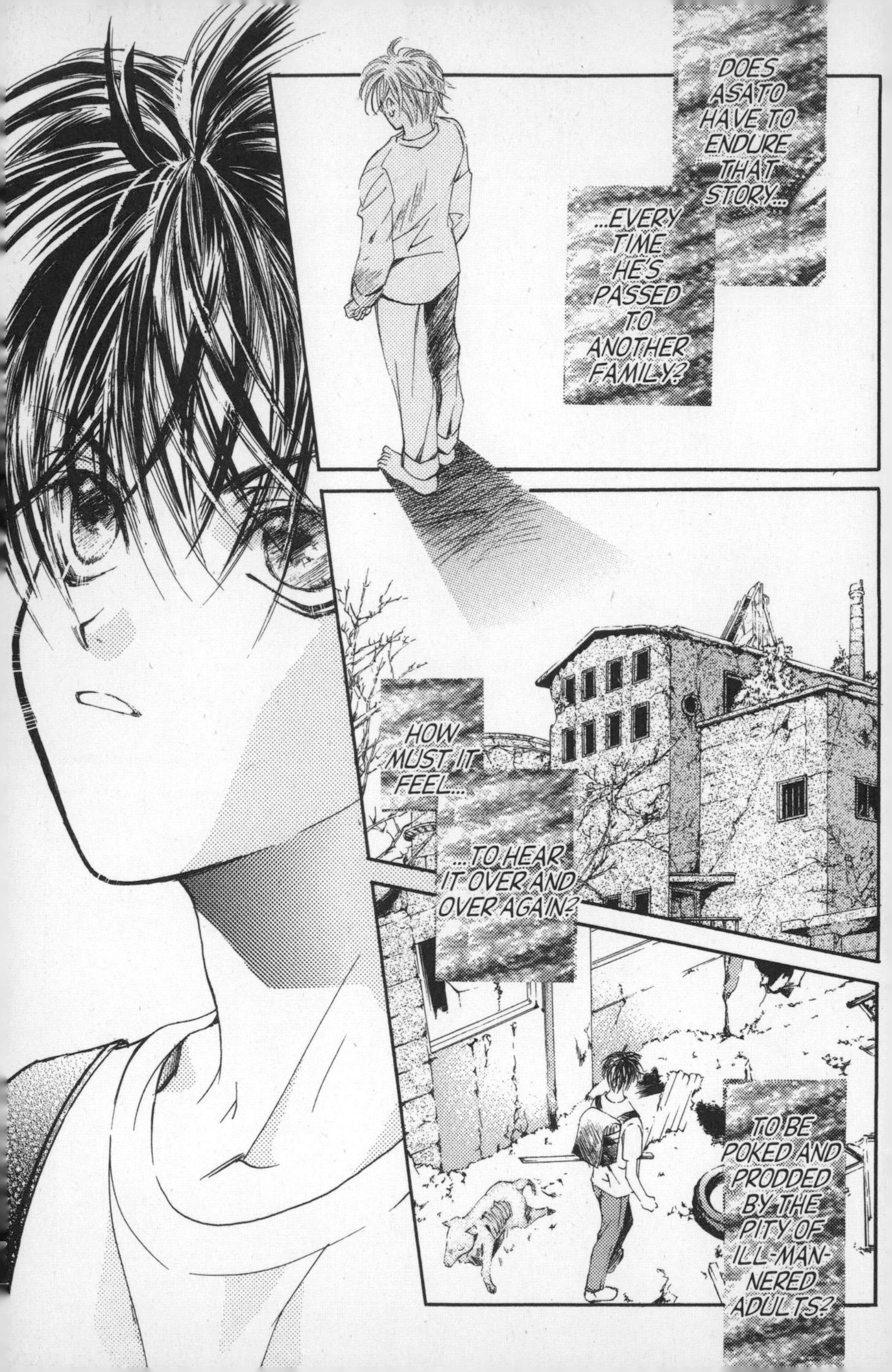
DOES ASATO HAVE TO ENDURE THAT STORY...
...EVERY TIME HE'S PASSED TO ANOTHER FAMILY?
HOW MUST IT FEEL...
...TO HEAR IT OVER AND OVER AGAIN?
TO BE POKED AND PRODDED BY THE PITY OF ILL-MANNERED ADULTS?

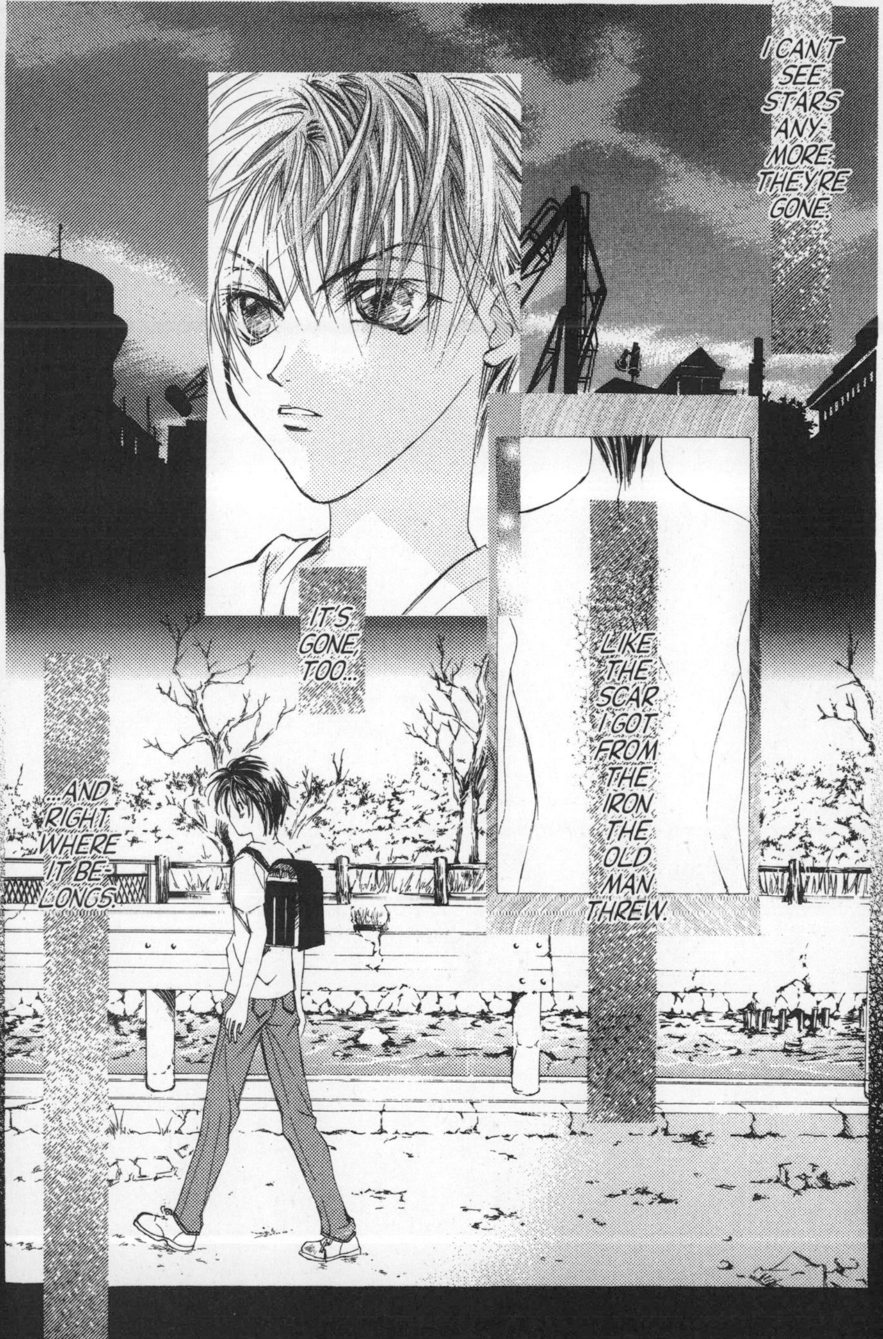
I CAN'T SEE STARS ANY-MORE. THEY'RE GONE.
IT'S GONE, TOO...
LIKE THE SCAR I GOT FROM THE IRON THE OLD MAN THREW.
...AND RIGHT WHERE IT BE-LONGS.

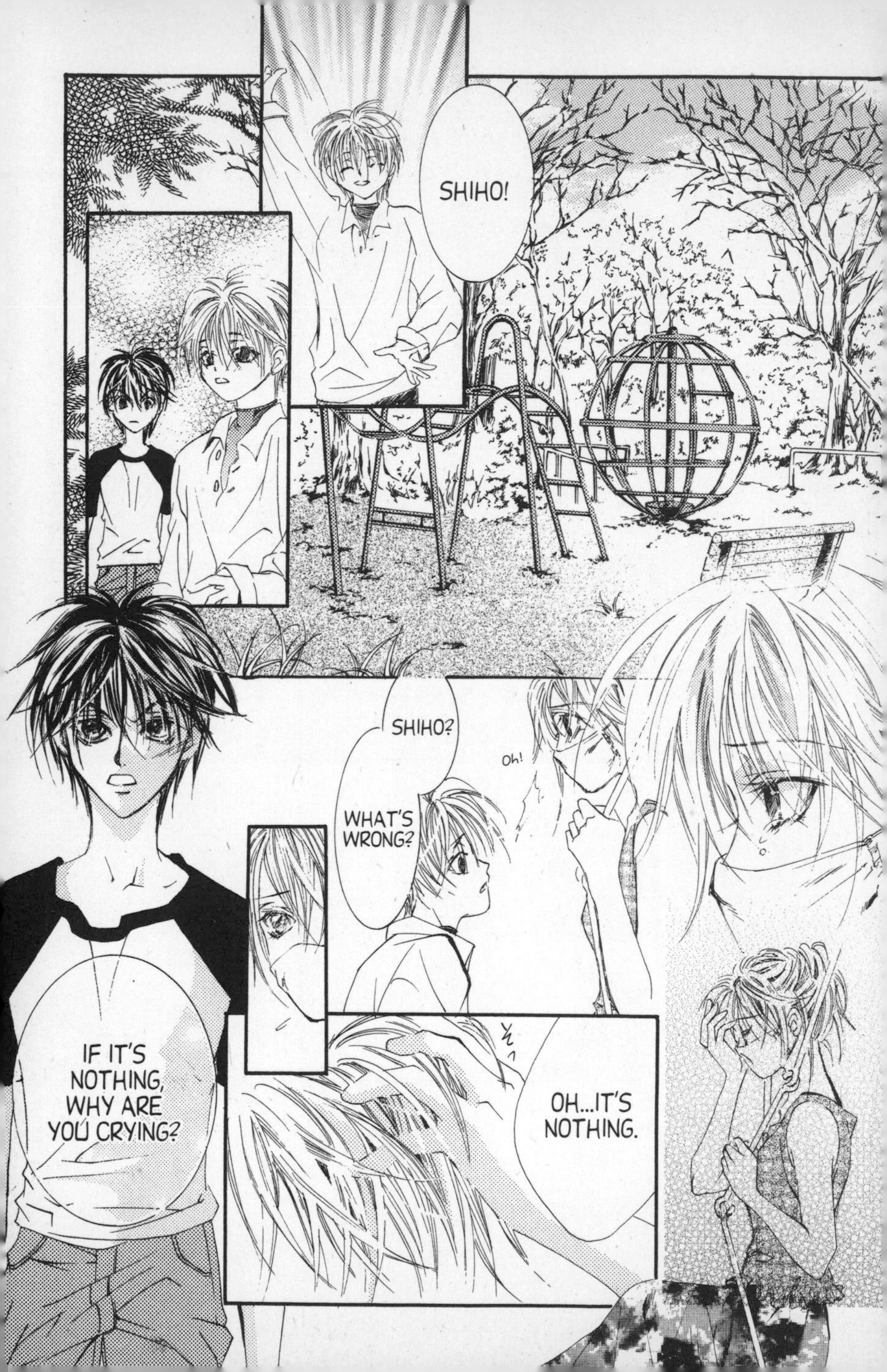
SHIHO!
SHIHO?
Oh!
WHAT'S WRONG?
OH...IT'S NOTHING.
IF IT'S NOTHING, WHY ARE YOU CRYING?

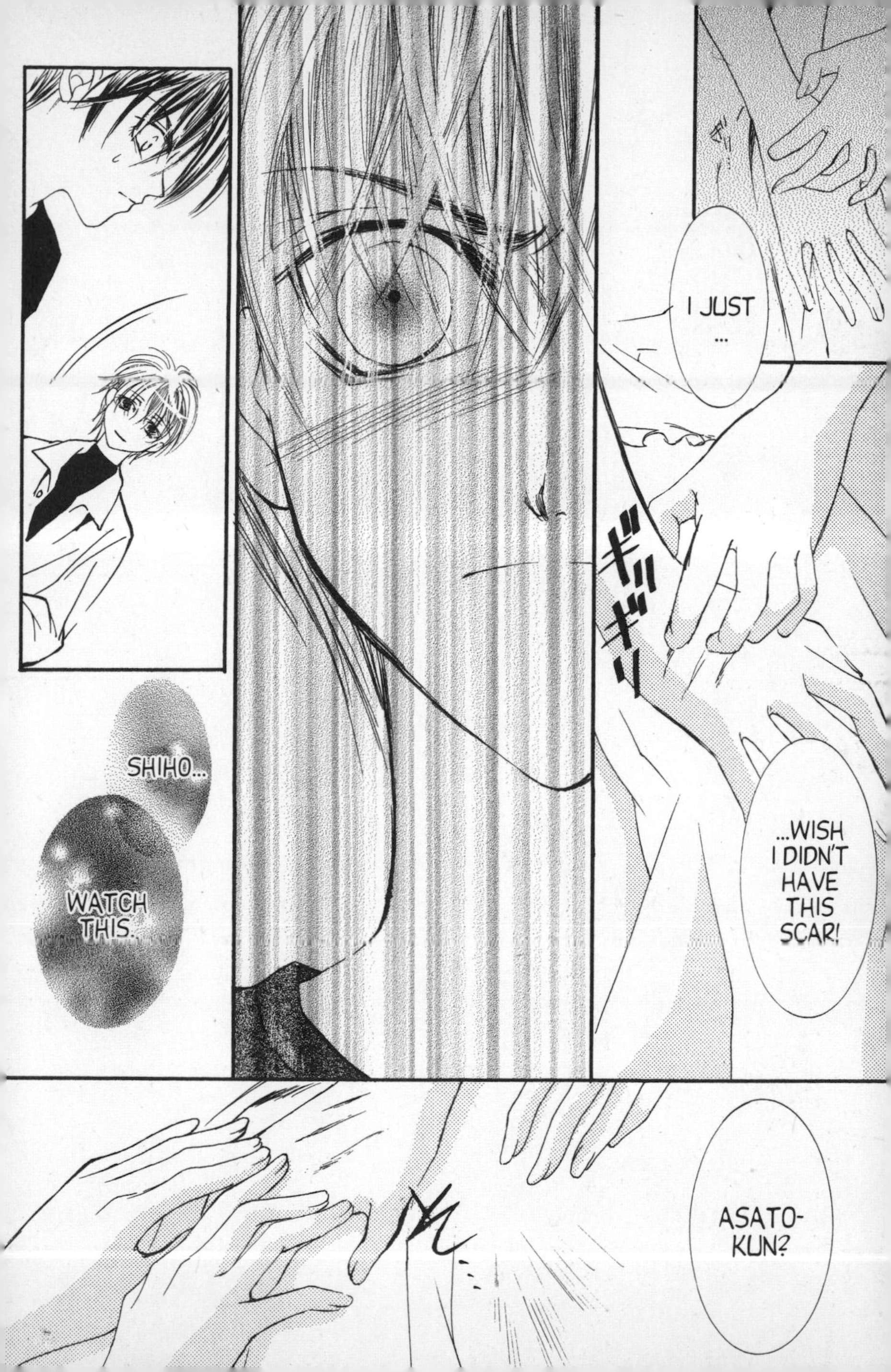
I JUST ...
...WISH I DIDN'T HAVE THIS SCAR!
SHIHO...
WATCH THIS.
ASATO-KUN?

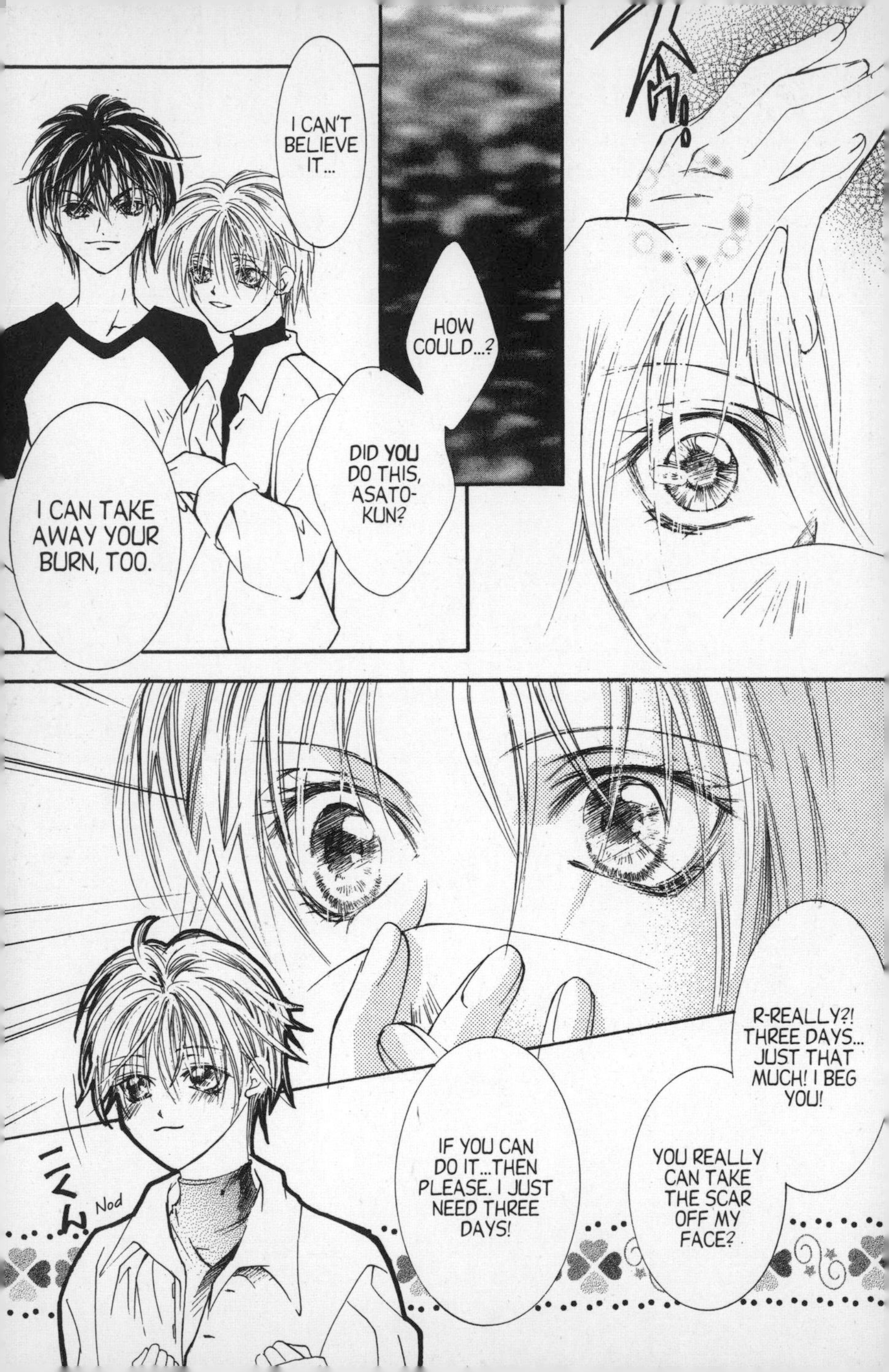
I CAN'T BELIEVE IT...
HOW COULD...?
DID YOU DO THIS, ASATO-KUN?
I CAN TAKE AWAY YOUR BURN, TOO.
R-REALLY?! THREE DAYS... JUST THAT MUCH! I BEG YOU!
YOU REALLY CAN TAKE THE SCAR OFF MY FACE?
IF YOU CAN DO IT...THEN PLEASE. I JUST NEED THREE DAYS!
Nod

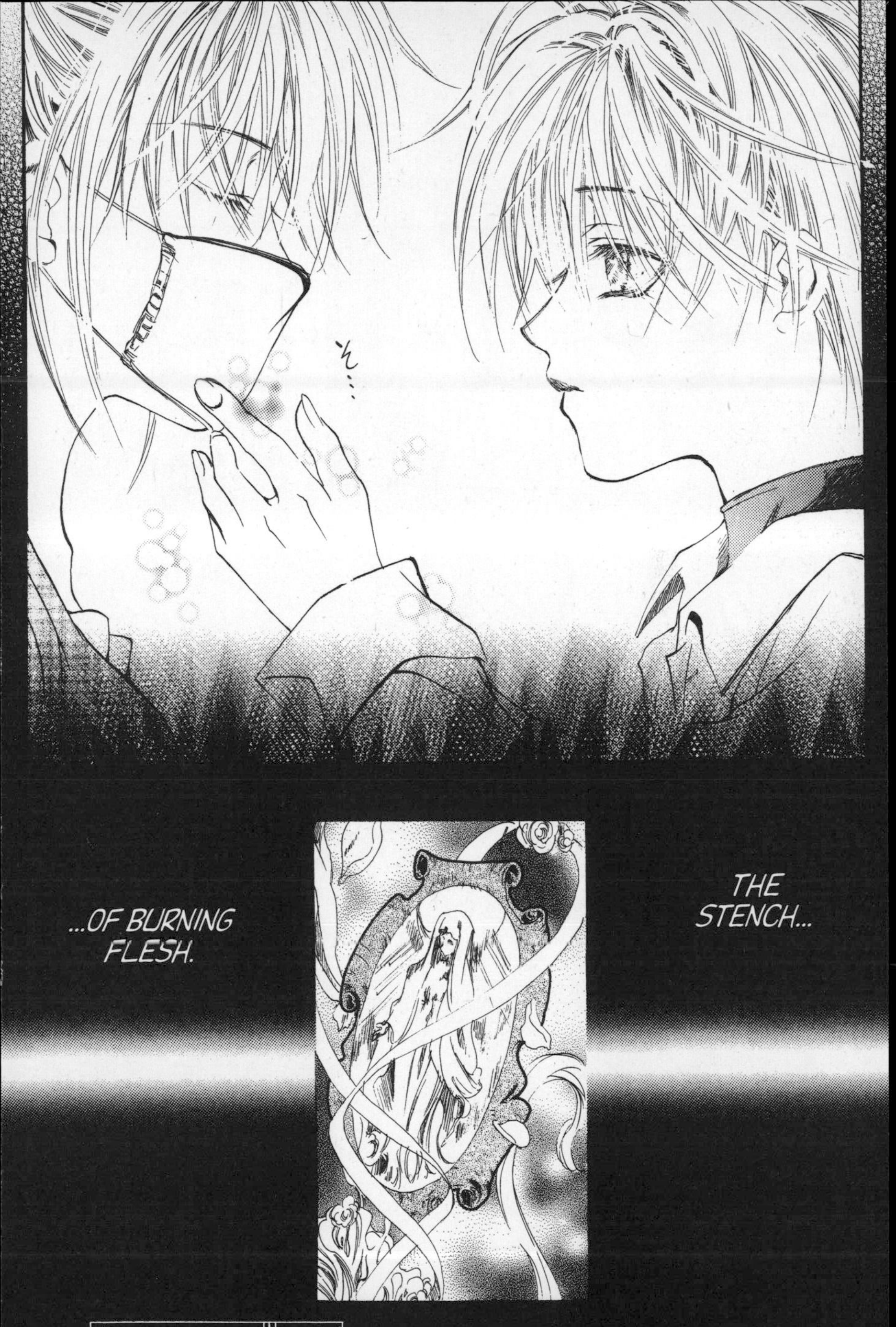
ん…
THE STENCH...
...OF BURNING FLESH.

傷 KIZ/KIDS 前編 END

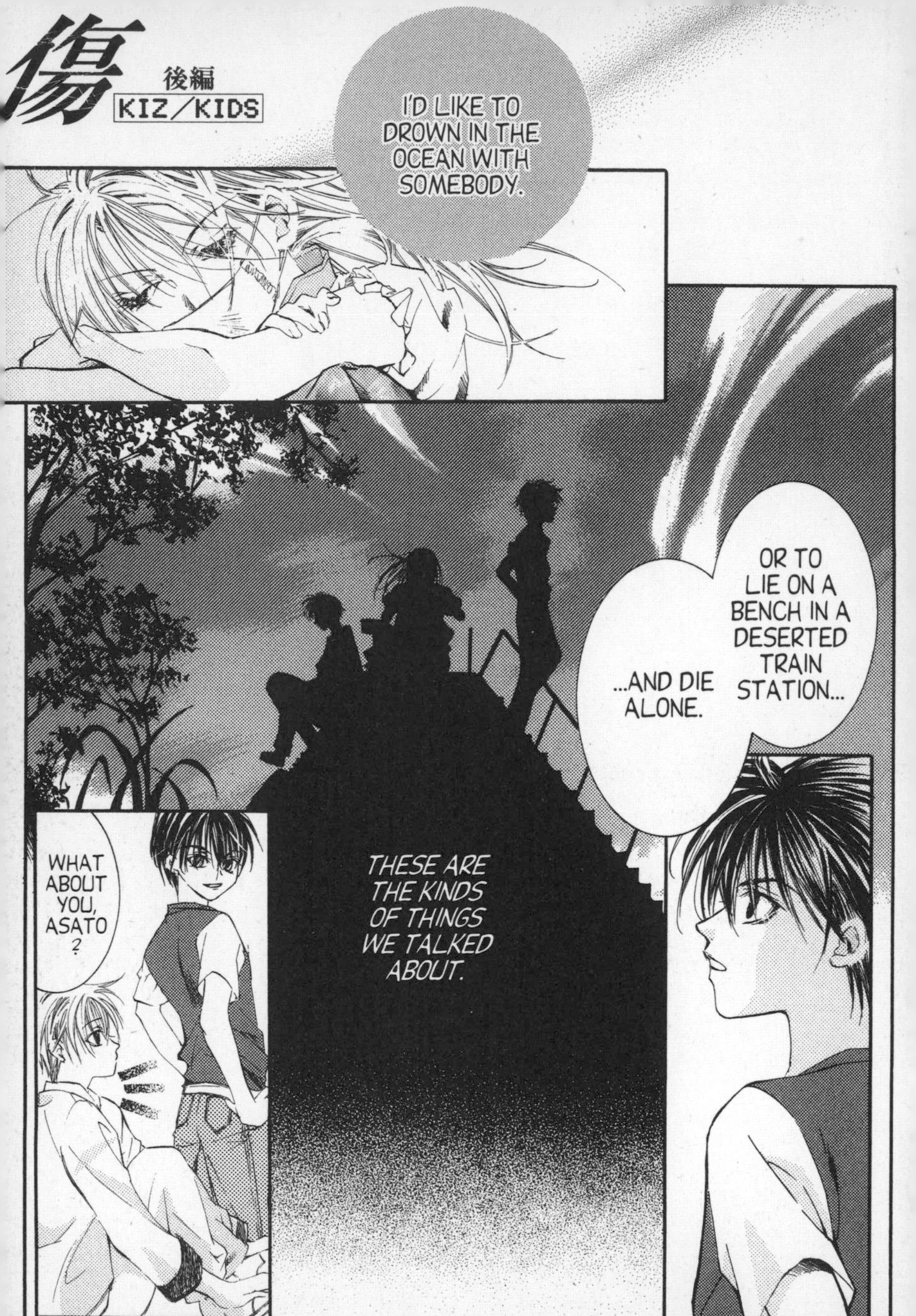
傷
後編
KIZ/KIDS
I'D LIKE TO DROWN IN THE OCEAN WITH SOMEBODY.
OR TO LIE ON A BENCH IN A DESERTED TRAIN STATION...
...AND DIE ALONE.
THESE ARE THE KINDS OF THINGS WE TALKED ABOUT.
WHAT ABOUT YOU, ASATO?

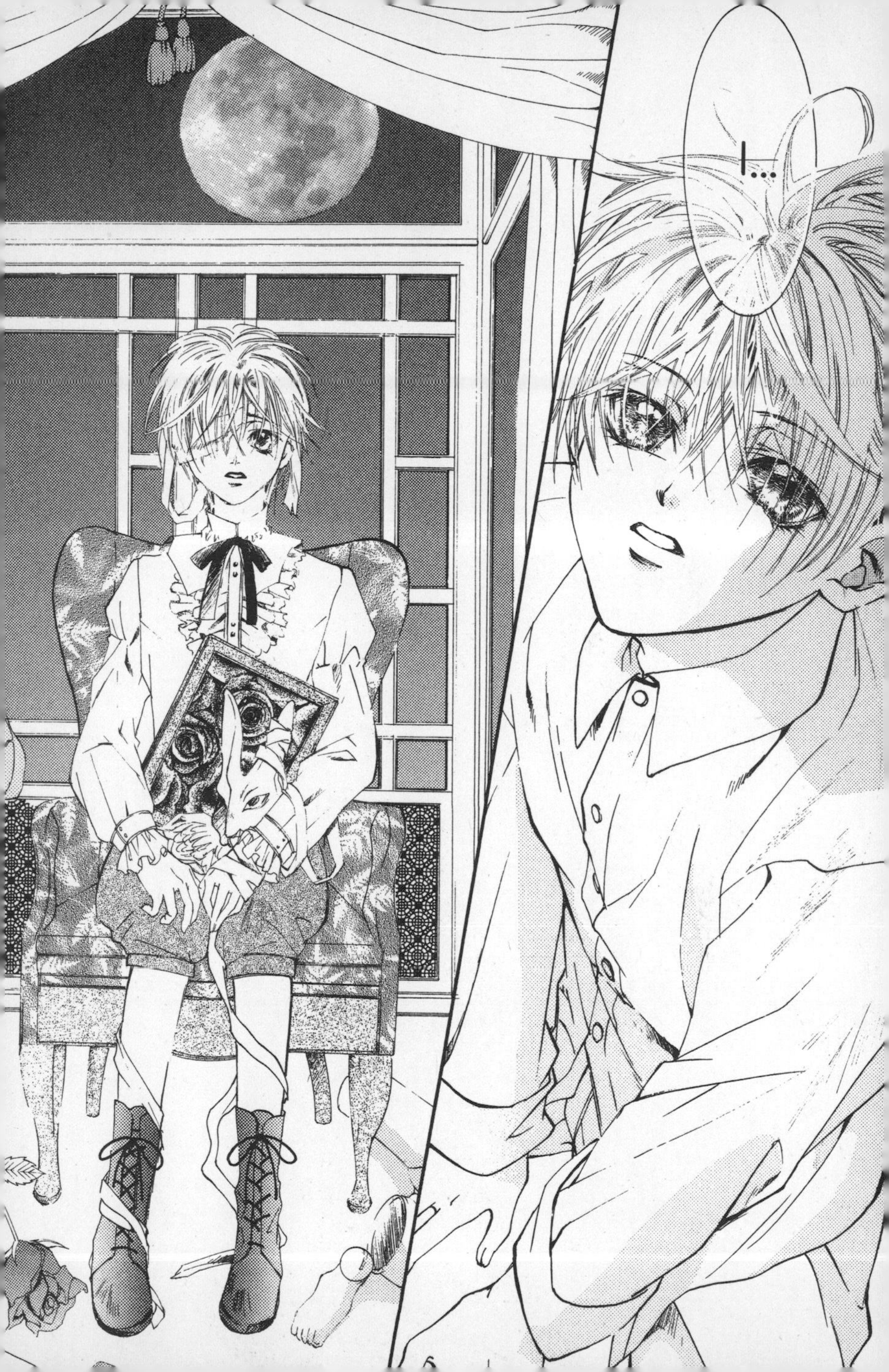
I...

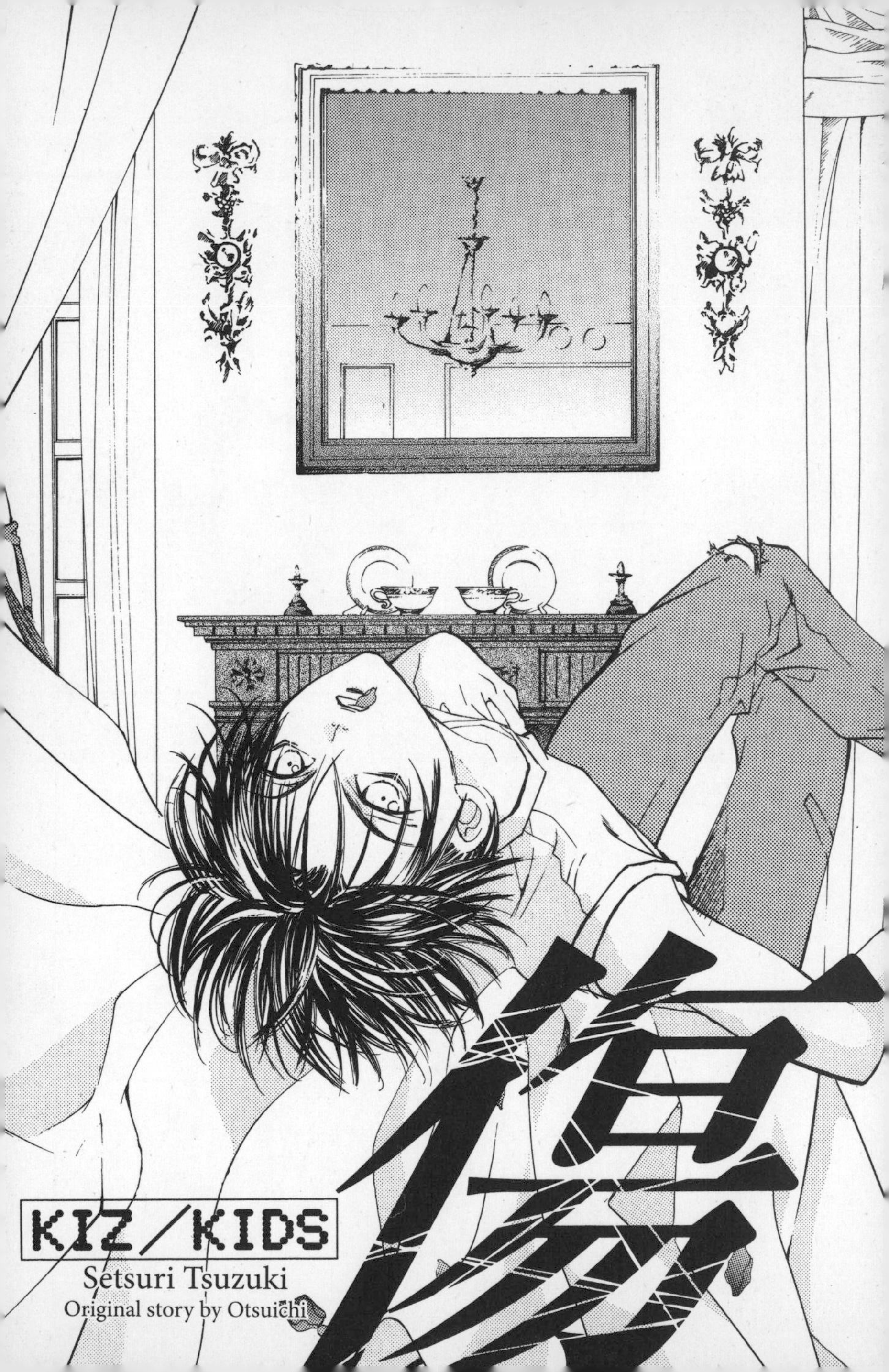
傷
KIZ/KIDS
Setsuri Tsuzuki
Original story by Otsuichi

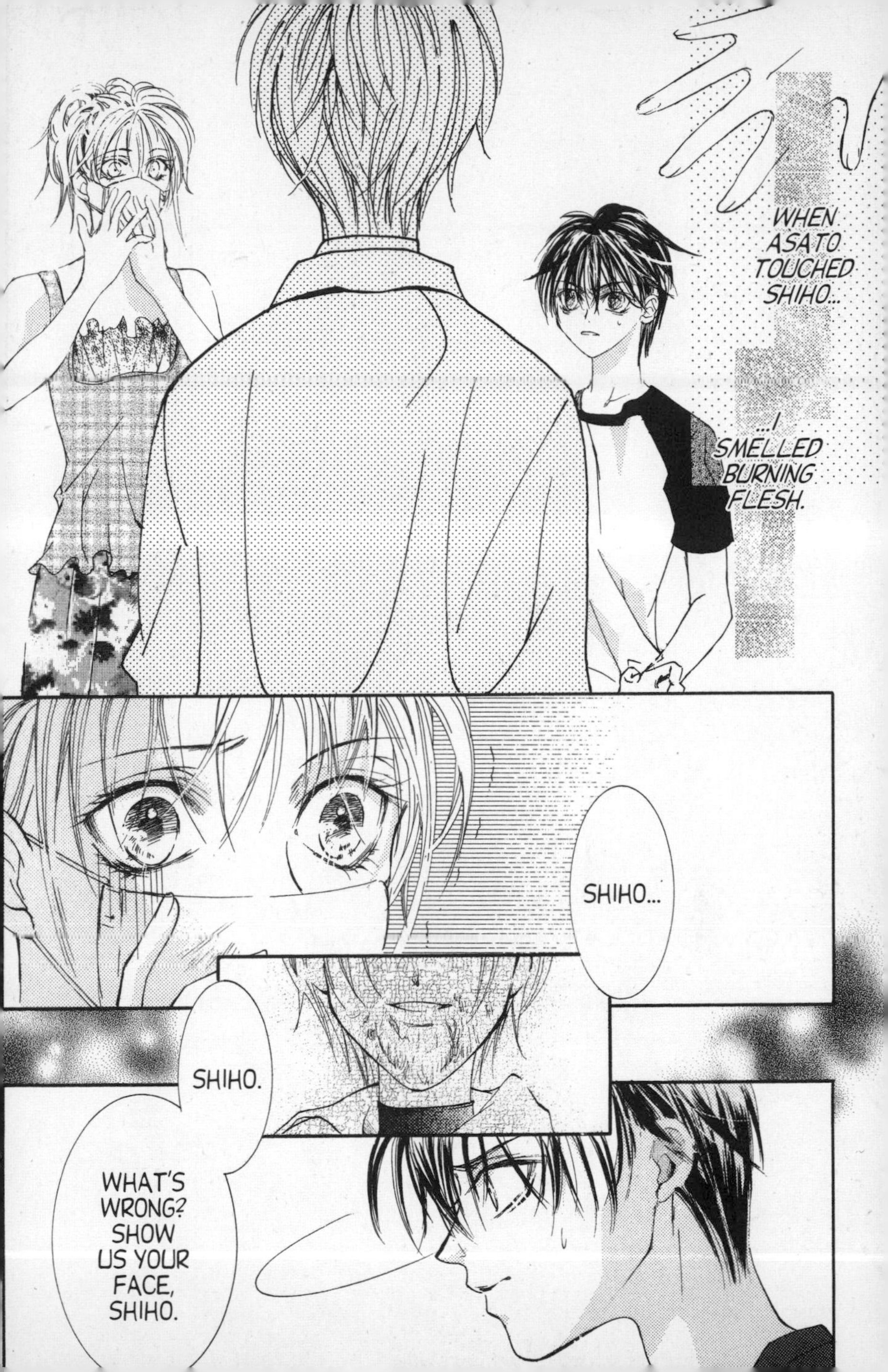
WHEN ASATO TOUCHED SHIHO...
...I SMELLED BURNING FLESH.
SHIHO...
SHIHO.
WHAT'S WRONG? SHOW US YOUR FACE, SHIHO.

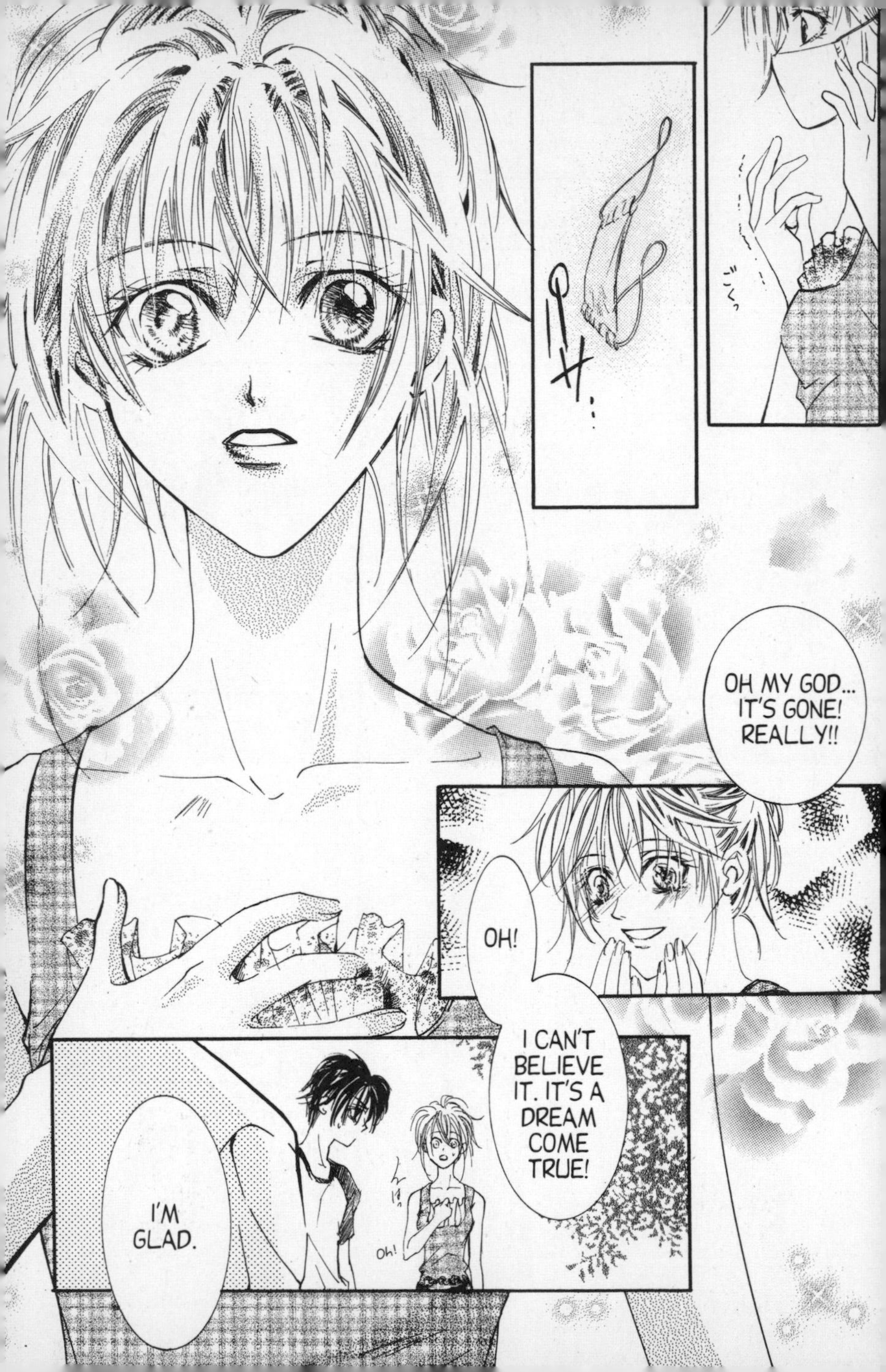
OH MY GOD... IT'S GONE! REALLY!!
OH!
I CAN'T BELIEVE IT. IT'S A DREAM COME TRUE!
Oh!
I'M GLAD.

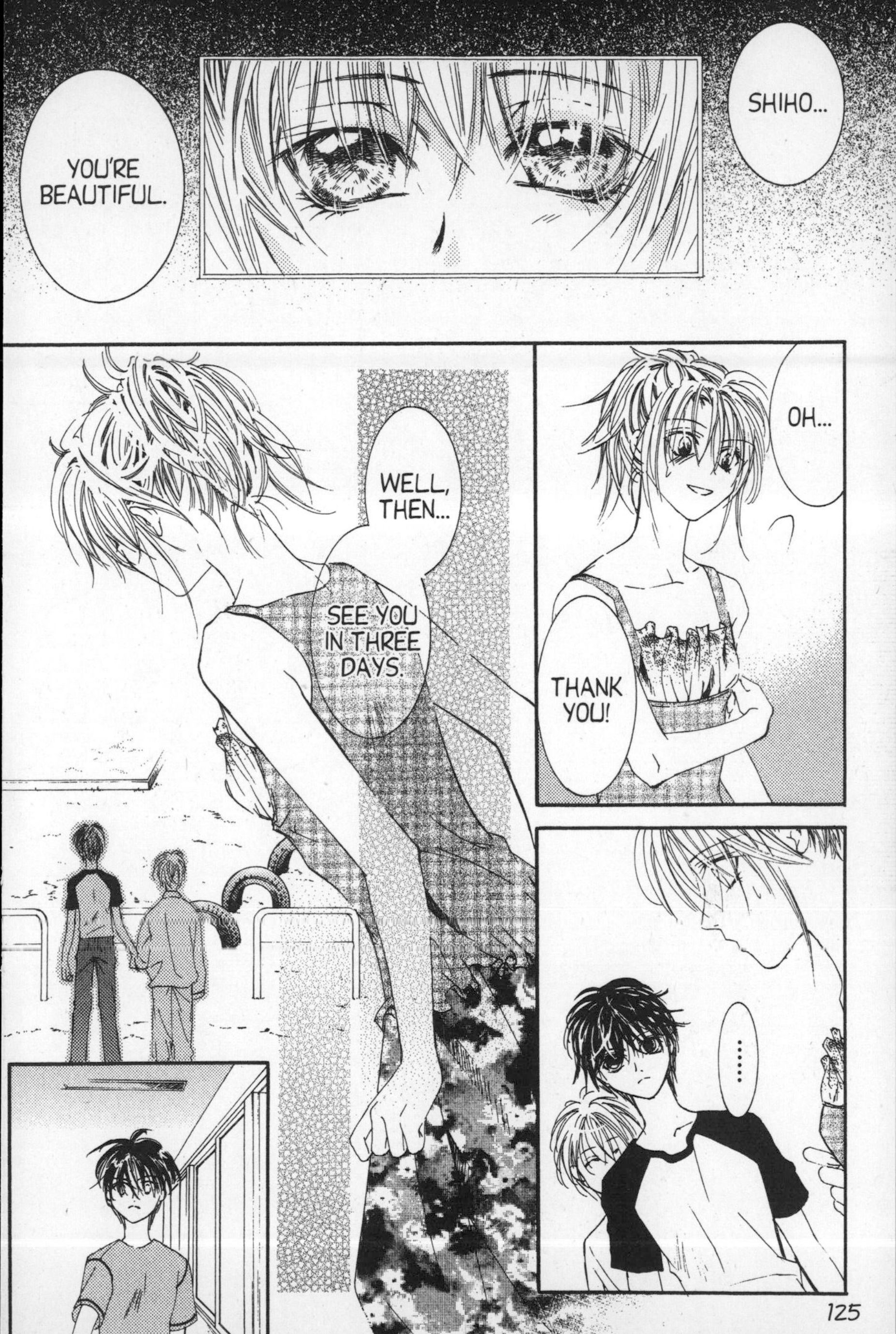
SHIHO...
YOU'RE BEAUTIFUL.
OH...
THANK YOU!
......
WELL, THEN...
SEE YOU IN THREE DAYS.

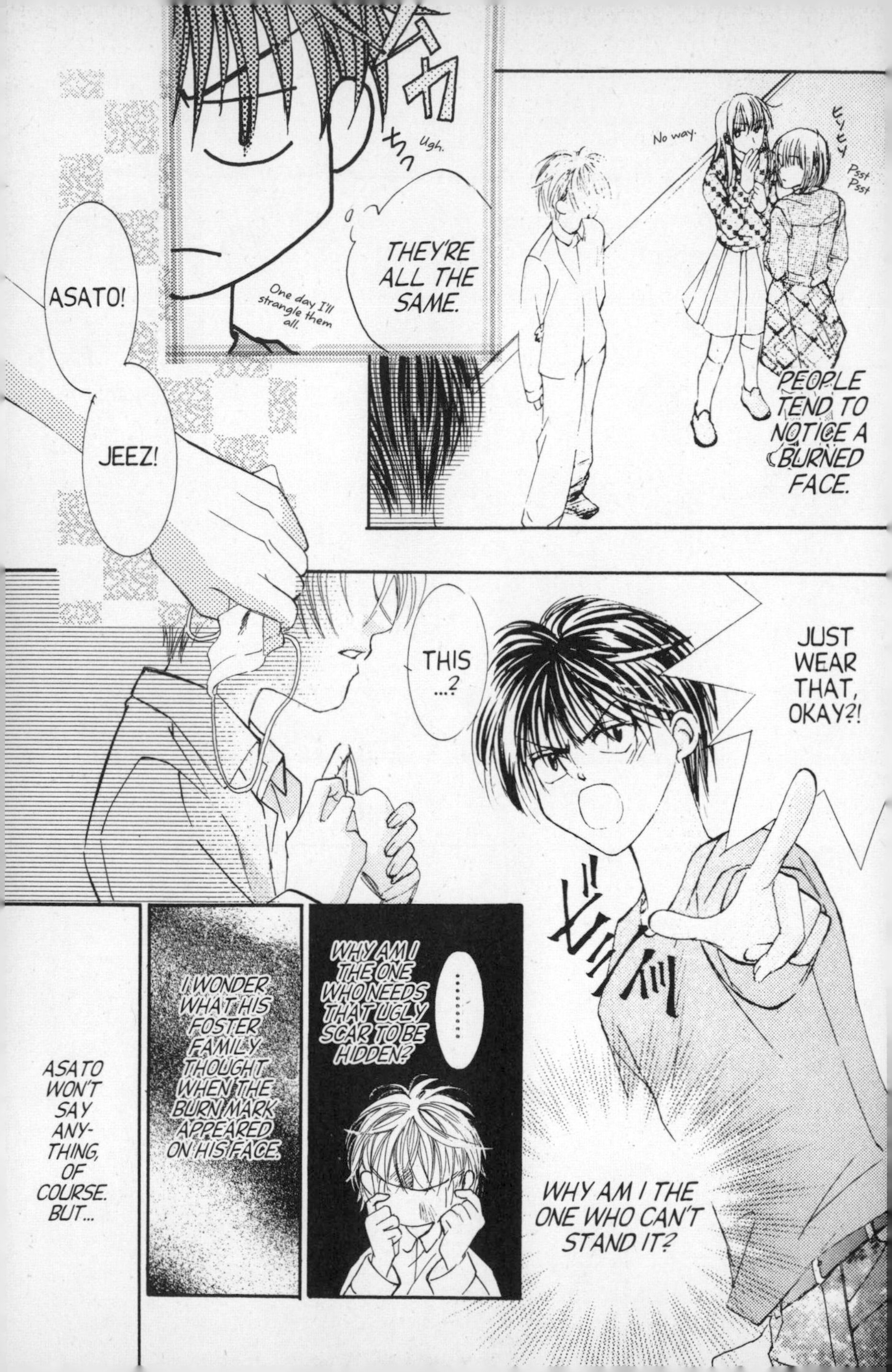
No way.
Psst Psst
PEOPLE TEND TO NOTICE A BURNED FACE.
Ugh.
THEY'RE ALL THE SAME.
One day I'll strangle them all.
ASATO!
JEEZ!
JUST WEAR THAT, OKAY?!
THIS ...?
WHY AM I THE ONE WHO CAN'T STAND IT?
WHY AM I THE ONE WHO NEEDS THAT UGLY SCAR TO BE HIDDEN?
....
I WONDER WHAT HIS FOSTER FAMILY THOUGHT WHEN THE BURN MARK APPEARED ON HIS FACE.
ASATO WON'T SAY ANY-THING, OF COURSE. BUT...

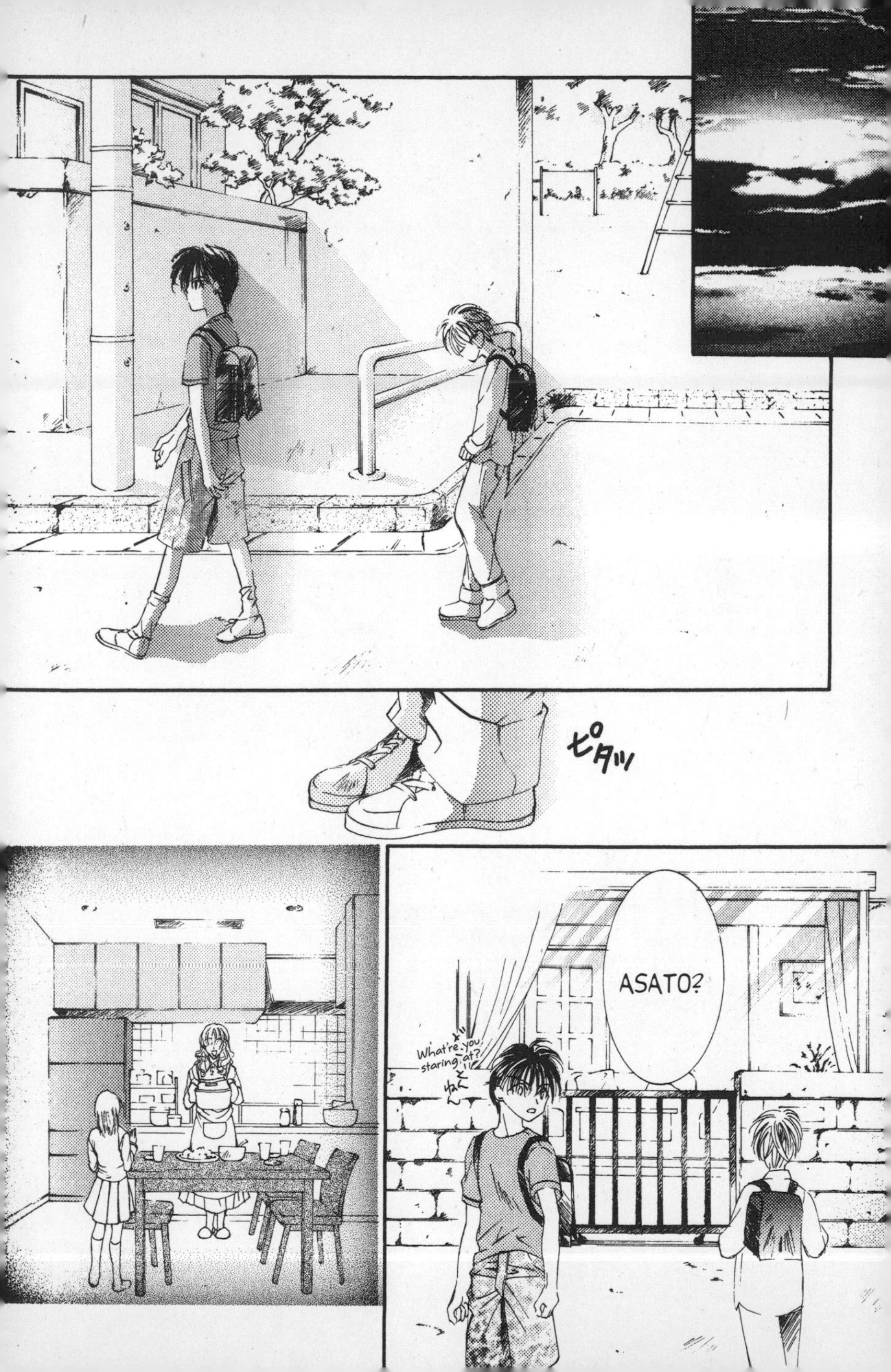
ピタッ
ASATO?
What're you staring at?

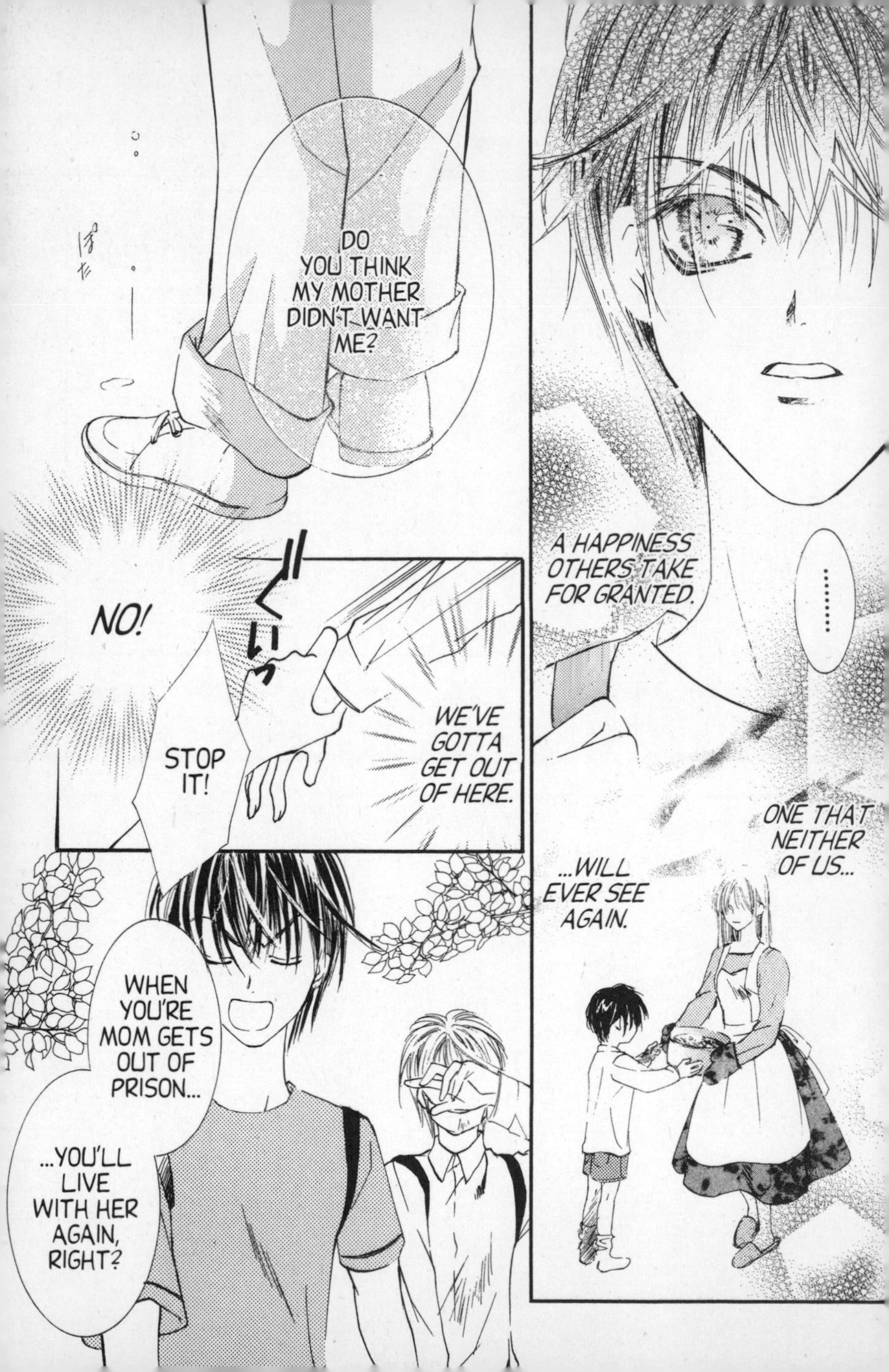
......
A HAPPINESS OTHERS TAKE FOR GRANTED.
ONE THAT NEITHER OF US...
...WILL EVER SEE AGAIN.
DO YOU THINK MY MOTHER DIDN'T WANT ME?
WE'VE GOTTA GET OUT OF HERE.
STOP IT!
NO!
WHEN YOU'RE MOM GETS OUT OF PRISON...
...YOU'LL LIVE WITH HER AGAIN, RIGHT?

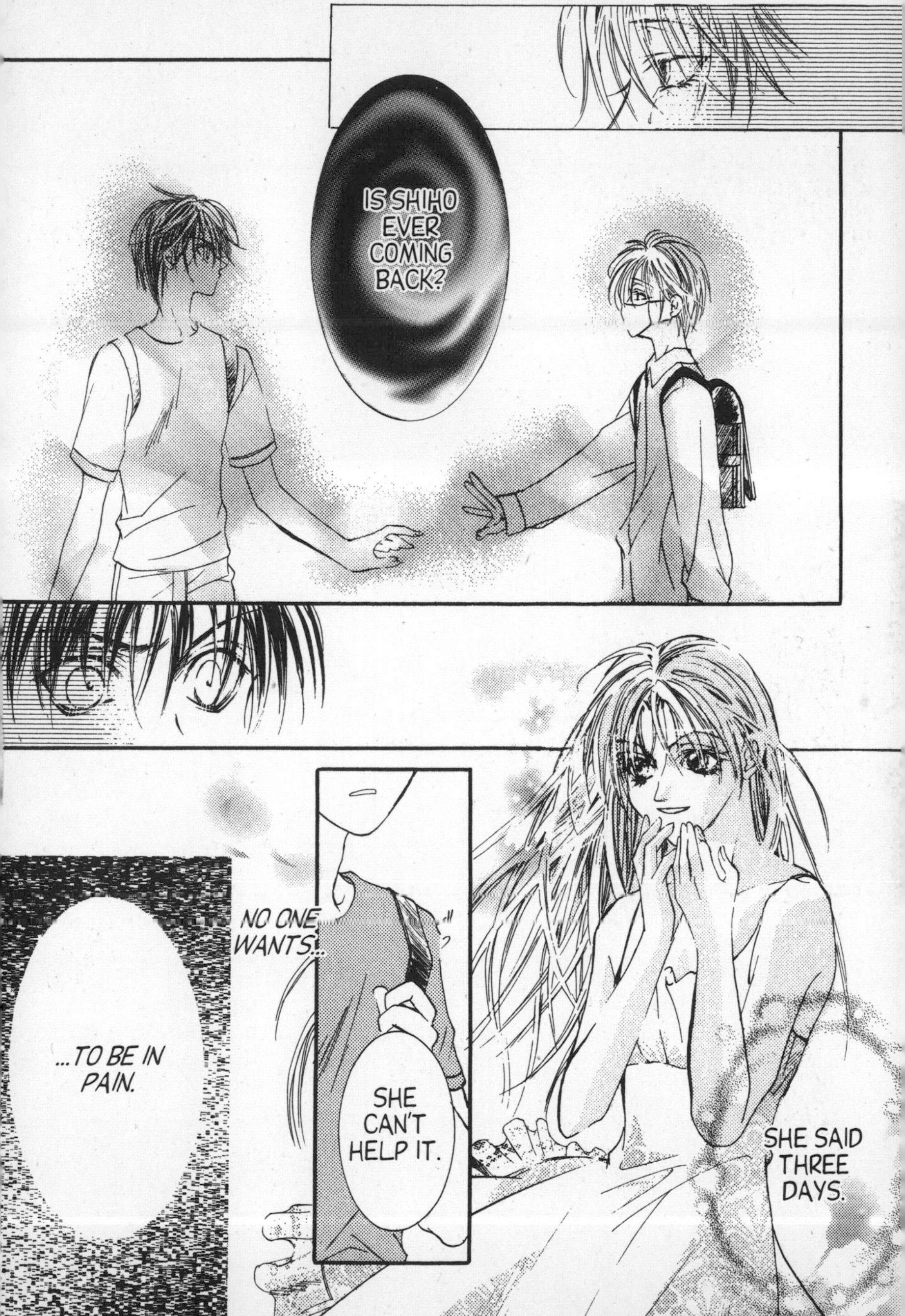
IS SHIHO EVER COMING BACK?
SHE SAID THREE DAYS.
SHE CAN'T HELP IT.
NO ONE WANTS...
...TO BE IN PAIN.

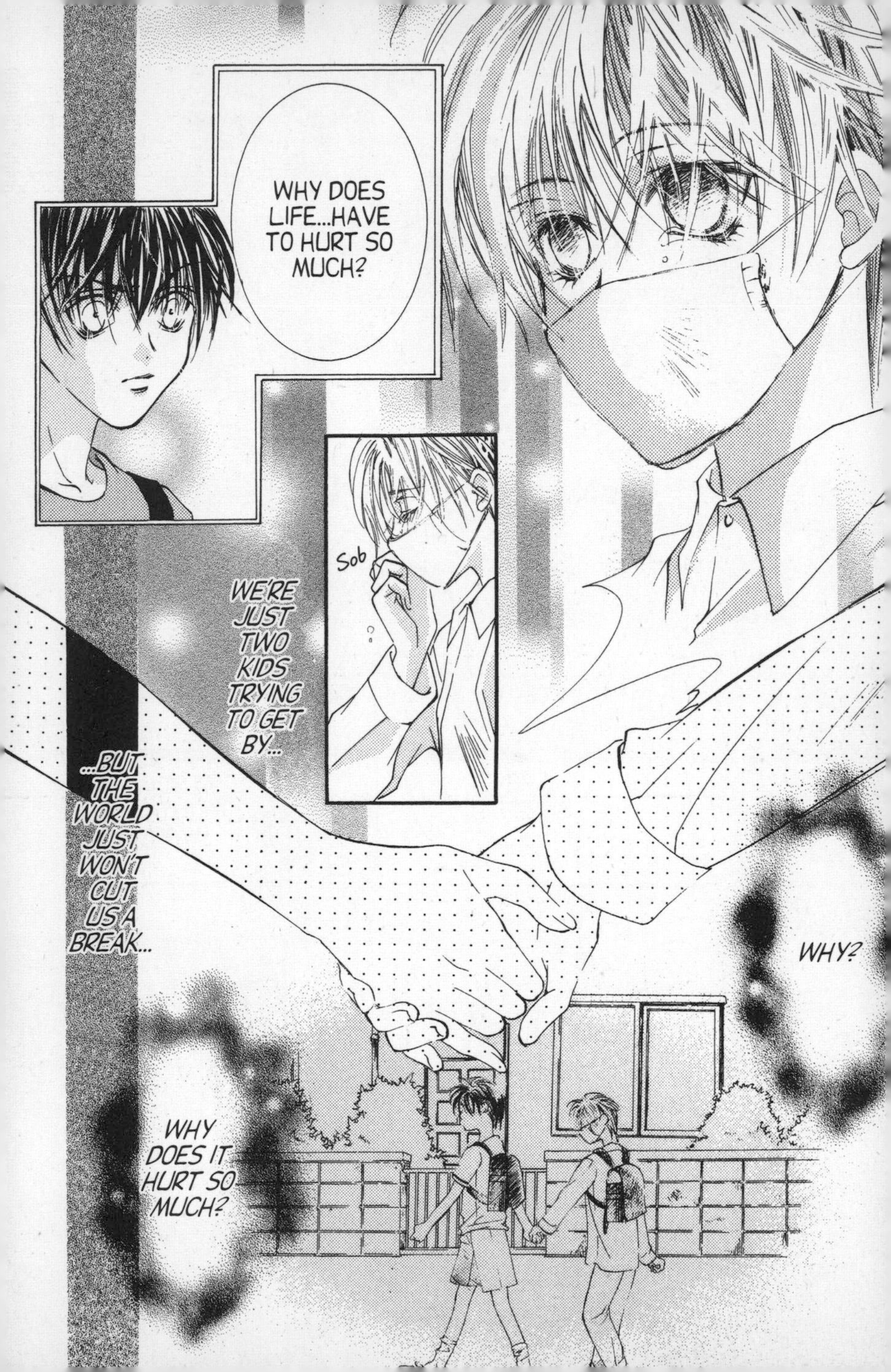
WHY DOES LIFE...HAVE TO HURT SO MUCH?
Sob
WE'RE JUST TWO KIDS TRYING TO GET BY...
...BUT THE WORLD JUST WON'T CUT US A BREAK...
WHY?
WHY DOES IT HURT SO MUCH?

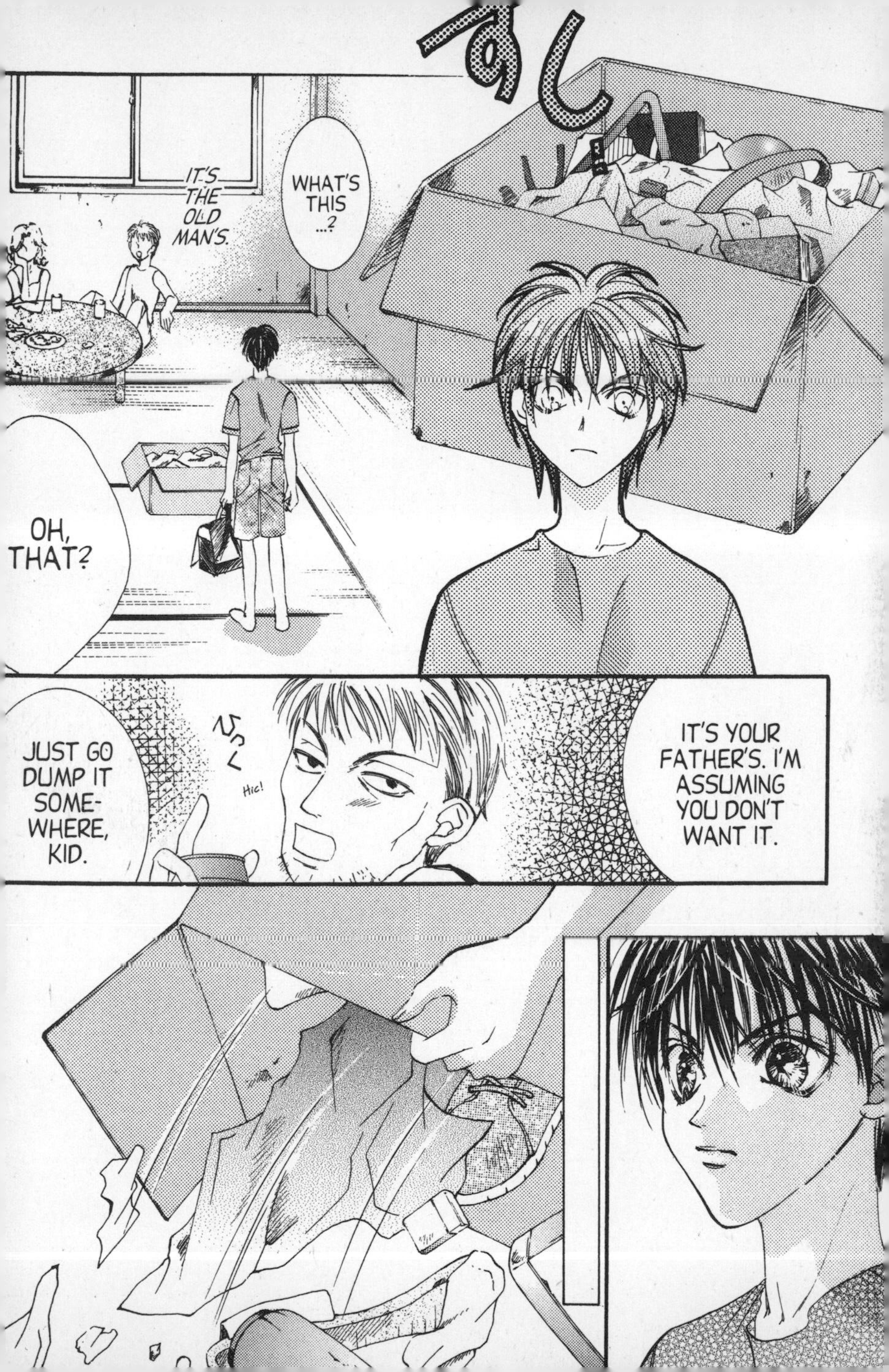
WHAT'S THIS ...?
IT'S THE OLD MAN'S.
OH, THAT?
IT'S YOUR FATHER'S. I'M ASSUMING YOU DON'T WANT IT.
Hic!
JUST GO DUMP IT SOME-WHERE, KID.

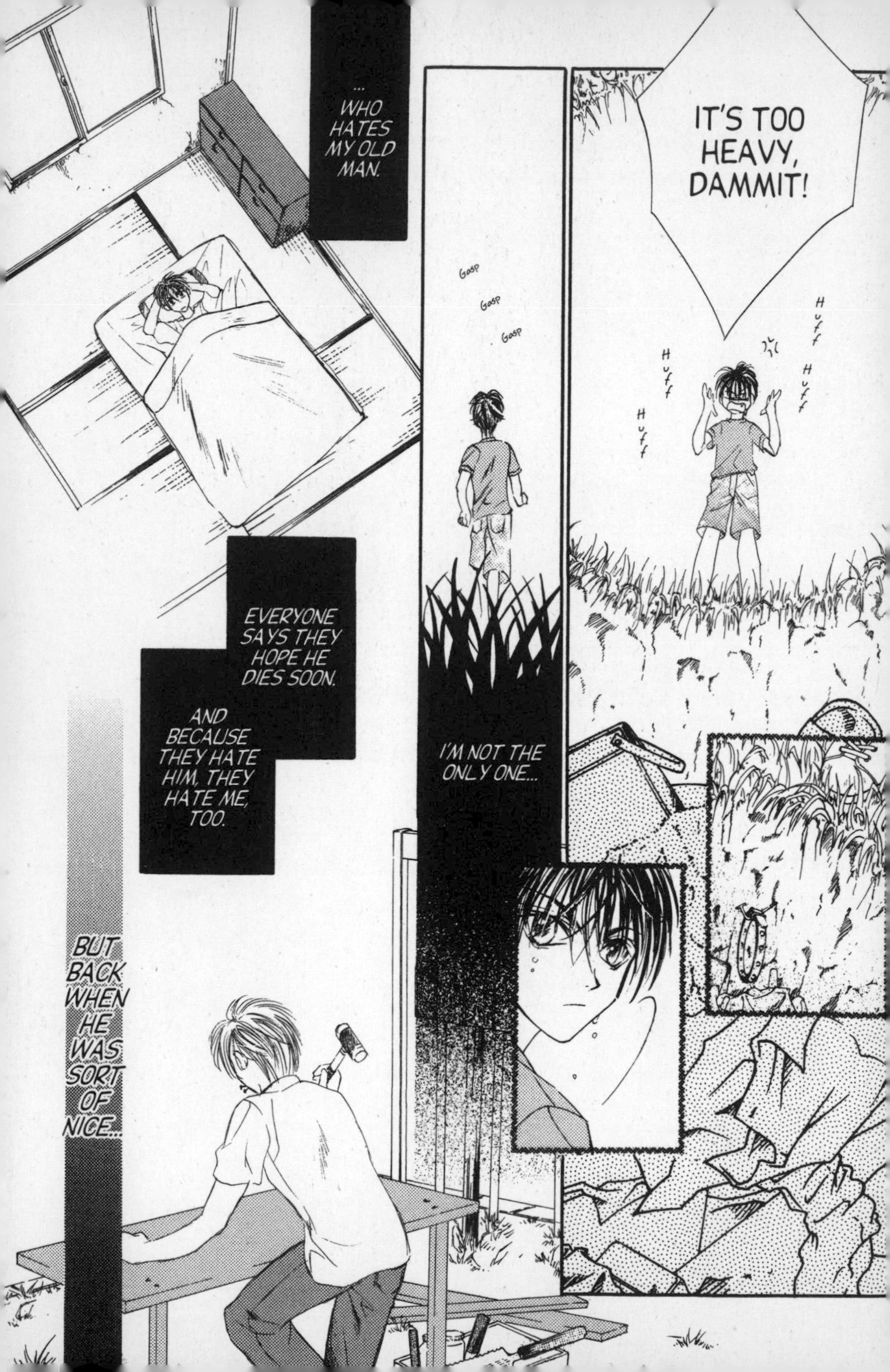
IT'S TOO HEAVY, DAMMIT!
Huff
Huff
Huff
Huff
Gasp
Gasp
Gasp
I'M NOT THE ONLY ONE...
... WHO HATES MY OLD MAN.
EVERYONE SAYS THEY HOPE HE DIES SOON.
AND BECAUSE THEY HATE HIM, THEY HATE ME, TOO.
BUT BACK WHEN HE WAS SORT OF NICE...

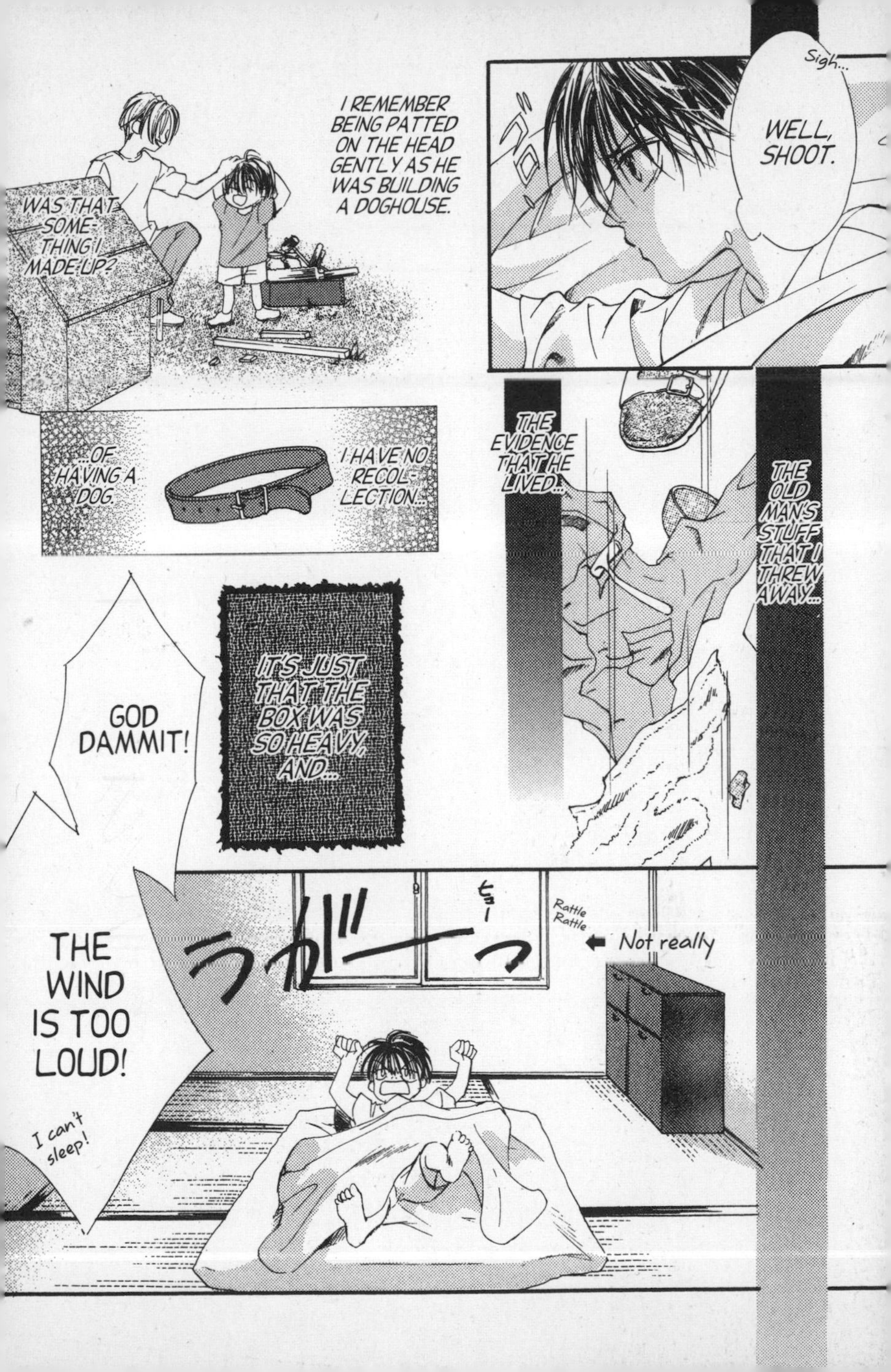
Sigh...
WELL, SHOOT.
I REMEMBER BEING PATTED ON THE HEAD GENTLY AS HE WAS BUILDING A DOGHOUSE.
WAS THAT SOME-THING I MADE UP?
THE OLD MAN'S STUFF THAT I THREW AWAY...
THE EVIDENCE THAT HE LIVED...
I HAVE NO RECOL-LECTION...
...OF HAVING A DOG.
IT'S JUST THAT THE BOX WAS SO HEAVY, AND...
GOD DAMMIT!
Rattle Rattle
Not really
THE WIND IS TOO LOUD!
I can't sleep!

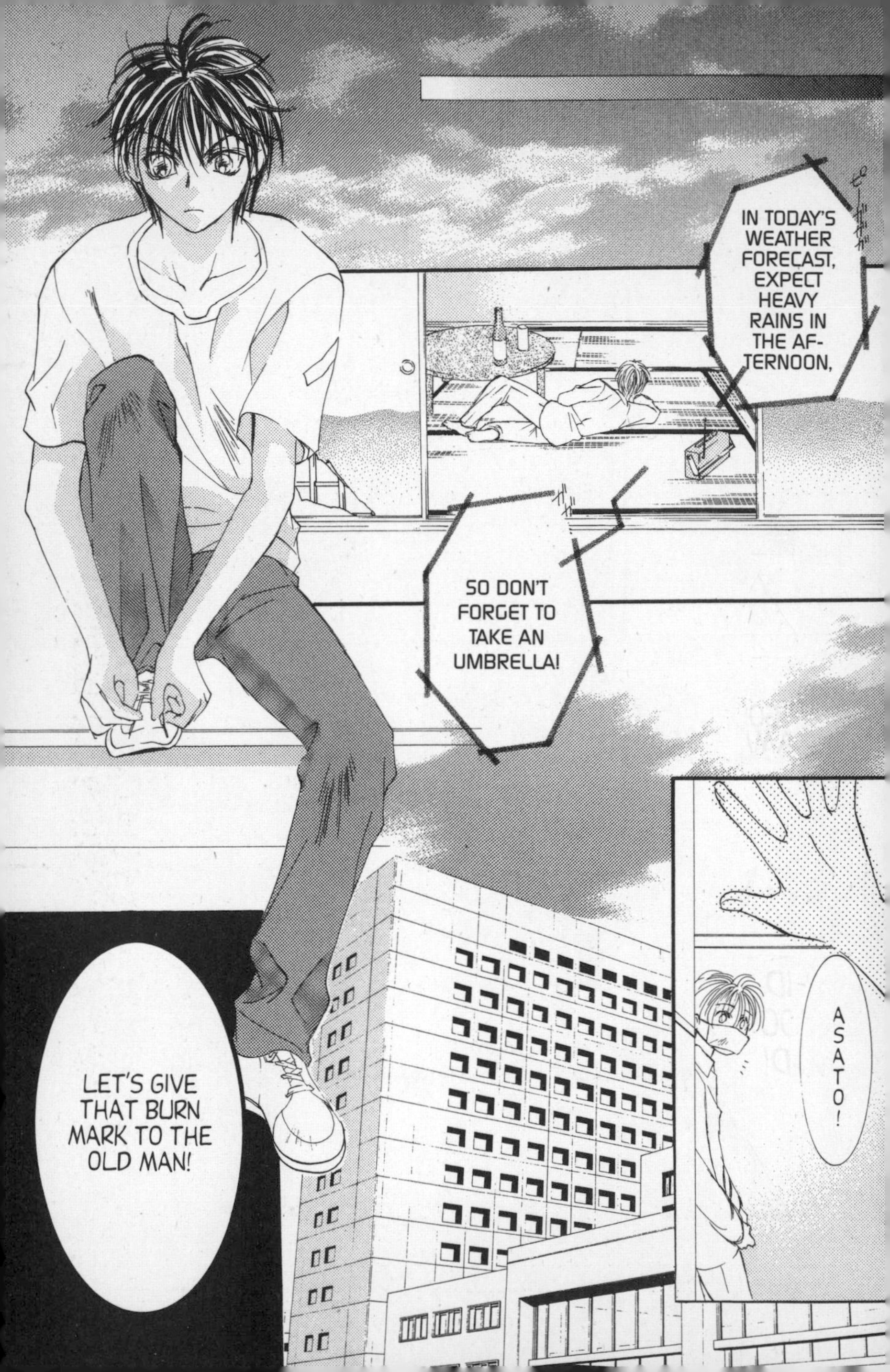
IN TODAY'S WEATHER FORECAST, EXPECT HEAVY RAINS IN THE AF-TERNOON,
SO DON'T FORGET TO TAKE AN UMBRELLA!
ASATO!
LET'S GIVE THAT BURN MARK TO THE OLD MAN!

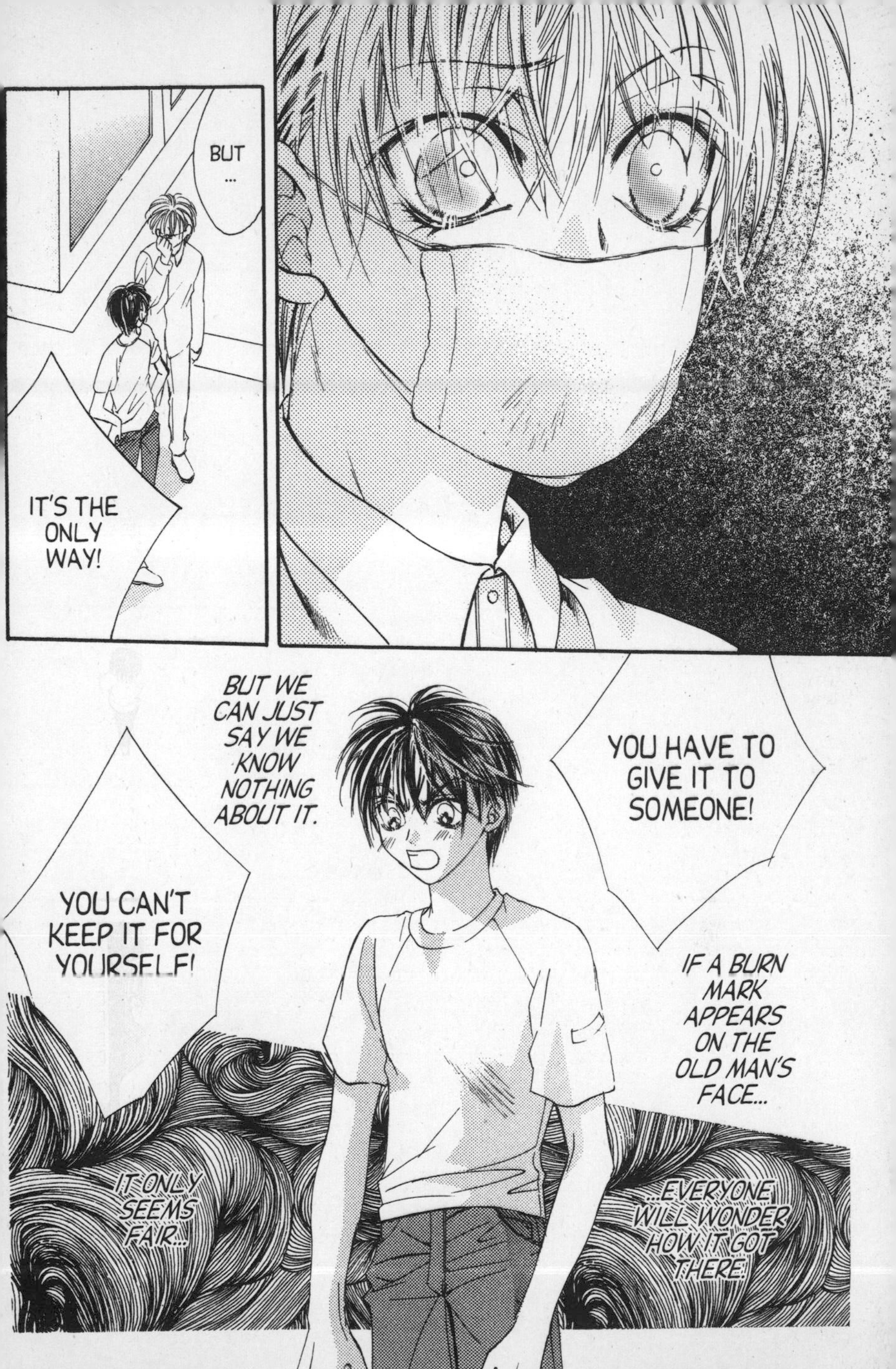
BUT ...
IT'S THE ONLY WAY!
YOU HAVE TO GIVE IT TO SOMEONE!
BUT WE CAN JUST SAY WE KNOW NOTHING ABOUT IT.
YOU CAN'T KEEP IT FOR YOURSELF!
IF A BURN MARK APPEARS ON THE OLD MAN'S FACE...
...EVERYONE WILL WONDER HOW IT GOT THERE.
IT ONLY SEEMS FAIR...

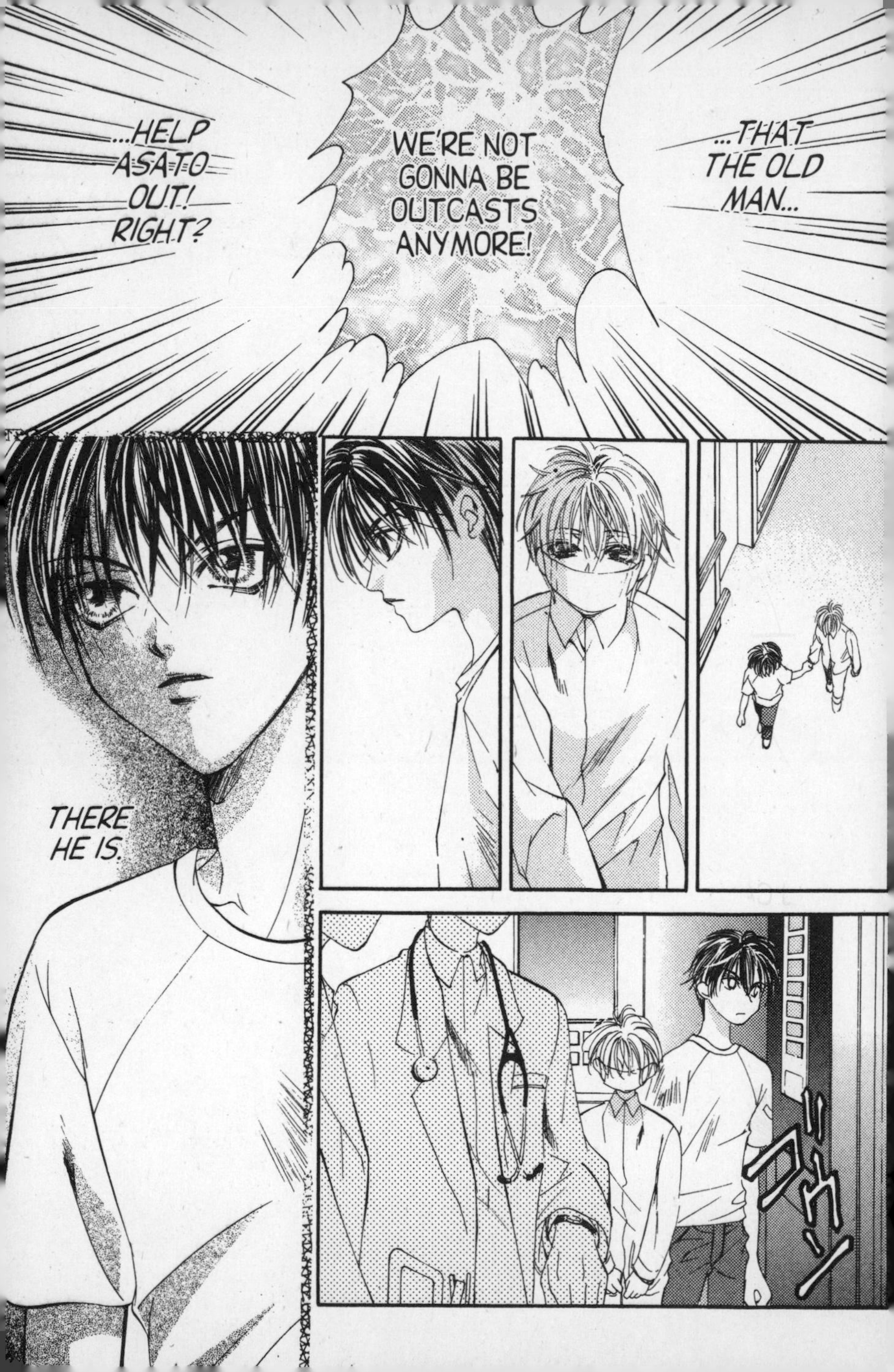
...THAT THE OLD MAN...
WE'RE NOT GONNA BE OUTCASTS ANYMORE!
...HELP ASATO OUT! RIGHT?
THERE HE IS.

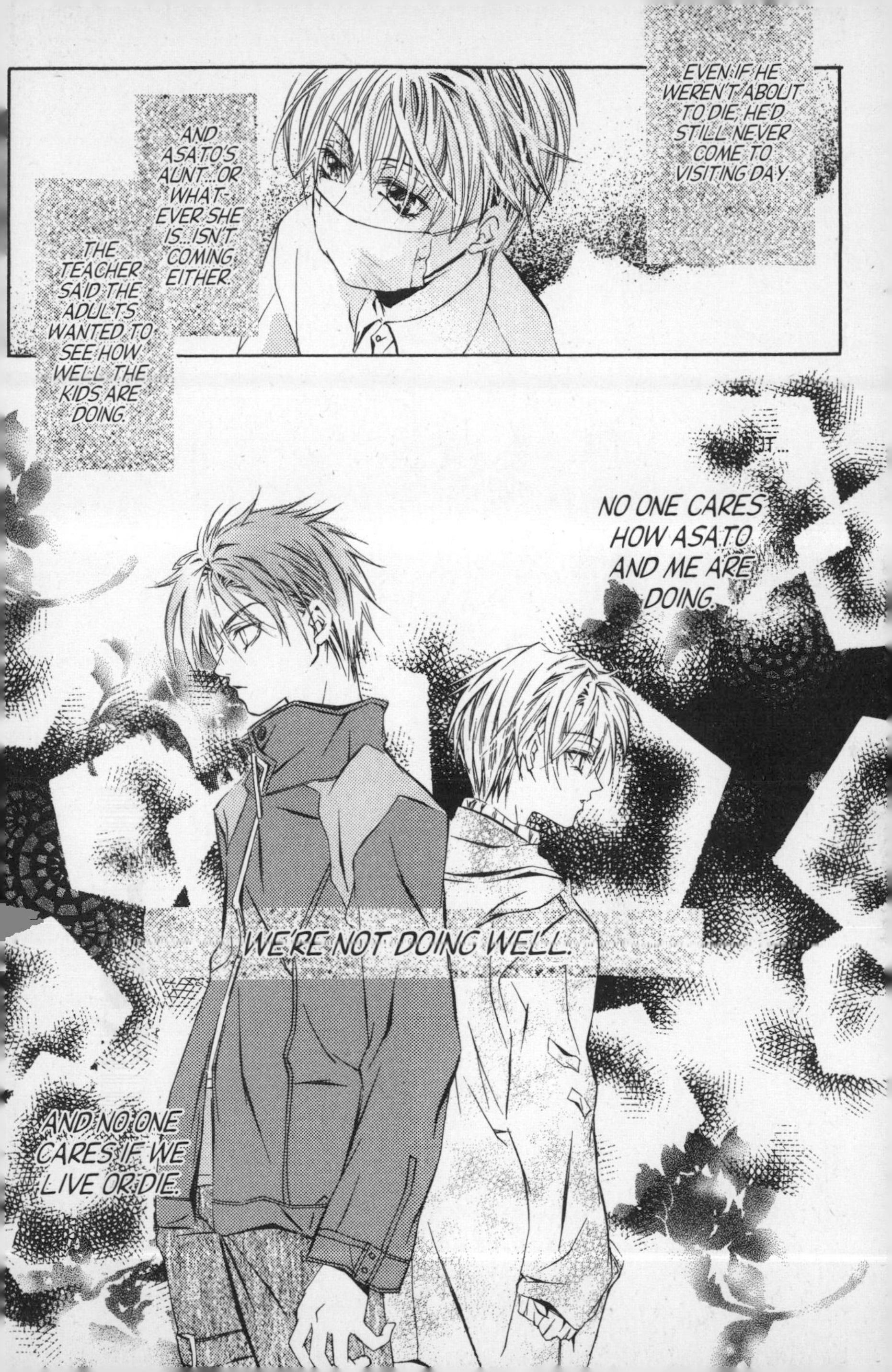
EVEN IF HE WEREN'T ABOUT TO DIE, HE'D STILL NEVER COME TO VISITING DAY.
AND ASATO'S AUNT...OR WHATEVER SHE IS...ISN'T COMING EITHER.
THE TEACHER SAID THE ADULTS WANTED TO SEE HOW WELL THE KIDS ARE DOING.
BUT...
NO ONE CARES HOW ASATO AND ME ARE DOING.
WE'RE NOT DOING WELL.
AND NO ONE CARES IF WE LIVE OR DIE.

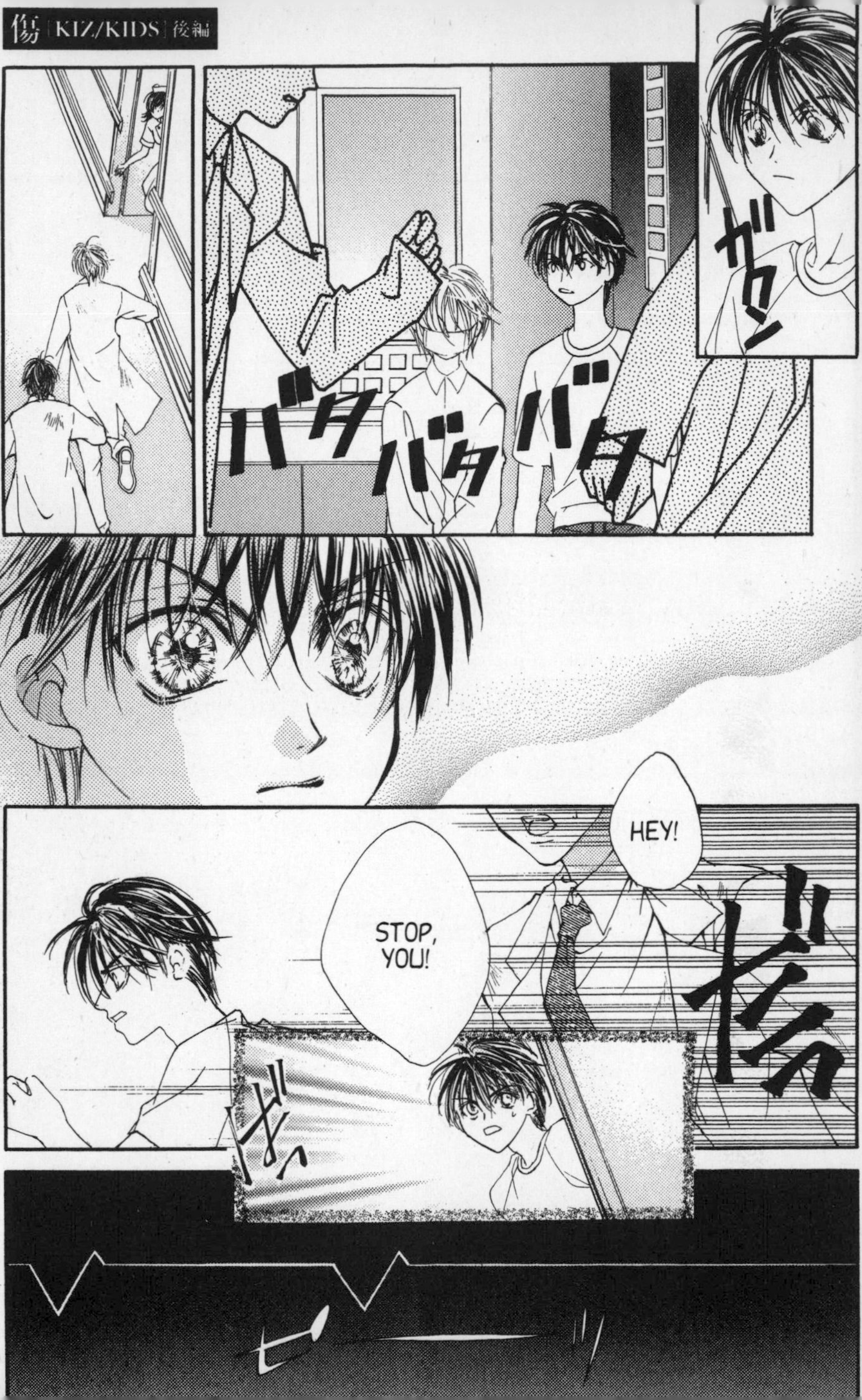
バタ
バタ
バタ
HEY!
STOP, YOU!

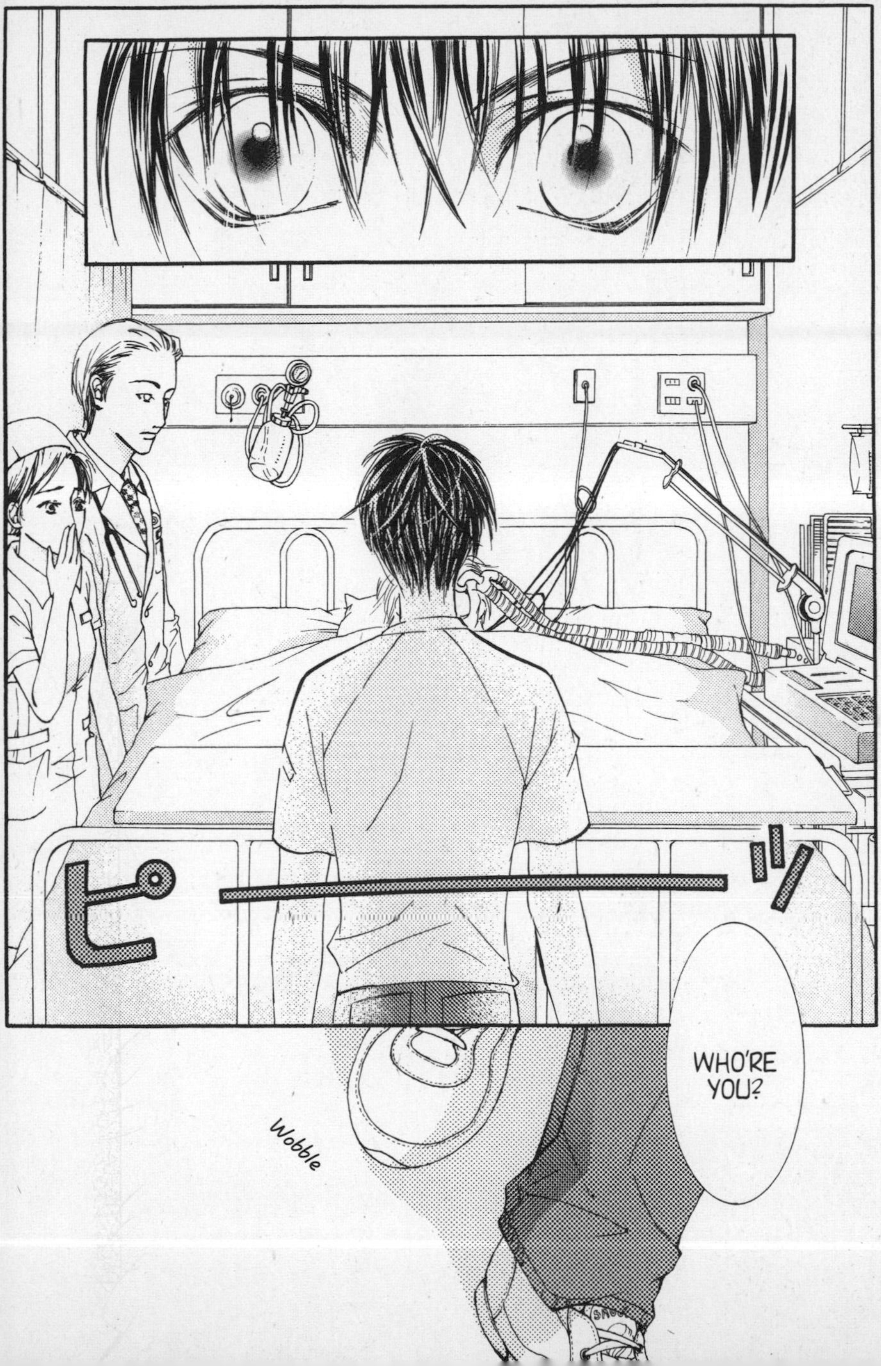
ピーーッ
WHO'RE YOU?
Wobble

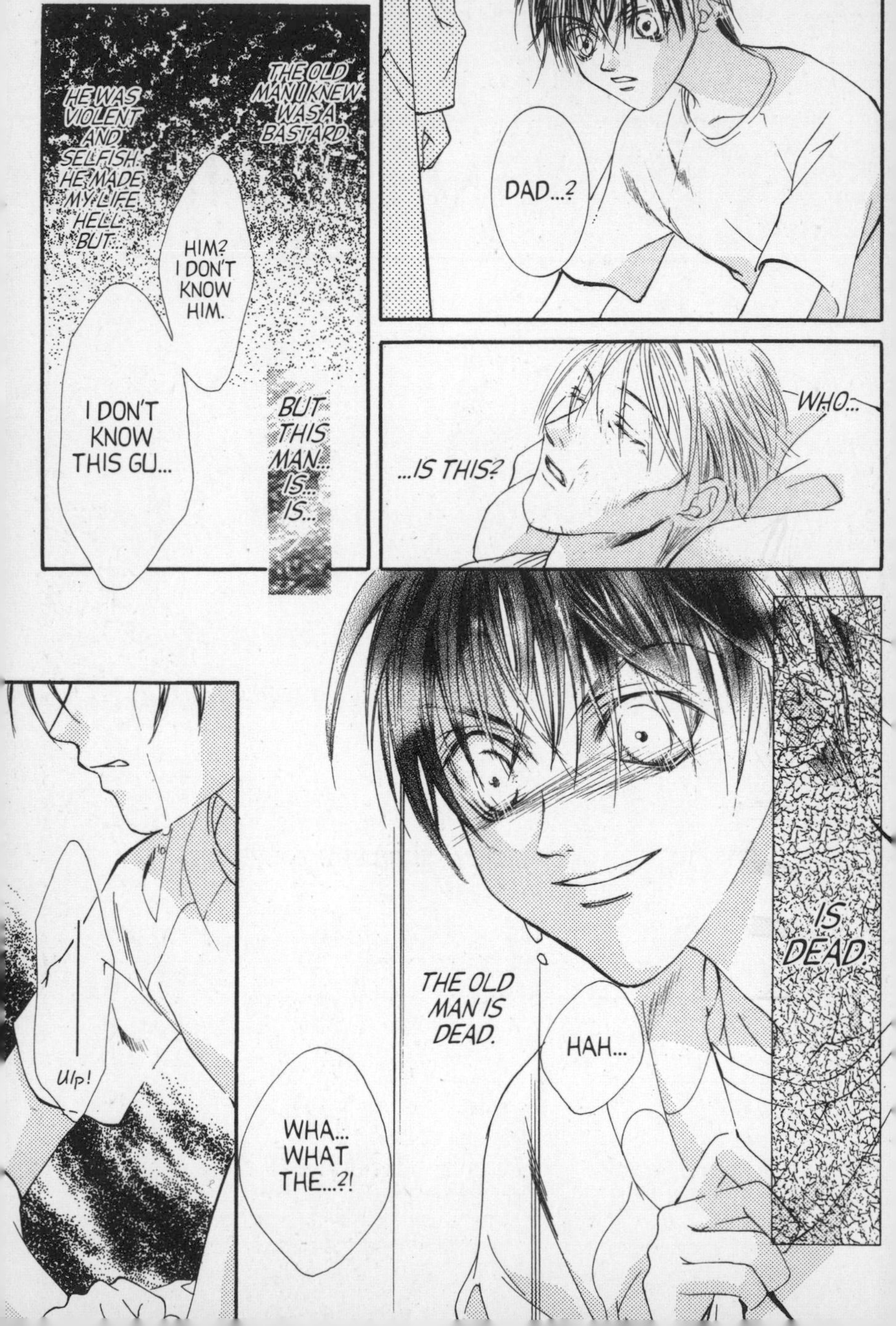
DAD...?
WHO...
...IS THIS?
THE OLD MAN I KNEW WAS A BASTARD.
HE WAS VIOLENT AND SELFISH. HE MADE MY LIFE HELL BUT...
HIM? I DON'T KNOW HIM.
BUT THIS MAN... IS... IS...
I DON'T KNOW THIS GU...
IS DEAD.
THE OLD MAN IS DEAD.
HAH...
WHA... WHAT THE...?!
Ulp!

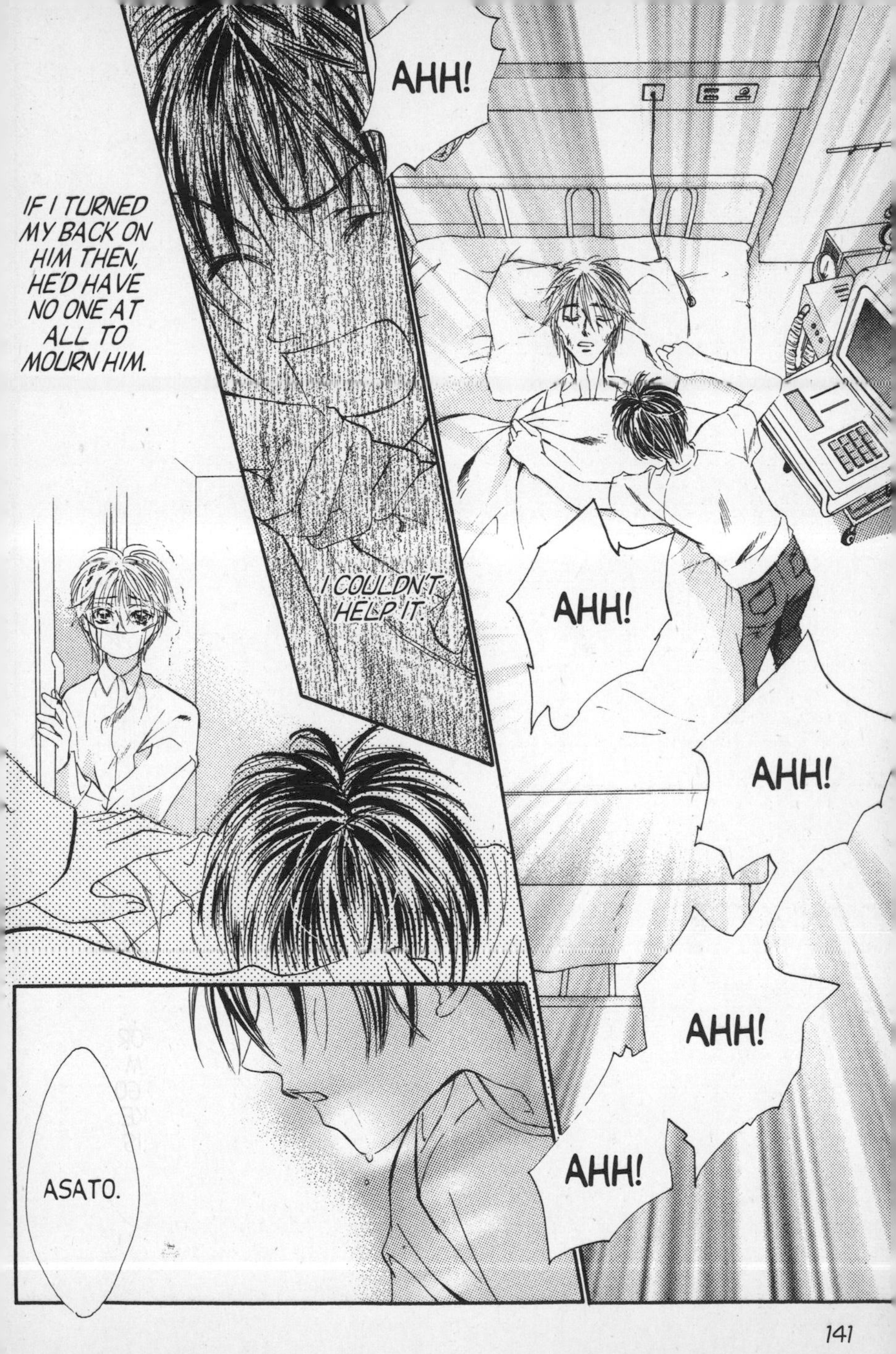
AHH!
AHH!
AHH!
AHH!
AHH!
IF I TURNED MY BACK ON HIM THEN, HE'D HAVE NO ONE AT ALL TO MOURN HIM.
I COULDN'T HELP IT.
ASATO.

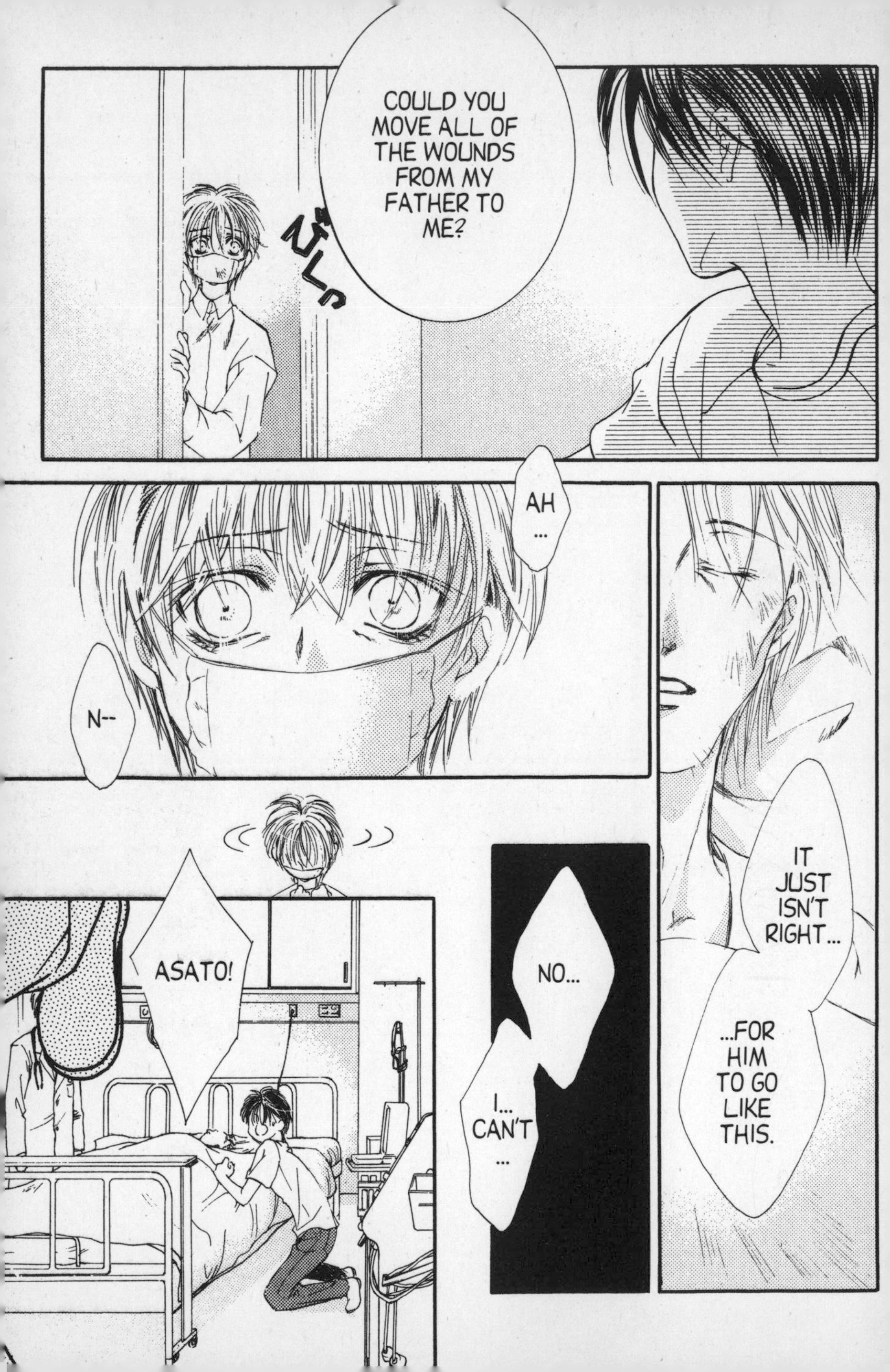
COULD YOU MOVE ALL OF THE WOUNDS FROM MY FATHER TO ME?
IT JUST ISN'T RIGHT...
...FOR HIM TO GO LIKE THIS.
AH ...
N--
NO...
I... CAN'T ...
ASATO!

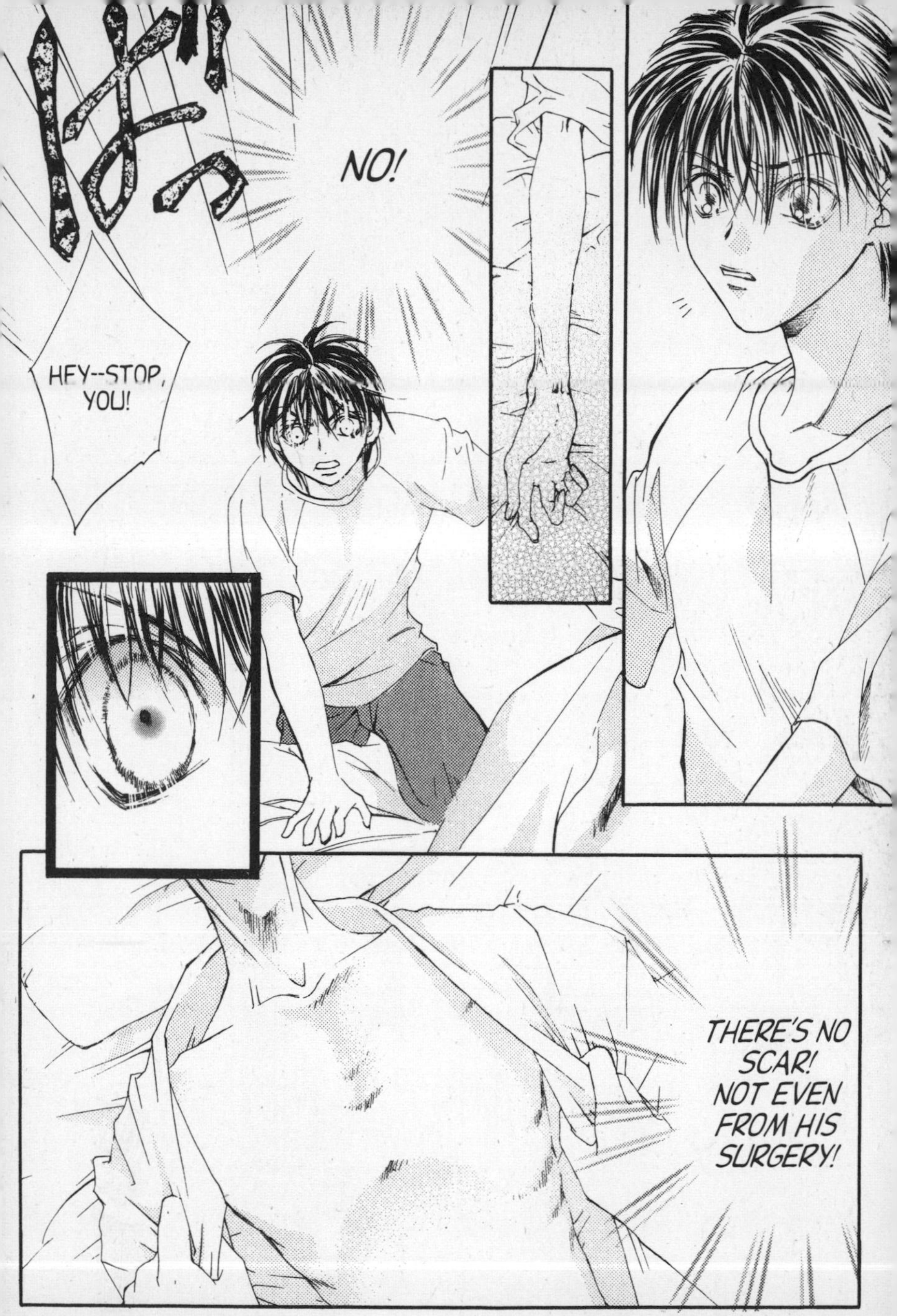
NO!
ぱっ
HEY--STOP, YOU!
THERE'S NO SCAR! NOT EVEN FROM HIS SURGERY!

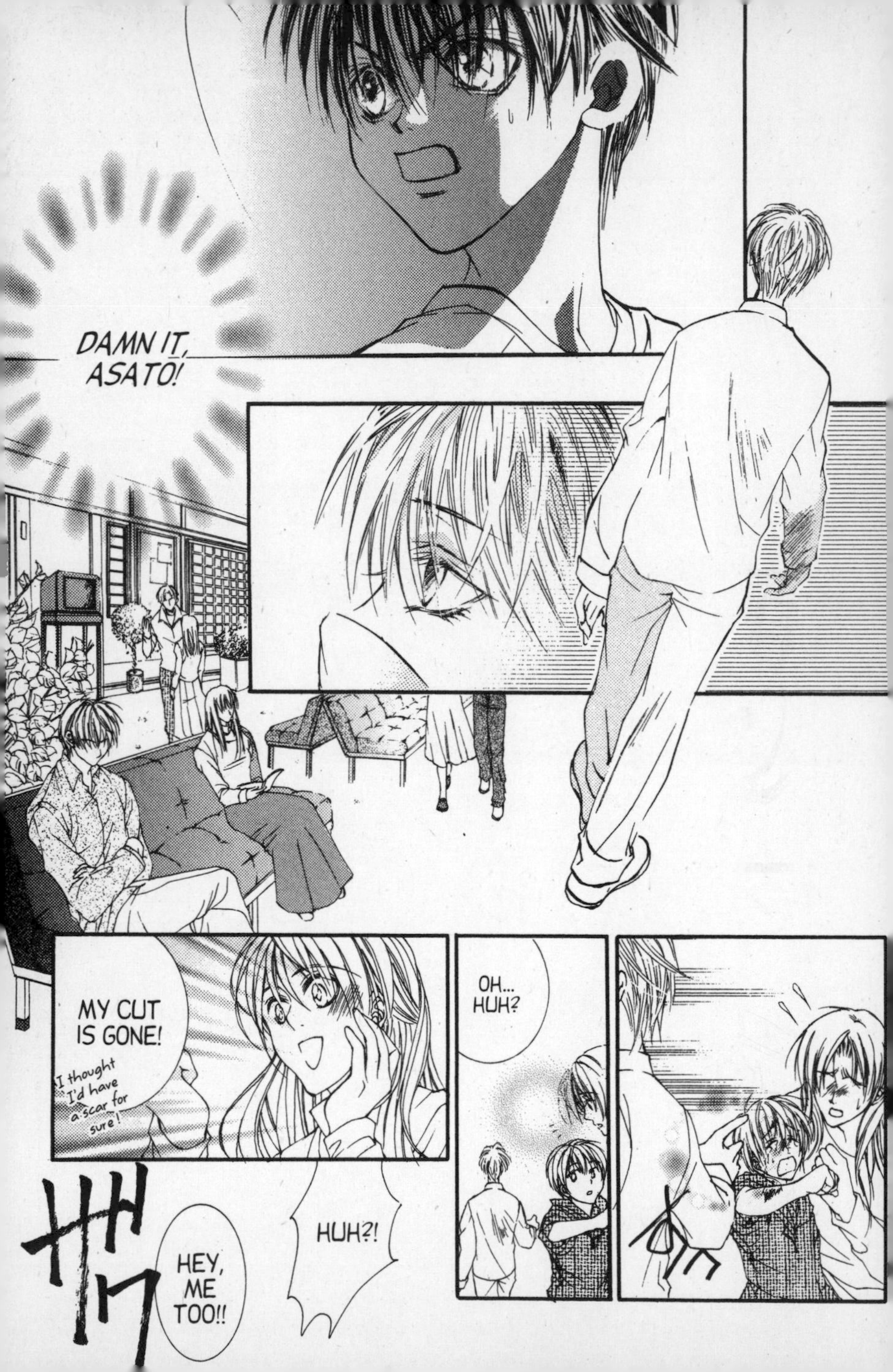
DAMN IT, ASATO!
OH... HUH?
MY CUT IS GONE!
I thought I'd have a scar for sure!
HUH?!
HEY, ME TOO!!

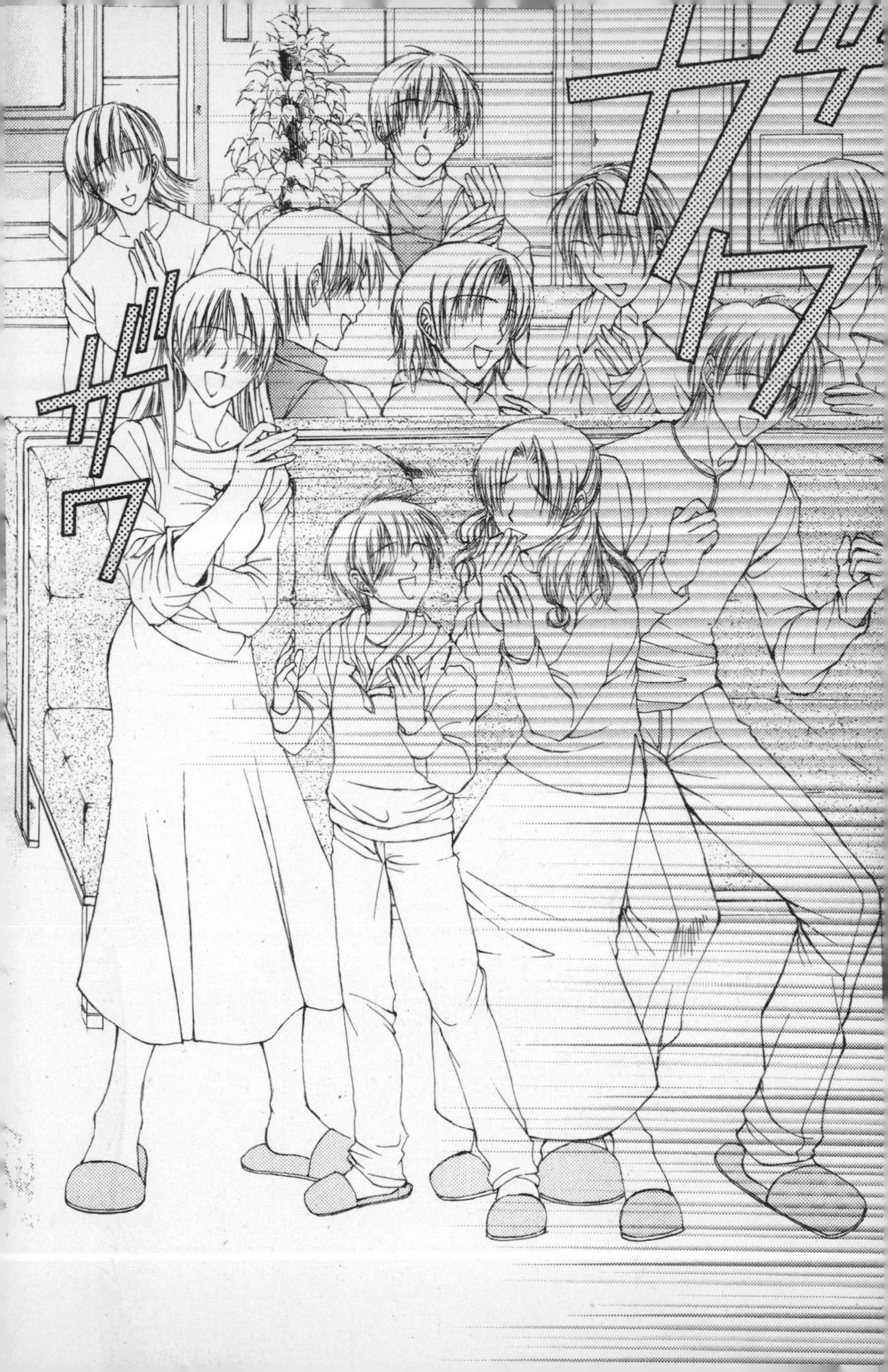
ザワ
ザワ

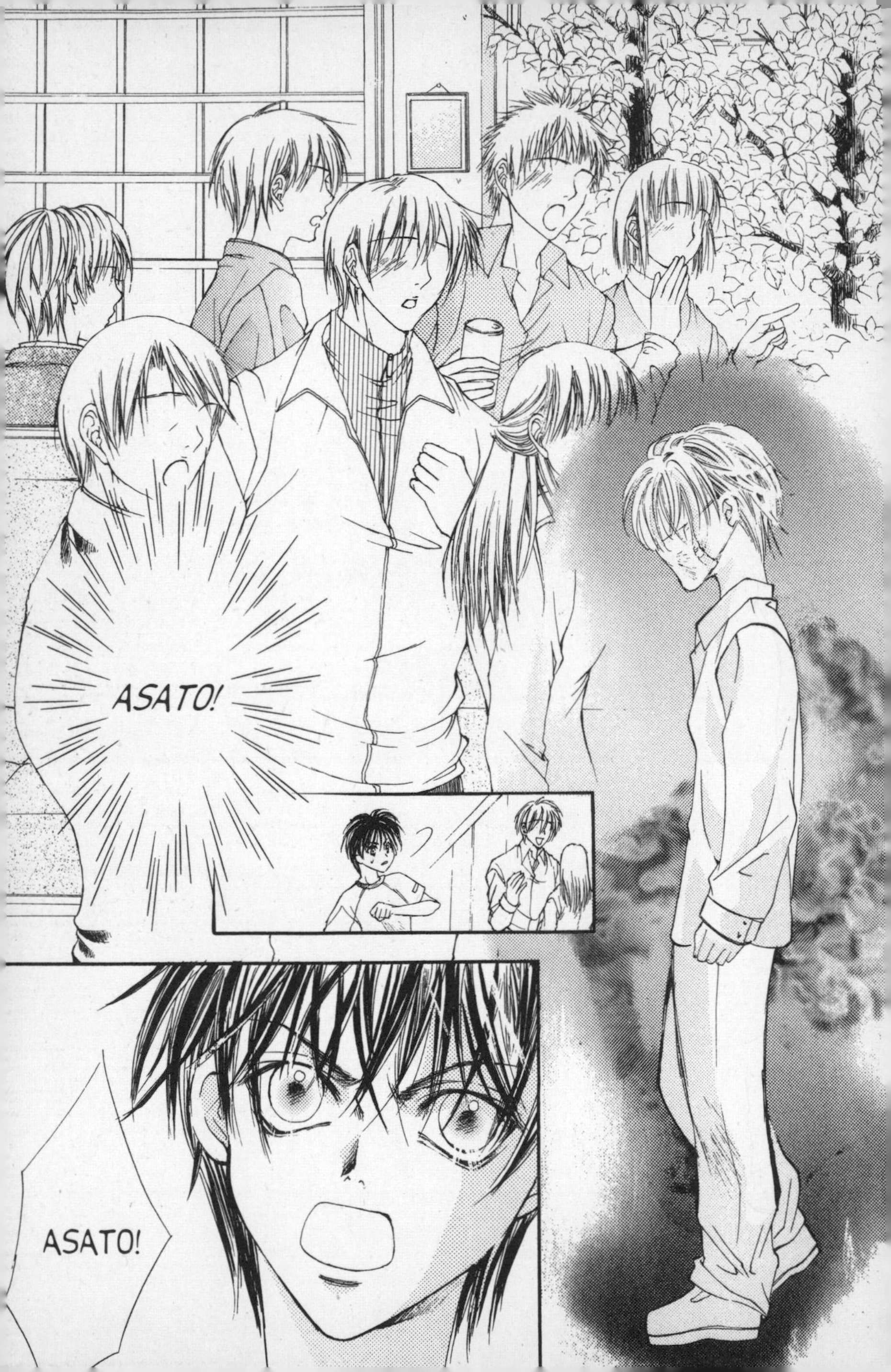
ASATO!
ASATO!

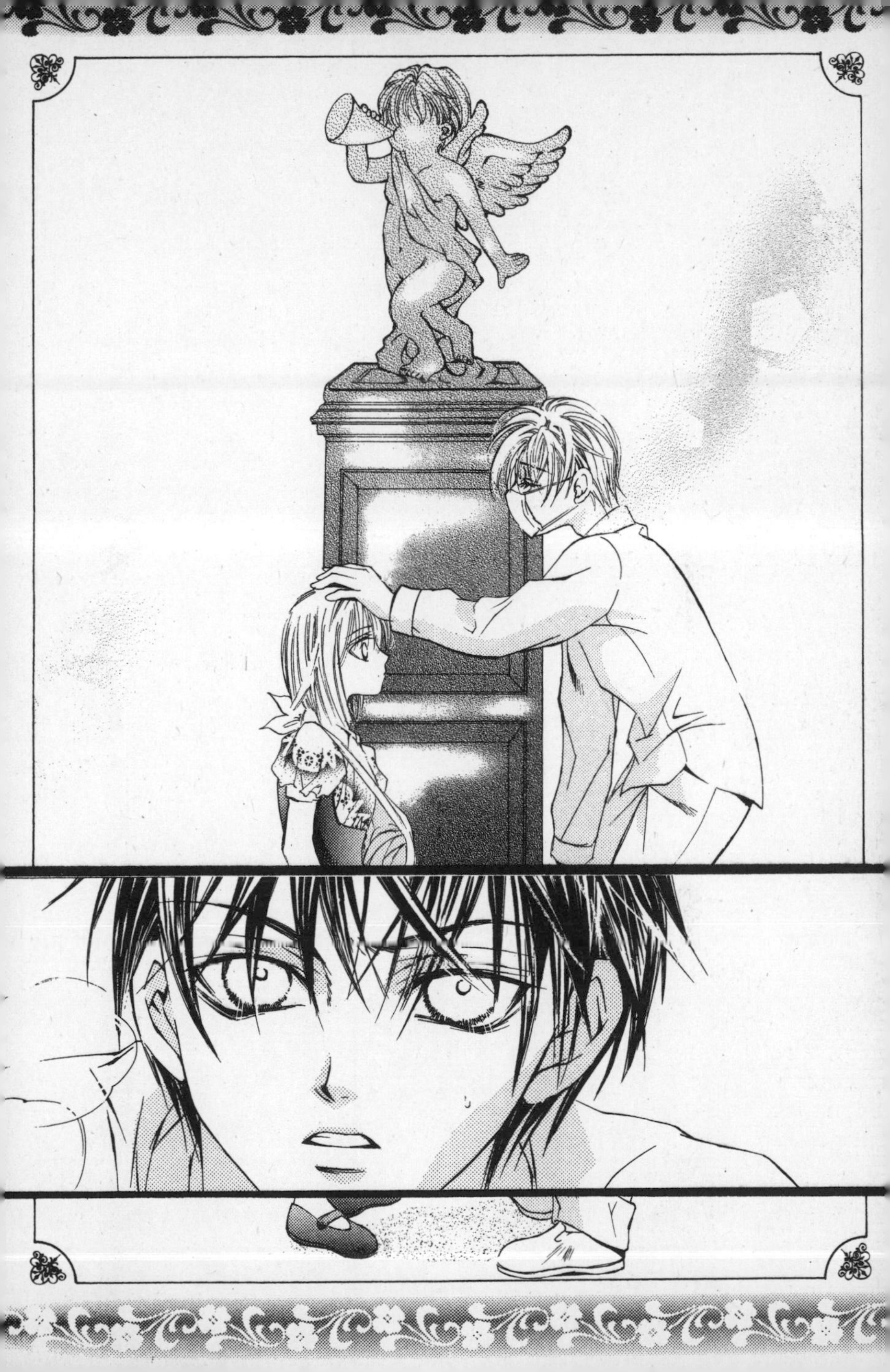

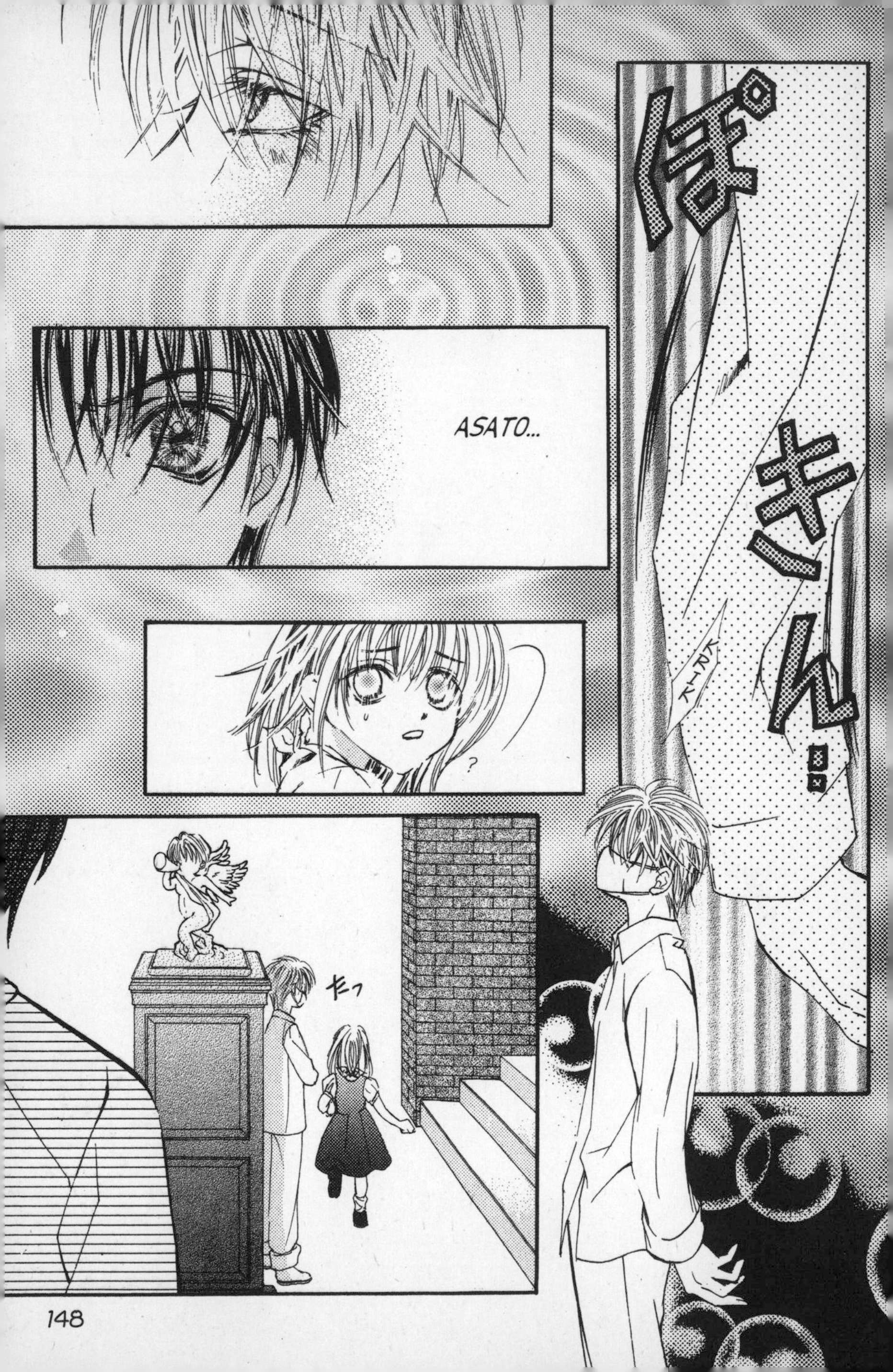
ぽきん!!
KRIK
ASATO...
?
たっ

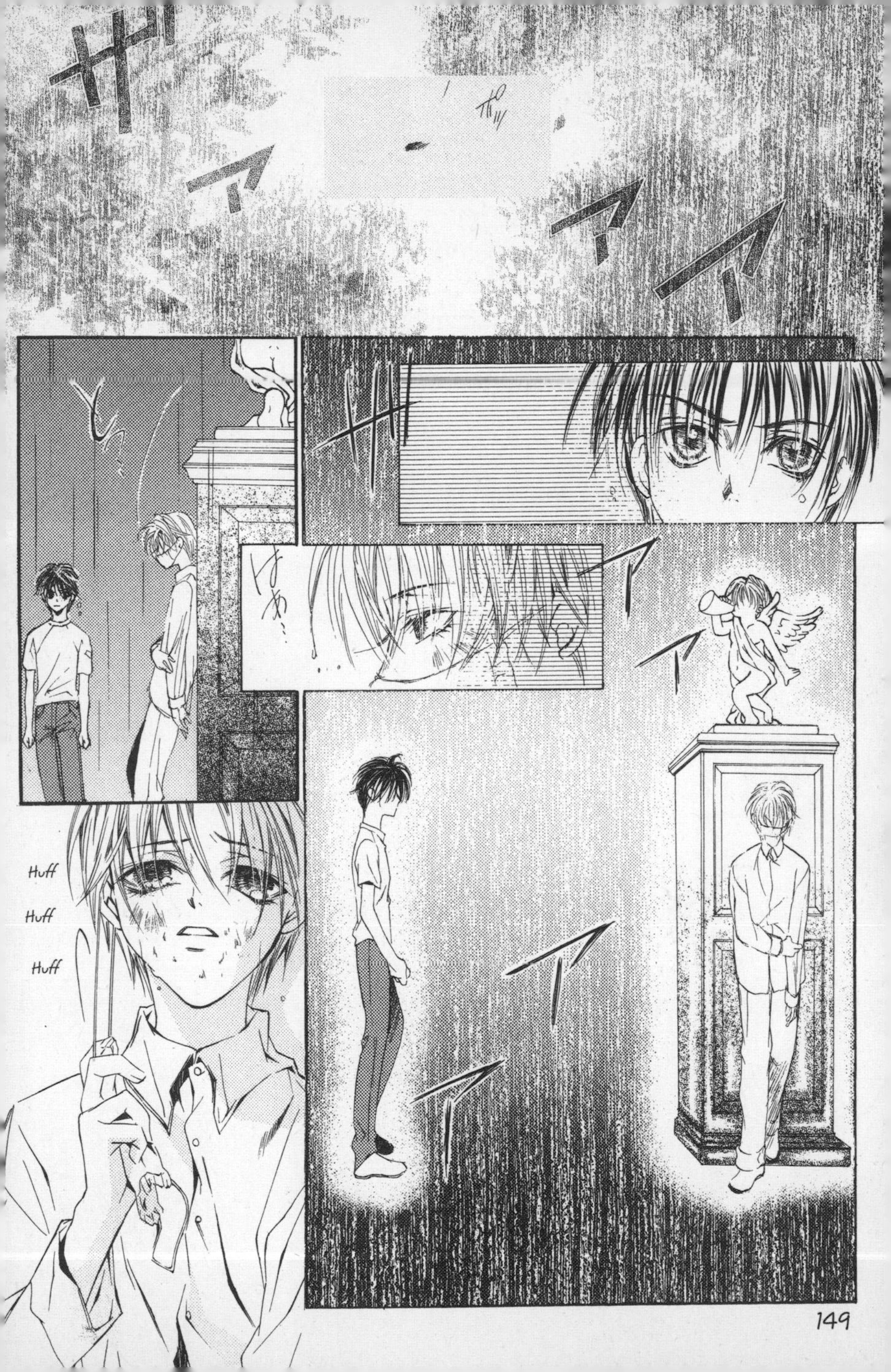
はぁ…
Huff
Huff
Huff

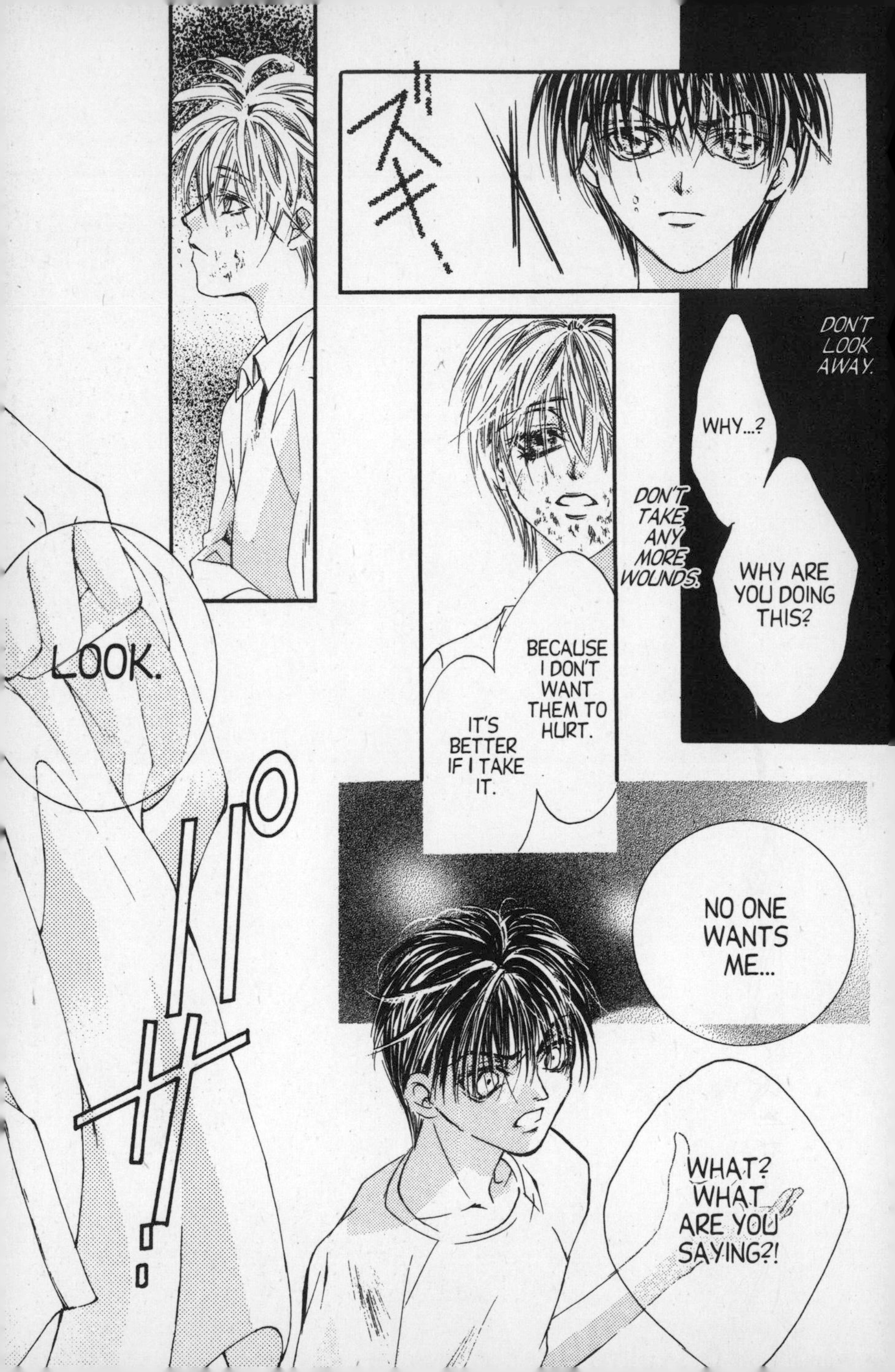

DON'T LOOK AWAY.
WHY...?
WHY ARE YOU DOING THIS?
DON'T TAKE ANY MORE WOUNDS.
BECAUSE I DON'T WANT THEM TO HURT.
IT'S BETTER IF I TAKE IT.
NO ONE WANTS ME...
WHAT? WHAT ARE YOU SAYING?!
LOOK.

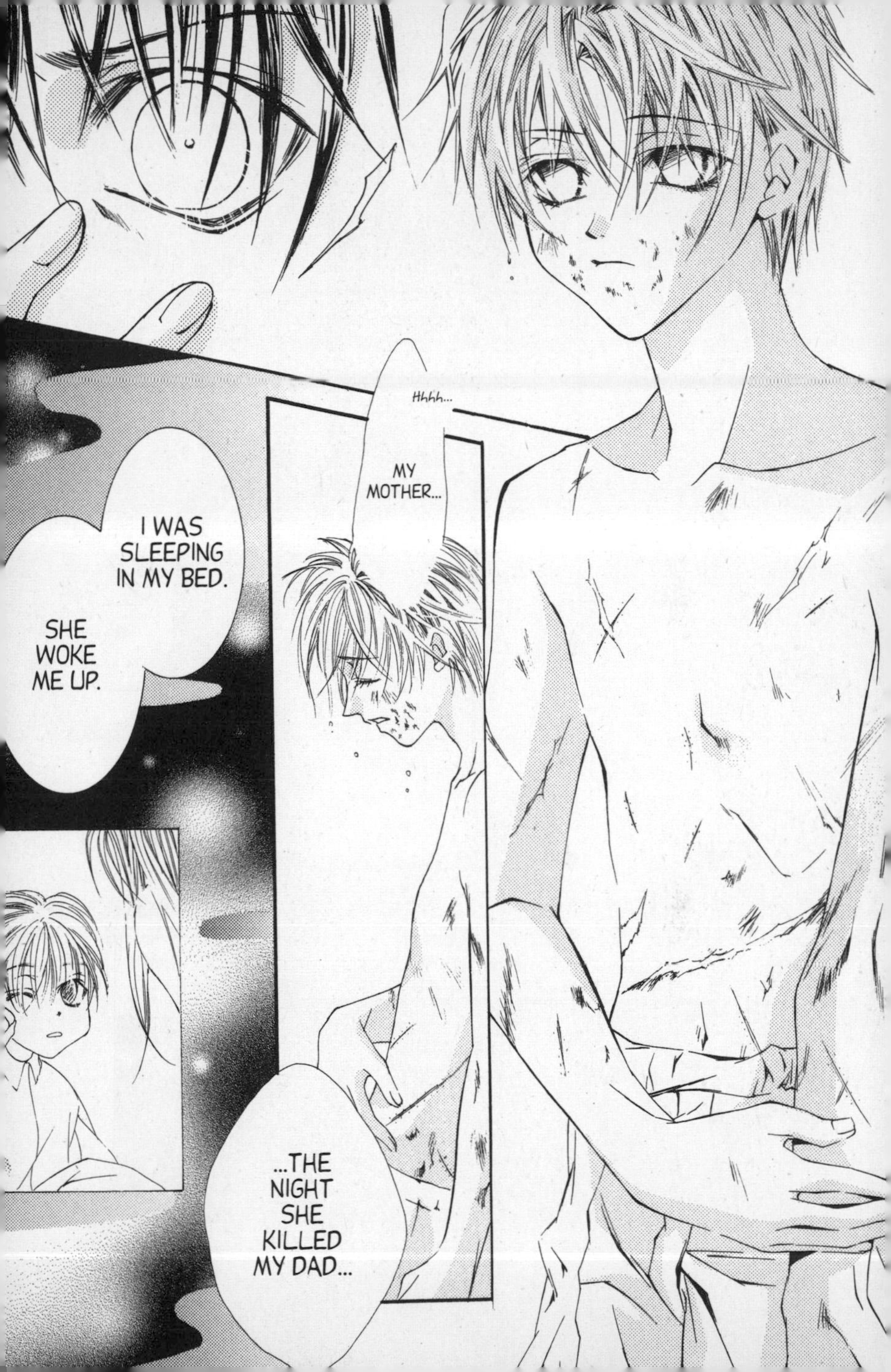
Hhhh...
MY MOTHER...
...THE NIGHT SHE KILLED MY DAD...
I WAS SLEEPING IN MY BED.
SHE WOKE ME UP.

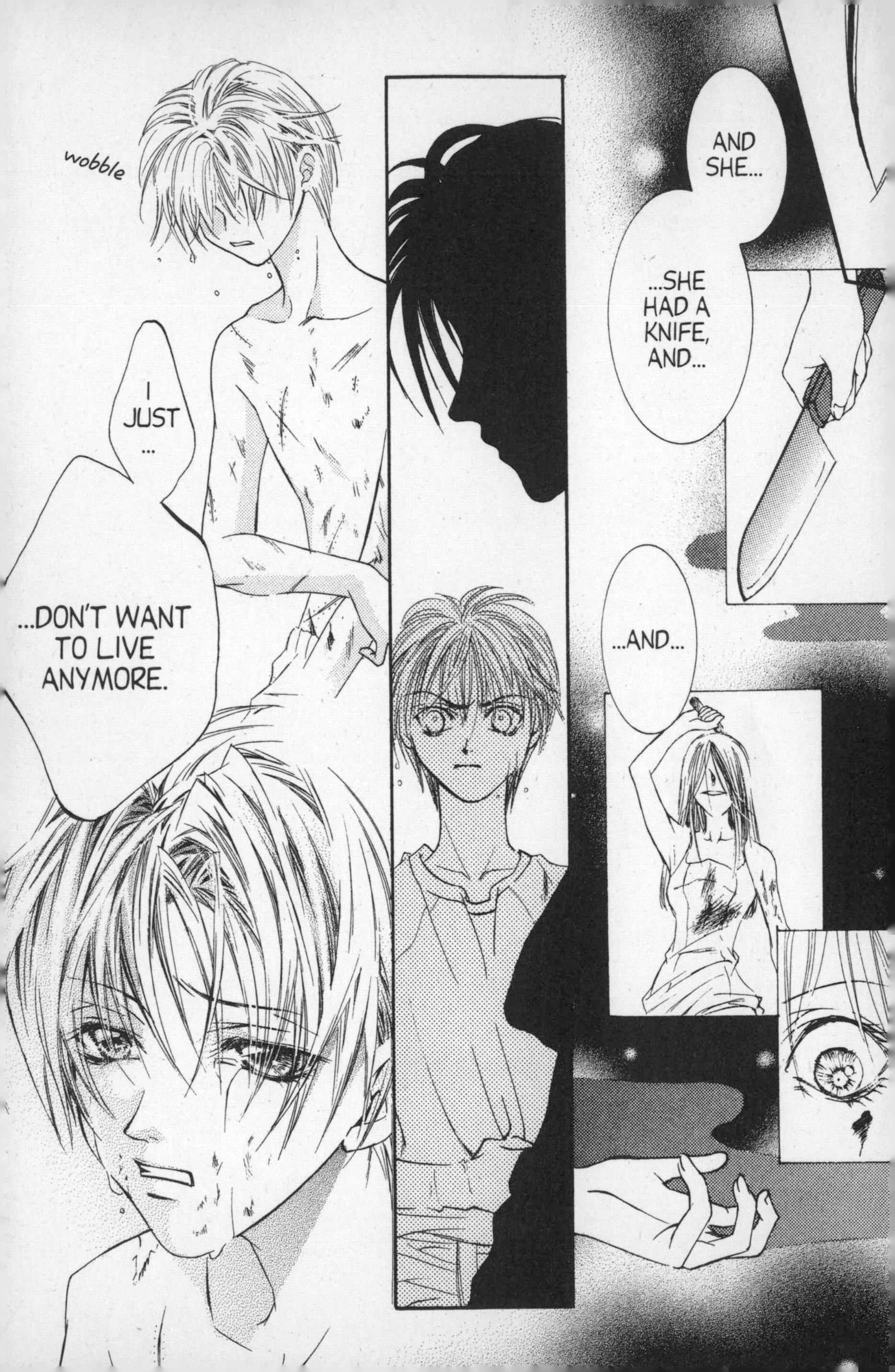
AND SHE...
...SHE HAD A KNIFE, AND...
...AND...
wobble
I JUST ...
...DON'T WANT TO LIVE ANYMORE.

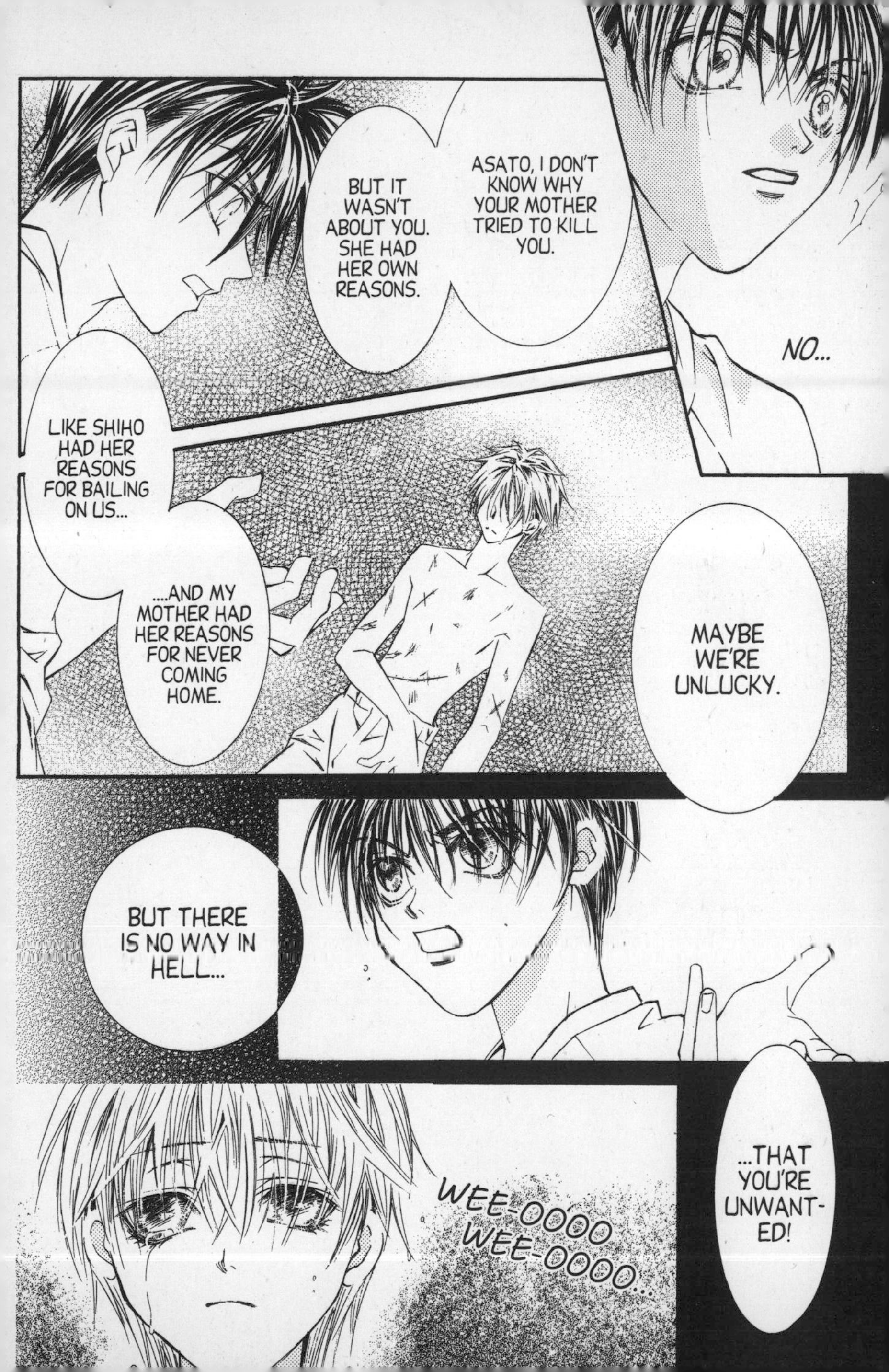
ASATO, I DON'T KNOW WHY YOUR MOTHER TRIED TO KILL YOU.
BUT IT WASN'T ABOUT YOU. SHE HAD HER OWN REASONS.
NO...
MAYBE WE'RE UNLUCKY.
LIKE SHIHO HAD HER REASONS FOR BAILING ON US...
....AND MY MOTHER HAD HER REASONS FOR NEVER COMING HOME.
BUT THERE IS NO WAY IN HELL...
...THAT YOU'RE UNWANT-ED!
WEE-OOOO WEE-OOOO...

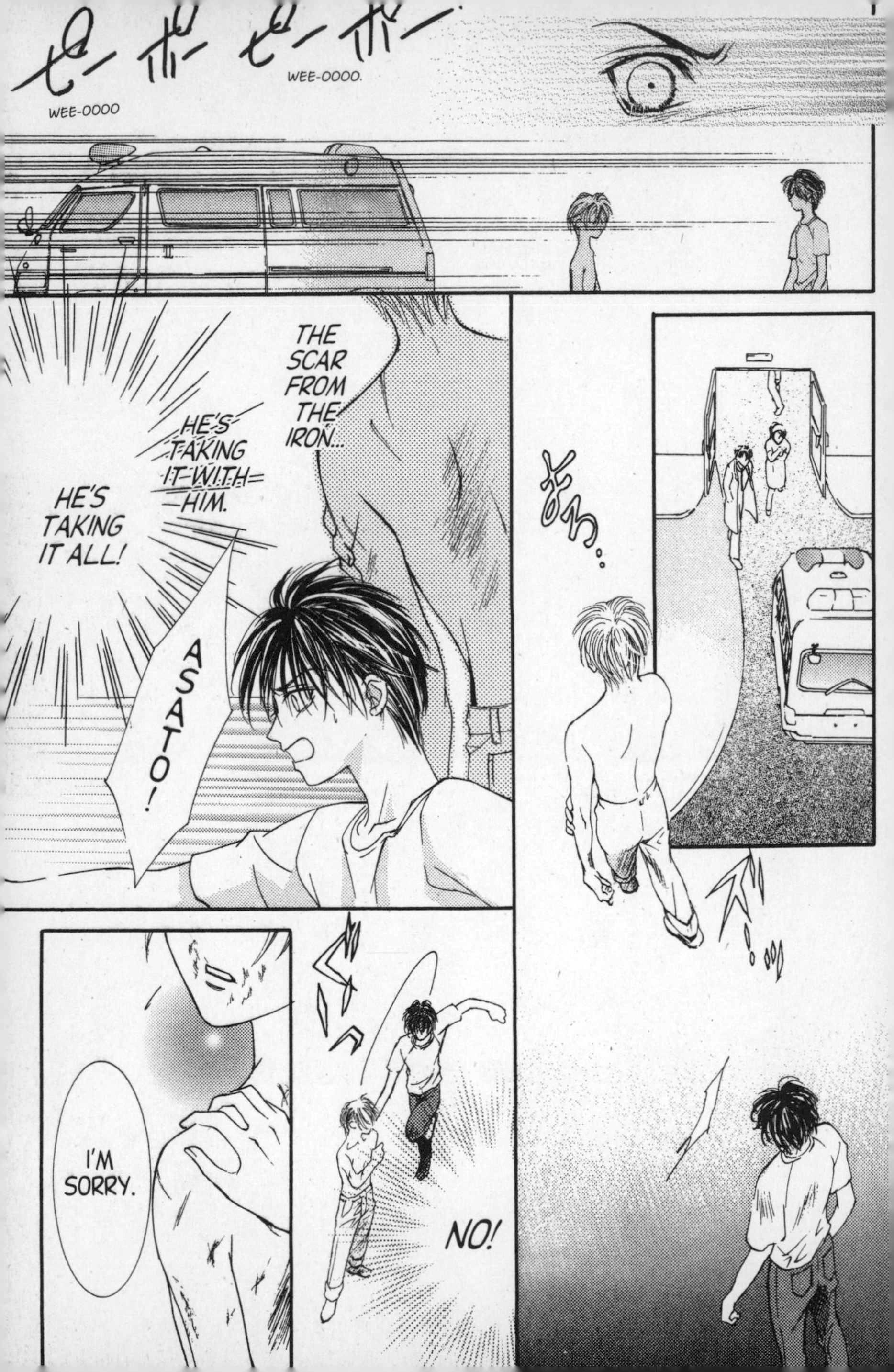
ピーポーピーポー
WEE-OOOO
WEE-OOOO.
THE SCAR FROM THE IRON...
HE'S TAKING IT WITH HIM.
HE'S TAKING IT ALL!
ASATO!
NO!
I'M SORRY.

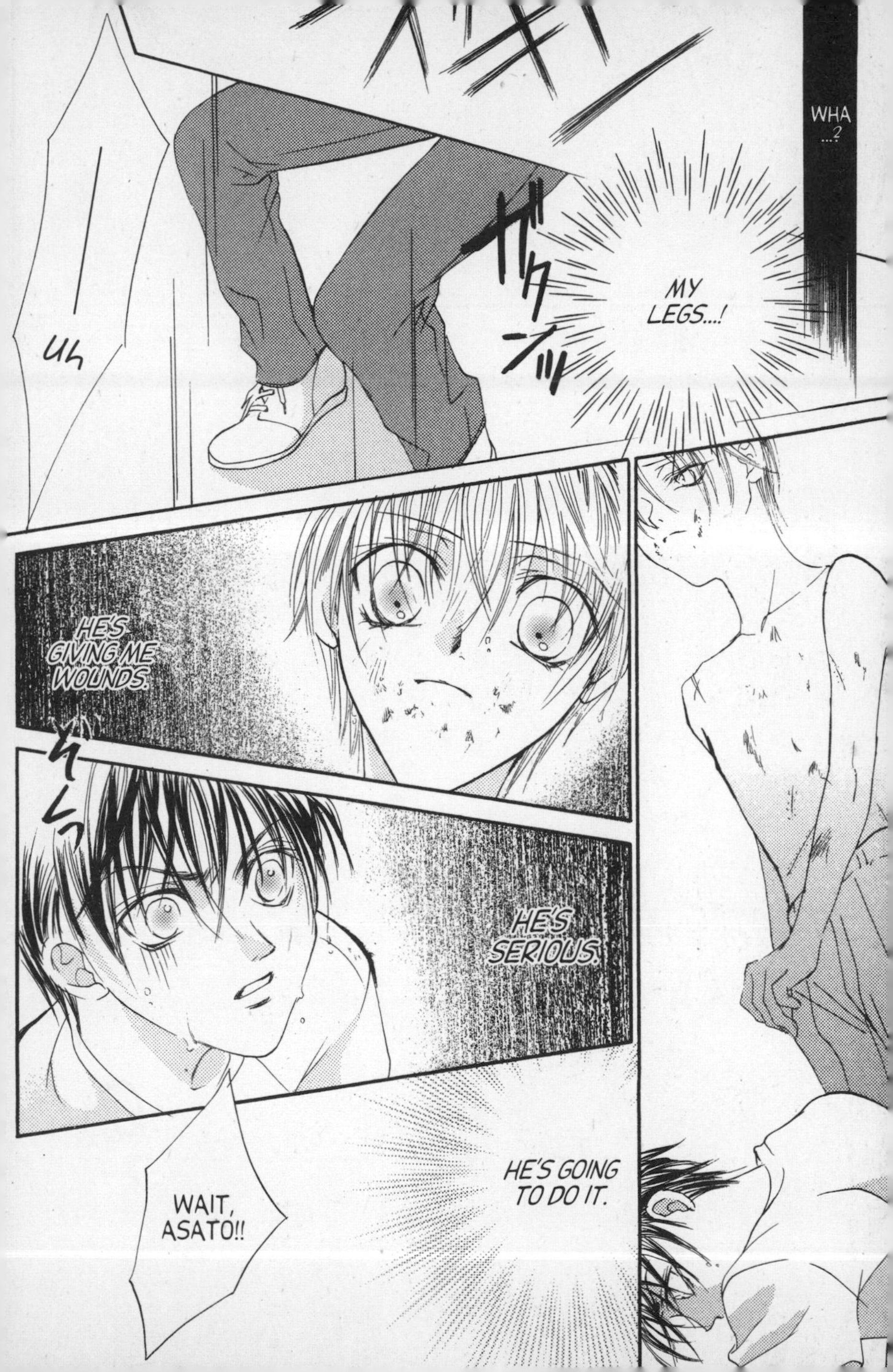
WHA ...?
ガクンッ
MY LEGS...!
uh
HE'S GIVING ME WOUNDS.
HE'S SERIOUS.
HE'S GOING TO DO IT.
WAIT, ASATO!!

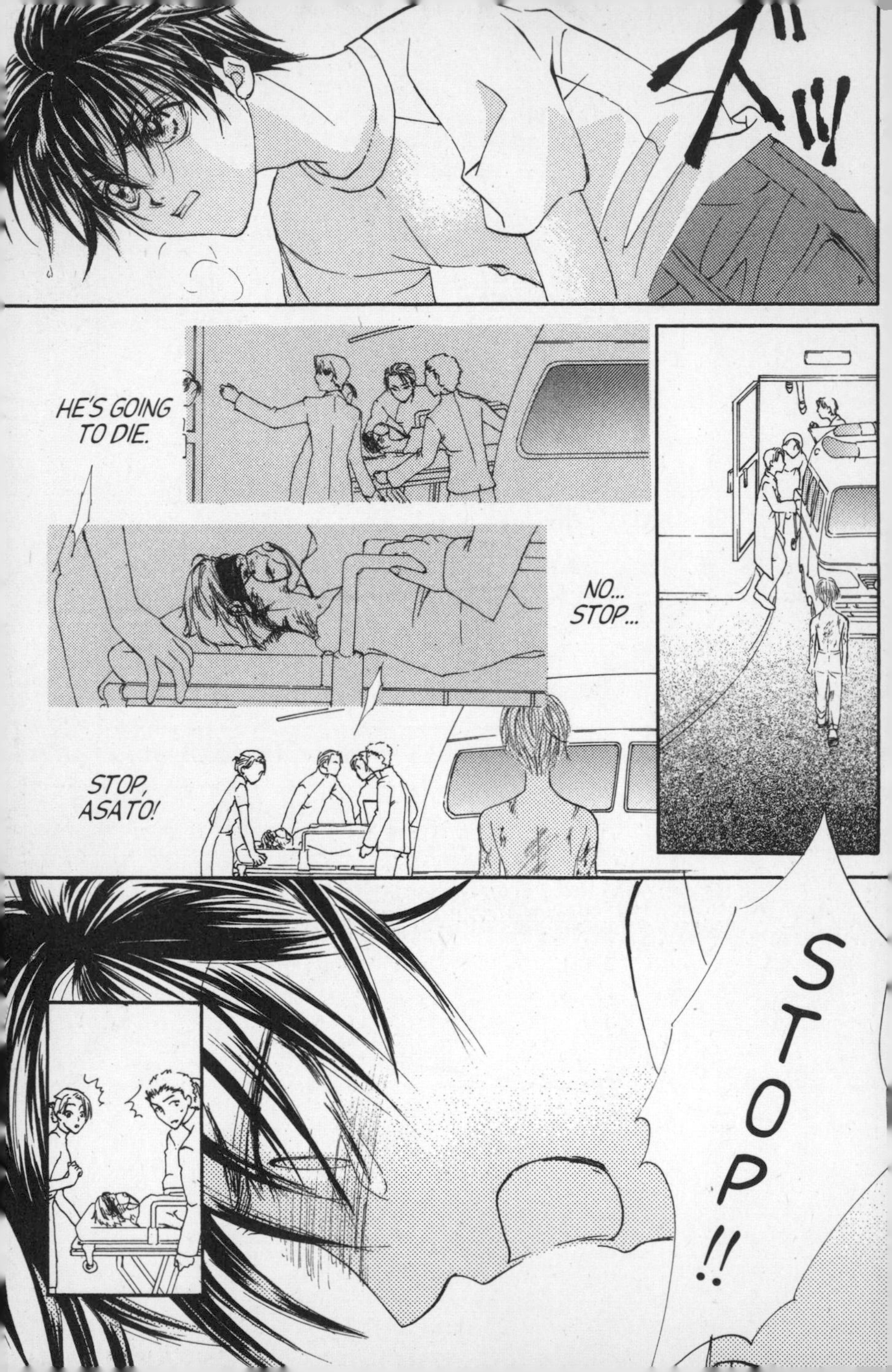
HE'S GOING TO DIE.
NO... STOP...
STOP, ASATO!
STOP!!

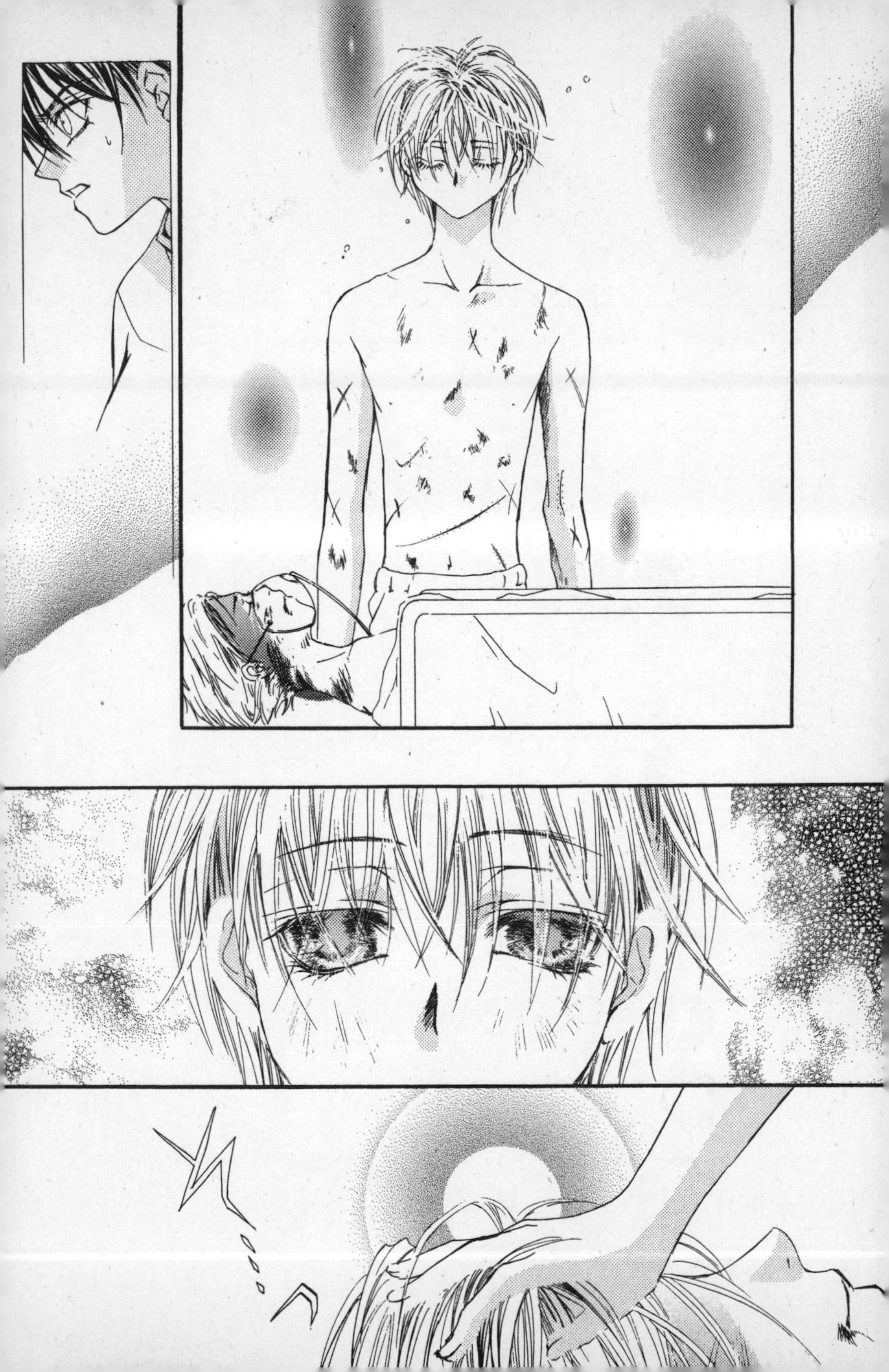

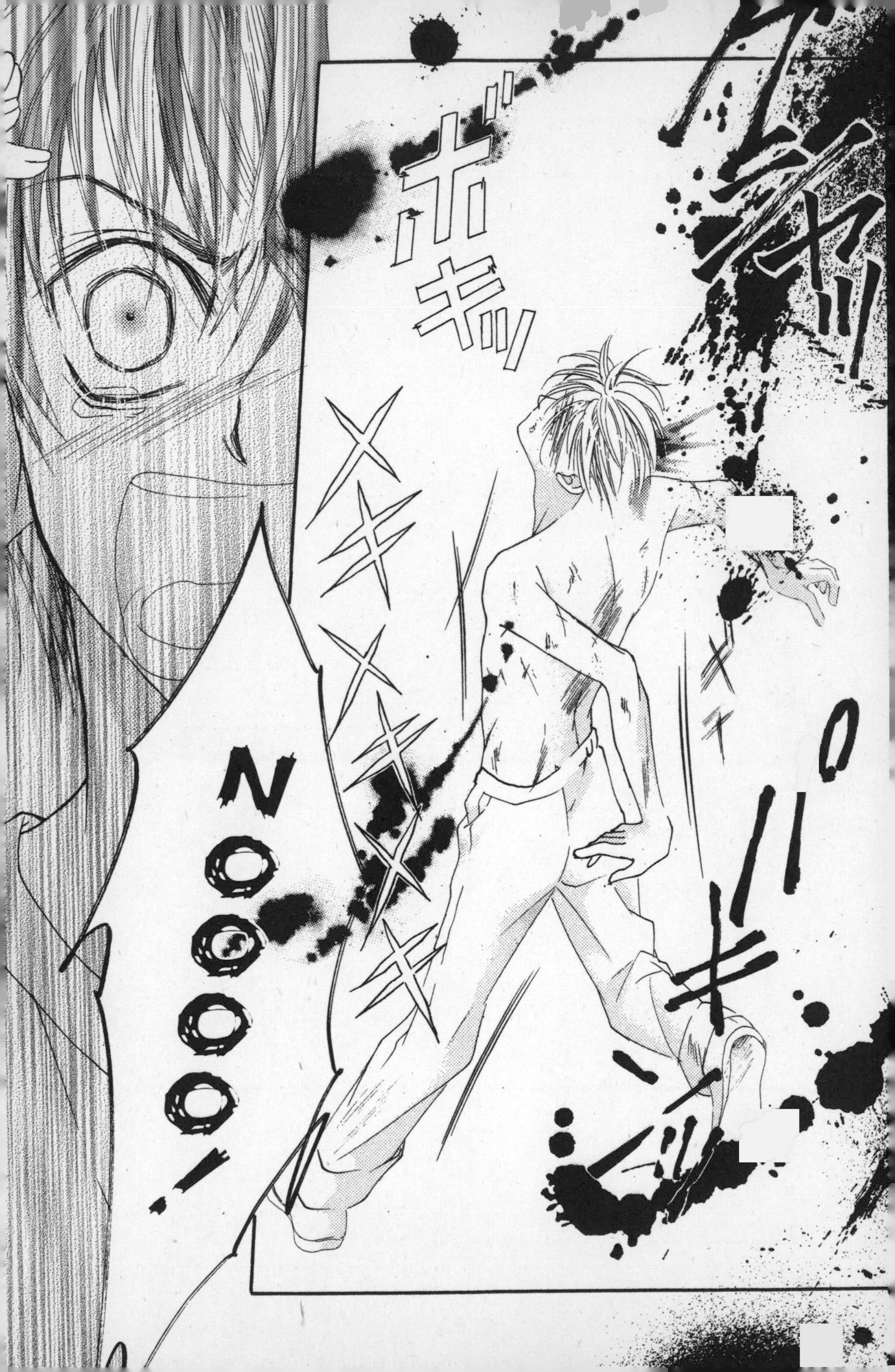

ボキッ
NOOOOO!

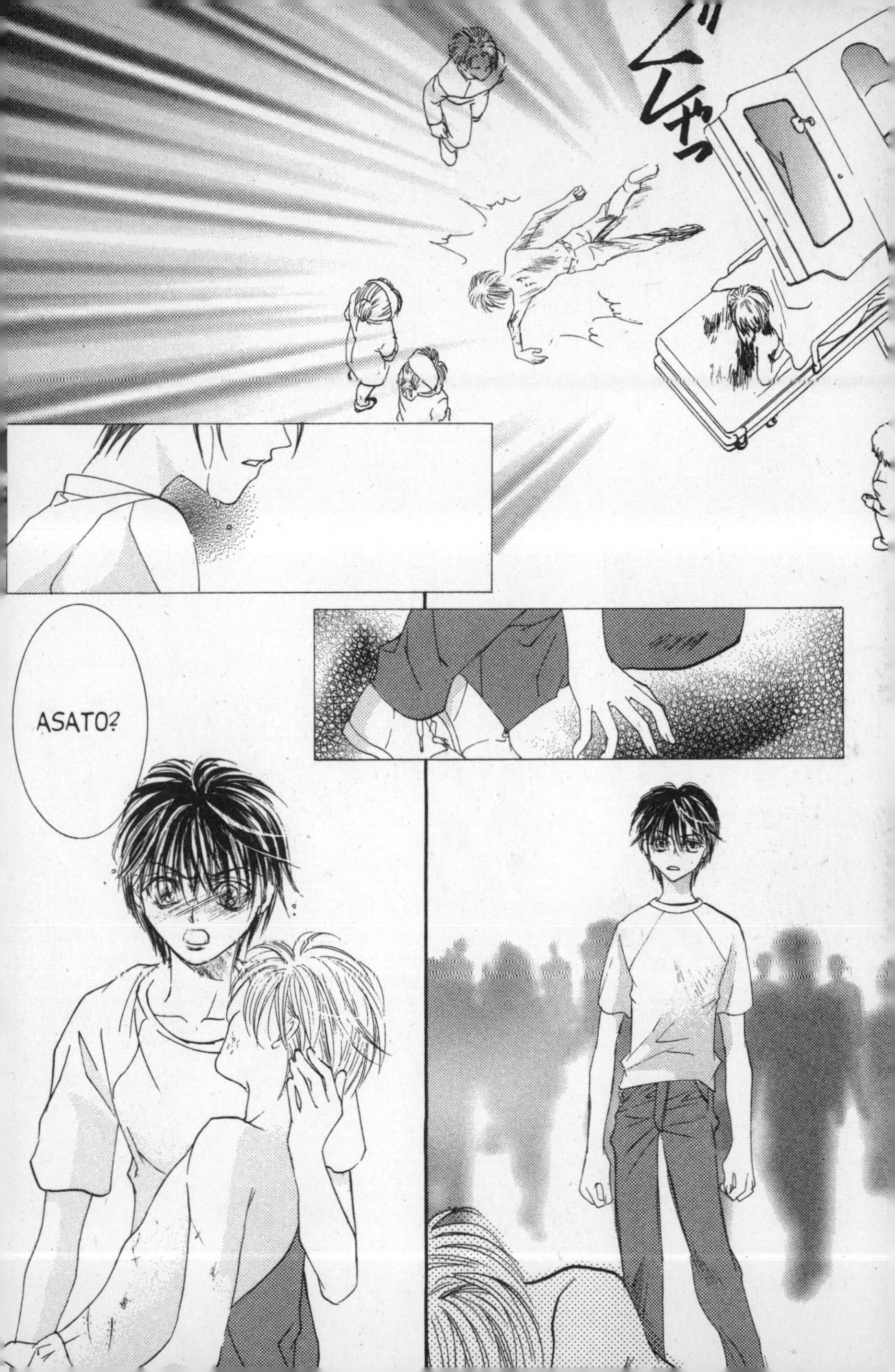
ASATO?

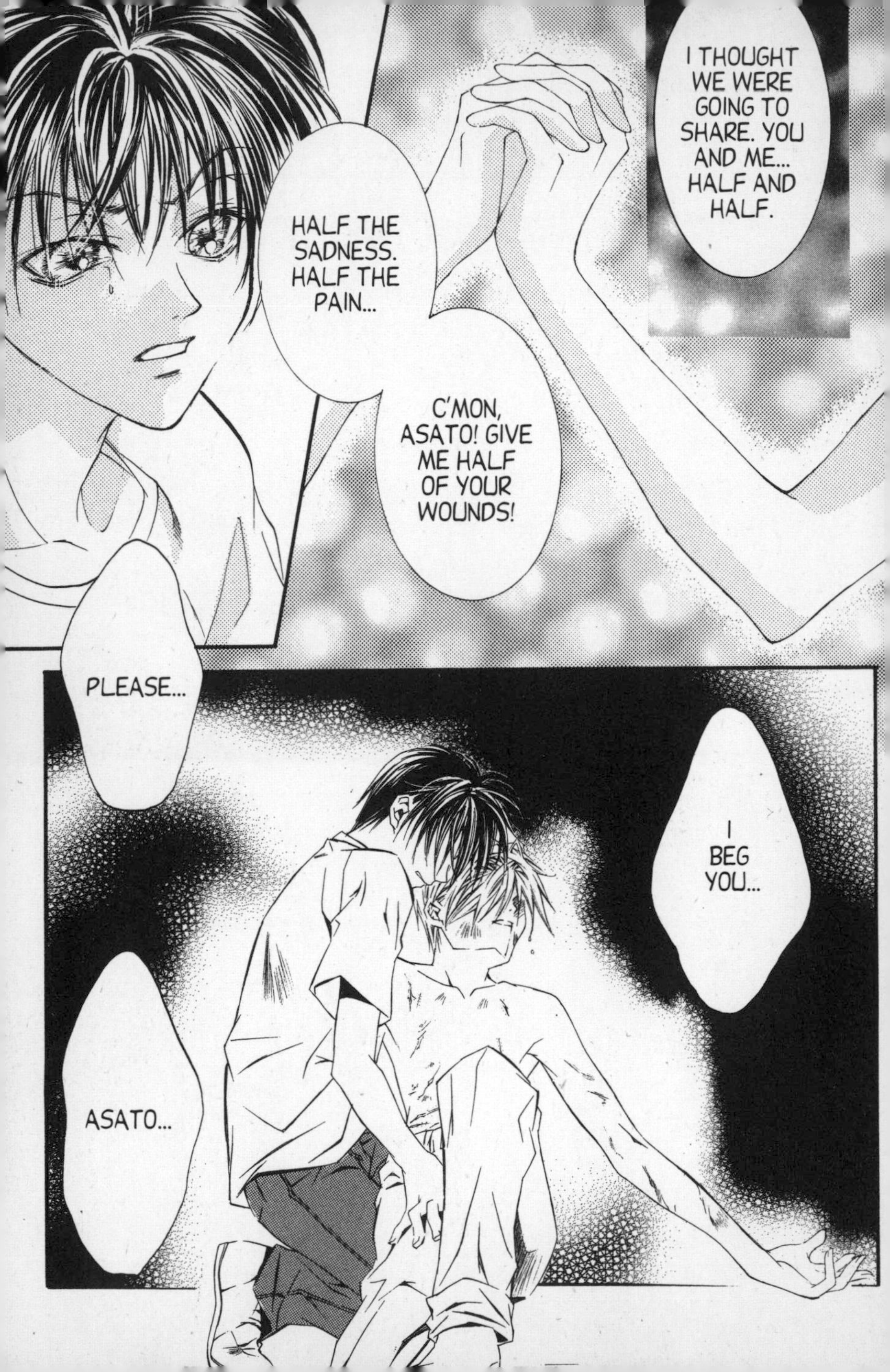
I THOUGHT WE WERE GOING TO SHARE. YOU AND ME... HALF AND HALF.
HALF THE SADNESS. HALF THE PAIN...
C'MON, ASATO! GIVE ME HALF OF YOUR WOUNDS!
PLEASE...
I BEG YOU...
ASATO...

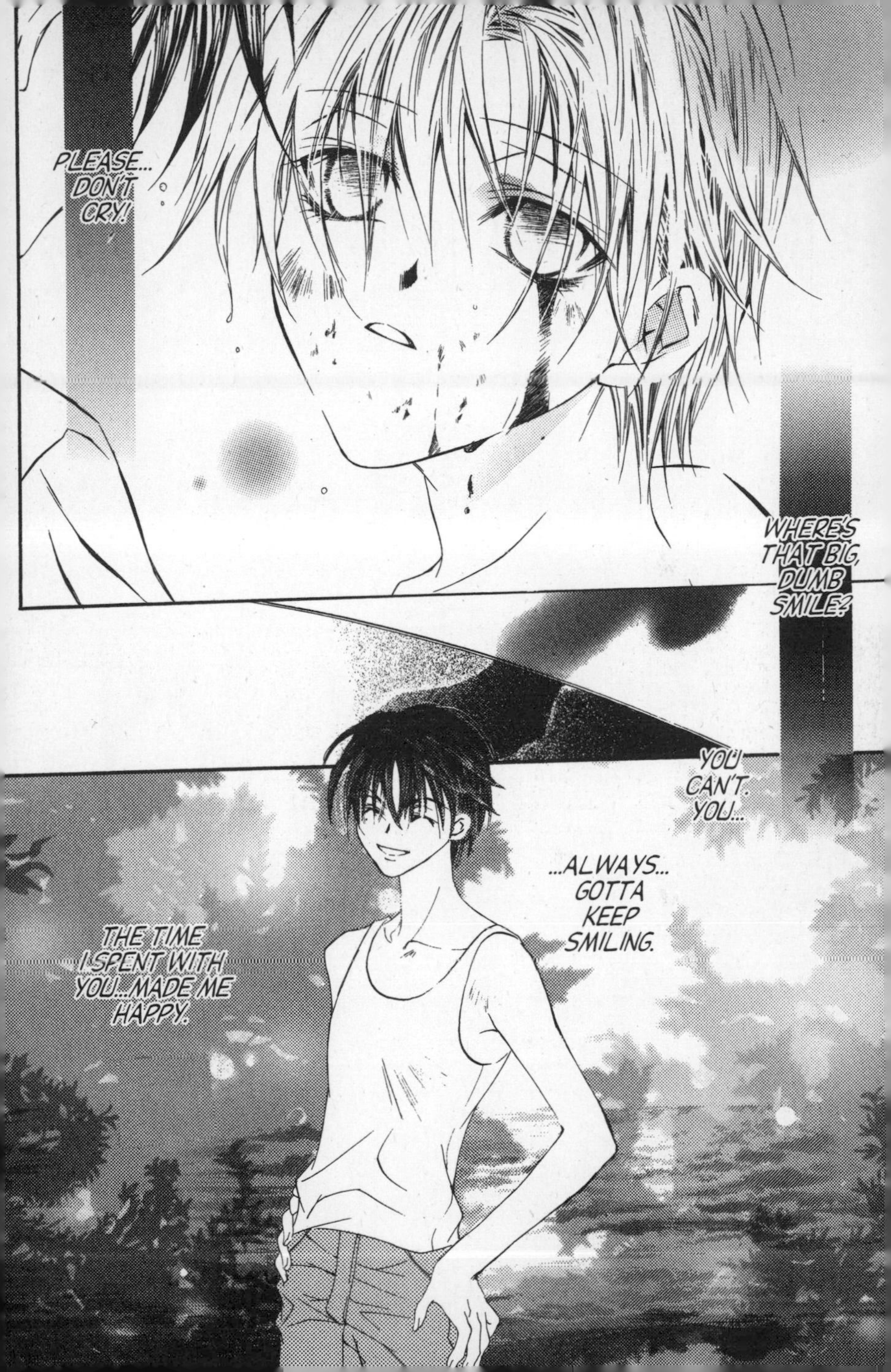
PLEASE... DON'T CRY!
WHERE'S THAT BIG, DUMB SMILE?
YOU CAN'T. YOU...
...ALWAYS... GOTTA KEEP SMILING.
THE TIME I SPENT WITH YOU...MADE ME HAPPY.

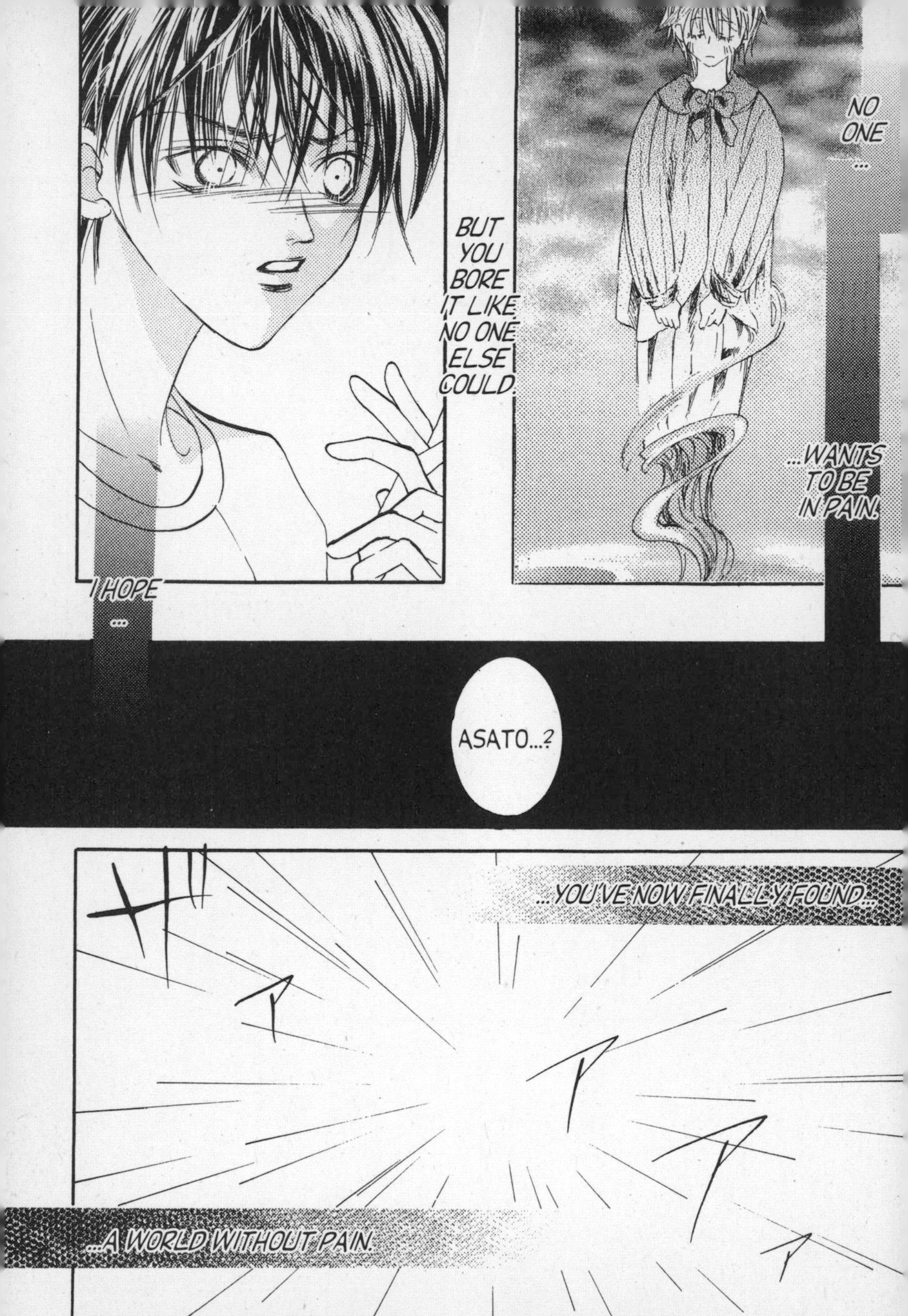
NO ONE ...
...WANTS TO BE IN PAIN.
BUT YOU BORE IT LIKE NO ONE ELSE COULD.
I HOPE ...
ASATO...?
...YOU'VE NOW FINALLY FOUND...
...A WORLD WITHOUT PAIN.

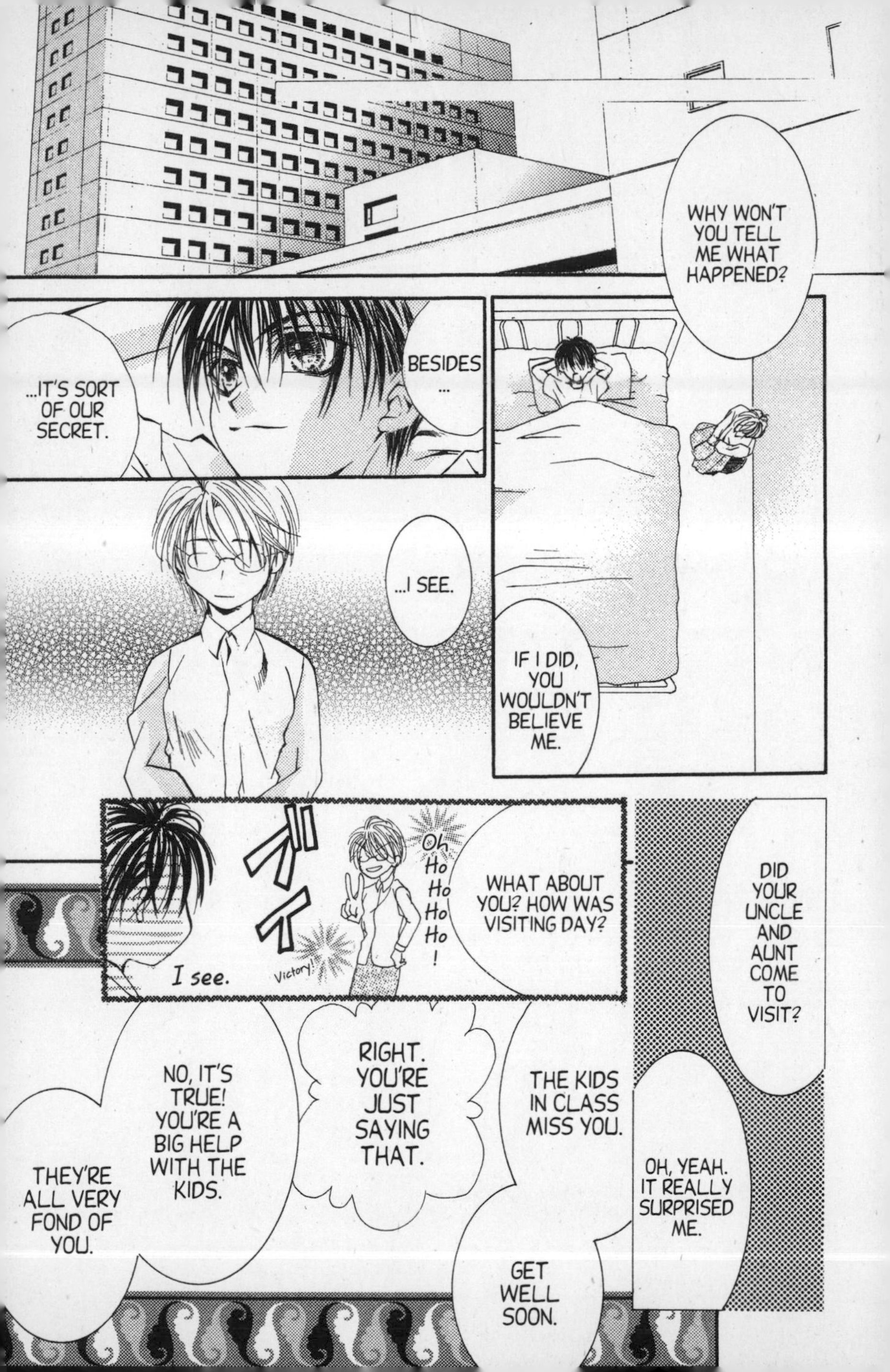
WHY WON'T YOU TELL ME WHAT HAPPENED?
IF I DID, YOU WOULDN'T BELIEVE ME.
BESIDES ...
...IT'S SORT OF OUR SECRET.
...I SEE.
DID YOUR UNCLE AND AUNT COME TO VISIT?
OH, YEAH. IT REALLY SURPRISED ME.
WHAT ABOUT YOU? HOW WAS VISITING DAY?
Oh Ho Ho Ho Ho!
Victory!
I see.
THE KIDS IN CLASS MISS YOU.
GET WELL SOON.
RIGHT. YOU'RE JUST SAYING THAT.
NO, IT'S TRUE! YOU'RE A BIG HELP WITH THE KIDS.
THEY'RE ALL VERY FOND OF YOU.

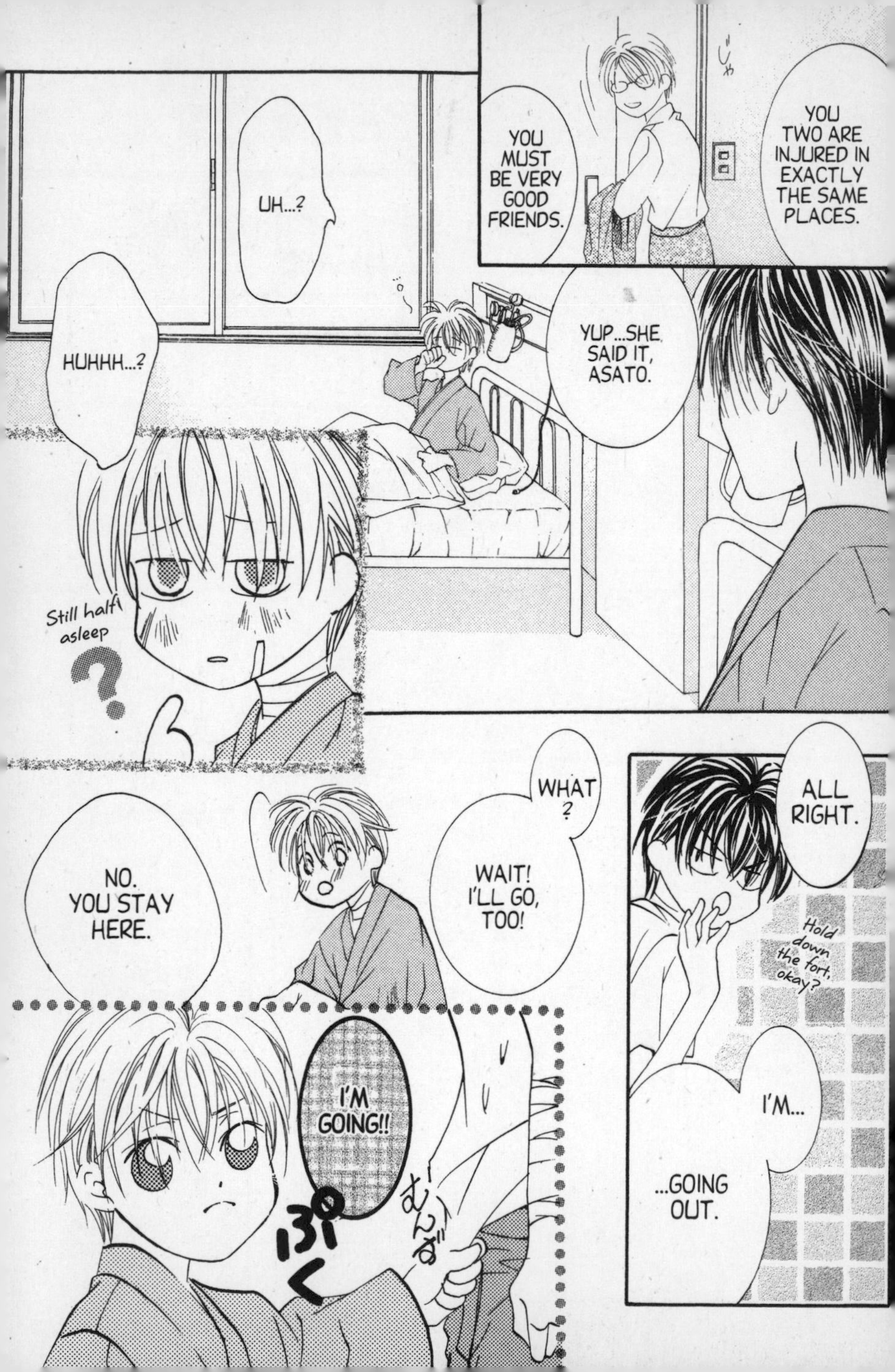
YOU TWO ARE INJURED IN EXACTLY THE SAME PLACES.
YOU MUST BE VERY GOOD FRIENDS.
YUP...SHE SAID IT, ASATO.
UH...?
HUHHH...?
Still half asleep
ALL RIGHT.
Hold down the fort, okay?
I'M...
...GOING OUT.
WHAT?
WAIT! I'LL GO, TOO!
NO. YOU STAY HERE.
I'M GOING!!
むんず
ぷく

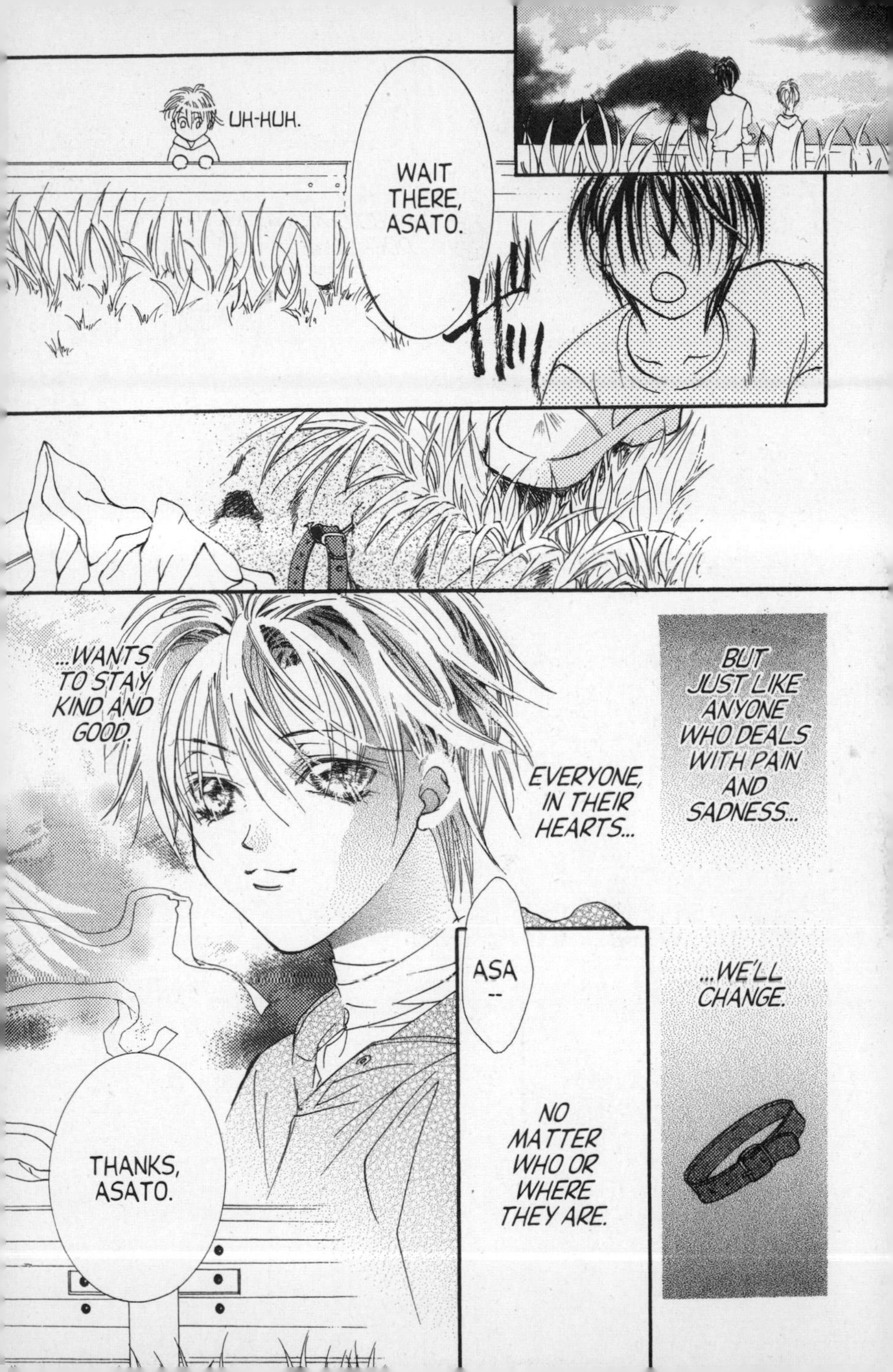
WAIT THERE, ASATO.
UH-HUH.
BUT JUST LIKE ANYONE WHO DEALS WITH PAIN AND SADNESS...
...WE'LL CHANGE.
NO MATTER WHO OR WHERE THEY ARE.
EVERYONE, IN THEIR HEARTS...
...WANTS TO STAY KIND AND GOOD.
ASA --
THANKS, ASATO.

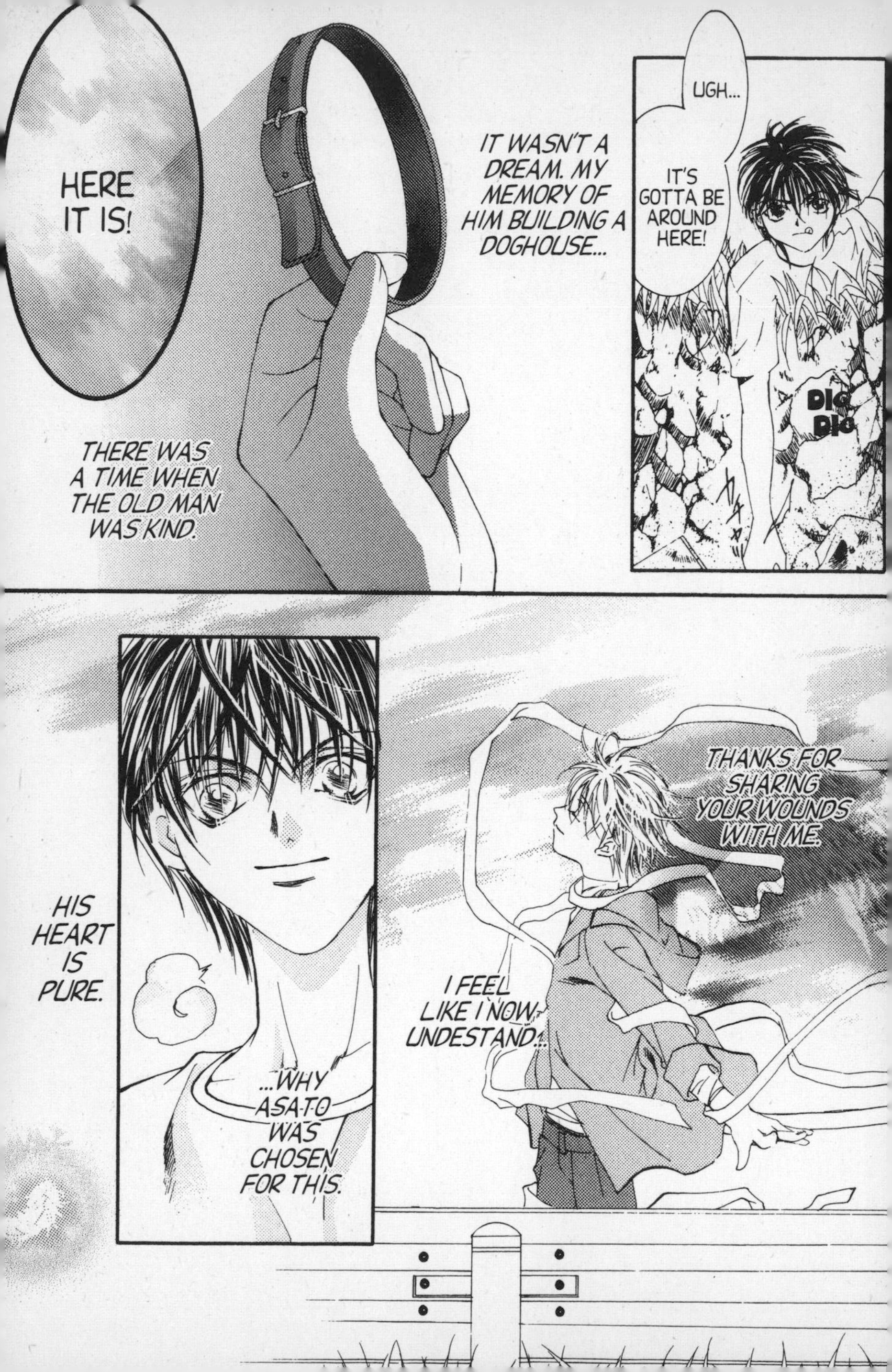
UGH...
IT'S GOTTA BE AROUND HERE!
DIG DIG
IT WASN'T A DREAM. MY MEMORY OF HIM BUILDING A DOGHOUSE...
HERE IT IS!
THERE WAS A TIME WHEN THE OLD MAN WAS KIND.
THANKS FOR SHARING YOUR WOUNDS WITH ME.
I FEEL LIKE I NOW UNDESTAND...
HIS HEART IS PURE.
...WHY ASATO WAS CHOSEN FOR THIS.

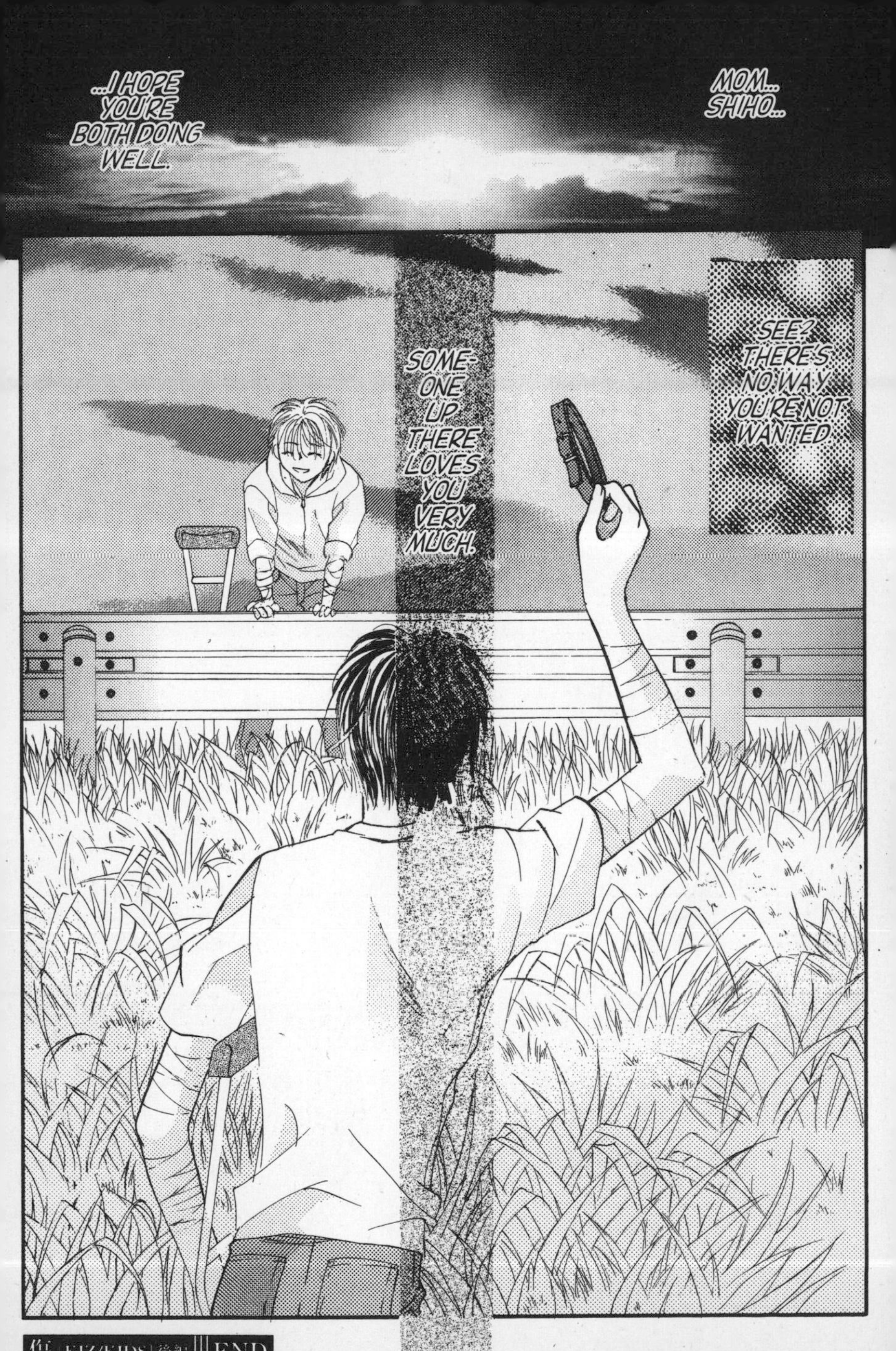
MOM... SHIHO...
...I HOPE YOU'RE BOTH DOING WELL.
SEE? THERE'S NO WAY YOU'RE NOT WANTED
SOME-ONE UP THERE LOVES YOU VERY MUCH.

傷 KIZ/KIDS 後編 END

Postscript
I'll be discussing the manga, so please read it first!
I'M TSUZUKI, THE MAIN ARTIST.
THANKS FOR BUYING THIS BOOK.
BEFORE I START ...
Heh Heh...
I'D LIKE TO THANK OTSUICHI-SENSEI.
And to apologize, for basically everything.
Heh Heh...
I learned a lot from this experience.
Kneel
IT WAS MY FIRST WORK WITH AN ORIGINAL AUTHOR...
NOT TO MENTION MY FAVORITE WRITER!
Before I received this assignment, I had already gotten my own book signed!
Just a big ol' fangirl
So embarrassed!
FOR SOME, THAT'S ENOUGH LUCK TO LAST A LIFETIME.
ANYWAY. RATHER THAN BEMOAN WHAT I COULD HAVE DONE BETTER, I'LL GIVE YOU A BEHIND-THE-SCENES ANECDOTE!
Runs Away
PRIOR TO WORKING ON "CALLING YOU," I HAD ONLY BEEN TO HANEDA AIRPORT TWICE.
EVEN AFTER I FINISHED THE ROUGH MANGA LAYOUT, I STILL HAD NO IDEA WHAT IT LOOKED LIKE.
PLEASE, LET ME GO...JUST THIS ONCE!
Eh, screw it, I'm going.
WHAT?!
EDITOR
Seconds to dead-line!

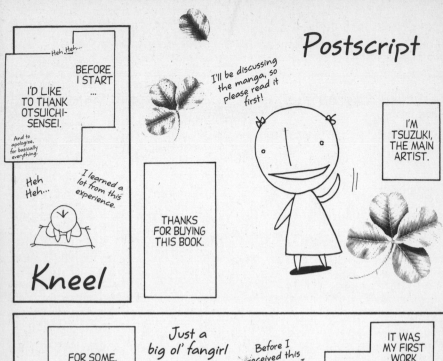

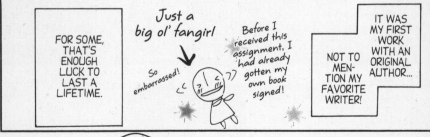

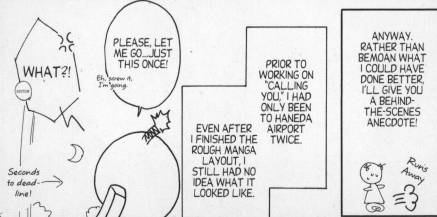

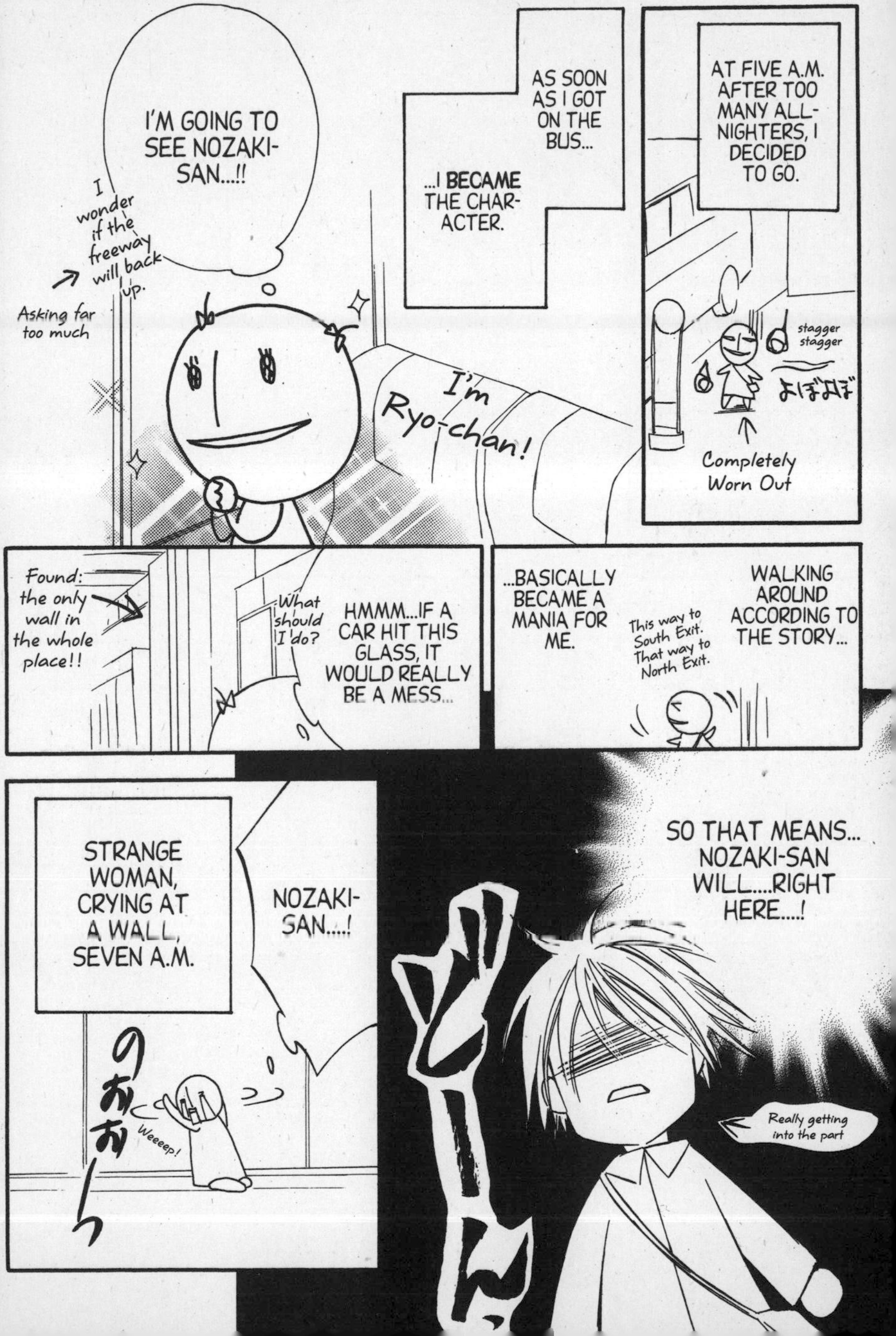
AT FIVE A.M. AFTER TOO MANY ALL-NIGHTERS, I DECIDED TO GO.
stagger stagger
よぼよぼ
Completely Worn Out
AS SOON AS I GOT ON THE BUS...
...I BECAME THE CHARACTER.
I'M GOING TO SEE NOZAKI-SAN...!!
I wonder if the freeway will back up.
Asking far too much
I'm Ryo-chan!
WALKING AROUND ACCORDING TO THE STORY...
...BASICALLY BECAME A MANIA FOR ME.
This way to South Exit. That way to North Exit.
HMMM...IF A CAR HIT THIS GLASS, IT WOULD REALLY BE A MESS...
What should I do?
Found: the only wall in the whole place!!
SO THAT MEANS... NOZAKI-SAN WILL....RIGHT HERE....!
Really getting into the part
NOZAKI-SAN....!
STRANGE WOMAN, CRYING AT A WALL, SEVEN A.M.
のおおーっ
Weeeep!

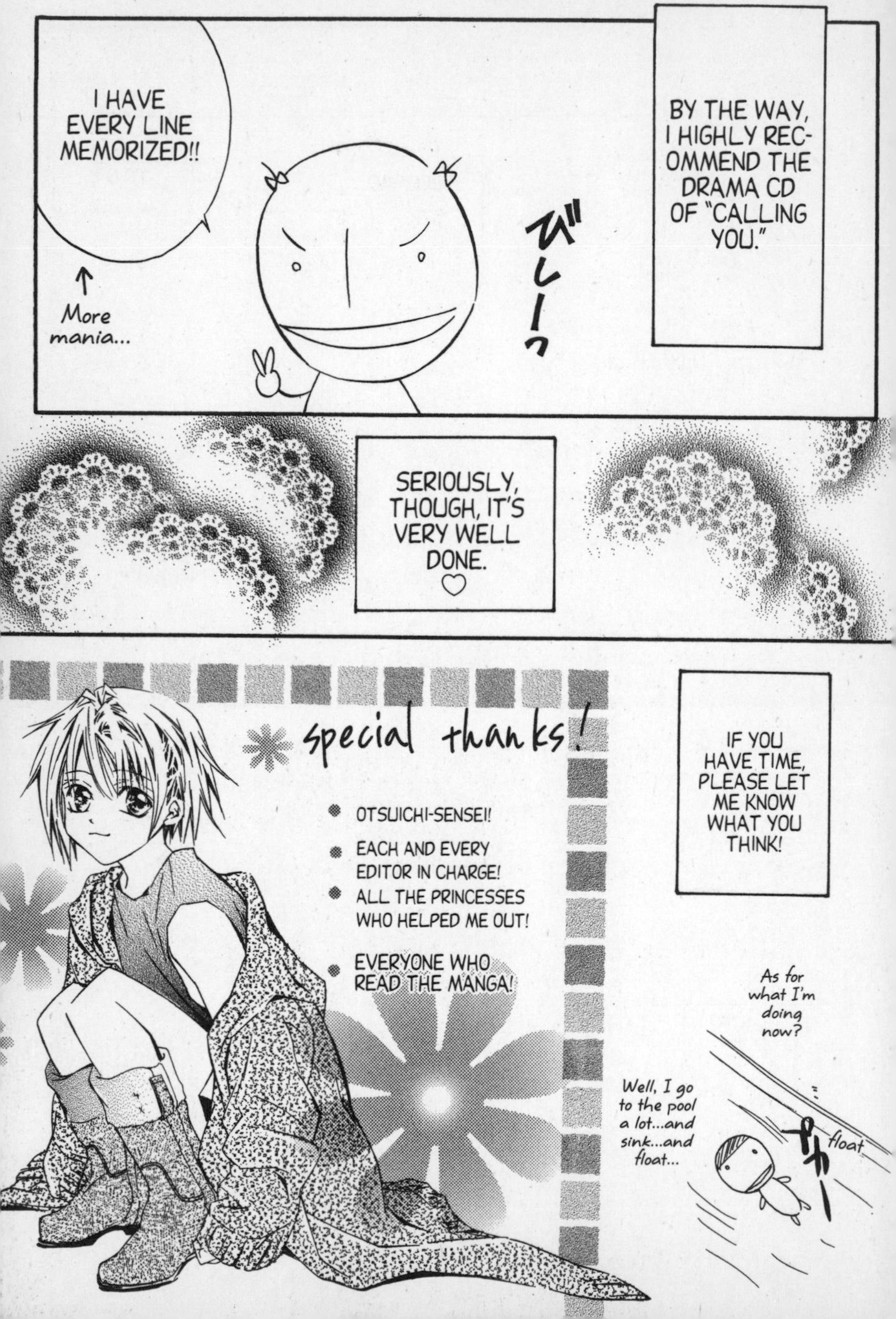
BY THE WAY, I HIGHLY REC-OMMEND THE DRAMA CD OF "CALLING YOU."
びしーっ
I HAVE EVERY LINE MEMORIZED!!
More mania...
SERIOUSLY, THOUGH, IT'S VERY WELL DONE. ♡
IF YOU HAVE TIME, PLEASE LET ME KNOW WHAT YOU THINK!
As for what I'm doing now?
Well, I go to the pool a lot...and sink...and float...
float
special thanks!
OTSUICHI-SENSEI!
EACH AND EVERY EDITOR IN CHARGE!
ALL THE PRINCESSES WHO HELPED ME OUT!
EVERYONE WHO READ THE MANGA!

I'm Otsuichi, the author of the original story. Time passes so quickly! Are you doing well? I spend pretty much every day at a family restaurant, working and reading. Since I go there so often, the waiters all know me. When I came in the other day, a waiter said, "Your usual table is ready." So I guess now I'll have to start ordering real food, instead of just getting a drink...

By the way, how did you like Tsuzuki-sensei's manga? I'd love to hear your thoughts. Though personally, I found it very hard to look at the pages. Not because it was bad or anything...it's just that, as the author of the original story, I felt like someone was tickling me in the side. I actually screamed a number of times while reading it. Not good.

If I hadn't been running every day in the park, I think I might have had a heart attack. You see, I wrote both "Kizu" and "Calling You" back when I was in college. It's embarrassing enough to read sentences I wrote back then...but when it's in pictures, the embarrassment is doubled!

By the way, I met Tsuzuki-sensei at a party last year. She looked so beautiful in her dress.

I remember thinking, "Wow! She's the one who's doing the art? Do bits of screen tone sheet float around her when she takes a bath?" Ah, manga-ka...such mystique.

Let's all write her letters of encouragement!

–Otsuichi
November 12, 2002

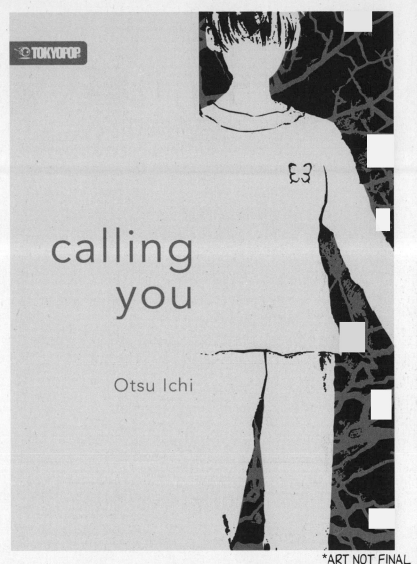

*ART NOT FINAL

AND COMING SOON TO POP FICTION:
THE NOVEL--CALLING YOU!

IN STORES JUNE 2007. CHECK IT OUT!

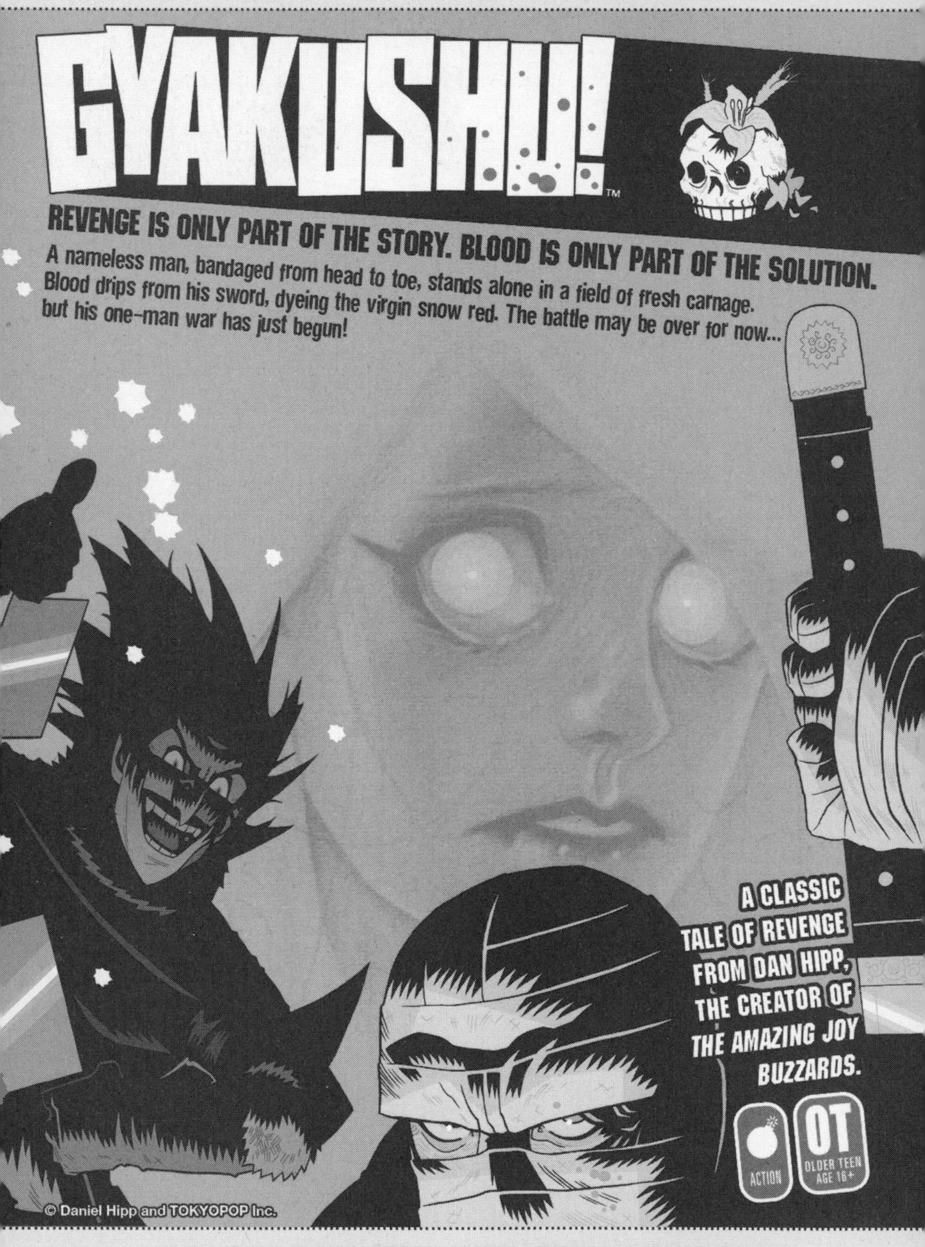
GYAKUSHU!™
REVENGE IS ONLY PART OF THE STORY. BLOOD IS ONLY PART OF THE SOLUTION.
A nameless man, bandaged from head to toe, stands alone in a field of fresh carnage. Blood drips from his sword, dyeing the virgin snow red. The battle may be over for now... but his one-man war has just begun!
A CLASSIC TALE OF REVENGE FROM DAN HIPP, THE CREATOR OF THE AMAZING JOY BUZZARDS.
ACTION
OT OLDER TEEN AGE 16+
© Daniel Hipp and TOKYOPOP Inc.

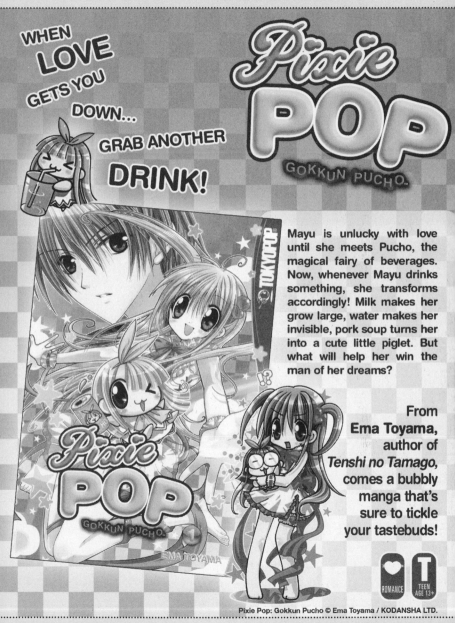

TOKYOPOP MANGA SUPPLEMENT

WHEN LOVE GETS YOU DOWN... GRAB ANOTHER DRINK!

Pixie POP
GOKKUN PUCHO.

Mayu is unlucky with love until she meets Pucho, the magical fairy of beverages. Now, whenever Mayu drinks something, she transforms accordingly! Milk makes her grow large, water makes her invisible, pork soup turns her into a cute little piglet. But what will help her win the man of her dreams?

From Ema Toyama, author of Tenshi no Tamago, comes a bubbly manga that's sure to tickle your tastebuds!

ROMANCE

T
TEEN
AGE 13+

Pixie Pop: Gokkun Pucho © Ema Toyama / KODANSHA LTD.

FOR MORE INFORMATION VISIT: WWW.TOKYOPOP.COM

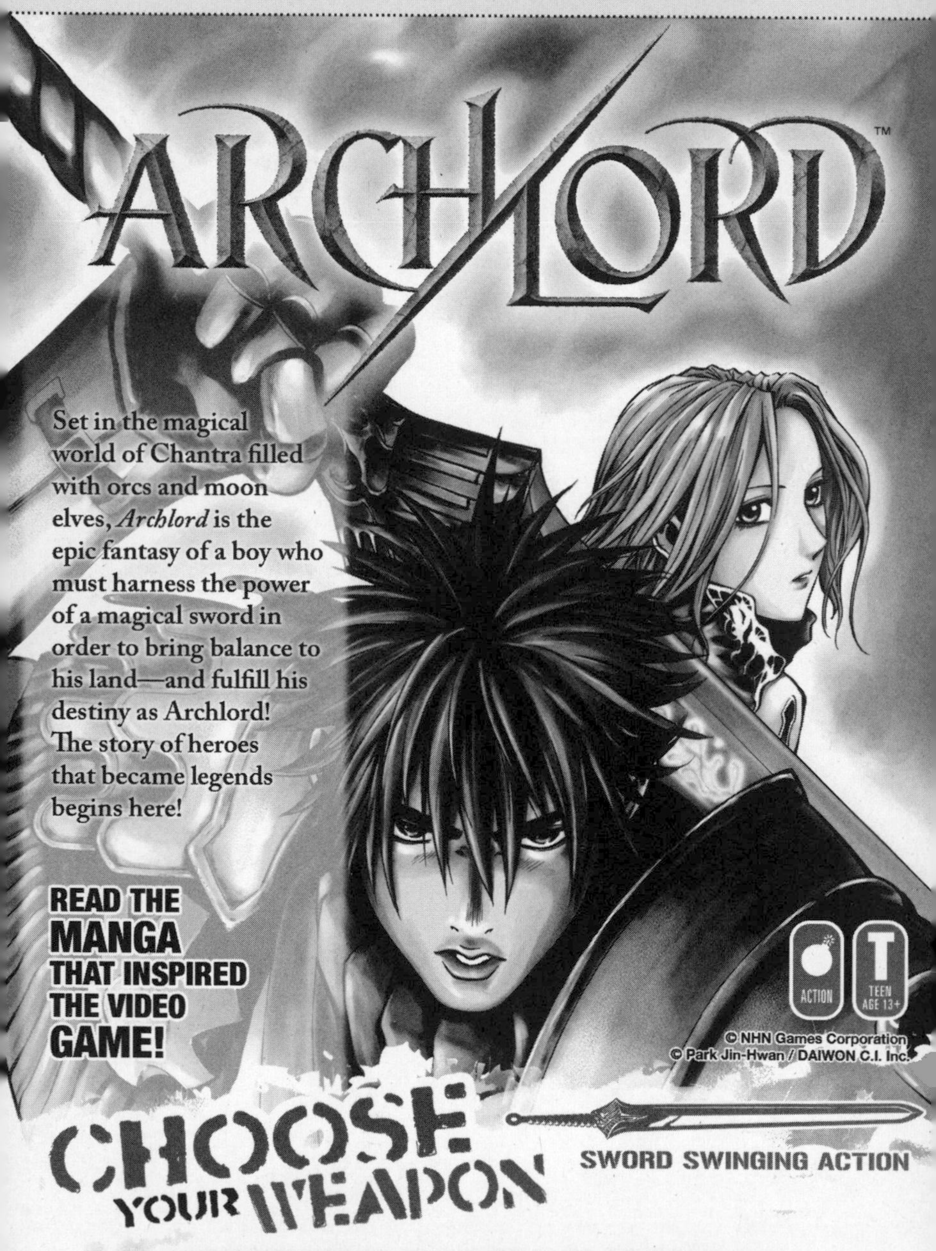
ARCHLORD™
Set in the magical world of Chantra filled with orcs and moon elves, *Archlord* is the epic fantasy of a boy who must harness the power of a magical sword in order to bring balance to his land—and fulfill his destiny as Archlord! The story of heroes that became legends begins here!
READ THE MANGA THAT INSPIRED THE VIDEO GAME!
ACTION
T TEEN AGE 13+
© NHN Games Corporation
© Park Jin-Hwan / DAIWON C.I. Inc.
CHOOSE YOUR WEAPON
SWORD SWINGING ACTION
FOR MORE INFORMATION VISIT: WWW.TOKYOPOP.COM

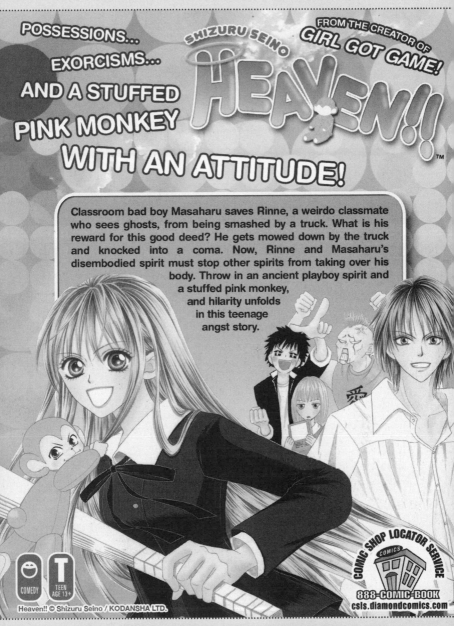

TOKYOPOP MANGA SUPPLEMENT

POSSESSIONS...
EXORCISMS...
AND A STUFFED
PINK MONKEY
WITH AN ATTITUDE!

SHIZURU SEINO

FROM THE CREATOR OF
GIRL GOT GAME!

HEAVEN!!™

Classroom bad boy Masaharu saves Rinne, a weirdo classmate
who sees ghosts, from being smashed by a truck. What is his
reward for this good deed? He gets mowed down by the truck
and knocked into a coma. Now, Rinne and Masaharu's
disembodied spirit must stop other spirits from taking over his
body. Throw in an ancient playboy spirit and
a stuffed pink monkey,
and hilarity unfolds
in this teenage
angst story.

COMEDY

T
TEEN
AGE 13+

Heaven!! © Shizuru Seino / KODANSHA LTD.

COMIC SHOP LOCATOR SERVICE
COMICS
888-COMIC-BOOK
csls.diamondcomics.com

FOR MORE INFORMATION VISIT: WWW.TOKYOPOP.COM

TOKYOPOP MANGA SUPPLEMENT

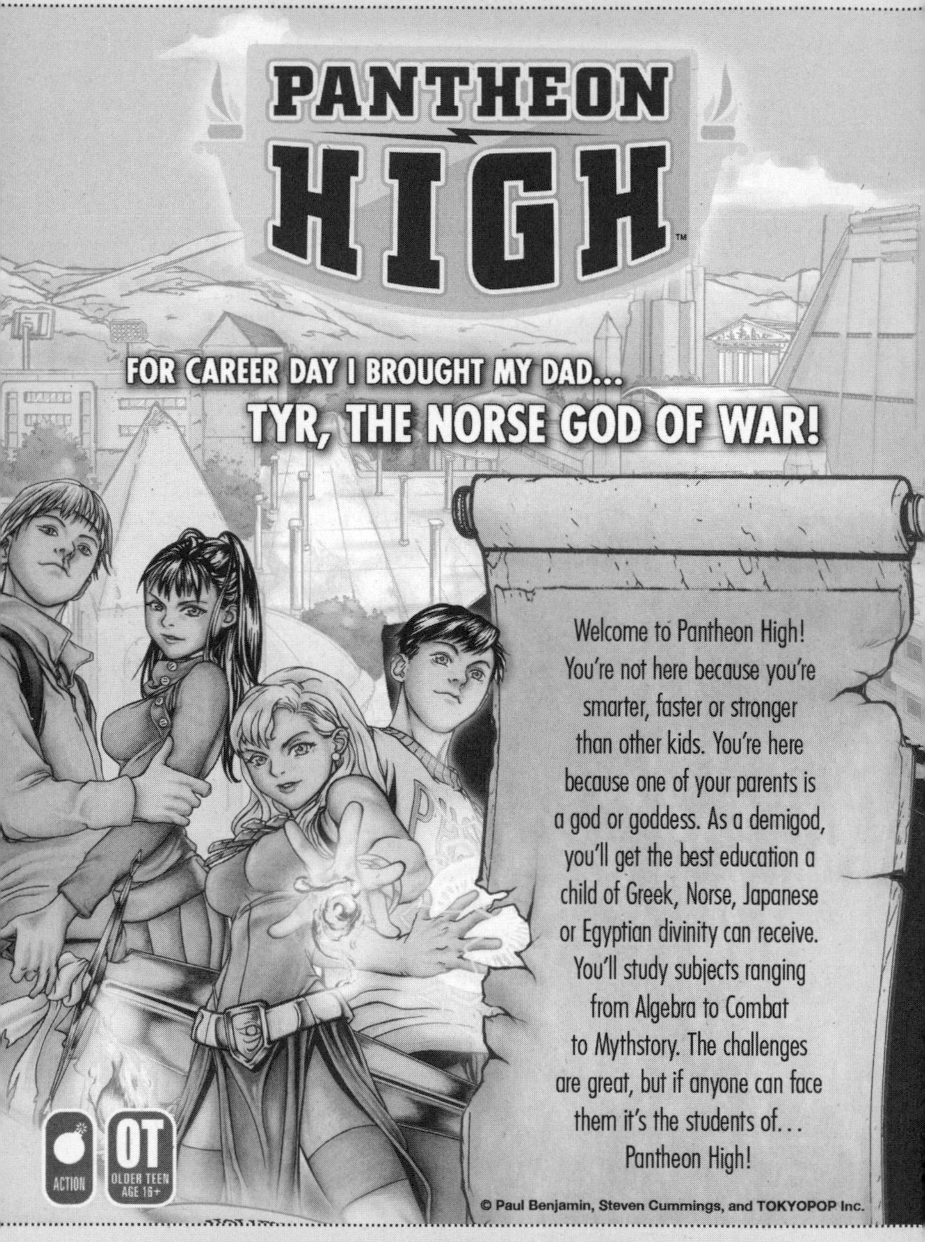

PANTHEON HIGH

FOR CAREER DAY I BROUGHT MY DAD...
TYR, THE NORSE GOD OF WAR!

Welcome to Pantheon High! You're not here because you're smarter, faster or stronger than other kids. You're here because one of your parents is a god or goddess. As a demigod, you'll get the best education a child of Greek, Norse, Japanese or Egyptian divinity can receive. You'll study subjects ranging from Algebra to Combat to Mythstory. The challenges are great, but if anyone can face them it's the students of... Pantheon High!

© Paul Benjamin, Steven Cummings, and TOKYOPOP Inc.

ACTION

OT
OLDER TEEN
AGE 16+

FOR MORE INFORMATION VISIT: WWW.TOKYOPOP.COM

STOP!

This is the back of the book.
You wouldn't want to spoil a great ending!

This book is printed "manga-style," in the authentic Japanese right-to-left format. Since none of the artwork has been flipped or altered, readers get to experience the story just as the creator intended. You've been asking for it, so TOKYOPOP® delivered: authentic, hot-off-the-press, and far more fun!

DIRECTIONS

If this is your first time reading manga-style, here's a quick guide to help you understand how it works.

It's easy... just start in the top right panel and follow the numbers. Have fun, and look for more 100% authentic manga from TOKYOPOP®!

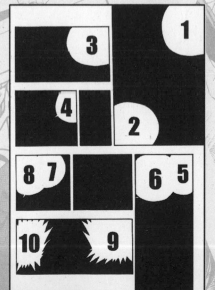

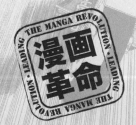

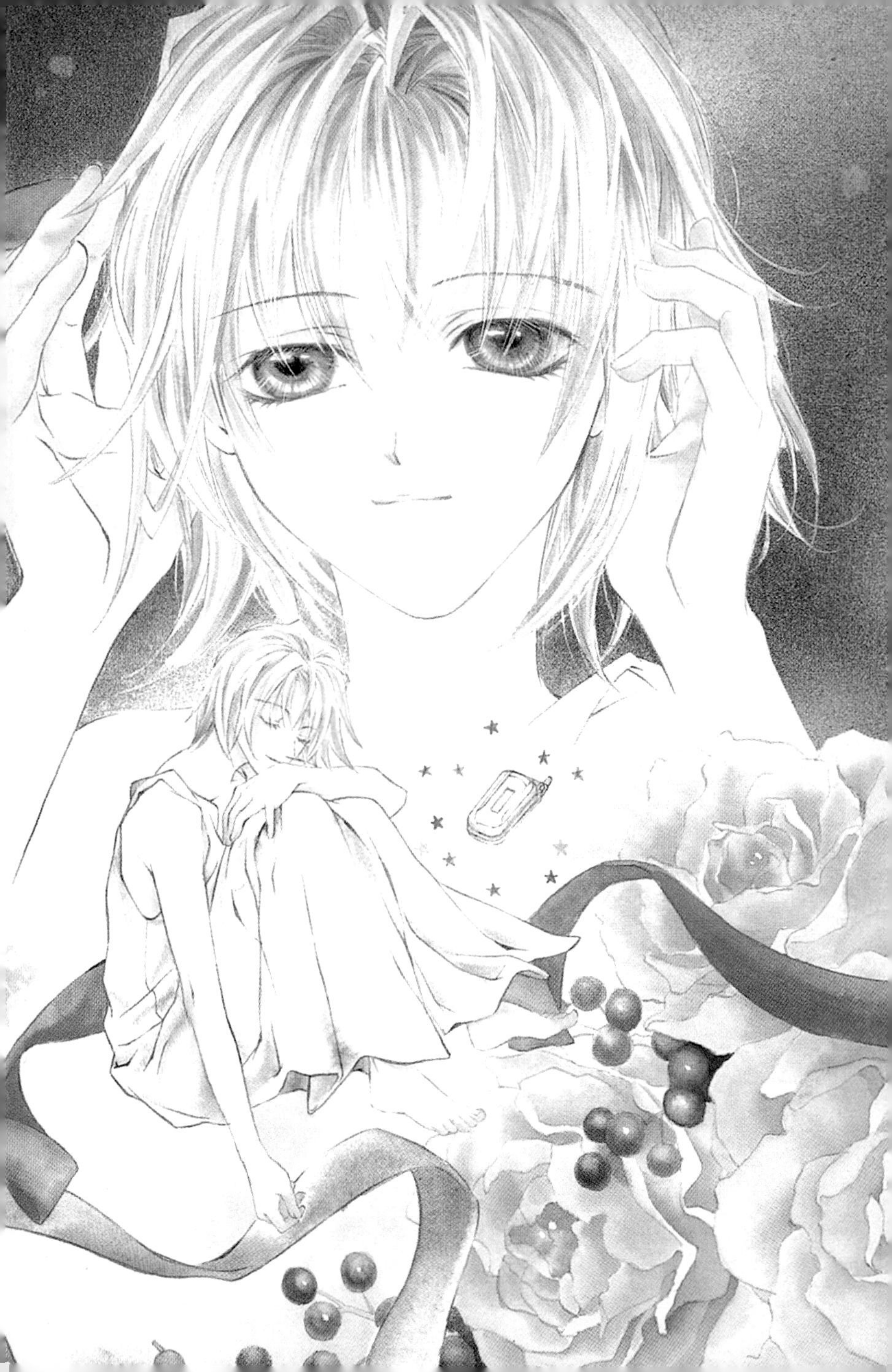

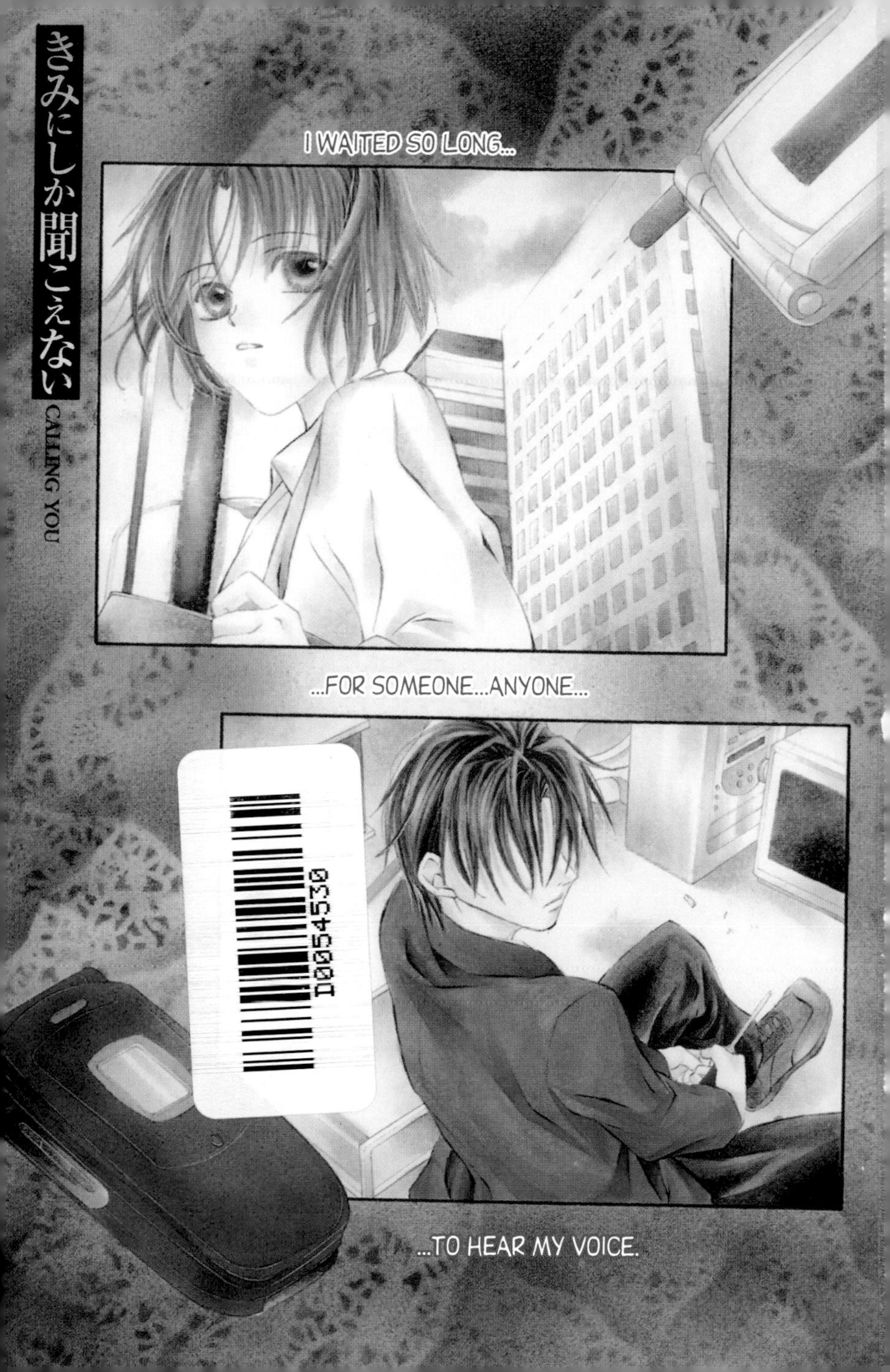
きみにしか聞こえない
CALLING YOU
I WAITED SO LONG...
...FOR SOMEONE...ANYONE...
...TO HEAR MY VOICE.